WORDS OF WISDOM FROM SHAKESPEARE

"Taffeta phrases, silken terms precise, three-piled hyperboles, spruce affectation, figures pedantical" (*Love's Labor's Lost*) . . . you will find all these and more in this comprehensive, easy-to-use, and thoroughly enjoyable collection of timeless poetry, proverbs, and sayings from the most quotable author in literary history. For example:

"Though this be madness, yet there is method in't."
Hamlet, II, ii, 207

"This bud of love, by summer's ripening breath,
May prove a beauteous flower when next we meet."
Romeo and Juliet, II, ii, 121

"O, beware, my lord, of jealousy!
It is the green-eyed monster, which doth mock
The meat it feeds on." *Othello*, III, iii, 165

"Look like the innocent flower,
But be the serpent under it." *Macbeth*, I, v, 66

"Better a witty fool than a foolish wit." *Twelfth Night*, I, v, 35

"Now my charms are all o'erthrown,
And what strength I have's mine own." *The Tempest*,
Epilogue, 1

MARGARET MINER and HUGH RAWSON have collaborated on two previous books of quotations: The *New International Dictionary of Quotations* (Signet) and *A Dictionary of Quotations from the Bible* (Meridian). Hugh Rawson is also the author of *Rawson's Dictionary of Euphemisms & Other Doubletalk*, *Wicked Words*, and *Devious Derivations*.

A DICTIONARY OF QUOTATIONS ✂ FROM ✂ SHAKESPEARE

A TOPICAL GUIDE TO OVER 3,000 GREAT PASSAGES FROM THE PLAYS, SONNETS, AND NARRATIVE POEMS

Selected by Margaret Miner
and Hugh Rawson

A MERIDIAN BOOK

MERIDIAN
Published by the Penguin Group
Penguin Books USA Inc., 375 Hudson Street, New York, New York 10014, U.S.A.
Penguin Books Ltd, 27 Wrights Lane, London W8 5TZ, England
Penguin Books Australia Ltd, Ringwood, Victoria, Australia
Penguin Books Canada Ltd, 10 Alcorn Avenue, Toronto, Ontario, Canada M4V 3B2
Penguin Books (N.Z.) Ltd, 182–190 Wairau Road, Auckland 10, New Zealand

Penguin Books Ltd, Registered Offices:
Harmondsworth, Middlesex, England

Published by Meridian, an imprint of Dutton Signet,
a division of Penguin Books USA Inc.
Previously published in a Dutton edition.

First Meridian Printing, September, 1996
10 9 8 7 6 5 4 3 2

REGISTERED TRADEMARK—MARCA REGISTRADA

The Library of Congress has catalogued the Dutton edition as follows:

Shakespeare, William, 1564–1616.
A dictionary of quotations from Shakespeare : a topical guide to
over 3,000 great passages from the plays, sonnets, and narrative
poems / selected by Margaret Miner and Hugh Rawson.
p.   cm.
ISBN 0-525-93451-0 (hc.)
ISBN 0-452-00127-2 (pbk.)
1. Shakespeare, William, 1564–1616—Dictionaries, indexes, etc.
2. Shakespeare, William, 1564–1616—Quotations.   3. Quotations,
English—Indexes.   I. Miner, Margaret.   II. Rawson, Hugh.
III. Title.
PR2892.S4177   1992
822.3'3—dc20   92–1354
                                                             CIP

Printed in the United States of America
Original hardcover design by Julian Hamer

In Memory of Stuart Flexner

Introduction

George Bernard Shaw was always looking over his shoulder at Shakespeare, and he didn't much like what he saw. "With the single exception of Homer, there is no eminent writer, not even Sir Walter Scott, whom I can despise so entirely as I despise Shakespeare when I measure my mind against his," wrote Shaw in the *Saturday Review* of September 26, 1896. Several months later, in a letter to Ellen Terry, GBS explained: "My capers are part of a bigger design than you think: Shakespeare, for instance, is to me one of the Towers of the Bastille, and down he must come" (January 27, 1897).

Poor Shaw. Shakespeare's social consciousness may not have been very well developed by Shaw's lights, but the Tower shows no signs of cracking. Shaw would make anybody's short list of the greatest playwrights of modern times, but when one asks who was the greatest English playwright of all time, Shakespeare's is the only name that comes to mind.

Nor does one have to go very far to find the reason why. Shaw himself had the answer. In another *Saturday Review* article (December 5, 1896), he put it this way: "Even when Shakespeare in his efforts to be a social philosopher, does rise for an instant to the level of a sixth-rate Kingsley, his solemn self-complacency infuriates me. And yet, so wonderful is his art, that it is not easy to disentangle what is unbearable from what is irresistible."

"And yet, so wonderful is his art." The compliment is backhanded, with the quibbling, carping "yet," but it is nevertheless true. Shakespeare is, as Shaw grudgingly admits, "irresistible." Time after time, in line after line, seemingly without effort (he is said to have hardly ever blotted out a phrase), Shakespeare managed to articulate emotions and thoughts with unmatched clarity and beauty.

"The better part of valor is discretion," "A hit, a very palpable hit," "More in sorrow than in anger," "Neither a borrower nor a lender be," "Sweets to the sweet," "To sleep—perchance to dream." So strong are his images, so wonderful his turns of phrase, that it is difficult to approach the same subjects without falling into his language. Many of his expressions have attained the status of clichés, which is another way of saying that his thoughts have permanently affected our own.

The overwhelming evidence is contained in, among other places, dictionaries of quotations. In Bartlett's *Familiar Quotations* (15th edition, 1980), the eminently quotable Shaw takes up three and a half columns, a lot more space than most writers, but hardly comparable to the 130 occupied by Shakespeare. This ratio is not unusual. In *The Penguin Dictionary of Quotations* (1960), Shaw fills three columns and Shakespeare ninety-six. In *The Concise Oxford Dictionary of Quotations* (1981), Shaw fills three columns and Shakespeare sixty-eight. Our own *New International Dictionary of Quotations* (1986) has forty-three quotations from Shaw to 266 from Shakespeare. In all instances, Shakespeare's only rival is the Bible. (Showing where our intellectual debts lie: In the four collections just mentioned, Shakespeare and the Bible together account for anywhere from 12 percent of the whole, in the case of Bartlett's, to 21 percent, in the *Concise Oxford*.)

The focus of *A Dictionary of Quotations from Shakespeare* is on quotations that are likely to be of practical use to writers and speakers today. While we include the most famous long passages in full, in balance we lean toward the concise and generally applicable. For example, from *Richard II,* of course we have "This royal throne of kings, this sceptered isle . . . " But we also include "Forget, forgive, conclude and be agreed" and "Rage must be withstood . . . lions make leopards tame."

A special attempt also has been made to include quotations that are relevant to modern times and present-day problems—environmental concerns, for instance, as in a line from the opening scene of *Macbeth* that could be used to describe a helicopter flight over Los Angeles, "Hover through the fog and filthy air." Similarly, the observation from *The Tempest* "There be some sports are painful" has been widely rediscovered in this age of physical fitness.

In a more serious area, the sections on "Crime" and "Danger and Dangerous People" are substantial, for like the Elizabethans, we are acutely aware of living in a violent and unpredictable society.

This collection of about three thousand quotations is organized to give the reader three chances to find the quotations he or she wants. First, the quotations are grouped by topic. The topic headings are printed in boldface capital letters along the left-hand margins of the pages, beginning with

ACTION

ACTION, PROMPT

ACTORS AND ACTING

and running through more than four hundred categories to

WRITING

YOUNG IN SPIRIT, THE

YOUTH

Second, since many quotations might be filed logically under one or more topical headings, the dictionary includes many cross-references to related subjects. These are printed in small capitals, preceded by the words "See" or "See also." For example, under the entry ADVICE, the reference is "See also WISDOM, WORDS OF." Occasionally a fragment of a quote is given under one heading and a longer passage including the fragment is given elsewhere. In such instances, the words "More at," followed by a cross-reference in small capitals, will lead the reader from the shorter to the longer version.

Finally, readers who half-recall a quote may consult the keyword index in the back of the book, where "salad days," for example, will refer them to the full quotation, "My salad days, / When I was green in judgment," which is filed under "Youth."

Within categories, quotations are arranged alphabetically by title of play (not counting articles such as "the"), and by numerical sequence. Thus, *The Merchant of Venice* is alphabetized ahead of *A Midsummer Night's Dream,* and *Henry VI* comes ahead of *Henry VIII.* As exceptions to this rule, *King John* and *King Lear* are filed under "K."

The quotations in this book are drawn not only from Shakespeare's plays but from his sonnets and other poems. The location of each passage in the complete work is identified by act, scene or verse, and beginning line. Acts, scenes, and verses are given in Roman numerals, line numbers in Arabic. Thus the position of "A harmless necessary cat" in *The Merchant of Venice* is given as IV,i,55.

Different editors of Shakespeare have divided the acts and scenes of some plays in different ways over the years, with the result that the same passage may be in different places in different editions. For this dictionary, we have followed one of the most widely used sets of texts, the Signet Classic Shakespeare Series, published by the New American Library/ Dutton Division of Penguin USA, and edited by Professor Sylvan Barnet, of Tufts University.

The only kind of change that we have made in some lines in the Signet editions is the traditional one of replacing certain contractions with full words. Thus, "th' " and "wand'ring," for example, usually appear in this collection as "the" and "wandering." We have done this more often in prose than poetry, and usually when the contraction doesn't indicate much if any difference in pronunciation.

Approximately 45 percent of the quotations in this dictionary have been annotated with information about who is speaking, the context, Shakespeare's sources, historical references, the meanings of particular words in Elizabethan times, theatrical history, and so on.

Our hope is that the reader will find familiar treasures here without difficulty, along with some unexpected and intriguing surprises. For truly, Shakespeare is a joy. One cannot improve upon the appreciation accorded him by Ben Jonson, a rival playwright but one with the grace to recognize the immortal accomplishments of a friend and colleague. His tribute, entitled "To the Memory of My Beloved, the Author, Mr. William Shakespeare," was included in the First Folio edition of Shakespeare's plays (1623):

> Soul of the Age!
> The applause, delight, the wonder of our stage!
> My Shakespeare rise! . . .
> Thou art a monument without a tomb,
> And art alive while thy book doth live,
> And we have wits to read and praise to give.

Shakespeare and His Works

William Shakespeare was born in 1564 in Stratford-upon-Avon, a market town in the English Midlands. His father, John, was a glovemaker, a dealer in agricultural produce, and a municipal official; his mother, Mary Arden, was the daughter of a well-to-do farmer. The first evidence of Shakespeare's existence is his baptism, recorded April 26 in the parish registry of Holy Trinity on the southern edge of town. The tradition that he was born three days before, on Sunday the 23rd, is appealing, because it would make his birthday coincide with St. George's Day, honoring England's patron saint. It also makes a fearful symmetry, for Shakespeare died on an April 23, fifty-two years later, in 1616.

In between, Shakespeare was a husband, father, actor, poet, and playwright. He married at eighteen a woman who was eight years older, Anne Hathaway. Their first child, Susanna, was born in 1583, followed by twins, Hamnet and Judith, in 1585. Hamnet died young, aged eleven, but the daughters lived to have families of their own. Their children had no children, however, so the last of Shakespeare's direct descendants was a granddaughter who died in 1670.

Shakespeare went to London in the 1580s. It is not known exactly when or why. He may have joined up with the Queen's Men, one of the five companies of traveling players that visited Stratford in 1587. Legend has it that he fled Stratford in order to avoid punishment for poaching. Once in London, he is said to have supported himself with odd jobs as a printer's devil and as a hired man for a livery stable, holding horses while his betters attended the theater. No real evidence exists for these stories.

By 1592, however, Shakespeare was well established not only as an actor but as a playwright. This is certain, thanks to an attack published that year by a rival, Robert Greene, on "an upstart crow . . . that with his tiger's heart wrapped in a player's hide, supposes he is . . . the only Shake-scene in the country." And there are later references to Shakespeare as a "principal comedian" and a "principal tragedian." He is reported to have been particularly effective as the ghost in *Hamlet* and as Adam in *As You Like It*.

Shakespeare prospered. In 1594, he became a charter member of a theatrical company, the Lord Chamberlain's Men, later renamed the King's Men. In 1596, the Shakespeare family was granted a coat of arms. In 1597, William purchased the second-largest house in Stratford. In 1599, his acting company moved into the newly opened Globe Theater, in which Shakespeare had a one-tenth interest. (He is the only Elizabethan drama-tist known to have received a share of a theater's profits.) In 1611, he retired.

Shakespeare made his will on March 25, 1616. He sought to keep his estate intact by leaving most of it to his daughter Susanna. His wife received, famously, the "second-best bed with the furniture." This may have been the bed they slept in, as opposed to the bed for guests, which was a better one, being less often used. Less than a month after making his will, Shakespeare was dead. On April 25, 1616, he was buried in the chancel of the church in which he had been baptized.

Aside from real estate and other worldly goods, Shakespeare left thirty-seven plays, 154 sonnets, and several longer poems. The exact numbers are in dispute. Shakespeare wrote only some parts of some of the plays, so different scholars come up with different totals. Some credit him with *Two Noble Kinsmen* (written with John Fletcher), which would in-crease the number of plays to thirty-eight. And suggestions continue to be made that he might have written other sonnets and poems of the period.

Even in cases where the authorship is certain, the dates of composi-tion almost always depend on guesswork. The sonnets were published in 1609 but probably written at least a decade earlier. The dates of the other poems also are uncertain. For example, it was once thought that Shake-speare wrote *Venus and Adonis* before coming to London, but scholars now believe that it and *The Rape of Lucrece* were written in the period 1592–94, when playwrights had time on their hands because London's theaters were closed because of plague. As for the plays, their dates of composition generally must be deduced from entries in the register of the Company of Stationers; allusions to historical events; references in the works of other writers; mentions of them in diaries, account books, letters, and other records; and, of course, stylistic analysis. In most cases, there is plenty of room for argument.

Eighteen of the plays were published within Shakespeare's lifetime in small books called quartos. These vary a great deal in character, and quarto editions of the same play differ from one another in a number of instances. Some quartos have the plays in finished form; other texts are very rough, perhaps based on actors' memories or shorthand notes rather than written scripts.

In 1623, seven years after Shakespeare's death, two actor friends, John Heminges and Henry Condell, collected thirty-six of his plays into what has come to be known as the First Folio. (*Pericles* is the only play in the official canon missing from this collection.) Some of the play texts in the First Folio are the same as those in previously published quarto editions. In other cases, new material seems to have been added or else cuts and condensations have been made. This complicates the dating problem, since it raises the possibility that some topical allusions may have been inserted while revising plays composed some years earlier.

With all these caveats, it remains possible to devise at least a rough chronology of Shakespeare's works. The following listing is taken from Sylvan Barnet's general preface to the Signet Classic Shakespeare Series.

PLAYS

1588–93	The Comedy of Errors
1588–94	Love's Labor's Lost
1590–91	2 Henry VI
1590–91	3 Henry VI
1591–92	1 Henry VI
1592–93	Richard III
1592–94	Titus Andronicus
1593–94	The Taming of the Shrew
1593–95	The Two Gentlemen of Verona
1594–96	Romeo and Juliet
1595	Richard II
1594–96	A Midsummer Night's Dream
1596–97	King John
1596–97	The Merchant of Venice
1597	1 Henry IV
1597–98	2 Henry IV
1598–1600	Much Ado About Nothing
1598–99	Henry V
1599–1600	Julius Caesar
1599–1600	As You Like It
1599–1600	Twelfth Night
1600–1601	Hamlet
1597–1601	The Merry Wives of Windsor
1601–1602	Troilus and Cressida

1602–1604	All's Well That Ends Well
1603–1604	Othello
1604–1605	Measure for Measure
1605–1606	King Lear
1605–1606	Macbeth
1606–1607	Antony and Cleopatra
1605–1608	Timon of Athens
1607–1609	Coriolanus
1608–1609	Pericles
1609–10	Cymbeline
1610–11	The Winter's Tale
1611–12	The Tempest
1612–13	Henry VIII

POEMS

1592	Venus and Adonis
1593–94	The Rape of Lucrece
1593–1600	Sonnets
1600–1601	The Phoenix and the Turtle

Acknowledgments

Many thanks are due family members who generously helped with the index, especially Bill Fuller, and also Mary E. Miner, and Nat and Catherine Rawson.

Rosemary Ahern did a fine job of editing and shepherding the book through the publication process.

In the town hall in Washington, Connecticut, Janet Hill, Dorothy Hill, and Kathy Gollow kindly helped us cover work that we rather neglected while finishing this volume.

ACTION

[1] Action is eloquence. *Coriolanus,* III,ii,76.

[2] What's done cannot be undone. *Macbeth,* V,i,71.

[3] It makes us, or it mars us, think on that. *Othello,* V,i,4. (Iago urging Roderigo into a sword fight.)

See also ACTION, PROMPT; BATTLES; BOLDNESS; DANGER; DECISION, MOMENT OF; DOING.

ACTION, PROMPT

[4]   That we would do
We should do when we would, for this "would" changes,
And hath abatements and delays as many
As there are tongues, are hands, are accidents. *Hamlet,* IV,vii,118.

[5] A little fire is quickly trodden out;
Which, being suffered, rivers cannot quench. *Henry VI, Part Three,* IV, viii,7. (A fire *suffered* is one permitted to burn.)

[6] If it were done when 'tis done, then 'twere well
It were done quickly. *Macbeth,* I,vii,1. (Macbeth is speaking of the assassination of Duncan. *Done* at the beginning of the quote means "finished," with no ongoing consequences. See also VIOLENCE.)

[1] Let's lack no discipline, make no delay,
For, lords, tomorrow is a busy day. *Richard III,* V,iii,17.

See also ACTION; BOLDNESS; DECISION, MOMENT OF; DELAY; DOING; IMPUL-
SIVITY; LATENESS.

ACTORS AND ACTING.   See THEATER.

ADVANTAGE

[2] Now, infidel, I have you on the hip! *The Merchant of Venice,* IV,i,333.
(Gratiano to Shylock. To have someone *on the hip* refers to an advanta-
geous hold in wrestling; see also a similar comment by Shylock to Antonio
under REVENGE.)

ADVERSITY

[3]   I am a man whom fortune hath cruelly scratched. *All's Well That Ends
Well,* V,ii,28.

[4] O, how full of briers is this working-day world! *As You Like It,* I,iii,11.

[5] Sweet are the uses of adversity,
Which, like the toad, ugly and venomous,
Wears yet a precious jewel in his head. *As You Like It,* II,i,12. (The jewel,
in this case, is the joy of a simple life deep in the country, in the Forest
of Arden. For grace in adversity, see GRACE. The ancient legend that toads,
snakes, dragons, and so on, bear a precious, magical jewel in their heads
originated in India.)

[6]   The whips and scorns of time,
The oppressor's wrong, the proud man's contumely,
The pangs of despised love, the law's delay,
The insolence of office, and the spurns
That patient merit of the unworthy takes. *Hamlet,* III,i,70. (More at SUI-
CIDE.)

[7] That's wormwood. *Hamlet,* III,ii,187. (In some editions the line is:
"Wormwood, wormwood." Hamlet says this as an aside referring to a
bitter truth. *Wormwood* is a bitter herb and the key ingredient in the
dangerous drink absinthe. In the Bible, Wormwood is the name of the star
that appears at the end of the world. In *Jeremiah,* the term is used to refer
to harsh adversity, or a cruel experience. Curiously, *Chernobyl* means
"wormwood.")

[8] The strawberry grows underneath the nettle. *Henry V,* I,i,60. (Proverbial.)

¹ There is some soul of goodness in things evil,
Would men observingly distill it out. *Henry V,* IV,i,4.

²   When fortune means to men most good,
She looks upon them with a threatening eye. *King John,* III,iii,119. (One of a series of remarks by Cardinal Pandulph on the lines of "It's always darkest before dawn." He is attempting to cheer up the French dauphin following a battlefield defeat.)

³ O ye gods, ye gods! Must I endure all this? *Julius Caesar,* IV,iii,41.

⁴   Man's nature cannot carry
The affliction nor the fear. *King Lear,* III,ii,48. (The earl of Kent, speaking of the violent storm that seems to have driven the failing king into madness.)

⁵   The rain it raineth every day. *King Lear,* III,ii,77. (Shakespeare uses the same phrase in *Twelfth Night,* V,i,394.)

⁶   Where the greater malady is fixed,
The lesser is scarce felt. *King Lear,* III,iv,8. (Lear, in mental anguish, scarcely minds the wind and rain that are buffeting him.)

⁷   The worst is not
So long as we can say "This is the worst." *King Lear,* IV,i,27.

⁸   We are not the first
Who with best meaning have incurred the worst. *King Lear,* V,iii,4. (For *best meaning* read "meaning to do what is best.")

⁹   There was never yet philosopher
That could endure the toothache patiently. *Much Ado About Nothing,* V,i,35. (See also PHILOSOPHY, *Romeo and Juliet,* III,iii,55)

¹⁰ One writ with me in sour misfortune's book! *Romeo and Juliet,* V,iii,82. (Romeo speaking of Juliet, whom he believes to be dead.)

¹¹ Rough winds do shake the darling buds of May. *Sonnet 18,* 3. (More at MORTALITY.)

¹² My grief lies onward and my joy behind. *Sonnet 50,* 14.

¹³ O, benefit of ill; now I find true
That better is by evil still made better. *Sonnet 119,* 9.

¹⁴ Misery acquaints a man with strange bedfellows. *The Tempest,* II,ii,40. (See also ALLIES, the quote from *The Merchant of Venice.*)

[1]   The fire in the flint
Shows not till it be struck. *Timon of Athens,* I,i,22.

See also ANXIETY AND WORRY; BAD TIMES; DESPAIR; FORTUNE; INJUSTICE; LIFE; POVERTY; RUIN; SUFFERING; TROUBLE.

ADVICE

[2] Do not, as some ungracious pastors do,
Show me the steep and thorny way to heaven,
Whiles, like a puffed and reckless libertine,
Himself the primrose path of dalliance treads
And recks not his own rede. *Hamlet,* I,iii,47. (Ophelia to her brother, Laertes. The last line means "And does not follow his own advice." Incidentally, the primrose path is mentioned in *Macbeth* as well; see TEMPTATION.)

[3]   Good counselors lack no clients. *Measure for Measure,* I,ii,109.

See also WISDOM, WORDS OF.

AGE.   See GENERATIONS; MIDDLE AGE; OLD AGE; YOUTH.

AGGRESSION

[4] Priests pray for enemies, but princes kill. *Henry VI, Part Two,* V,ii,71.

[5]   Appetite, an universal wolf
. . .
Must make perforce a universal prey
And last eat up himself. *Troilus and Cressida,* I,iii,121. (From Ulysses' great speech on the necessity of order; see BAD TIMES and ORDER.)

See also AMBITION; ANGER; COMPETITION; PASSION; SUCCESS; VIOLENCE.

AIR POLLUTION

[6] Hover through the fog and filthy air. *Macbeth,* I,i,11. (From the witches' chants in the opening scene.)

ALCOHOL.   See DRINKING.

ALLIES

[7] Nature teaches beasts to know their friends. *Coriolanus,* II,i,6.

[8] Never so few, and never yet more need. *Henry IV, Part Two,* I,i,215.

[1] Now join your hands, and with your hands your hearts. *Henry VI, Part Three*, IV,vi,39.

[2] Nature hath framed strange fellows in her time. *The Merchant of Venice*, I,i,51. (For bedfellows in misery, see ADVERSITY, the quote from *The Tempest*.)

See also FRIENDS; LOYALTY.

AMBITION

[3] Wilt thou be lord of all the world? *Antony and Cleopatra*, II,vii,61. (Menas to Pompey. He repeats the question two lines later in slightly different words: "Wilt thou be lord of the whole world?")

[4] Who does in the wars more than his captain can
Becomes his captain's captain; and ambition
(The soldier's virtue) rather makes choice of loss
Than gain which darkens him. *Antony and Cleopatra*, III,i,21. (Ventidius explaining why he does not intend to pursue a greater victory over the Parthians in the absence of Antony: fame at Antony's expense would hurt his career in the long run. See also POLITICS.)

[5]   The very substance of the ambitious is merely the shadow of a dream. *Hamlet*, II,ii,262.

[6] Thou seek'st the greatness that will overwhelm thee. *Henry IV, Part Two*, IV,v,97. (The king to his son. He is accusing him of trying to usurp the throne "before thy hour be ripe," l.96.)

[7] Choked with ambition of the meaner sort. *Henry VI, Part One*, II,v,123. (A similar figure of speech appears in *Part Two:* "Virtue is choked with foul ambition"—see under BAD TIMES.)

[8] Banish the canker of ambitious thoughts. *Henry VI, Part Two*, I,ii,18.

[9] For a kingdom any oath may be broken. *Henry VI, Part Three*, I,ii,16.

[10]   I do but dream on sovereignty;
Like one that stands upon a promontory,
And spies a far-off shore where he would tread,
Wishing his foot were equal with his eye. *Henry VI, Part Three*, III,ii,134. (This is the future Richard III.)

[11]   Fling away ambition.
By that sin fell the angels. *Henry VIII*, III,ii,440.

[1] It is the bright day that brings forth the adder. *Julius Caesar* II,i,14.

[2]   Ambition's debt is paid. *Julius Caesar,* III,i,83. (Brutus after the assassination of Caesar.)

[3]   Ambition should be made of sterner stuff. *Julius Caesar,* III,ii,94. (From Mark Antony's funeral speech for Caesar. His preceding line is "When the poor hath cried, Caesar hath wept." Antony is answering the conspirators' claim that Caesar's ambition threatened the republic. Brutus had told the crowd: "As he [Caesar] was valiant, I honor him; but as he was ambitious, I slew him," 1.26.)

[4] Vaulting ambition, which o'erleaps itself
And falls on the other. *Macbeth,* I,vii,27. (Ambition leaps too boldly over a barrier and falls on the other side.)

[5] Let not light see my black and deep desires:
The eye wink at the hand; yet let that be
Which the eye fears, when it is done, to see. *Macbeth,* I,iv,51.

See also AGGRESSION; POWER; RUTHLESSNESS; SELF-INTEREST; SUCCESS.

AMBIVALENCE

[6] Her tongue will not obey her heart, nor can
Her heart inform her tongue; the swan's-down feather
That stands upon the swell at the full of tide,
And neither way inclines. *Antony and Cleopatra,* III,ii,47. (Antony commenting on the distress of his wife, Octavia, divided in affection between him and her brother, Octavius Caesar.)

[7]   Poor Brutus, with himself at war. *Julius Caesar,* I,ii,46. (Brutus speaking of himself.)

[8]   We would, and we would not. *Measure for Measure,* IV,iv,36.

[9] I do perceive here a divided duty. *Othello,* I,iii,179. (Desdemona referring to her obligations to her father and her husband.)

[10] O thou weed,
Who art so lovely fair, and smell'st so sweet,
That the sense aches at thee, would thou hadst never been born! *Othello,* IV,ii,66. (Othello torn between love and hate for Desdemona.)

ANGELS

[11] Angels are bright still, though the brightest fell. *Macbeth,* IV,iii,22.

[12]   His better angel. *Othello,* V,ii,205. (A guardian angel.)

[1]   A wingèd messenger of heaven
. . .
When he bestrides the lazy puffing clouds
And sails upon the bosom of the air. *Romeo and Juliet,* II,ii,28,31.

ANGER

[2] Rancor will out. *Henry VI, Part Two,* I,i,142. (A comment by the duke of Gloucester to his half uncle, the bishop of Winchester. The passage runs: " 'Tis not my speeches that you do mislike, / But 'tis my presence that doth trouble ye. / Rancor will out.")

[3] Could I come near your beauty with my nails,
I'd set my ten commandments in your face. *Henry VI, Part Two,* I,iii,143. (Eleanor, the duchess of Gloucester, to her nephew's new queen, Margaret of Anjou. The queen has just, allegedly by accident, boxed the duchess's ear.)

[4] Come not between the Dragon and his wrath. *King Lear,* I,i,124. (The *Dragon* is the emblem of England and as well of any ferocious being.)

[5] I understand a fury in your words. *Othello,* IV,ii,32. (A bewildered Desdemona to Othello.)

[6] Rage must be withstood.
. . . Lions make leopards tame. *Richard II,* I,i,174.

[7] To be in anger is impiety;
But who is man that is not angry? *Timon of Athens,* III,v,57.

See also DESPAIR AND RAGE; EMOTIONS; ENEMIES AND ENMITY; HATE.

ANIMALS

[8] I could endure anything before but a cat, and now he's a cat to me. *All's Well That Ends Well,* IV,iii,250. (Shakespeare apparently was not a cat lover. See also LIKES AND DISLIKES, the quote from *The Merchant of Venice.*)

[9] Hark, hark, the lark at heaven's gate sings. *Cymbeline,* II,iii,20. (More at MORNING.)

[10] The cock, that is the trumpet to the morn. *Hamlet,* I,i,150.

[11]   A beast that wants discourse of reason. *Hamlet,* I,ii,150. (Translation: a beast that lacks the ability to reason. More at DEATH AND GRIEF.)

[12]   Honeybees,
Creatures that by a rule in nature teach
The act of order to a peopled kingdom.

They have a king, and officers of sorts,
Where some like magistrates correct at home,
Others like merchants venture trade abroad,
Others like soldiers armèd in their stings
Make boot upon the summer's velvet buds. *Henry V,* I,ii,187. (And so on—this charming passage continues another ten lines. It is part of a general paean to order in society; see also ORDER. In the fourth line, *correct* could be read "impose discipline"; *make boot upon* means "plunder." See also below. Note one small masculine flaw in the passage: that reference to the honeybee *king.*)

[1] The singing masons building roofs of gold. *Henry V,* I,ii,198. (The bees building their honeycomb. See also above. These loving references to bees arose from Shakespeare's affection for the country and gardens; see also PLANTS AND FLOWERS.)

[2] The little dogs and all,
Tray, Blanch, and Sweetheart—see, they bark at me. *King Lear,* III,vi,61.

[3] I come, Graymalkin. *Macbeth,* I,i,8. (First Witch to her attendant spirit within a gray cat. Cats are traditional hosts of familiar spirits, although a toad named Paddock is also cited in the next line. At the opening of Act IV, the witches exclaim, "Thrice the brinded [brindled] cat hath mewed." The mewing may signal something outside the power of the occult.)

[4] It was the owl that shrieked, the fatal bellman,
Which gives the sternest good-night. *Macbeth,* II,ii,3. (The cry of owls supposedly portended death.)

[5] A falcon, towering in her pride of place. *Macbeth,* II,iv,12. (More at OMENS.)

[6] He doth nothing but talk of his horse. *The Merchant of Venice,* I,ii,39. (*He* is a Neapolitan prince whom Portia finds lacking as a potential husband. The prince boasts that he shoes his horse himself. "I am much afeared my lady his mother played false with a smith," observes Portia. See also INSULTS.)

[7] A harmless necessary cat. *The Merchant of Venice,* IV,i,55. (From a passage in which Shylock is talking about arbitrary dislikes. He wonders why some people can't stand harmless cats. See also LIKES AND DISLIKES.)

[8] To bring in—God shield us!—a lion among ladies, is
a most dreadful thing. For there is not a more fearful wild fowl
than your lion living. *A Midsummer Night's Dream,* III,i,30. (Bottom on the advisability of introducing a lion in a production of *Pyramus and Thisby.* His opinion is influenced by his having failed to win the role of the lion;

see also THEATER. Of course, being Bottom, he misspeaks in his excitement, calling the beast a *fowl.*)

[1] A very gentle beast, and of a good conscience. *A Midsummer Night's Dream,* V,i,227. (The lion in *Pyramus and Thisby.* See also above.)

[2] Master, I marvel how the fishes live in the sea. *Pericles,* II,i,29. (More at COMPETITION.)

[3] Give me another horse! *Richard III,* V,iii,178. (In a dream Richard anticipates his desperate need for a mount. See below.)

[4] A horse! A horse! My kingdom for a horse! *Richard III,* V,iv,7,14. (One of the most famous lines ever written, the last words of Richard in the battle of Bosworth Field, which brought Henry VII to the throne.)

[5]   The lark, the herald of the morn. *Romeo and Juliet,* III,v,6. (More at MORNING.)

[6]   The lark at break of day arising
From sullen earth, sings hymns at heaven's gate. *Sonnet 29,* 11.

[7]   Apes
With foreheads villainous low. *The Tempest,* IV,i,248. (Caliban fears that he and his companions will be magically transformed into barnacles or apes. Large apes were believed to be dangerous.)

[8]   Get thee away, and take
Thy beagles with thee. *Timon of Athens,* IV,iii,175. (Timon to Alcibiades. The quote may be directed to anyone accompanied by one pooch too many, but the "beagles" here are two ladies of easy morals. *Beagle* was a moderately contemptuous term for a woman, similar to today's *broad.* It could be used affectionately, as in "She's a beagle true-bred, and one that adores me," *Twelfth Night,* II,iii,179. The term seems to be derived from Old French, meaning "one who bays" or "gapes.")

[9] The owl, night's herald. *Venus and Adonis,* 531.

See also RIDING (for more on horses).

ANTONY, MARK.   See DEATH AND GRIEF; EPITAPHS; LOVE,
                                    EXPRESSIONS OF.

ANXIETY AND WORRY

[10] So shaken as we are, so wan with care. *Henry IV, Part One,* I,i,1. (A great opening line, spoken by the king, the once relentless Henry Bolingbroke, now worn and haunted by the assassination of Richard II, by which

Bolingbroke became King Henry IV. Shakespeare added years to Henry IV's age to heighten the contrast between him and his son, called Hal and Harry—the future Henry V. Historically, Henry IV was thirty-seven at the critical battle of Shrewsbury. Prince Hal, the hero of the battle, was sixteen. Hotspur, his rival, whom Shakespeare portrays as about the same age as Hal, was actually thirty-nine.)

¹ O polished perturbation! Golden care!
That keep'st the ports of slumber open wide
To many a watchful night! *Henry IV, Part Two,* IV,v,23. (The *golden care* here is the crown lying beside the sleeping Henry IV.)

² Care is no cure, but rather corrosive,
For things that are not to be remedied. *Henry VI, Part One,* III,iii,3.

³   Men are flesh and blood, and apprehensive. *Julius Caesar,* III,i,67.

⁴ Your mind is tossing on the ocean. *The Merchant of Venice,* I,i,8.

⁵   It keeps on the windy side of care. *Much Ado About Nothing,* II,i,310. (Beatrice is speaking of her "merry heart." For *windy* read "windward.")

⁶   Though care killed a cat, thou hast mettle enough in thee to kill care. *Much Ado About Nothing,* V,i,132. (We are more familiar with cats killed by curiosity. But Bartlett's *Familiar Quotations* has a couple of references to care and cats: from the *Shirburn Ballads,* 1585, "Let care kill a cat, / We'll laugh and grow fat," and from Ben Jonson, *Every Man in His Humor,* 1598, "Hang sorrow, care'll kill a cat.")

⁷   Where care lodges, sleep will never lie. *Romeo and Juliet,* II,iii,36. (More at OLD AGE.)

⁸ When day's oppression is not eased by night,
But day by night and night by day oppressed. *Sonnet 28, 3.*

⁹ Past cure I am, now reason is past care,
And frantic-mad with evermore unrest. *Sonnet 147, 9.* (The poet is distraught at the infidelity of his mistress.)

¹⁰ My mind is troubled, like a fountain stirred;
And I myself see not the bottom of it. *Troilus and Cressida,* III,iii,310.

APPARITIONS

¹¹ Whether in sea or fire, in earth or air,
The extravagant and erring spirit hies
To his confine. *Hamlet,* I,i,153. (Translation: [At cock's crow] the spirit that has left its domain and is wandering returns to its proper place. See

also OCCULT, THE. According to tradition, Shakespeare himself first played the ghost.)

[1] Angels and ministers of grace defend us!
Be thou a spirit of health or goblin damned,
Bring with thee airs from heaven or blasts from hell,
Be thy intents wicked or charitable,
Thou com'st in such a questionable shape
That I will speak to thee. *Hamlet,* I,iv,38. (Hamlet to the ghost of his father. *Health,* in the second line, means "goodness." *Questionable shape* means "in a form that seems capable of being questioned." On the issue of whether or not Shakespeare intended the audience to accept the ghost as real or imagined, Samuel Taylor Coleridge made the point that Hamlet is relaxed and behaving normally until the moment that the ghost appears. His reaction here, and that of his companions, indicates that the ghost is a genuine being. See also *Macbeth,* III,iv,107, below.)

[2]   What may this mean
That thou, dead corse, again in complete steel,
Revisits thus the glimpses of the moon,
Making night hideous, and we fools of nature
So horridly to shake our disposition
With thoughts beyond the reaches of our souls?
Say, why is this? Wherefore? What should we do? *Hamlet,* I,iv,51. (More from the passage quoted above.)

[3] Art thou some god, some angel, or some devil,
That mak'st my blood cold, and my hair to stare? *Julius Caesar,* IV,iii,278. (Brutus to Caesar's ghost. *To stare* means "to stand upright.")

[4] The earth hath bubbles as the water has,
And these are of them. *Macbeth,* I,iii,79. (Banquo speaking of the witches.)

[5] Is this a dagger which I see before me,
The handle toward my hand? Come, let me clutch thee.
I have thee not, and yet I see thee still.
Art thou not, fatal vision, sensible
To feeling as to sight, or art thou but
A dagger of the mind, a false creation,
Proceeding from the heat-oppressèd brain? *Macbeth,* II,i,33. (Later, at the dinner attended by the ghost of Banquo, Lady Macbeth speaks of "the air-drawn dagger," III,iv,63.)

[6] Hence, horrible shadow!
Unreal mockery, hence! *Macbeth,* III,iv,107. (Macbeth to the ghost of Banquo. The phrase *unreal mockery* is ammunition for those who dispute

Coleridge's view that the apparitions in *Hamlet* and *Macbeth* should be accepted as real ghosts; see above, *Hamlet*, I,iv,38. See also MADNESS.)

1   Be not afraid of shadows. *Richard III*, V,iii,216. (More at FEAR.)

See also OCCULT, THE.

APPEARANCES

2 Bear a fair presence, though your heart be tainted. *Comedy of Errors*, III,ii,13. (Good advice in a play in which appearances govern the plot. This lighthearted farce, involving two sets of identical twins, is the basis of the Rodgers and Hart musical *The Boys from Syracuse*.)

3 Seems, madam? Nay, it is. I know not "seems." *Hamlet*, I,ii,76. (Hamlet to his mother, who has asked why the death of his father seems to be so painful to him. See also SORROW AND SADNESS.)

4   I perchance hereafter shall think meet
To put an antic disposition on. *Hamlet*, I,v,171.

5   The devil hath power
To assume a pleasing shape. *Hamlet*, II,ii,611.

6 I have heard of your paintings, well enough. God hath given you one face, and you make yourselves another. *Hamlet*, III,i,144. (Hamlet to Ophelia.)

7   There's no art
To find the mind's construction in the face:
He was a gentleman on whom I built
An absolute trust. *Macbeth*, I,iv,11. (The king, Duncan, speaking of the thane of Cawdor, just executed for treason. The speech is sometimes misinterpreted to mean that it is not difficult to find the mind's construction in the face. But in context it is clear that the meaning is just the opposite. Incidentally, the king arrives at an equally bad reading of character in trusting the thane's successor, Macbeth. See also below.)

8 Your face, my Thane, is as a book where men
May read strange matters. *Macbeth*, I,v,63. (Lady Macbeth to her husband. She advises him to assume an appearance of innocence; see DECEPTIVENESS.)

9   His face is the worst thing about him. *Measure for Measure*, II,i,155.

10 Mislike me not for my complexion,
The shadowed livery of the burnished sun. *The Merchant of Venice*, II,i,1. (Portia's Moroccan suitor speaks. *Shadowed livery* roughly translates as "dark uniform.")

¹ Some there be that shadows kiss;
Such have but a shadow's bliss. *The Merchant of Venice,* II,ix,65.

² The world is still deceived with ornament. *The Merchant of Venice,* III,ii,74.

³ Thus ornament is but the guilèd shore
To a most dangerous sea. *The Merchant of Venice,* III,ii,97.

⁴ To be a well-favored man is the gift of fortune. *Much Ado About Nothing,* III,iii,14.

⁵ Opinion's but a fool that makes us scan
The outward habit for the inward man. *Pericles,* II,ii,55. (*Opinion* refers to public opinion.)

⁶   By his face straight shall you know his heart. *Richard III,* III,iv,53.

See also BEARDS; BEAUTY; FASHION; GUILT; LIES AND DECEIT.

ARGUMENTS

⁷   The Retort Courteous . . . the Quip Modest . . . the Reply Churlish . . . the Reproof Valiant . . . the Countercheck Quarrelsome; and so to the Lie Circumstantial and the Lie Direct. *As You Like It,* V,iv,73. (Touchstone outlining the stages of an argument. He concludes that only an *If*—a hypothetical—can settle such a matter: "Your If is the only peacemaker. Much virtue in If," l.102.)

⁸   Beware
Of entrance to a quarrel. *Hamlet,* I,iii,65. (More at WISDOM, WORDS OF.)

⁹ Good reasons must of force give place to better. *Julius Caesar,* IV,iii,202.

¹⁰ He draweth out the thread of his verbosity finer than the staple of his argument. *Love's Labor's Lost,* V,i,18. (For *staple* read "fiber.")

¹¹ It were a goot [good] motion if we leave our pribbles and prabbles. *The Merry Wives of Windsor,* I,i,54. (*Pribbles and prabbles* are petty disagreements.)

¹²   In the managing of quarrels you may say he is wise, for either he avoids them with great discretion, or undertakes them with a most Christianlike fear. *Much Ado About Nothing,* II,iii,188.

¹³ Harp not on that string, madam; that is past. *Richard III,* IV,iv,363. (Richard III to his sister-in-law Elizabeth. His complaint about her nagging is fairly outrageous, considering that he murdered her sons.)

¹⁴ Thy head is as full of quarrels as an egg is full of meat. *Romeo and Juliet,* III,i,23.

¹   Be it sun or moon or what you please.
And if you please to call it a rush-candle,
Henceforth I vow it shall be so for me. *The Taming of the Shrew,* IV,v,13.
(Kate determined to avoid an argument with Petruchio, even if he calls the
sun the moon. See also MANIPULATION.)

See also NEGOTIATION; REASONS; TALK.

ARMIES.   See DEFENSE; SOLDIERS; WAR.

ARTS.   See CENSORSHIP; DANCE; INSPIRATION; MUSIC; POETRY;
                                  STORIES; THEATER; WRITING.

ATHENS.   See CITIES.

AUTHORITY.   See CENSORSHIP; HIGH POSITION; LEADERS; ORDER;
                                         POWER.

B

BAD TIMES

[1] The time is out of joint. O cursèd spite,
That ever I was born to set it right! *Hamlet,* I,v,188.

[2]   He doth bestride a bleeding land,
Gasping for life. *Henry IV, Part Two,* I,i,206.

[3]   These days are dangerous:
Virtue is choked with foul ambition,
And charity chased hence by rancor's hand. *Henry VI, Part Two,* III,i,142.

[4] The weight of this sad time we must obey. *King Lear,* V,iii,325.

[5] Bleed, bleed, poor country. *Macbeth,* IV,iii,31. (See also TYRANNY.)

[6] The bay trees in our country are all withered,
And meteors fright the fixèd stars of heaven,
The pale-faced moon looks bloody on the earth,
And lean-looked prophets whisper fearful change;
Rich men look sad, and ruffians dance and leap,
The one in fear to lose what they enjoy,
The other to enjoy by rage and war.
These signs forerun the death or fall of kings. *Richard II,* II,iv,8. (See also
OMENS.)

[7]   This world is grown so bad
That wrens make prey where eagles dare not perch. *Richard III,* I,iii,69.
(The last line is similar to "For fools rush in where angels fear to tread,"

Alexander Pope, *Essay on Criticism,* but with the sense that common people are flourishing at the expense of aristocrats.)

[1] Then everything include itself in power,
Power into will, will into appetite,
And appetite, an universal wolf,
So doubly seconded with will and power,
Must make perforce an universal prey,
And last eat up himself. *Troilus and Cressida,* I,iii,119. (Ulysses here describes the ascendance of greed and passion that follows a breakdown in social order and authority; see also ORDER; REVOLUTION.)

See also ADVERSITY; DANGER; REVOLUTION; TYRANNY; WAR.

BALDNESS

[2]   What he hath scanted men in hair, he hath given them in wit. *The Comedy of Errors,* II,ii,80. (A few lines earlier, in response to the comment "There's a time for all things," 1.64, the same character, Dromio of Syracuse, quips, "There's no time for a man to recover his hair that grows bald by nature," 1.71.)

BANISHMENT AND EXILE

[3]   Our exiled friends abroad
That fled the snares of watchful tyranny. *Macbeth,* V,viii,66.

[4] Must I not serve a long apprenticehood
To foreign passages, and in the end,
Having my freedom, boast of nothing else
But that I was a journeyman to grief? *Richard II,* I,iii,270. (Bolingbroke faced with banishment. *A journeyman to grief* means "a worker in the employ of grief.")

[5] Eating the bitter bread of banishment. *Richard II,* III,i,21.

[6] Ha, banishment? Be merciful, say "death";
For exile hath more terror in his look,
Much more than death. Do not say "banishment." *Romeo and Juliet,* III,iii,12.

BATTLES.   See WAR.

BEARDS

[7] I could not endure a husband with a beard on his face. *Much Ado About Nothing,* II,i,29.

BEAUTY

1   An angel; or, if not,
An earthly paragon. *Cymbeline,* III,vi,43.

2   My beauty, though but mean,
Needs not the painted flourish of your praise. *Love's Labor's Lost,* II,i,13.

3   "The heavenly rhetoric of thine eye." *Love's Labor's Lost,* IV,iii,59.
(From a sonnet by the love-smitten Longaville. Berowne calls it "pure,
pure idolatry.")

4   Beauty is a witch. *Much Ado About Nothing,* II,i,177. (More at LOVE
AND LOVERS.)

5   That whiter skin of hers than snow,
And smooth as monumental alabaster. *Othello,* V,ii,4.

6 Beauty itself doth of itself persuade
The eyes of men without an orator. *The Rape of Lucrece,* 29.

7 This silent war of lilies and of roses,
Which Tarquin viewed in her fair face's field. *The Rape of Lucrece,* 71.
(Beauty's color is red, virtue's white.)

8 All orators are dumb when beauty pleadeth. *The Rape of Lucrece,* 268.

9   O, she doth teach the torches to burn bright!
It seems she hangs upon the cheek of night
As a rich jewel in an Ethiop's ear—
Beauty too rich for use, for earth too dear! *Romeo and Juliet,* I,v,46.
(Romeo at first sight of Juliet.)

10 She speaks, yet she says nothing. *Romeo and Juliet,* II,ii,12. (The balcony
scene. Juliet's beauty speaks to Romeo.)

11 From fairest creatures we desire increase,
That thereby beauty's rose might never die. *Sonnet 1,* 1. (A plea to the
patron of the sonnets, Shakespeare's friend Henry Wriothesley, earl of
Southampton, to marry and father children. The dedication of the sonnets
is to Mr. W.H., "the only begetter of these ensuing sonnets." Since "Mr."
may not be correct for an earl, other suggestions have been made as to the
identity of W.H. But there seems little doubt that Shakespeare wrote the
poems for Southampton and dedicated them to him, as well.)

12 Shall I compare thee to a summer's day?
Thou art more lovely and more temperate. *Sonnet 18,* 1. (More at MORTAL-
ITY.)

[1] The ornament of beauty is suspect. *Sonnet 70, 3.*

[2] When in the chronicle of wasted time
I see descriptions of the fairest wights,
And beauty making beautiful old rhyme
In praise of ladies dead and lovely knights;
Then, in the blazon of sweet beauty's best,
Of hand, of foot, of lip, of eye, of brow,
I see their antique pen would have expressed
Even such a beauty as you master now. *Sonnet 106, 1.* (In the first two lines, *wasted* means "past," and *wights* means "people.")

[3] There's nothing ill can dwell in such a temple.
If the ill spirit have so fair a house,
Good things will strive to dwell with it. *The Tempest,* I,ii,458. (Miranda speaking of Ferdinand.)

[4]   'Tis beauty truly blent, whose red and white
Nature's own sweet and cunning hand laid on.
Lady, you are the cruelest she alive
If you will lead these graces to the grave,
And leave the world no copy. *Twelfth Night,* I,v,239. (Very much the same argument that Shakespeare made in the early sonnets. See, for example, *Sonnet 1* above.)

See also APPEARANCES; CLEOPATRA; GRACE; ROMEO AND JULIET; WOMEN.

BEGINNINGS

[5]   The game's afoot! *Henry V,* III,i,32. (More at WAR. A similar phrase appears in *Cymbeline,* "The game is up," III,iii,107.)

[6]   The true beginning of our end. *A Midsummer Night's Dream,* V,i,111. (*End* here means "purpose." In modern times, when Napoleon's army was halted after the Battle of Borodino in the 1812 Russian campaign, Talleyrand said, *"Voilà le commençement de la fin"*—"There is the beginning of the end." After the British under General Bernard Montgomery defeated Field Marshal Erwin Rommel at El Alamein in 1942, Winston Churchill said, "Now this is not the end. It is not even the beginning of the end. But it is, perhaps, the end of the beginning.")

See also ENDINGS.

BETRAYAL

[7] *Et tu, Brutè?* Then fall Caesar. *Julius Caesar,* III,i,77. (The Latin phrase was popularly accepted as Caesar's last words.)

¹ This was the most unkindest cut of all. *Julius Caesar,* III,ii,185. (Antony speaking of the wound in Caesar's body inflicted by Brutus. It was, according to Plutarch, a wound in the groin.)

See also CONSPIRACY; TREASON.

BIRDS.

See ANIMALS.

BOASTING.

See BRAGGING.

BODY

² O, that this too too sullied flesh would melt,
Thaw, and resolve itself into a dew. *Hamlet,* I,ii,129. (More at DEPRESSION. *Sullied* is sometimes given as *solid;* either may be correct.)

³ O flesh, flesh, how art thou fishified! *Romeo and Juliet,* II,iv,39. (A curiously memorable remark by Mercutio, part of a punning tease of Romeo, who, Mercutio insists, resembles "a dried herring." In *The Tempest,* the clown Trinculo accuses Caliban of having "a very ancient and fishlike smell," II,ii,26.)

See also APPEARANCES; BALDNESS; BEAUTY; BEARDS; BRAIN, THE; FATNESS; HEALTH; SICKNESS; THINNESS.

BOLDNESS

⁴   We ready are to try our fortunes
To the last man. *Henry IV, Part Two,* IV,ii,43.

⁵   I'll take my chance. *King John,* I,i,151. (The entire line is "Brother, take you my land, I'll take my chance," spoken by Philip the Bastard, an illegitimate son of Richard I, a character invented by Shakespeare. Here the Bastard impetuously renounces claim to an inheritance in order to serve Queen Elinor—Eleanor of Aquitaine, Richard's mother—on a campaign in France.)

⁶ Who dares not stir by day must walk by night. *King John,* I,i,172. (In other words, timidity increases difficulty.)

⁷ Be bloody, bold, and resolute! *Macbeth,* IV,i,79.

⁸ Have you no modesty, no maiden shame,
No touch of bashfulness? *A Midsummer Night's Dream,* III,ii,285.

⁹ To horse, to horse, urge doubts to them that fear. *Richard II,* II,i,299.

See also ACTION; ACTION, PROMPT; COURAGE; DETERMINATION; DANGER; IMPULSIVITY; OPPORTUNITY; RISK; SUCCESS.

BOOKS.   See EDUCATION; READING.

BOYS.   See YOUTH.

BRAGGING

1   Who knows himself a braggart,
Let him fear this; for it will come to pass
That every braggart will be found an ass. *All's Well That Ends Well,*
IV,iii,349. (Spoken by Parolles, quite a boaster himself—his name means
Talker or Braggart, from the French *paroles,* "words." Dr. Johnson in *The
Plays of William Shakespeare* noted that Parolles has "many of the linea-
ments of Falstaff and seems to be the character which Shakespeare de-
lighted to draw, a fellow that had more wit than virtue." See also the
description of Pistol below.)

2   He hath a killing tongue and a quiet sword; by the means whereof
'a breaks words, and keeps whole weapons. *Henry V,* III,ii,34. (A boy's
comment on the boastful but cowardly Pistol. The boy also notes that
despite Pistol's threats, "'A never broke any man's head but his own, and
that was against a post when he was drunk," l.41. *'A* means "he.")

See also PUBLIC RELATIONS; TALK.

BRAIN, THE

3   [The] brain,
Which some suppose the soul's frail dwelling house. *King John,* V,vii,2.

See also MIND.

BRAVERY.   See BOLDNESS; COURAGE.

BRIBERY

4   You yourself
Are much condemned to have an itching palm,
To sell and mart your offices for gold
To undeservers. *Julius Caesar,* IV,iii,9. (Brutus to Cassius.)

5   Give him gold; and though authority be a stubborn bear, yet he
is oft led by the nose with gold. Show the inside of your purse
to the outside of his hand, and no more ado. *The Winter's Tale,* IV,iv,808.

BRITAIN.   See ENGLAND AND THE ENGLISH.

BROTHERS.   See FAMILY.

BUSINESS

[1] Sell when you can. *As You Like It,* III,v,60.

[2]   Every man hath business and desire. *Hamlet,* I,v,130.

[3]   In the way of bargain, mark ye me,
I'll cavil on the ninth part of a hair. *Henry IV, Part One,* III,i,138.

[4] Great business must be wrought ere noon. *Macbeth,* III,v,22.

[5] He is well paid that is well satisfied. *The Merchant of Venice,* IV,i,415.

[6] My business was great, and in such a case as mine a man may strain
courtesy. *Romeo and Juliet,* II,iv,53. (Romeo's business was love.)

[7]   You do as chapmen do,
Dispraise the thing that you desire to buy. *Troilus and Cressida,* IV,i,75.
(Chapmen traded and sold cheap goods.)

[8]   Let me have no lying; it becomes none but tradesmen. *The Winter's
Tale,* IV,iv,726.

See also CONTRACTS; MONEY; NEGOTIATION; RISK.

BUYING AND SELLING.   See BUSINESS.

CAESAR. See JULIUS CAESAR.

CAPITAL PUNISHMENT. See PUNISHMENT.

CARE. See ANXIETY AND WORRY; CAREFULNESS; HELP; KINDNESS.

CAREFULNESS

[1] Wisely and slow. They stumble that run fast. *Romeo and Juliet,* II,iii,94. (Friar Lawrence to Romeo. Similarly, E. B. White's Charlotte the spider, advised Wilbur, the nervous pig: "Never hurry, never worry.")

See also DISCRETION; PRUDENCE.

CASSIUS. See DANGEROUS PEOPLE.

CATS. See ANIMALS.

CENSORSHIP

[2] Art made tongue-tied by authority. *Sonnet 66, 9.*

CEREMONY

[3] What have kings that privates have not too,
Save ceremony, save general ceremony?
And what art thou, thou idol Ceremony? *Henry V,* IV,i,243. (More at HIGH POSITION.)

1 The sauce to meat is ceremony;
Meeting were bare without it. *Macbeth,* III,iv,37. (A dinner party is not complete without gracious attention to guests.)

See also MANNERS.

CHANCE

2 If Hercules and Lichas play at dice
Which is the better man, the greater throw
May turn by fortune from the weaker hand. *The Merchant of Venice,* II,i,32. (Lichas was Hercules' page.)

3 As good luck would have it. *The Merry Wives of Windsor,* III,v,81. (A traditional phrase.)

4 So we profess
Ourselves to be the slaves of chance, and flies
Of every wind that blows. *The Winter's Tale,* IV,iv,543.

5 The odds for high and low's alike. *The Winter's Tale,* V,i,207. (Chance is the same for those in high position as for those of low estate.)

See also FATE; FORTUNE; OPPORTUNITY; RISK.

CHANGE

6 Presume not that I am the thing I was. *Henry IV, Part Two,* V,v,57. (The young Henry V rejecting his old but rowdy friend Falstaff.)

7 Bless thee, Bottom! Bless thee! Thou art translated. *A Midsummer Night's Dream,* III,i,119. (Quince's somewhat inarticulate reaction upon first sight of Bottom with an ass's head.)

CHARITY.   See GIVING; MERCY.

CHASTITY.   See INNOCENCE; SEX; VIRTUE.

CHILDREN

8 Barnes are blessings. *All's Well That Ends Well,* I,iii,26. (*Barnes* means "bairns," or "children.")

9 At first, the infant,
Mewling and puking in the nurse's arms.
Then the whining schoolboy, with his satchel
And shining morning face, creeping like snail
Unwillingly to school. *As You Like It,* II,vii,143. (The unforgettable passage on childhood from the "seven ages of man" speech; see LIFE.)

[1] The pleasing punishment that women bear. *The Comedy of Errors,* I,i,46. (The reference is to childbirth, in this case the birth of twins. For a very difficult birth, see *Richard III* below.)

[2] "One fair daughter, and no more,
The which he lovèd passing well." *Hamlet,* II,ii,416. (Hamlet is quoting from a ballad on the story of Jephtha, the Old Testament leader, who sacrificed his only child in a bargain made with the Lord to gain victory over the Ammonites. Hamlet's reference to this chilling story is directed to Polonius, who has just one daughter, Ophelia.)

[3]   See, sons, what things you are!
How quickly nature falls into revolt
When gold becomes her object! *Henry IV, Part Two,* IV,v,64. (The king, supposing that his son Harry has taken his crown with the intention to depose him. Subsequently he challenges his son with this suspicion, and the prince defends his good intentions. See below.)

[4] *Prince.* I never thought to hear you speak again.
King. Thy wish was father, Harry, to that thought. *Henry IV, Part Two,* IV,v,91. (The prince had picked up the crown when his father, the king, was asleep. He explains that he thought his father was near death.)

[5]   'Tis a happy thing
To be the father unto many sons. *Henry VI, Part Three,* III,ii,104.

[6]   Men ne'er spend their fury on a child. *Henry VI, Part Three,* V,v,57. (Not true then—the child referred to, the Prince of Wales, has just been murdered—and not true now.)

[7] Grief fills the room up of my absent child,
Lies in his bed, walks up and down with me,
Puts on his pretty looks, repeats his words,
Remembers me of all his gracious parts,
Stuffs out his vacant garments with his form. *King John,* III,iii,93. (Constance of Brittany mourning the capture of her son Arthur, who later dies. Some scholars think that her grief alludes to the death of Shakespeare's son, Hamnet, in August 1596. But the play may have been written before that date.)

[8]   My boy, my Arthur, my fair son!
My life, my joy, my food, my all the world!
My widow-comfort, and my sorrows' cure! *King John,* III,iii,103. (Constance of Brittany lamenting her son. See also above.)

[9]   Now, our joy,
Although our last and least. *King Lear,* I,i,84. (Lear speaking of Cordelia.)

¹ Ingratitude! thou marble-hearted fiend,
More hideous when thou showest thee in a child
Than the sea-monster. *King Lear,* I,iv,266. (The king in a state of parental outrage. See also below.)

² How sharper than a serpent's tooth it is
To have a thankless child. *King Lear,* I,iv,295.

³ Those pelican daughters. *King Lear,* III,iv,75. (Lear referring to Goneril and Regan. The pelican, according to myth, pierces its breast and feeds its blood to its children.)

⁴ Tigers, not daughters. *King Lear,* IV,ii,40.

⁵ All my pretty ones? *Macbeth,* IV,iii,216. (Macduff when he learns of the murder of his children. More at FAMILY.)

⁶ The boy was the very staff of my age, my very prop. *The Merchant of Venice,* II,ii,66. (Old Gobbo, believing his son Lancelot to be dead.)

⁷ My own flesh and blood to rebel! *The Merchant of Venice,* III,i,32. (Shylock, incredulous at his daughter's betrayal.)

⁸ I had rather adopt a child than get it. *Othello,* I,iii,189. (*Get* means "beget." Brabantio is wildly upset to learn of his daughter's marriage to Othello.)

⁹ A grievous burden was thy birth to me;
Tetchy and wayward was thy infancy. *Richard III,* IV,iv,168. (The duchess of York to her son Richard III. Sir Thomas More in *The History of Richard III,* one of Shakespeare's sources, wrote: "It is for truth reported that the Duchess his mother had so much ado in her travail that she could not be delivered of him uncut, and that he came into the world with the feet forward.")

¹⁰ Earth hath swallowèd all my hopes but she;
She is the hopeful lady of my earth. *Romeo and Juliet,* I,ii,14. (Capulet speaking of his daughter, Juliet. The poor man is later bewildered by Juliet's rebellion. He and his wife had wanted more children, he says, adding, "But now I see this one is one too much," III,v,167. See also below.)

¹¹ Hang, beg, starve, die in the streets,
For, by my soul, I'll ne'er acknowledge thee. *Romeo and Juliet,* III,v,194. (A blustering Capulet unconvincingly disowning Juliet.)

¹² Die single and thine image dies with thee. *Sonnet 3,* 14. (From one of the many sonnets in which Shakespeare urges his friend and patron Southampton to marry and have children. See also PARENTS.)

[1] I have done nothing but in care of thee,
Of thee my dear one, thee my daughter. *The Tempest,* I,ii,16. (Prospero to Miranda.)

[2] She is peevish, sullen, froward,
Proud, disobedient, stubborn, lacking duty,
Neither regarding that she is my child
Nor fearing me as if I were her father. *The Two Gentlemen of Verona,* III,i,68. (*Froward* means "willful.")

[3] A gallant child . . . makes old hearts fresh. *The Winter's Tale,* I,i,40.

[4] He makes a July's day short as December. *The Winter's Tale,* I,ii,169. (King Polixenes of Bohemia speaking of his son, who keeps him busy. "He's all my exercise, my mirth, my matter," the king comments, l.166).

[5] Thou met'st with things dying, I with things new born. *The Winter's Tale,* III,iii,112. (A shepherd happily announcing his discovery of an abandoned baby girl—Perdita, daughter of the king and queen of Sicily.)

See also PARENTS; YOUTH.

CHOICE

[6] There's small choice in rotten apples. *The Taming of the Shrew,* I,i,134. (Proverbial.)

See also DECISION, MOMENT OF; WILL.

CHRISTIANS

[7] O father Abram, what these Christians are,
Whose own hard dealings teaches them suspect
The thoughts of others! *The Merchant of Venice,* I,iii,157. (An ironic comment by Shylock.)

See also HOLY LAND; RELIGION.

CHRISTMAS

[8] Some say that ever 'gainst that season comes
Wherein our Savior's birth is celebrated,
This bird of dawning singeth all night long,
And then, they say, no spirit dare stir abroad,
The nights are wholesome, then no planets strike,
No fairy takes, nor witch hath power to charm:
So hallowed and so gracious is that time. *Hamlet* I,i,158. (In a charming digression, Marcellus recounts this Christmas legend that comes to his

mind after the ghost of Hamlet's father "faded on the crowing of the cock," 1.157. The cock is the bird of dawning that sings all night in the Christmas season. In the first line above, *'gainst* means "just before." *No planets strike* means "no planets bring bad luck." In the next line, *takes* means "bewitches.")

CITIES

[1] What is the city but the people? *Coriolanus,* III,i,198.

[2] I hope to see London once ere I die. *Henry IV, Part Two,* V,iii,61.

[3]   I have walked about the streets,
Submitting me unto the perilous night. *Julius Caesar,* I,iii,46.

[4]   Cloud-kissing Ilion. *The Rape of Lucrece,* 1370. (A reference to Troy.)

[5]   This coward and lascivious town. *Timon of Athens,* V,iv,1. (Alcibiades speaking of Athens.)

[6]   Rome is but a wilderness of tigers. *Titus Andronicus,* III,i,54. (Romans are beasts of prey.)

CLEANLINESS

[7]   Bid them wash their faces,
And keep their teeth clean. *Coriolanus,* II,iii,64. (Coriolanus's contemptuous advice for the citizens of Rome.)

CLEOPATRA

[8]   My serpent of old Nile. *Antony and Cleopatra,* I,v,25. (Cleopatra mentions that Antony affectionately refers to her this way.)

[9]   I was
A morsel for a monarch. *Antony and Cleopatra,* I,v,30. (Cleopatra commenting on her relationship with Caesar. Later, Antony says to her, "I found you as a morsel cold upon / Dead Caesar's trencher," III,xiii,116. In the book *Cleopatra: Histories, Dreams and Distortions,* Lucy Hughes-Hallett describes the historical Cleopatra as a shrewd, practical ruler. She had strong, almost masculine features, with a hooked nose. She was, in sum, a monarch—not a morsel.)

[10] The barge she sat in, like a burnished throne,
Burned on the water: the poop was beaten gold;
Purple the sails, and so perfumèd that
The winds were lovesick with them; the oars were silver,
Which to the tune of flutes kept stroke and made

The water which they beat to follow faster,
As amorous of their strokes. For her own person,
It beggared all description: she did lie
In her pavilion, cloth-of-gold of tissue,
O'erpicturing that Venus where we see
The fancy outwork nature: on each side her
Stood pretty dimpled boys, like smiling Cupids,
With divers-colored fans, whose wind did seem
To glow the delicate cheeks which they did cool,
And what they undid did. *Antony and Cleopatra,* II,ii,197. (One of the most gorgeous speeches in all Shakespeare. In 1845, Théophile Gautier described Cleopatra as "the most complete woman ever to have existed, the most womanly woman and the most queenly queen." Blaise Pascal asserted, "Cleopatra's nose, had it been shorter, the whole face of the world would have been changed," *Pensées,* 1670.)

[1] Age cannot wither her, nor custom stale
Her infinite variety: other women cloy
The appetites they feed, but she makes hungry
Where most she satisfies. *Antony and Cleopatra,* II,ii,241.

[2] I am fire, and air; my other elements
I give to baser life. *Antony and Cleopatra,* V,ii,289. (Cleopatra committing suicide. According to ancient science, the other two, baser, elements constituting the person were earth and water. Incidentally, with lines like "I am fire, and air," it is hard to credit that the great Sarah Siddons turned down the chance to appear in the 1813 production staged by her brother, John Philip Kendall. But she explained that she would hate herself if she played the part as it ought to be played.)

[3] She looks like sleep,
As she would catch another Antony
In her strong toil of grace. *Antony and Cleopatra,* V,ii,345. (Octavius Caesar looking upon the dead Cleopatra. See also NOBILITY. A *toil* is a net or snare.)

CLOTHING. See FASHION.

COMFORT

[4] That comfort comes too late;
'Tis like a pardon after execution. *Henry VIII,* IV,ii,120.

[5] I do not ask you much—
I beg cold comfort. *King John,* V,vii,41. (King John asks for relief in death

and, literally, for cold to soothe the burning of the poison that is killing him. Possibly he suffered ergotism, a fungus infection of rye and other grains that caused many painful deaths in the Middle Ages. *Cold comfort* in this grim context is rather different from the cold-porridge comfort mentioned in *The Tempest;* see below.)

¹ Patch grief with proverbs. *Much Ado About Nothing,* V,i,17.

² Charm ache with air and agony with words. *Much Ado About Nothing,* V,i,26.

³　　Of comfort no man speak. *Richard II,* III,ii,144. (The lead-in to Richard's "death of kings" speech. See HIGH POSITION.)

⁴ He receives comfort like cold porridge. *The Tempest,* II,i,10. (See also the quote from *King John* above.)

See also COMPANY; HELP; REMEDIES.

COMMON SENSE

⁵　　I know a hawk from a handsaw. *Hamlet,* II,ii,388. (A clever saying, in that *hawk* refers to both a bird and a kind of pickax, and *handsaw* resembles *hernshaw,* or *heronsew,* from the Old French *heronceau,* a young heron. This sentence sounds proverbial but actually seems to have been original with Shakespeare.)

⁶ I have a good eye, uncle; I can see a church by daylight. *Much Ado About Nothing,* II,i,81.

See also WISDOM, WORDS OF; WIT.

COMPANY

⁷　　Society is no comfort
To one not sociable. *Cymbeline,* IV,ii,12.

⁸　　I myself am best
When least in company. *Twelfth Night,* I,iv,37.

See also GUESTS.

COMPARISONS

⁹ Comparisons are odorous. *Much Ado About Nothing,* III,v,15. (Often misquoted as "Comparisons are odious.")

¹⁰ Compare her face with some that I shall show,
And I will make thee think thy swan a crow. *Romeo and Juliet,* I,ii,89.

¹ Shall I compare thee to a summer's day? *Sonnet 18,* 1. (More at MORTAL-ITY.)

² My mistress's eyes are nothing like the sun;
Coral is far more red than her lips' red;
If snow be white, why then her breasts are dun;
If hairs be wires, black wires grow on her head. *Sonnet 130,* 1. (Shake-speare's mood in the sonnets is often anguished, the style sometimes forced. Here he is having fun. He concludes, "I grant I never saw a goddess go; / My mistress when she walks treads on the ground. / And yet, by heaven, I think my love as rare / As any she belied with false compare.")

COMPETITION

³ Two stars keep not their motion in one sphere. *Henry IV, Part One,* V,iv,64. (The prince, the future Henry V, to Hotspur. The message is that there isn't room for the two of them in England: "Nor can one England brook a double reign / Of Harry Percy and the Prince of Wales," l.65.)

⁴ *Third Fisherman.* Master, I marvel how the fishes live in the sea.
First Fisherman. Why, as men do a-land: the great ones eat up the little ones. *Pericles,* II,i,29.

See also AGGRESSION; AMBITION; SUCCESS.

COMPLAINTS

⁵ Thou art the Mars of malcontents. *The Merry Wives of Windsor,* I,iii,103.

CONCEIT.   See PRIDE; VANITY.

CONCLUSIONS

⁶ This denoted a foregone conclusion. *Othello,* III,iii,425.

CONFLICT.   See ARGUMENTS; VIOLENCE; WAR.

CONFUSION

⁷ My thoughts are whirlèd like a potter's wheel;
I know not where I am, nor what I do. *Henry VI, Part One,* I,v,19.

⁸ Confusion now hath made his masterpiece. *Macbeth,* II,iii,68. (More at CRIME.)

⁹   All is uneven,
And everything is left at six and seven. *Richard II,* II,ii,120.

CONSCIENCE

[1] Thus conscience does make cowards of us all. *Hamlet,* III,i,83. (In this context, *conscience* means "consciousness," or the ability to think. More at THOUGHT.)

[2] O shame, where is thy blush? *Hamlet,* III,iv,83. (More at SEX.)

[3] A peace above all earthly dignities,
A still and quiet conscience. *Henry VIII,* III,ii,379.

[4]   Some certain dregs of conscience are yet within me. *Richard III,* I,iv,122.

[5]   It [conscience] makes a man a coward. A man cannot steal, but it accuseth him; a man cannot swear, but it checks him; a man cannot lie with his neighbor's wife, but it detects him. . . . It beggars any man that keeps it. It is turned out of towns and cities for a dangerous thing, and every man that means to live well endeavors to trust to himself and live without it. *Richard III,* I,iv,136. (Hesitating to act, this would-be murderer instead talks compulsively. Eventually his accomplice has to strike down the victim.)

[6] Every man's conscience is a thousand men. *Richard III,* V,ii,17. (Right makes might.)

[7] O coward conscience, how dost thou afflict me! *Richard III,* V,iii,180. (Richard's conscience has finally awakened. See also below.)

[8] My conscience hath a thousand several tongues,
And every tongue brings in a several tale,
And every tale condemns me for a villain. *Richard III,* V,iii,194. (For *several* read "separate.")

[9] Conscience is but a word that cowards use,
Devised at first to keep the strong in awe;
Our strong arms be our conscience, swords our law! *Richard III,* V,iii,310. (Preparing for battle, Richard rejects his tormenting conscience.)

See also GUILT.

CONSPICUOUS CONSUMPTION

[10]   [The poor King Reignier] whose large style
Agrees not with the leanness of his purse. *Henry VI, Part Two,* I,i,111. (Reignier, the duke of Anjou, is remembered chiefly through this line. He was the father of the beautiful Margaret of Anjou, who married Henry VI.)

[1]   What needs these feasts, pomps, and vainglories? *Timon of Athens,* I,ii,253.

See also LUXURY; MONEY; RICH, THE; VANITY.

CONSPIRACY

[2] Open-eyed conspiracy
His time doth take.
If of life you keep a care,
Shake off slumber and beware. *The Tempest,* II,i,305. (*Open-eyed* means "wakeful," "alert.")

See also BETRAYAL; DANGER; TREASON.

CONTRACTS

[3] If you repay me not on such a day,
In such a place, such sum or sums as are
Expressed in the condition, let the forfeit
Be nominated for an equal pound
Of your fair flesh, to be cut off and taken
In what part of your body pleaseth me. *The Merchant of Venice,* I,iii,143. (One of the most famous legal contracts in all literature. The bargain has a fairy-tale quality—but is grounded in the real world by Shakespeare's knack for legal language and the vivid character of Shylock. Antonio, confident to the point of arrogance, accepts the gruesome terms of the loan: "I'll seal to such a bond, / And say there is much kindness in the Jew.")

[4] Let him look to his bond. *The Merchant of Venice,* III,i,46. (Shylock after learning that Antonio's ship has been wrecked.)

[5] Is it so nominated in the bond? *The Merchant of Venice,* IV,i,258. (Also, " 'Tis not in the bond," l.261. Shylock's obsession with the terms of the bond leads to his undoing, as Portia eventually argues that the bond includes no mention of blood, and that, if while cutting the pound of flesh, he sheds a drop of Christian blood, then his lands and goods are confiscate to the state of Venice and he will be executed.)

[6] I have no joy of this contract tonight. *Romeo and Juliet,* II,ii,117. (More at IMPULSIVITY.)

See also BUSINESS; NEGOTIATION.

CONVERSIONS

[7]   I do not shame
To tell you what I was, since my conversion

So sweetly tastes, being the thing I am. *As You Like It,* IV,iii,136. (Oliver, sounding for all the world as pleased with himself as any contemporary born-again Christian.)

COUNTRY LIFE

¹ Hath not old custom made this life more sweet
Than that of painted pomp? Are not these woods
More free from peril than the envious court? *As You Like It,* II,i,2. (The rightful duke speaking of pastoral life in the Forest of Arden. Near Stratford stood a forest by this name [from the Celtic *ard,* "high" or "great," plus *den,* "a wooded valley"]. Shakespeare's mother, Mary Arden, was from an important local family. The name also refers to Ardennes—the play is set in France—and Eden, the ultimate country place.)

²   This our life, exempt from public haunt,
Finds tongues in trees, books in the running brooks,
Sermons in stones, and good in everything. *As You Like It,* II,ii,15. (*Public haunt* means "people" or "society." The lines are a continuation of the speech quoted above.)

³ Under the greenwood tree
Who loves to lie with me,
And turn his merry note
Unto the sweet bird's throat,
Come hither, come hither, come hither.
Here shall he see no enemy
But winter and rough weather. *As You Like It,* II,v,1. ("Who loves to lie with me" did not meet nineteenth-century standards for nice invitations. In the Rev. James Plumtre's collection of Shakespeare's songs, the phrase was changed to "Who loves to work with me," even though work was absolutely not done in the Forest of Arden. See below.)

⁴ Who doth ambition shun
And loves to live in the sun,
Seeking the food he eats,
And pleased with what he gets,
Come hither, come hither, come hither. *As You Like It,* II,v,34.

⁵ O God! methinks it were a happy life,
To be no better than a homely swain;
To sit upon a hill as I do now,
To carve out dials quaintly, point by point. *Henry VI, Part Three,* II,v,21. (The beleaguered king imagines the life of a shepherd, whittling a sundial, calculating the hours of his life and how they will be spent in peaceful pursuits. See more below and also at TIME.)

¹ Ah, what a life were this! how sweet! how lovely!
Gives not the hawthorn-bush a sweeter shade
To shepherds looking on their silly sheep,
Than doth a rich embroidered canopy
To kings that fear their subjects' treachery? *Henry VI, Part Three,* II,v,41.

² This castle hath a pleasant seat; the air
Nimbly and sweetly recommends itself
Unto our gentle senses. *Macbeth,* I,vi,1. (King Duncan commenting on the
charm of Macbeth's castle. Banquo, taking up the theme, notes that
martins nest there, and "the air is delicate," l.9. The sweetness of the air
probably was in contrast to the atmosphere around many castles, considering the lack of plumbing and running water.)

See also NATURE.

COURAGE

³ 'Tis true that we are in great danger;
The greater therefore should our courage be. *Henry V,* IV,i,1.

⁴   Courage mounteth with occasion. *King John,* II,i,82. (One finds courage when it is needed.)

⁵ I dare do all that may become a man;
Who dares do more is none. *Macbeth,* I,vii,46. (Macbeth to his wife,
asserting that unwillingness to commit murder is not cowardice but de-
cency. Later Macbeth tries to conquer his terror at the appearance of the
ghost of Banquo by announcing, "What man dare, I dare," III,iv,100.)

⁶ *Macbeth.* If we should fail?
Lady Macbeth. We fail?
But screw your courage to the sticking-place,
And we'll not fail. *Macbeth,* I,vii,58.

See also BOLDNESS; DANGER; FEAR; RESISTANCE.

COURTSHIP.   See LOVE AND LOVERS; MEN AND WOMEN; SEX.

COWARDICE.   See FEAR.

CRAFTINESS

⁷ Though this be madness, yet there is method in it. *Hamlet,* II,ii,207. (See
also MADNESS.)

⁸ I know a trick worth two of that. *Henry IV, Part One,* II,i,38.

¹ The fox barks not when he would steal the lamb. *Henry VI, Part Two,* III,i,55.

² Bait the hook well! This fish will bite. *Much Ado About Nothing,* II,iii,111.

³ My purpose is indeed a horse of that color. *Twelfth Night,* II,iii,167. (Maria intends to play a trick on Malvolio.)

⁴ Here comes the trout that must be caught with tickling. *Twelfth Night,* II,v,21. (Maria again. *Trout* has a sexual meaning as well as the literal one.)

See also DECEPTIVENESS; LIES AND DECEIT.

CRIME

⁵ Beauty provoketh thieves sooner than gold. *As You Like It,* I,iii,108. (Rosalind, preparing to flee with her cousin Celia through the Forest of Arden, fears they may meet rapists as well as thieves. Rural journeys were always dangerous, especially after nightfall. Rosalind disguises herself as a man and adopts a swashbuckling manner to discourage attackers; see MEN AND WOMEN.)

⁶　　Foul deeds will rise,
Though all the earth o'erwhelm them, to men's eyes. *Hamlet,* I,ii,257. (Similar to "Murder will out." See the first quote from *The Merchant of Venice,* below, and the quote from *Richard III,* I,iv,286.)

⁷ Murder most foul, as in the best it is,
But this most foul, strange, and unnatural. *Hamlet,* I,v,27. (The ghost of Hamlet's father, speaking of his own murder.)

⁸　　Murder, though it have no tongue, will speak. *Hamlet,* II,ii,605. (See below, *The Merchant of Venice,* II,ii,79, and *Richard III,* I,iv,286, for notes on other similar quotations.)

⁹ O, my offense is rank, it smells to heaven;
It hath the primal eldest curse upon it,
A brother's murder. *Hamlet,* III,iii,36.

¹⁰ With all his crimes broad blown, as flush as May. *Hamlet,* III,iii,81. (Hamlet speaks of his father's dying without the sacrament of confession. *Blown* means "in bloom," "full." *Flush* means "full of life.")

¹¹　　A purse of gold most resolutely snatched on Monday night and most dissolutely spent on Tuesday morning. *Henry IV, Part One,* I,ii,34. (From a speech by Prince Hal on the ebb and flow of fortune among his disreputable friends.)

¹² I'll starve ere I'll rob a foot further. *Henry IV, Part One,* II,ii,21. (Falstaff threatening to reform, as was his custom.)

[1] A plague upon it when thieves cannot be true to one another! *Henry IV, Part One,* II,ii,27. (Falstaff disgusted.)

[2] See how the blood is settled in his face.
. . . his face is black and full of blood,
His eyeballs further out than when he lived,
Staring full ghastly like a strangled man. *Henry VI, Part Two,* III,ii,160,168. (From a lengthy, fascinating passage in which the earl of Warwick examines the corpse and deathbed of the duke of Gloucester and explains why the evidence points to murder by strangulation. An early and rare example of forensic reasoning. Based on circumstantial evidence, the earl has a shrewd idea who the murderers are: "Who finds the heifer dead, and bleeding fresh, / And sees fast by a butcher with an ax, / But will suspect 'twas he that made the slaughter?" l.188.)

[3] Why, I can smile, and murder whiles I smile. *Henry VI, Part Three,* III,ii,182. (More at EVIL. See also below.)

[4] I have no brother, I am like no brother;
And this word "love," which graybeards call divine,
Be resident in men like one another
And not in me: I am myself alone. *Henry VI, Part Three,* V,vi,80. (The future Richard III is a classic sociopath, incapable of love or friendship, at least as portrayed by Shakespeare; the members of the Richard III Society vehemently disagree. At any rate, when Richard here says he is like no brother, he means that his twisted body has made him different from other men. He does have a brother, Clarence, one of his several victims. In another line, he says of himself: "I, that have neither pity, love, nor fear," l.68. Here he is boasting. Later he despairs. See also AMBITION; DANGEROUS PEOPLE; DESPAIR; EVIL.)

[5] Corruption wins not more than honesty. *Henry VIII,* III,ii,444. (Cardinal Wolsey teaching a lesson learned the hard way.)

[6]   The work we have in hand,
Most bloody, fiery, and most terrible. *Julius Caesar,* I,iii,129. (Cassius on the assassination of Caesar.)

[7] Between the acting of a dreadful thing
And the first motion, all the interim is
Like a phantasma, or a hideous dream. *Julius Caesar,* II,i,63. (Brutus contemplating striking down Caesar. More of the passage is below.)

[8]   The state of a man,
Like to a little kingdom, suffers then
The nature of an insurrection. *Julius Caesar,* II,i,67. (Brutus continues to

describe his turbulent, nightmarish state of mind. His sense that his self has been divided or taken over is reported quite commonly by murderers.)

[1] Let's be sacrificers, but not butchers. *Julius Caesar,* II,i,166. (Brutus making a distinction between styles of assassination. See also below.)

[2] Let's carve him as a dish fit for the gods. *Julius Caesar,* II,i,173. (Brutus again. Plutarch, Shakespeare's main source, notes that Brutus struck Caesar in the groin.)

[3]   Pity, like a naked newborn babe,
Striding the blast, or heaven's cherubin horsed
Upon the sightless couriers of the air,
Shall blow the horrid deed in every eye,
That tears shall drown the wind. *Macbeth,* I,vii,21. (Macbeth imagining the universal horror if he assassinates Duncan. See also VIOLENCE and JUSTICE.)

[4]   Thou sure and firm-set earth,
Hear not my steps, which way they walk, for fear
The very stones prate of my whereabout. *Macbeth,* II,i,56. (On stones that speak, see the note on the first *Merchant of Venice* quote below.)

[5] I go, and it is done: the bell invites me.
Hear it not, Duncan, for it is a knell
That summons thee to heaven, or to hell. *Macbeth,* II,i,62.

[6] Confusion now hath made his masterpiece,
Most sacrilegious murder hath broke ope
The Lord's anointed temple, and stole thence
The life of the building. *Macbeth,* II,iii,68.

[7]   Ere the bat hath flown
His cloistered flight, ere to black Hecate's summons
The shard-borne beetle with his drowsy hums
Hath rung night's yawning peal, there shall be done
A deed of dreadful note. *Macbeth,* III,ii,40. (Macbeth telling his wife that Banquo and his son will be murdered. *Shard-borne* means either "borne on hard, scaly wings" or "bred in dung." Macbeth then implores the night to come and "with thy bloody and invisible hand" to accomplish the murder; see NIGHT.)

[8]   Blood will have blood.
Stones have been known to move and trees to speak;
Augures and understood relations have
By maggot-pies and choughs and rooks brought forth
The secretest man of blood. *Macbeth,* III,iv,123. (*Understood relations* are

reports that are comprehended, in this case from chattering birds. A *maggot-pie* is a magpie. The notion that birds inform and informers are birds continues in modern slang. For similar quotes, see below: *The Merchant of Venice* and the quote from *Richard III,* I,iv,286.)

1 I am in blood
Stepped in so far that, should I wade no more,
Returning were as tedious as go o'er. *Macbeth,* III,iv,137.

2 Yet who would have thought the old man to have had so much blood in him? *Macbeth,* V,i,42. (The sleepwalking Lady Macbeth.)

3 Every true man's apparel fits your thief. *Measure for Measure,* IV,ii,44. (Ambiguous, but may mean an honest man's clothes will suit a thief very nicely, or, one cannot easily judge by appearance between the honest man and a thief.)

4 Truth will come to light; murder cannot be hid long. *The Merchant of Venice,* II,ii,79. (The proverbial saying "Murder will out" was used in various forms by numerous authors, including Chaucer and Cervantes as well as Shakespeare. In an 1838 address at Harvard Divinity School, Emerson wrote, "Murder will speak out of stone walls." In the Bible, stones that speak out appear in *Habakkuk* 2:11, "The stone shall cry out of the wall"; and in *Luke* 19:40. See also the quote from Act I of *Hamlet,* above; the second quote from *Macbeth,* below, and from *Richard III,* I,iv,286.

5 *Bassanio.* Do all men kill the things they do not love?
Shylock. Hates any man the thing he would not kill? *The Merchant of Venice,* IV,i,66. (Dialogue on whether Shylock should go ahead and cut out a pound of flesh from Antonio, whom he does not love—altered by Oscar Wilde in *The Ballad of Reading Gaol,* "Each man kills the thing he loves.")

6 Flat burglary as ever was committed. *Much Ado About Nothing,* IV,ii,49.

7 The robbed that smiles, steals something from the thief. *Othello,* I,iii,204.

8 They love not poison that do poison need. *Richard II,* V,vi,38. (Boling-broke rebuking the murderer that he himself set on King Richard.)

9 I do love thee so
That I will shortly send thy soul to heaven,
If heaven will take the present at our hands. *Richard III,* I,i,118. (A little joke by the future Richard III, referring to his brother Clarence, who stands between him and the throne. See above under *Henry VI, Part III.*)

10 This will out. *Richard III,* I,iv,286. (Said by a murderer. Proverbial. Similar to Chaucer's "Mordre wol out, certeyn, it wol nat faille," "The

Prioress's Tale." A chilling line in *The Duchess of Malfi,* IV,ii,260, reads: "Other sins only speak; murder shrieks out." See also the note above for *The Merchant of Venice,* II,ii,79.)

1   His complexion is perfect gallows. *The Tempest,* I,i,30. (Translation: He looks like someone who'll end up on the gallows.)

2 We are not thieves, but men that much do want. *Timon of Athens,* IV,iii,422.

3 All that you meet are thieves. *Timon of Athens,* IV,iii,453.

4   Crimes . . .
Are not inherited. *Timon of Athens,* V,iv,37. (An Athenian senator trying to persuade Alcibiades not to make war on all Athenians because of the crimes of a few.)

5   A snapper-up of unconsidered trifles. *The Winter's Tale,* IV,iii,26. (In other words, a thief, here named Autolycus. One of his specialties is stealing linen hung out to bleach. For a lyric reference to sheets on a hedge, see SPRING. Later, Autolycus sings happily of "Lawn [linen] as white as driven snow," IV,iv,220.)

See also BRIBERY; DANGEROUS PEOPLE; DISHONESTY; EVIL; GUILT; LAW AND LAWYERS; LIES AND DECEIT; PUNISHMENT; TREASON; VIOLENCE; WILD AND WANTON PEOPLE.

CRISIS.   See ADVERSITY; ALLIES; BAD TIMES; DANGER; DECISION, MOMENT OF; REVOLUTION.

CRITICISM

6   Better a little chiding than a great deal of heartbreak. *The Merry Wives of Windsor,* V,iii,10.

7   I am nothing if not critical. *Othello,* II,i,117.

8 The raven chides blackness. *Troilus and Cressida,* II,iii,213. (Shakespeare used proverbial sayings liberally.)

See also INSULTS; SELF-CRITICISM.

CRUELTY.   See CRIME; DANGEROUS PEOPLE; EVIL; PUNISHMENT; RUTHLESSNESS; VIOLENCE.

CRYING. See WEEPING.

CURSES

[1] A plague a both your houses!
They have made worms' meat of me. *Romeo and Juliet,* III,i,108. (Mercutio, fatally wounded by Tybalt.)

See also DESPAIR AND RAGE; TALK, PLAIN AND FANCY.

CUSTOM. See HABIT AND CUSTOM.

DANCE

[1] I am for other than dancing measures. *As You Like It,* V,iv,193. (Said by melancholy Jaques, who declines to dance.)

[2] You and I are past our dancing days. *Romeo and Juliet,* I,v,33.

[3] Come unto these yellow sands,
And then take hands.
Curtsied when you have and kissed
The wild waves whist,
Foot it featly here and there. *The Tempest,* I,ii,375. (*Kissed the wild waves whist* refers, somewhat unclearly, to kisses hushing the waves into silence.)

[4] I can cut a caper. *Twelfth Night,* I,iii,117.

[5] When you do dance, I wish you
A wave o' the sea, that you might ever do
Nothing but that—move still, still so. *The Winter's Tale,* IV,iv,140.

DANGER

[6] He must have a long spoon that must eat with the devil. *The Comedy of Errors,* IV,iii,65. (Proverbial. In Chaucer, the saying goes "Therfore behoveth hire a full long spoon / That shal ete with a feend," "The Squire's Tale" in *The Canterbury Tales.*)

[7] O, the blood more stirs
To rouse a lion than to start a hare! *Henry IV, Part One,* I,iii,195.

¹ Out of this nettle, danger, we pluck this flower, safety. *Henry IV, Part One*, II,iii,9.

² I must go and meet with danger there,
Or it will seek me in another place
And find me worse provided. *Henry IV, Part Two*, II,iii,48. (The earl of Northumberland, resolving to join the rebel force. A similar attitude toward danger is expressed by Brutus in *Julius Caesar* when he insists on engaging the enemy at Philippi; see under OPPORTUNITY. But Northumberland, unlike Brutus, changed his mind and retreated to a safe haven in Scotland.)

³ Beware the ides of March. *Julius Caesar*, I,ii,18. (A soothsayer to Caesar. The next day Caesar meets the soothsayer again and remarks, "The ides of March have come," to which the soothsayer replies, "Ay, Caesar, but not gone," III,i,1. The ides were March 15; the year was 44 B.C.)

⁴ Clouds, dews, and dangers come. *Julius Caesar*, V,iii,64.

⁵ Where we are
There's daggers in men's smiles. *Macbeth*, II,iii,141.

⁶ We have scorched the snake, not killed it. *Macbeth*, III,ii,13. (*Scorched* means "scored" or "cut." The term is sometimes written "scotched.")

⁷ She loved me for the dangers I had passed. *Othello*, I,iii,166. (More at LOVE AND LOVERS. See also STORIES.)

⁸ Lives like a drunken sailor on a mast,
Ready with every nod to tumble down
Into the fatal bowels of the deep. *Richard III*, III,iv,98. (The person who lives this way is one who trusts in the goodwill of Richard.)

See also ADVERSITY; BAD TIMES; BOLDNESS: CONSPIRACY; COURAGE; EVIL; OMENS; RISK; TROUBLE.

DANGEROUS PEOPLE

⁹ A dangerous and lascivious boy. *All's Well That Ends Well*, IV,iii,232. (Thus Parolles describes Bertram, the Count Rousillon—unfortunately, without realizing that it is Bertram to whom he is speaking. "[He] is a whale to virginity," Parolles continues, "and devours all the fry.")

¹⁰ Though I am not splenitive and rash,
Yet have I in me something dangerous,
Which let thy wisdom fear. *Hamlet*, V,i,263. (Hamlet to Laertes. *Splenitive* means "hot-tempered," the spleen being considered the organ governing anger.)

¹   I am myself alone. *Henry VI, Part Three,* V,vi,83. (The future Richard III. More at CRIME. See also EVIL and the quote from *Richard III* below.)

² Yond Cassius has a lean and hungry look;
He thinks too much: such men are dangerous. *Julius Caesar,* I,ii,194.
(Caesar is speaking. The passage begins: "Let me have men about me that are fat, / Sleek-headed men, and such as sleep a-nights," l.193. In Plutarch, Shakespeare's main source, Caesar remarks, "I like not his pale looks," and adds, "These pale-visaged and carrion-lean people, I fear them most.")

³   He reads much,
He is a great observer, and he looks
Quite through the deeds of men. He loves no plays.
. . . he hears no music.
Seldom he smiles, and smiles in such a sort
As if he mocked himself. *Julius Caesar,* I,ii,201.

⁴ Such men as he be never at heart's ease
Whiles they behold a greater than themselves,
And therefore are they very dangerous. *Julius Caesar* I,ii,208.

⁵ Child Rowland to the dark tower came;
His word was still, "Fie, foh, and fum,
I smell the blood of a British man." *King Lear,* III,iv,185. (A nursery or nonsense rhyme, perhaps from a lost ballad, spoken by Edgar. *Child* refers to a candidate for knighthood. *Rowland* is Charlemagne's nephew, the hero of *The Song of Roland. His word was still* means "his saying was always.")

⁶ *Second Murderer.* I am one, my liege,
Whom the vile blows and buffets of the world
Hath so incensed that I am reckless what
I do to spite the world.
First Murderer. And I another
So weary with disasters, tugged with fortune,
That I would set my life on any chance,
To mend it or be rid on it. *Macbeth,* III,i,108.

⁷   Fit for treasons, stratagems, and spoils. *The Merchant of Venice,* V,i,85. (Shakespeare's opinion of the person who is not moved by music; see MUSIC.)

⁸ She was a vixen when she went to school;
And though she be but little, she is fierce. *A Midsummer Night's Dream,* III,ii,324.

1   I play the villain. *Othello,* II,iii,336. (Iago speaks.)

2 The love of wicked men converts to fear,
That fear to hate. *Richard II,* V,i,66.

3   Take heed of yonder dog!
Look when he fawns he bites; and when he bites,
His venom tooth will rankle to the death.
Have not to do with him, beware of him.
Sin, death, and hell have set their marks on him
And all their ministers attend on him. *Richard III,* I,iii,288. (Queen Margaret, no sweetheart herself, on the subject of the future Richard III. In a March 13, 1991, article in the *Wall Street Journal,* Cynthia Crossen listed some of the flaws traditionally ascribed to Richard III. He was said to have been born with teeth and claws, as well as the more probable hunchback and withered arm. As an adult he ate live frogs and killed his nephews. Ms. Crossen also described the zealous efforts by members of the Richard III Society to set the record straight. All lies, they say, invented by Henry VII, who defeated Richard and took over the throne.)

4 A devil, a born devil, on whose nature
Nurture can never stick. *The Tempest,* IV,i,188. (Prospero on Caliban.)

5   He's a very devil. *Twelfth Night,* III,iv,284. (Sir Toby speaking of Cesario, who is really Viola.)

See also CRIME; EVIL; RUTHLESSNESS; WILD AND WANTON PEOPLE.

DEATH

6   The dead are well. *Antony and Cleopatra,* II,v,33. (Spoken by Cleopatra and identified as a common saying. The meaning is that the dead are well out of the world's suffering. Or the dead are well and in heaven.)

7   Make death proud to take us. *Antony and Cleopatra,* IV,xv,87. (Cleopatra speaking of the burial of Antony. The whole passage reads: "We'll bury him; and then, what's brave, what's noble, / Let's do it after the high Roman fashion, / And make death proud to take us." See also DEATH AND GRIEF; GREATNESS.)

8 If thou and nature can so gently part,
The stroke of death is as a lover's pinch,
Which hurts, and is desired. *Antony and Cleopatra,* V,ii,294. (Cleopatra observing the death of her servant Iras just before putting the asp to her own breast; see also GREATNESS; SUICIDE.)

9 Hold death awhile at the arm's end. *As You Like It,* II,vi,9. (Orlando to his old servant Adam, who is weak from lack of food.)

[1]   A great reckoning in a little room. *As You Like It,* III,iii,14. (A. L. Rowse notes that here Shakespeare may have been alluding to Christopher Marlowe's death. The line recalls Marlowe's "Infinite riches in a little room," *The Jew of Malta.* Marlowe himself died of a knife wound incurred in a fight in a room in an inn at Deptford. The fight may have been over the bill. Here Touchstone says that obscure poetry "strikes a man more dead than a great reckoning in a little room." The reckoning would be the bill for the room.)

[2] Death, that dark spirit. *Coriolanus,* II,i,166.

[3] Fear no more the heat of the sun
Nor the furious winter's rages;
Thou thy worldly task hast done,
Home art gone and ta'en thy wages.
Golden lads and girls all must,
As chimney-sweepers, come to dust. *Cymbeline,* IV,ii,258. (The burial song continues with the two singers alternating lines and couplets, including the one below. The next quote after that is from the same passage, but is not part of the song.)

[4] Quiet consummation have,
And renownèd be thy grave. *Cymbeline,* IV,ii,280.

[5] The ground that gave them first has them again.
Their pleasures here are past, so is their pain. *Cymbeline,* IV,ii,289.

[6]   The sure physician, Death. *Cymbeline,* V,iv,7.

[7]   All that lives must die,
Passing through nature to eternity. *Hamlet,* I,ii,72.

[8] Cut off even in the blossoms of my sin,
Unhouseled, disappointed, unaneled,
No reckoning made, but sent to my account
With all my imperfections on my head.
O, horrible! O, horrible! Most horrible! *Hamlet,* I,v,76. (The ghost of Hamlet's father, deploring having been suddenly murdered, with no chance to confess his sins and receive absolution. An orderly and religious death was an important chivalric ideal. *Unhouseled, disappointed, unaneled* translates: without the Eucharist, unabsolved, without the sacrament of extreme unction.)

[9] The undiscovered country, from whose bourn
No traveler returns. *Hamlet,* III,i,79. (More at SUICIDE.)

[10] He is dead and gone, lady,
He is dead and gone;

At his head a grass-green turf,
At his heels a stone. *Hamlet,* IV,v,29. (Song sung by Ophelia, grieving for her father.)

¹ *Hamlet.* Has this fellow no feeling of his business? 'A sings in gravemaking. *Horatio.* Custom hath made it in him a property of easiness. *Hamlet,* V,i,66. (Hamlet is speaking of the gravedigger. Horatio's answer means: He's so used to the work, it doesn't bother him.)

² *Hamlet.* Who is to be buried in it?
Clown. One that was a woman, sir; but, rest her soul, she's dead.
Hamlet. How absolute the knave is! *Hamlet,* V,i,136. (See also TALK, PLAIN AND FANCY.)

³ Alas, poor Yorick! *Hamlet,* V,i,185. (See MORTALITY.)

⁴   This fell sergeant, Death,
Is strict in his arrest. *Hamlet,* V,ii,337.

⁵ Now cracks a noble heart. Good night, sweet Prince. *Hamlet,* V,ii,360. (More at HAMLET.)

⁶   O proud Death,
What feast is toward in thine eternal cell? *Hamlet,* V,ii,365. (*Toward* means "about to happen," "in preparation." Fortinbras is referring to the death of so many so suddenly, including Hamlet.)

⁷   The end of life cancels all bands. *Henry IV, Part One,* III,ii,157. (*Bands* refers to promises, obligations, bonds. Essentially proverbial. See the same idea under *The Tempest* below.)

⁸ Doomsday is near. Die all, die merrily. *Henry IV, Part One,* IV,i,133. (Hotspur before the battle of Shrewsbury.)

⁹   Thou owest God a death. *Henry IV, Part One,* V,i,126. (Prince Hal to the frightened Falstaff before the battle of Shrewsbury. Falstaff replies, " 'Tis not due yet: I would be loath to pay him before his day," l.127. The word *death* may have been pronounced as *debt,* adding a pun to the joke. The same theme is taken up more seriously in *Part Two;* see below.)

¹⁰ Death, as the Psalmist saith, is certain to all, all shall die. *Henry IV, Part Two,* III,ii,39.

¹¹ A man can die but once. We owe God a death. *Henry IV, Part Two,* III,ii,242. (Spoken stoically by Feeble. This recalls the joking exchange between Hal and Falstaff on the same theme in *Part One.* Incidentally, Falstaff repeatedly teases Feeble—who is far braver than he—about his name, for example: "Let that suffice, most forcible Feeble," III,ii,171.)

¹² His cares are now all ended. *Henry IV, Part Two,* V,ii,3.

¹ He's in Arthur's bosom, if ever man went to Arthur's bosom. 'A made a finer end, and went away and it had been any christom child. *Henry V,* II,iii,9. (Hostess Quickly announcing the death of Falstaff. *'A* means "he." *Christom child* refers to a child in a christening robe; the correct term was actually *chrisom.* More below.)

² Then I felt to his knees, and so upward, and upward, and all was as cold as any stone. *Henry V,* II,iii,25. (Hostess Quickly describing the death of Falstaff; the conclusion of the speech quoted above.)

³   Death's dishonorable victory. *Henry VI, Part One,* I,i,20.

⁴ He dies, and makes no sign. *Henry VI, Part Two,* III,iii,29. (Cardinal Beaufort on his deathbed does not hear or does not respond when asked to hold up his hand to show that he is thinking of heaven's bliss. In delirium, the cardinal admitted involvement in the murder of his half nephew, the duke of Gloucester; see also JUDGING OTHERS and the next quote below.)

⁵ So bad a death argues a monstrous life. *Henry VI, Part Two,* III,iii,30. (The earl of Warwick on the death of the cardinal. The king, more verbose, comments: "Ah, what a sign it is of evil life, / Where death's approach is seen so terrible," l.5)

⁶   Dead as a doornail. *Henry VI, Part Two,* IV,x,42. (A common saying.)

⁷ Why, what is pomp, rule, reign, but earth and dust?
And, live we how we can, yet die we must. *Henry VI, Part Three,* V,ii,27.

⁸   Farewell!
And when you would say something that is sad,
Speak how I fell. I have done, and God forgive me. *Henry VIII,* II,i,134. (The duke of Buckingham on his way to be executed.)

⁹ He gave his honors to the world again,
His blessèd part to heaven, and slept in peace. *Henry VIII,* IV,ii,29. (The passage refers to Cardinal Wolsey, who died ruined. Katherine [Catherine of Aragon], once a victim of Wolsey's ambition, responds, "So may he rest. His faults lie gently on him!" But then she goes on to enumerate those faults, beginning with, "He was a man / Of an unbounded stomach [arrogance].")

¹⁰ Cowards die many times before their deaths;
The valiant never taste of death but once.
Of all the wonders that I yet have heard,
It seems to me most strange that men should fear,
Seeing that death, a necessary end,
Will come when it will come. *Julius Caesar,* II,ii,32. (Caesar is speaking.)

1   He that cuts off twenty years of life
Cuts off so many years of fearing death. *Julius Caesar,* III,i,101.

2   Live a thousand years,
I shall not find myself so apt to die. *Julius Caesar* III,i,159.

3   Then burst his mighty heart. *Julius Caesar,* III,ii,188. (From Antony's funeral speech. He tells the Roman crowd that at the sight of Brutus among the conspirators, Caesar ceased resisting and covered his face. This follows Plutarch's account.)

4 Death, death, O, amiable, lovely death! *King John,* III,iii,25. (Constance of Brittany in despair at the loss of her son, Arthur. For a less melodramatic, more touching passage from this scene, see CHILDREN. Eventually, Constance dies of sorrow.)

5   'Tis strange that death should sing!
I am the cygnet to this pale faint swan,
Who chants a doleful hymn to his own death,
And from the organ-pipe of frailty sings
His soul and body to their lasting rest. *King John,* V,vii,20. (Prince Henry attending to the dying King John. Swans were said to sing only as they died.)

6   Now my soul hath elbow-room. *King John,* V,vii,28.

7 What surety of the world, what hope, what stay,
When this was now a king, and now is clay? *King John,* V,vii,68.

8   Men must endure
Their going hence, even as their coming hither:
Ripeness is all. *King Lear,* V,ii,9. (See also the note on the same passage at OLD AGE.)

9 Vex not his ghost: O, let him pass! He hates him
That would upon the rack of this tough world
Stretch him out longer. *King Lear,* V,iii,315. (The earl of Kent advising Edgar to let Lear die. The *ghost* is the departing spirit.)

10   Nothing in his life
Became him like the leaving it. He died
As one that had been studied in his death,
To throw away the dearest thing he owed
As 'twere a careless trifle. *Macbeth,* I,iv,7. (Wonderful lines for a character who does not even appear in the play, the treacherous thane of Cawdor, who is executed and whose title and property are awarded to Macbeth. *Owed,* by the way, means "owned.")

1   It is a knell
That summons thee to heaven, or to hell. *Macbeth,* II,i,63. (More at
CRIME.)

2   The sleeping and the dead
Are but as pictures. 'Tis the eye of childhood
That fears a painted devil. *Macbeth,* II,ii,52. (Lady Macbeth deriding her
husband for his unwillingness to return to the chambers where the murdered Duncan lies, guarded by drunken, sleeping soldiers.)

3   Duncan is in his grave;
After life's fitful fever he sleeps well.
Treason has done his worst: nor steel, nor poison,
Malice domestic, foreign levy, nothing,
Can touch him further. *Macbeth,* III,ii,22.

4 Be absolute for death. *Measure for Measure,* III,i,5. (This means "Be absolutely prepared to die." The duke, Vincentio, is advising Claudio to expect
death; thus death will be easier if it comes, and life sweeter if he is spared.
The duke continues, "Reason thus with life: If I do lose thee, I do lose a
thing / That none but fools would keep; a breath thou art, / Servile to all
the skyey influences," 1.6. The last phrase means "heavenly influences,"
i.e., the stars, chance, fate.)

5   I find I seek to die,
And seeking death, find life. *Measure for Measure,* III,i,42. (Claudio re-
sponding to the duke's urging to prepare for death without fear in order
to live fully. See above and also LIFE.)

6 The sense of death is most in apprehension,
And the poor beetle that we tread upon
In corporal sufferance finds a pang as great
As when a giant dies. *Measure for Measure,* III,i,78. (The first line means
that the feeling of death is mostly in the imagination.)

7 If I must die,
I will encounter darkness as a bride,
And hug it in mine arms. *Measure for Measure,* III,i,83.

8 Ay, but to die, and go we know not where,
To lie in cold obstruction and to rot,
This sensible warm motion to become
A kneaded clod; and the delighted spirit
To bathe in fiery floods, or to reside
In thrilling region of thick-ribbèd ice;
To be imprisoned in the viewless winds,

And blown with restless violence round about
The pendent world. *Measure for Measure,* III,i,118. (*Obstruction* means "in a rigid state"; *motion* means "a living thing"; *pendent* means "hanging in space.")

1   The young gentleman . . . is indeed deceased, or as you would say in plain terms, gone to heaven. *The Merchant of Venice,* II,ii,61.

2 Put out the light, and then put out the light. *Othello,* V,ii,7. (Othello with a lantern at Desdemona's bedside, resolving to murder her. He thinks aloud that while he can relight the lantern, once Desdemona is dead, "I know not where is that Promethean heat / That can thy light relume. When I have plucked the rose, / I cannot give it vital growth again; / It needs must wither," l.12.)

3 More are men's ends marked than their lives before;
The setting sun and music at the close,
As the last taste of sweets in sweetest last,
Writ in remembrance more than things long past. *Richard II,* II,i,11.

4 The ripest fruit first falls. *Richard II,* II,i,153. (Proverbial.)

5 The worst is death, and death will have his day. *Richard II,* III,ii,103.

6   Of comfort no man speak.
Let's talk of graves, of worms, and epitaphs.
. . .
Let's choose executors and talk of wills. *Richard II,* III,ii,144,148. (More of the passage follows, as Richard sees too late what lies ahead.)

7 And nothing can we call our own, but death
And that small model of the barren earth
Which serves as paste and cover to our bones.
For God's sake let us sit upon the ground
And tell sad stories of the death of kings. *Richard II,* III,ii,152. (More at HIGH POSITION.)

8 A little, little grave, an obscure grave. *Richard II,* III,iii,153. (More at HIGH POSITION.)

9 O Lord, methought what pain it was to drown!
What dreadful noise of water in mine ears!
What sights of ugly death within mine eyes!
Methoughts I saw a thousand fearful wracks;
A thousand men that fishes gnawed upon. *Richard III,* I,iv,21.

10   The kingdom of perpetual night. *Richard III,* I,iv,47. (A common phrase dating back at least to Catullus: "When our brief light has set, there's the kingdom of perpetual night," *Carmina I.*)

[1] How oft when men are at the point of death
Have they been merry! *Romeo and Juliet,* V,iii,88. (Romeo notes that jailers
call this mood a "lightning before death," 1.90.)

[2]   Beauty's ensign yet
Is crimson in thy lips and in thy cheeks,
And death's pale flag is not advancèd there. *Romeo and Juliet,* V,iii,94.
(Romeo speaking of Juliet. For Romeo's last words, see SUICIDE.)

[3] Tired with all these, for restful death I cry. *Sonnet 66,* 1. (*These* are the
wrongs and injustices of the world.)

[4]   He that dies pays all debts. *The Tempest,* III,ii,136. (See also the
quote from *Henry IV, Part One* above.)

[5] Hector is dead; there is no more to say. *Troilus and Cressida,* V,x,22.

[6] Come away, come away, death,
And in sad cypress let me laid.
Fly away, fly away, breath;
I am slain by a fair cruel maid. *Twelfth Night,* II,iv,51.

[7] Tell me, what blessings I have here alive,
That I should fear to die? *The Winter's Tale,* III,ii,105.

See also DEATH AND GRIEF; DEATHBED STATEMENTS AND FINAL WORDS;
ENDINGS; EPITAPHS; MORTALITY; SUICIDE.

DEATH AND GRIEF

[8] Moderate lamentation is the right of the dead, excessive grief the enemy
to the living. *All's Well That Ends Well,* I,i,59.

[9]   The crown of the earth doth melt. My lord!
O, withered is the garland of the war,
The soldier's pole is fallen: young boys and girls
Are level now with men. The odds is gone,
And there is nothing left remarkable
Beneath the visiting moon. *Antony and Cleopatra,* IV,xv,63. (Cleopatra
mourning the death of Antony. The term *odds* means "measure," "stan-
dard of value." *Pole* has a double meaning, both "standard" or "flag" and
"polestar.")

[10]   To persever
In obstinate condolement is a course
Of impious stubbornness. 'Tis unmanly grief.
It shows a will most incorrect to heaven. *Hamlet,* I,ii,92. (Claudius trying
to talk Hamlet out of mourning for his father.)

1   A beast that wants discourse of reason
Would have mourned longer. *Hamlet,* I,ii,150. (Hamlet on his mother's
rapid recovery from grief after the death of his father.)

2 Nay then, let the devil wear black, for I'll have a suit of sables. O heavens!
Die [sic] two months ago, and not forgotten yet? Then there's hope a great
man's memory may outlive his life half a year. *Hamlet,* III,ii,133. (Another
bitter comment from Hamlet on the limited mourning for his father. *Sable*
refers to the color black used for mourning, as well as to the fur.)

3 Lay her in the earth,
And from her fair and unpolluted flesh
May violets spring! *Hamlet,* V,i,240. (Laertes at the burial of Ophelia. See
also RELIGION, Laertes to the priest.)

4 Hung be the heavens with black, yield day to night! *Henry VI, Part One,*
I,i,1. (The opening lines of the play, which begins with the funeral of
Henry V.)

5 These arms of mine shall be thy winding-sheet;
My heart, sweet boy, shall be thy sepulcher,
For from my heart thine image ne'er shall go. *Henry VI, Part Three,*
II,v,114. (A father grieving over his son whom he has inadvertently killed
in battle.)

6 Howl, howl, howl, howl! O, you are men of stones:
Had I your tongues and eyes, I'd use them so
That heaven's vault should crack. She's gone for ever. *King Lear,* V,iii,259.
(Lear grieving for the murdered Cordelia. More below.)

7 Thou'lt come no more,
Never, never, never, never, never. *King Lear,* V,iii,309. (Lear mourning his
daughter Cordelia. See also above.)

8 Death lies on her like an untimely frost
Upon the sweetest flower of all the field. *Romeo and Juliet,* IV,v,28. (Capulet grieving over Juliet, his only child. See also CHILDREN.)

9 No longer mourn for me when I am dead
Than you shall hear the surly sullen bell
Give warning to the world that I am fled
From this vile world with vilest worms to dwell. *Sonnet 71,* 1.

10 For he being dead, with him is beauty slain,
And, beauty dead, black chaos comes again. *Venus and Adonis,* 1.1019.
(The idea that chaos follows loss appears also in *Othello,* III,iii,90; see
LOVE, EXPRESSIONS OF.)

See also EPITAPHS; SORROW AND SADNESS.

DEATHBED STATEMENTS AND FINAL WORDS

1 Not Caesar's valor hath o'erthrown Antony,
But Antony's hath triumphed on itself. *Antony and Cleopatra,* IV,xv,14.
(Antony after fatally wounding himself with his sword.)

2 I am dying, Egypt, dying; only
I here importune death awhile, until
Of many thousand kisses the poor last
I lay upon thy lips. *Antony and Cleopatra,* IV,xv,18. (Antony, in his last
minutes of life, to Cleopatra.)

3 Heaven take my soul, and England keep my bones! *King John,* IV,iii,10.
(Dying words of the young Duke Arthur, King John's nephew. He is killed
leaping from a castle wall in an attempt to escape imprisonment—not
knowing that his release was imminent.)

4   Soft you, a word or two before you go.
I have done the state some service, and they know't.
No more of that. I pray you, in your letters,
When you shall these unlucky deeds relate,
Speak of me as I am. Nothing extenuate,
Nor set down aught in malice. Then must you speak
Of one that loved not wisely, but too well. *Othello,* V,ii,334.

5 They say the tongues of dying men
Enforce attention like deep harmony.
. . .
For they breathe truth that breathe their words in pain. *Richard II,* II,i,5,8.
(A formulation of the traditional belief that deathbed statements are due
special consideration. In law, their evidentiary status is stronger than that
of ordinary statements. In *Othello,* the dying Emilia connects the immi-
nence of death with the truth of her vindication of Desdemona: "So come
my soul to bliss as I speak true," V,ii,247.)

6 Mount, mount, my soul; thy seat is up on high,
Whilst my gross flesh sinks downward here to die. *Richard II,* V,v,111.

7   A plague a both your houses!
They have made worms' meat of me. *Romeo and Juliet,* III,i,108. (Mercutio, fatally wounded by Tybalt.)

8   O, here
Will I set up my everlasting rest
And shake the yoke of inauspicious stars
From this world-wearied flesh. Eyes, look your last! *Romeo and Juliet,*
V,iii,109. (Romeo, preparing to take poison.)

See also SUICIDE.

DECEIT.   See CRAFTINESS; DECEPTIVENESS; DISHONESTY; HYPOCRISY; LIES AND DECEIT.

DECEPTIVENESS

[1] Smooth runs the water where the brook is deep. *Henry VI, Part Two,* III,i,53.

[2]   Look like the innocent flower,
But be the serpent under it. *Macbeth,* I,v,66.

[3] To have what we would have, we speak not what we mean. *Measure for Measure,* II,iv,118.

See also CRAFTINESS; DISHONESTY; HYPOCRISY; LIES AND DECEIT.

DECISION, MOMENT OF

[4] There is a tide in the affairs of men. *Julius Caesar,* IV,iii,217. (More at OPPORTUNITY.)

[5]   This is the night
That either makes me or fordoes me quite. *Othello,* V,i,128.

See also ACTION; BOLDNESS; RISK.

DECLINE

[6]   We have seen better days. *As You Like It,* II,vii,120.

[7] O Hamlet, what a falling-off was there. *Hamlet,* I,v,47. (The ghost of Hamlet's father, speaking of his wife's remarriage to his brother, his murderer.)

[8] Farewell! A long farewell to all my greatness! *Henry VIII,* III,ii,351. (More at GREATNESS.)

[9] The sun of Rome is set. Our day is gone;
Clouds, dews, and dangers come; our deeds are done! *Julius Caesar,* V,iii,63.

[10] I have a kind of alacrity in sinking. *The Merry Wives of Windsor,* III,v,12.

[11] Men shut their doors against a setting sun. *Timon of Athens,* I,ii,147.

[12]   His days and times are past. *Timon of Athens,* II,i,21.

See also ENDINGS; MIDDLE AGE; OLD AGE; PAST, THE; RUIN.

DEFENSE

[13] For peace itself should not so dull a kingdom
(Though war nor no known quarrel were in question)

But that defenses, musters, preparations
Should be maintained, assembled, and collected,
As were a war in expectation. *Henry V,* II,iv,16.

[1] In cases of defense, 'tis best to weigh
The enemy more mighty than he seems. *Henry V,* II,iv,43.

See also RESISTANCE; SECURITY; WAR.

DELAY

[2]   Delays have dangerous ends. *Henry VI, Part One,* III,ii,33.

[3] Now 'tis the spring, and weeds are shallow-rooted;
Suffer them now, and they'll o'ergrow the garden. *Henry VI, Part Two,*
III,i,31.

[4]   We burn daylight. *Romeo and Juliet,* I,iv,43.

See also ACTION, PROMPT; LATENESS; THOUGHT (*Hamlet,* III,i,83).

DEMOCRACY

[5]   The fool multitude that choose by show. *The Merchant of Venice,*
II,ix,25.

See also PUBLIC, THE.

DENMARK

[6] Something is rotten in the state of Denmark. *Hamlet,* I,iv,90.

DEPRESSION

[7]   Everything about you demonstrating a careless desolation. *As You
Like It,* III,ii,373. (The end of a speech in which Rosalind enumerates signs
of self-neglect and despondency characteristic of a man in love—signs
resembling those of clinical depression.)

[8]   It is a melancholy of mine own, compounded of many simples,
extracted from many objects, and indeed the sundry contemplation of my
travels, in which my often rumination wraps me in a most humorous
sadness. *As You Like It,* IV,i,15. (Jaques speaking. He suffers, albeit
comically, from a chronic, gloomy cynicism.)

[9] How is it that the clouds still hang on you? *Hamlet,* I,ii,66. (Claudius to
Hamlet.)

[10] O that this too too sullied flesh would melt,
Thaw, and resolve itself into a dew,

Or that the Everlasting had not fixed
His canon 'gainst self-slaughter. O, God, God,
How weary, stale, flat, and unprofitable
Seems to me all the uses of this world! *Hamlet,* I,ii,129. (*Sullied* in the first line is sometimes given as *solid.* The Signet edition editor, Edward Hubler, points out that "solid" fits better with "melt." *Canon* means "law." This and the speech below are classic expressions of melancholy, or what we would call depression. According to A. C. Bradley's *Shakespearean Tragedy,* Elizabethans associated a melancholic temperament with a tendency toward volatile, intense moods, whether of delight or sorrow. This is certainly characteristic of Hamlet.)

[1]   I have of late, but
wherefore I know not, lost all my mirth, forgone all
custom of exercises; and indeed, it goes so heavily
with my disposition that this goodly frame, the
earth, seems to me a sterile promontory; this most
excellent canopy, the air, look you, this brave
o'erhanging firmament, this majestical roof fretted
with golden fire: why, it appeareth nothing to me
but a foul and pestilent congregation of vapors. *Hamlet,* II,ii,303.

[2]   Yet to me, what is this quintessence of dust? Man delights not me; nor woman neither. *Hamlet,* II,ii,316. (The conclusion of the speech above. The *quintessence of dust* is mankind. See HUMAN NATURE AND HUMANKIND.)

[3] Tomorrow, and tomorrow, and tomorrow,
Creeps in this petty pace from day to day. *Macbeth,* V,v,19. (Macbeth concluding that life is wearisome and meaningless, no more than a tale told by an idiot; see LIFE.)

[4]   These dreary dumps. *Titus Andronicus,* I,i,392. (The phrase refers to a melancholic, depressed mood, such as might afflict one viewing this drama, called by T. S. Eliot "one of the stupidest and most uninspired plays ever written." Especially depressing is the modern revival of interest in the play, based on the fact that rape, murder, mutilation, etc. are such timely subjects. Peter Brook staged a version at Stratford in England, with Laurence Olivier and Vivien Leigh. In the 1980s, Deborah Warner and the Royal Shakespeare Company revived the play within their standard repertory. A reference to the dumps also appears in *Romeo and Juliet,* IV,v,129: "And doleful dumps the mind oppress.")

See also DEATH AND GRIEF; DESPAIR; LONELINESS; SORROW AND SADNESS; SUICIDE.

DESIRE

1   Who riseth from a feast
With that keen appetite that he sits down? *The Merchant of Venice,* II,vi,8.
(More below.)

2   All things that are
Are with more spirit chasèd than enjoyed. *The Merchant of Venice,* II,vi,12.
(This speech on appetite and desire continues with an extended metaphor
involving a ship setting out on a voyage; see SHIPS AND SAILING.)

3 Desire my pilot is, beauty my prize. *The Rape of Lucrece,* 279.

See also ENVY; GREED; PASSION; SEX.

DESPAIR

4 O now, forever
Farewell the tranquil mind. Farewell content! *Othello,* III,iii,344. (More at
WAR.)

5 I shall despair. There is no creature loves me;
And if I die, no soul will pity me. *Richard III,* V,iii,201. (Richard III paying
the price for a life of violence and duplicity. See also CRIME and EVIL.)

6 Come weep with me—past hope, past care, past help! *Romeo and Juliet,*
IV,i,45. (Juliet—age fourteen—speaks.)

7   My ending is despair. *The Tempest,* Epilogue, 15. (Prospero speaks.
The quote usually is cut off here, but this is not actually a tragic moment.
The next line is "Unless I be relieved by prayer." *Prayer* refers to his plea
to the audience for applause and an approving end to the performance.)

See also DEPRESSION; DESPAIR AND RAGE; SUICIDE.

DESPAIR AND RAGE

8   O sun,
Burn the great sphere thou movest in: darkling stand
The varying shore of the world! *Antony and Cleopatra,* IV,xv,9. (*Darkling*
means "in darkness." *Shore* in some editions appears as *star.* This curse is
called down by Cleopatra at the sight of Antony mortally wounded.)

9 Blow, winds, and crack your cheeks. Rage, blow!
You cataracts and hurricanoes, spout
Till you have drenched our steeples, drowned the cocks.
You sulph'rous and thought-executing fires,

Vaunt-couriers of oak-cleaving thunderbolts,
Singe my white head. And thou, all-shaking thunder,
Strike flat the thick rotundity o' th' world,
Crack Nature's molds, all germains spill at once,
That makes ingrateful man. *King Lear,* III,ii,1. (*Hurricanoes* are water-spouts. *Cocks* are weathercocks, or weathervanes. *Thought-executing* is ambiguous, referring possibly both to action as quick as thought and action in response to thought. *Vaunt-couriers* are forward scouts. *Germains* are the seeds of life.

This is one of the most demanding speeches in classical theater. The actor must convey power and rage within the character of a broken and aged father. A modern actor who mastered the role most brilliantly was Sir Laurence Olivier.)

DETACHMENT

[1] I am gone, though I am here. *Much Ado About Nothing,* IV,i,291.

DETECTION.   See CRIME.

DETERMINATION

[2]   My fate cries out
And makes each petty artere in this body
As hardy as the Nemean lion's nerve. *Hamlet,* I,iv,81. (Hamlet determining to follow the beckoning ghost of his father. The Nemean lion is the mythical lion killed by Hercules; *nerve* means "sinews.")

[3] Fight till the last gasp. *Henry VI, Part One,* I,ii,127.

See also BOLDNESS; PERSEVERANCE; RESISTANCE.

DEVIL

[4] This is the foul fiend Flibbertigibbet. He begins at curfew, and walks till the first cock. He gives the web and the pin, squints the eye, and makes the harelip; mildews the white wheat, and hurts the poor creature of earth. *King Lear,* III,iv,116. (*Curfew* is nine in the morning, and *first cock* is midnight. The *web and the pin* is a cataract in the eye. *White* means "ripening.")

[5] The Prince of Darkness is a gentleman. *King Lear,* III,iv,146.

See also EVIL.

DISAPPOINTMENT

[6] Oft expectation fails, and most oft there
Where most it promises. *All's Well That Ends Well,* II,i,144.

DISCRETION

[1] The better part of valor is discretion. *Henry IV, Part One,* V,iv,119. (Spoken by Falstaff, whose discretion might also be termed cowardice.)

See also CAREFULNESS; PRUDENCE.

DISHONESTY

[2] He will steal, sir, an egg out of a cloister. *All's Well That Ends Well,* IV,iii,263.

[3] He has everything that an honest man should not have; what an honest man should have, he has nothing. *All's Well That Ends Well,* IV,iii,272.

See also CRIME; HYPOCRISY; LIES AND DECEIT.

DISLIKES. See LIKES AND DISLIKES.

DISSIPATION. See DRINKING; SEX; WILD AND WANTON PEOPLE.

DOCTORS

[4] *Countess.* What hope is there of his Majesty's amendment?
Lafew. He hath abandoned his physicians. *All's Well That Ends Well,* I,i,14. (Actually, doctors come off relatively well in this play, considering that until recent times their remedies were often as dangerous as diseases. The heroine, Helena, is the daughter of a famous but not wealthy physician—there were such doctors then. Helena possesses some of her late father's secrets, and it is she who saves the king.)

[5] Kill thy physician, and the fee bestow
Upon the foul disease. *King Lear,* I,i,165. (This line can be taken a couple of different ways, but it is not a literal recommendation. The earl of Kent is trying to warn Lear that he is making a terrible mistake, rewarding evil and destroying virtue. The physician here is akin to the always imperiled bearer of bad news; see NEWS.)

[6] With the help of a surgeon he might yet recover, and yet prove an ass. *A Midsummer Night's Dream,* V,i,312.

[7] The patient dies while the physician sleeps. *The Rape of Lucrece,* 904. (More at INJUSTICE.)

[8] Trust not the physician. *Timon of Athens,* IV,iii,438.

See also HEALTH; MEDICINE; PROFESSIONS; SICKNESS.

DOGS.   See ANIMALS.

DOING

[1] If to do were as easy as to know what were good to do, chapels had been churches, and poor men's cottages princes' palaces. *The Merchant of Venice,* I,ii,12.

[2] O, what men dare do! What men may do! What men daily do, not knowing what they do! *Much Ado About Nothing,* IV,i,18.

[3] Things won are done, joy's soul lies in the doing. *Troilus and Cressida,* I,ii,299. (Cressida referring to sexual pursuit. See also at SEX.)

[4]   What you do
Still betters what is done. *The Winter's Tale,* IV,iv,135. (Spoken by a man in love—Prince Florizel.)

See also ACTION; EFFORT.

DOUBT

[5]   No hinge nor loop
To hang a doubt on. *Othello,* III,iii,362. (Iago is promising absolute proof of Desdemona's infidelity; see PROOF.)

[6]   Modest doubt is called
The beacon of the wise. *Troilus and Cressida,* II,ii,15.

See also SELF-DOUBT.

DOVER CLIFFS

[7]   How fearful
And dizzy 'tis to cast one's eyes so low!
The crows and choughs that wing the midway air
Show scarce so gross as beetles. Half way down
Hangs one that gathers sampire, dreadful trade!
Methinks he seems no bigger than his head.
The fishermen that walk upon the beach
Appear like mice; and yond tall anchoring bark
Diminished to her cock; her cock, a buoy
Almost too small for sight. The murmuring surge
That on the unnumbered idle pebble chafes
Cannot be heard so high. *King Lear,* IV,vi,12. (*Choughs* are a kind of crow; *sampire* is an herb that grows on Dover Cliffs; *cock* is a dinghy.)

DREAMERS

[1] He is a dreamer, let us leave him. *Julius Caesar,* I,ii,24. (A bad decision by Caesar. *He* is the soothsayer warning to beware the ides of March. See DANGER.)

[2]   It seems to me
That yet we sleep, we dream. *A Midsummer Night's Dream,* IV,i,196.

[3] I have had a dream, past the wit of man to say what dream it was. *A Midsummer Night's Dream,* IV,i,208. (See also NONSENSE.)

[4] Dream on, dream on. *Richard III,* V,iii,172.

See also FAIRIES (the Queen Mab passage from *Romeo and Juliet*); SLEEP AND DREAMS.

DREAMS.   See DREAMERS; SLEEP AND DREAMS.

DRINKING

[5] Though I look old, yet I am strong and lusty,
For in my youth I never did apply
Hot and rebellious liquors in my blood. *As You Like It,* II,iii,47. (*Rebellious* means "causing the body to rebel.")

[6]   Falser than vows made in wine. *As You Like It,* III,v,73.

[7] We'll teach you to drink deep ere you depart. *Hamlet,* I,ii,175.

[8]   It is a custom
More honored in the breach than the observance. *Hamlet,* I,iv,15. (Hamlet is referring to the custom of draining a cup of wine in a single swallow when making a toast. See HABIT AND CUSTOM.)

[9]   I will make it felony to drink small beer. *Henry VI, Part Two,* IV,ii,66. (Jack Cade is calling not for prohibition of alcohol, but rather prohibition of weak beer.)

[10] That which hath made them drunk hath made me bold;
What hath quenched them hath given me fire. *Macbeth,* II,ii,1. (Lady Macbeth, speaking of Duncan's drunken, sleeping bodyguards.)

[11] *Macduff.* What three things does drink especially provoke?
Porter. Marry, sir, nose-painting, sleep, and urine. Lechery, sir, it provokes and unprovokes; it provokes the desire, but it takes away the performance: therefore much drink may be said to be an equivocator with lechery: it makes him and it mars him; it sets him on and it takes him off; it persuades him and disheartens him; makes him stand to and not stand to; in conclu-

sion, equivocates him in a sleep, and giving him the lie, leaves him. *Macbeth*, II,iii,29. (From the porter's scene, the one comic moment in the play. Interrupting a grim multiple murder, it is as odd and unexpected as life itself.)

[1] I drink to the general joy of the whole table. *Macbeth*, III,iv,90.

[2] I have very poor and unhappy brains for drinking; I could well wish courtesy would invent some other custom of entertainment. *Othello*, II,iii,31. (Cassio, Iago's rival, admits to a weakness that Iago quickly exploits.)

[3] Potations pottle-deep. *Othello*, II,iii,52. (Drinks drained to the bottom of the goblet.)

[4] O thou invisible spirit of wine, if thou hast no name to be known by, let us call thee devil! *Othello*, II,iii,280. (Cassio speaks; see two quotes above and quote below.)

[5] O God, that men should put an enemy in their mouths to steal away their brains! that we should with joy, pleasance, revel, and applause transform ourselves into beasts! *Othello*, II,iii,288.

[6]   Good wine is a good familiar creature if it be well used. *Othello*, II,iii,308. (Iago's smug reply to Cassio's laments; see above.)

[7] Here's that which is too weak to be a sinner,
Honest water, which ne'er left man in the mire. *Timon of Athens*, I,ii,58. (Written on the water fountain in the market square of Stratford-on-Avon.)

[8] One draught above heat makes him a fool, the second mads him, and a third drowns him. *Twelfth Night*, I,v,131. (*Above heat* means "more than needed for warmth.")

See also WILD AND WANTON PEOPLE.

DUNCAN.   See VIRTUE.

E

EAGERNESS

[1] To business that we love we rise betime
And go to it with delight. *Antony and Cleopatra,* IV,iv,20.

[2] The day shall not be up so soon as I
To try the fair adventure of tomorrow. *King John,* V,v,21.

[3] Gallop apace, you fiery-footed steeds,
Toward Phoebus' lodging! *Romeo and Juliet,* III,ii,1. (Juliet calling upon the sun to move faster to the west so that night will fall and Romeo will arrive. In Greek legend Phoebus drove the chariot of the sun.)

[4] I am giddy; expectation whirls me round. *Troilus and Cressida,* III,ii,17. (Troilus anticipating a long-awaited rendezvous with Cressida.)

See also SPEED.

EAST, THE

[5] In the East my pleasure lies. *Antony and Cleopatra,* II,iii,41.

EDUCATION

[6] Thou art a scholar; speak to it, Horatio. *Hamlet,* I,i,42. (The frightened Marcellus asking Horatio to speak to the ghost of Hamlet's father.)

[7] 'Tis needful that the most immodest word
Be looked upon and learned. *Henry IV, Part Two,* IV,iv,70. (In learning a language, one must learn the bad words as well as the nice ones.)

¹ Never was such a sudden scholar made. *Henry V,* I,i,32. (The passage concludes "as in this king." The Archbishop of Canterbury is referring to the suddenly reformed character of Harry—now Henry V—following the death of his father.)

² Thou hast most traitorously corrupted the youth of the realm in erecting a grammar school: and whereas before, our forefathers had no other books but the score and the tally, thou hast caused printing to be used, and contrary to the King, his crown and dignity, thou hast built a paper mill. It will be proved to thy face that thou hast men about thee that usually talk of a noun and a verb, and such abhominable words as no Christian ear can endure to hear. *Henry VI, Part Two,* IV,vii,34. (Accusations by the peasant leader Jack Cade against Lord Say. Shakespeare had a feel for revolutionary rhetoric. Incidentally, the references to a printing press and paper mill are blatant anachronisms, possibly meant to be humorous.)

³ Away with him, away with him! He speaks Latin. *Henry VI, Part Two,* IV,vii,59. (Jack Cade, the Kentish revolutionary, ordering the execution of Lord Say. The nobleman, no doubt already doomed, made a little joke when asked what he thought of the county of Kent. *"Bona terra mala gens,"* he replied—"Good land, bad people.")

⁴ He was a scholar, and a ripe and good one;
Exceeding wise, fair-spoken, and persuading. *Henry VIII,* IV,ii,51. (More at WOLSEY, CARDINAL.)

⁵ Our court shall be a little academe,
Still and contemplative in living art. *Love's Labor's Lost,* I,i,13. (The king of Navarre, a lover of learning. In study and contemplation, he seeks "that honor which shall . . . make us heirs of all eternity," l.6.)

⁶ O, these are barren tasks, too hard to keep,
Not to see ladies, study, fast, not sleep! *Love's Labor's Lost,* I,i,47. (Berowne, said by A. L. Rowse to be modeled on Shakespeare himself, is not entranced by the spartan academy proposed by the king of Navarre. See also below.)

⁷ Study is like the heaven's glorious sun,
That will not be deep-searched with saucy looks.
Small have continual plodders ever won
Save base authority from others' books.
These earthly godfathers of heaven's lights,
That give a name to every fixèd star
Have no more profit of their shining nights
Than those that walk and wot not what they are. *Love's Labor's Lost,* I,i,84. (Berowne again; see above. *Earthly godfathers of heaven's lights* are astronomers.)

¹ He hath never fed of the dainties that are bred in a book. He hath not eat paper, as it were, he hath not drunk ink. *Love's Labor's Lost,* IV,ii,24. (Shakespeare was not nearly so well educated as Christopher Marlowe and others with whom he had to compete as a young man. He was a quick study, but enjoyed teasing scholars.)

² You two are book-men. *Love's Labor's Lost,* IV,ii,34.

³ She is not yet so old
But she may learn. *The Merchant of Venice,* III,ii,160.

⁴ The thrice-three Muses mourning for the death
Of Learning, late deceased in beggary. *A Midsummer Night's Dream,* V,i,52. (A thumbnail sketch of a play that Theseus rejects as inappropriate for a wedding celebration: "That is some satire, keen and critical, / Not sorting with a nuptial ceremony," l.54.)

⁵ Those that do teach young babes
Do it with gentle means and easy tasks. *Othello,* IV,ii,110.

⁶ No profit grows where is no pleasure taken.
In brief, sir, study what you most affect. *The Taming of the Shrew,* I,i,39. (*Affect* means "enjoy.")

⁷ You taught me language, and my profit on it
Is, I know how to curse. The red plague rid you
For learning me your language! *The Tempest,* I,ii,363. (Caliban to Prospero and Miranda. In *Learning to Curse* [1991], Stephen Greenblatt in the title essay explores the confrontation between the culture and attitudes of Western literate colonists versus those of "unlettered" peoples. Shakespeare had a similar theme in mind, as Europeans were beginning to wrestle with the concepts of the "natural man" and "noble savage." *Caliban* is probably a variation on "cannibal.")

⁸ Thou art a scholar! Let us therefore eat and drink. *Twelfth Night,* II,iii,13.

See also HISTORY; IGNORANCE; READING; SCIENCE.

EFFETENESS

⁹ The age is grown so picked that the toe of the peasant comes so near the heel of the courtier he galls his kibe. *Hamlet,* V,i,142. (Translation: The times have become so picky that if the toe of a peasant comes near the heel of a courtier, it irritates the sore there. Specifically, the kind of sore is a chilblain, a painful, often ulcerated swelling caused by cold. Chilblains formerly were a common affliction of the hands and feet.)

¹⁰ Came there a certain lord, neat and trimly dressed,
Fresh as a bridegroom, and his chin new reaped

Showed like a stubble land at harvest home.
He was perfumèd like a milliner,
And 'twixt his finger and his thumb he held
A pouncet box, which ever and anon
He gave his nose, and took't away again;
. . .
And as the soldiers bore dead bodies by,
He called them untaught knaves, unmannerly,
To bring a slovenly unhandsome corse
Betwixt the wind and his nobility. *Henry IV, Part One,* I,iii,32,41. (In a play full of great opening speeches, Hotspur here, in his first appearance, complains of being "pestered with a popinjay," l.49—an emissary from the king demanding that Hotspur turn over prisoners. See also SOLDIERS. A *pouncet box* is a perfume box; a *corse* is a corpse.)

¹   I could brain him with his lady's fan. *Henry IV, Part One,* II,iii,23.

² The wealthy, curlèd darlings of our nation. *Othello,* I,ii,67.

See also MANNERS.

EFFORT

³ Nothing will come of nothing. *King Lear,* I,i,92.

See also ACTION; BOLDNESS; DOING; IMPROVEMENTS.

ELITE, THE

⁴ We few, we happy few, we band of brothers. *Henry V,* IV,iii,60. (More at WAR.)

⁵ The choice and master spirits of this age. *Julius Caesar,* III,i,163.

⁶ I will not choose what many men desire,
Because I will not jump with common spirits
And rank me with the barbarous multitudes. *The Merchant of Venice,* II,ix,30.

⁷ This happy breed of men, this little world. *Richard II,* II,i,45. (More at ENGLAND AND ENGLISHMEN.)

See also GREATNESS; HONOR.

ELIZABETH I

⁸ This royal infant—heaven still move about her! *Henry VIII,* V,v,17. (The idea that a newborn comes from heaven to earth is most famously ex-

pressed in Wordsworth's "Intimations of Immortality" in the passage that begins "Our birth is but a sleep and a forgetting" and ends "Heaven lies about us in our infancy!")

1   Truth shall nurse her,
Holy and heavenly thoughts still counsel her.
She shall be loved and feared. Her own shall bless her. *Henry VIII,* V,v,28.
(For more of this passage, see PEACE.)

EMBARRASSMENT

2 What, must I hold a candle to my shames? *The Merchant of Venice,* II,vi,41.
(Jessica, dressed as a boy, would prefer to remain hidden in darkness.)

EMOTIONS

3   Are you like the painting of a sorrow,
A face without a heart? *Hamlet,* IV,vii,108.

4 You are not wood, you are not stones, but men. *Julius Caesar,* III,ii,144.

5 Who can be wise, amazed, temperate and furious,
Loyal and neutral, in a moment? No man. *Macbeth,* III,iii,110.

6 *Malcolm.* Dispute it like a man.
Macduff. I shall do so;
But I must also feel it as a man.
I cannot but remember such things were,
That were most precious to me. *Macbeth,* IV,iii,220. (Macduff is speaking of the murder of his wife and children. *Dispute it* means "fight back.")

7   A man whose blood
Is very snow-broth; one who never feels
The wanton stings and motions of the sense,
But doth rebate and blunt his natural edge
With profits of the mind, study and fast. *Measure for Measure,* I,iv,57.
(This frosty character is Lord Angelo, who is soon to be corrupted by lust for Isabella. A flawed play, but the role of Angelo has attracted some wonderful actors, including William Poel, at the end of the nineteenth century, who helped to restore the bowdlerized text; Charles Laughton, in 1933, who played the part as an outrageous sensualist; Emlyn Williams, in 1937, who struggled with temptation; and John Gielgud, in Peter Brook's 1950 production, who was memorably repressed and agonized.)

8   Ask your heart what it doth know. *Measure for Measure,* II,ii,137.

9   My heart is turned to stone; I strike it, and it hurts my hand. *Othello,* IV,i,184. (Othello resolving to murder Desdemona.)

¹   One fire burns out another's burning;
One pain is lessened by another's anguish. *Romeo and Juliet,* I,ii,46.

² Unmovèd, cold, and to temptation slow. *Sonnet 94,* 4. (More at VIRTUE.)

See also AMBIVALENCE; ANGER; ANXIETY AND WORRY; DEATH AND GRIEF; DEPRESSION; DESPAIR; DESPAIR AND RAGE; EAGERNESS; ENVY; FEAR; HAPPINESS; IMPULSIVITY; JEALOUSY; LOVE AND LOVERS; PASSION; SEX; SORROW AND SADNESS.

ENDINGS

³ All's well that ends well; still the fine's the crown.
What'er the course, the end is the renown. *All's Well That Ends Well,* IV,iv,35. (*Fines* means "end." The last part of the couplet is an embellishment of a proverb, which in Latin goes *Finis coronat opus,* "The end crowns the work." Used also in *Troilus and Cressida* and *Henry VI, Part Two;* see below. The phrase "All's well that ends well"—also proverbial—is repeated at V,i,25.)

⁴   The long day's task is done,
And we must sleep. *Antony and Cleopatra,* IV,xiv,35. (Antony speaking half literally after a day in battle, half in indirect acknowledgment that the time has come to take his own life. A similarly ambiguous phrase is used by Cleopatra's attendant Iras: "The bright day is done, / And we are for the dark," V,ii,193.)

⁵   I turn my back.
There is a world elsewhere. *Coriolanus,* III,iii,134.

⁶   That it should come to this. *Hamlet,* I,ii,137.

⁷   Let the end try the man. *Henry IV, Part Two,* II,ii,46. (*End* here is used in the sense of outcome.)

⁸ *La fin couronne les oeuvres. Henry VI, Part Two,* V,ii,28. (Another version of the proverb discussed above in the note to *All's Well That Ends Well.* It translates literally "The end crowns the works.")

⁹   He makes a swanlike end,
Fading in music. *The Merchant of Venice,* III,ii,44. (The swan was believed to sing only while dying.)

¹⁰ Here is my journey's end, here is my butt,
And very seamark of my utmost sail. *Othello,* V,ii,264. (The *butt* is the target, place aimed at; the *seamark* is a sign that the voyage has reached its farthest point.)

¹ The daintiest last, to make the end most sweet. *Richard II,* I,iii,68. (A metaphor based on dishes at a feast.)

²   The end crowns all,
And that old common arbitrator, Time,
Will one day end it. *Troilus and Cressida,* IV,v,223. (Hector speaking of the war between Troy and Greece. The first line is a variation of a proverb. See the first quote under this heading.)

See also BEGINNINGS; DEATH; DECLINE; ENDS AND MEANS; ENTROPY; SUICIDE.

ENDS AND MEANS

³ To do a great right, do a little wrong. *The Merchant of Venice,* IV,i,215. (Bassanio pleading that Shylock's pound-of-flesh contract be broken.)

⁴ A little harm done to a great good end. *The Rape of Lucrece,* 528.

See also MORALITY.

ENEMIES AND ENMITY

⁵   He is a lion
That I am proud to hunt. *Coriolanus,* I,i,236.

⁶   My nearest and dearest enemy. *Henry IV, Part One,* III,ii,123. (The king speaking to and of his son, the future Henry V.)

⁷ If the enemy is an ass and a fool and a prating coxcomb, is it meet, think you, that we should also, look you, be an ass and a fool and a prating coxcomb? *Henry V,* IV,i,78.

⁸ Heat not a furnace for your foe so hot
That it do singe yourself. *Henry VIII,* I,i,140.

See also ANGER; HATE; VIOLENCE; WAR.

ENGLAND AND THE ENGLISH

⁹   Britain's a world
By itself. *Cymbeline,* III,i,12.

¹⁰ *Hamlet.* Why was he sent to England?
Clown. Why, because 'he was mad. 'He shall recover his wits there; or, if 'he do not, 'tis no great matter there. *Hamlet,* V,i,152. (The person sent to England was Hamlet himself. The gravedigger does not recognize him.)

¹¹   It was always the trick of our English nation, if they have a good thing, to make it too common. *Henry IV, Part Two,* I,ii,223. (Falstaff to the Chief Justice.)

[1] O England, model to thy inward greatness,
Like little body with a mighty heart,
What mightst thou do, that honor would thee do,
Were all they children kind and natural! *Henry V,* II,Chorus,16. (Paraphrase: England, shape yourself on the model of your inward greatness, as
a little body with a mighty heart. What couldn't you do—which according
to honor you should do—if only all your children were kind and loyal as
natural children should be!)

[2]   "God for Harry, England and Saint George!" *Henry V,* III,1,34.
(More at WAR.)

[3] I thought upon one pair of English legs
Did march three Frenchmen. *Henry V,* III,vi,157. (The young king boasting that one English soldier is worth three Frenchmen.)

[4] That island of England breeds very valiant creatures: their mastiffs are of
unmatchable courage. *Henry V,* III,vii,145. (A French lord the night
before the battle of Agincourt. See also below.)

[5]   Give them great meals of beef, and iron and steel; they will eat like
wolves and fight like devils. *Henry V,* III,vii,156. (A more realistic assess-
ment of the English fighting man than the quote above. But since the
outnumbered English were short on beef and other rations, the French did
not expect a hard fight.)

[6] Let us be backed with God and with the seas
Which He hath given for fence impregnable,
And with their helps only defend ourselves;
In them and in ourselves our safety lies. *Henry VI, Part Three,* IV,i,43.
(This speech by Lord Hastings could possibly have been spoken, with
slight modernization, by Winston Churchill. Today, however, the seas
around Great Britain are no longer a "fence impregnable.")

[7] This England never did, nor never shall,
Lie at the proud foot of a conquerer
But when it first did help to wound itself. *King John,* V,vii,112. (The last
line is usually omitted.)

[8]   Naught shall make us rue
If England to itself do rest but true! *King John,* V,vii,117. (The last lines of
the play.)

[9] Where'er I wander, boast of this I can:
Though banished, yet a true-born Englishman. *Richard II,* I,iii,307.

[10] This royal throne of kings, this sceptered isle,
This earth of majesty, this seat of Mars,

This other Eden, demi-paradise,
This fortress built by Nature for herself
Against infection and the hand of war,
This happy breed of men, this little world,
This precious stone set in the silver sea
Which serves it in the office of a wall,
Or as a moat defensive to a house,
Against the envy of less happier lands,
This blessed plot, this earth, this realm, this England. *Richard II,* II,i,40.
(John of Gaunt's paean to his homeland. More below. The vision of
England as an Eden arises from the playwright's intense patriotism and
his love of his country's fields, forests, and gardens. See PLANTS AND
FLOWERS.)

[1] England, bound in with the triumphant sea,
Whose rocky shore beats back the envious siege
Of watery Neptune. *Richard II,* II,i,61.

[2]   England that was wont to conquer others
Hath made a shameful conquest of itself. *Richard II,* II,i,65.

See also DOVER CLIFFS.

ENNUI

[3]   My little body is aweary of this great world. *The Merchant of Venice,*
I,ii,1.

[4]   There is nothing left remarkable
Beneath the visiting moon. *Antony and Cleopatra,* IV,xv,67. (More at
DEATH AND GRIEF.)

ENTROPY

[5]   Thoughts, the slaves of life, and life, time's fool,
And time, that takes survey of all the world,
Must have a stop. *Henry IV, Part One,* V,iv,80. (The dying Hotspur to
Hal.)

[6] O ruined piece of nature! This great world
Shall so wear out to nought. *King Lear,* IV,vi,136. (Gloucester to the
demented Lear.)

ENVIRONMENT

[7] Clear wells spring not, sweet birds sing not,
Green plants bring not forth their dye.
Herds stands weeping, flocks all sleeping. *The Passionate Pilgrim,* xvii,25.

(A natural calamity brought about, in this case, by the death of Love, but much like the destruction now envisaged as a result of abuse of our environment.)

See also AIR POLLUTION; NATURE; PLANTS AND FLOWERS.

ENVY

1   Men that make
Envy and crookèd malice nourishment
Dare bite the best. *Henry VIII*, V,iii,43.

2   The apprehension of the good
Gives but the greater feeling to the worse. *Richard II*, I,iii,299. (More at THOUGHT.)

3 Desiring this man's art, and that man's scope,
With what I most enjoy contented least. *Sonnet 29*, 7. (Shakespeare desiring the art and range of another. Whom did he have in mind?)

EPITAPHS

4 His legs bestrid the ocean: his reared arm
Crested the world: his voice was propertied
As all the tunèd spheres, and that to friends;
But when he meant to quail and shake the orb,
He was as rattling thunder. For his bounty,
There was no winter in't: an autumn 'twas
That grew the more by reaping. *Antony and Cleopatra*, V,ii,82. (Cleopatra's epitaph for Antony. It concludes below.)

5 Think you there was or might be such a man
As this I dreamt of? *Antony and Cleopatra*, V,ii,92.

6   Death, in thy possession lies
A lass unparalleled. *Antony and Cleopatra*, V,ii,315. (Charmian speaking of Cleopatra.)

7   He shall have a noble memory. *Coriolanus*, V,vi,154. (Aufidius, speaking rather coolly of Coriolanus.)

8 Now cracks a noble heart. *Hamlet*, V,ii,360. (More at HAMLET.)

9   This earth that bears thee dead
Bears not alive so stout a gentleman. *Henry IV, Part One*, V,iv,91. (*Stout* here means "valiant." The Prince of Wales is speaking of Hotspur, whom he has just killed in battle. Hotspur's rebellion still rankles, however, as the prince concludes, "Thy ignominy sleep with thee in the grave, / But not remembered in thy epitaph," l.99.)

[1] I could have better spared a better man. *Henry IV, Part One,* V,iv,103. (The prince's affectionate epitaph for Falstaff, who appears, for the moment, to be dead.)

[2] Your son, my lord, has paid a soldier's debt:
He only lived until he was a man;
The which no sooner had his prowess confirmed
In the unshrinking station where he fought,
But like a man he died. *Macbeth,* V,viii,39. (Ross conveying the news of the death of young Siward. Siward's father replies, "Why then, God's soldier be he!" l.47. And adds, "He parted well and paid his score," l.52. The *unshrinking station* refers to the place where young Siward stood his ground.)

[3] Beauty, truth, and rarity,
Grace in all simplicity
Here enclosed, in cinders lie. *The Phoenix and the Turtle,* 53.

[4] Full fathom five thy father lies;
Of his bones are coral made;
Those are pearls that were his eyes;
Nothing of him that doth fade
But doth suffer a sea change
Into something rich and strange.
Sea nymphs hourly ring his knell. *The Tempest,* I,ii,397.

[5] His part is played, and though it were too short
He did it well. *The Two Noble Kinsmen,* V,iv,101. (Theseus speaking of the death of Arcite. The play is based on Chaucer's "The Knight's Tale," and was written in part by Shakespeare and in part by John Fletcher.)

See also DEATH AND GRIEF; JULIUS CAESAR.

EQUALITY

[6] We came into the world like brother and brother:
And now let's go hand in hand, not one before another. *The Comedy of Errors,* V,i,426. (The last lines of the play, spoken by Dromio of Ephesus to his twin, Dromio of Syracuse. Shakespeare himself was the father of twins: Hamnet and Judith.)

[7] The selfsame sun that shines upon his court
Hides not his visage from our cottage, but
Looks on alike. *The Winter's Tale,* IV,iv,448.

EVIL

1   Wicked meaning in a lawful deed. *All's Well That Ends Well,* III, vii,45. (A reference to wickedness within the law. In this case, the person meaning, or intending, evil is Bertram, who intends to commit adultery. The deed, however, will be lawful, as his wife, Helena, plans secretly to substitute herself for the other woman. The play is based upon a story in Boccaccio's *Decameron.*)

2 It is not, nor it cannot come to good. *Hamlet,* I,ii,158. (Hamlet refers to his mother's new marriage.)

3   All is not well.
I doubt some foul play. *Hamlet,* I,ii,255. (*Doubt* means "suspect.")

4 Something is rotten in the state of Denmark. *Hamlet,* I,iv,90.

5 O villain, villain, smiling, damnèd villain!
My tables—meet it is I set it down
That one may smile, and smile, and be a villain.
At least I am sure it may be so in Denmark. *Hamlet,* I,v,106. (Hamlet on his uncle, Claudius. For another smiling villain, see the quotes from *Henry VI, Part Three,* below. The reference to *tables* indicates that Hamlet is writing down his observations.)

6   Commit
The oldest sins the newest kind of ways? *Henry IV, Part Two,* IV,v,125. (More at WILD AND WANTON PEOPLE.)

7 There is some soul of goodness in things evil,
Would men observingly distill it out. *Henry V,* IV,i,4.

8 Why, I can smile, and murder whiles I smile,
And cry "Content" to that which grieves my heart,
And wet my cheeks with artificial tears,
And frame my face to all occasions. *Henry VI, Part Three,* III,ii,182. (The future Richard III reviewing the skills he can call upon to win the crown. Richard's speech concludes below. When the late Sir Laurence Olivier was preparing his cinematic interpretation of this role, he resolved to model himself on the legendary Broadway producer Jed Harris, whom he found to be without redeeming virtues. Olivier gleefully disclosed this in a television interview filmed shortly before he died. He added that he later heard that Mr. Harris was also the model for the voice of the Big, Bad Wolf in the Disney movie *The Three Little Pigs.*)

9 Can I do this, and cannot get a crown?
Tut, were it farther off, I'll pluck it down. *Henry VI, Part Three,* III,ii,194.

(The conclusion of the wonderful self-revelatory soliloquy of the future Richard III; see above. See also AMBITION; CRIME.)

[1] This bold bad man. *Henry VIII,* II,ii,43. (Cardinal Wolsey is the man.)

[2] Ye have angels' faces, but heaven knows your hearts. *Henry VIII,* III,i,144. (Queen Katherine to Cardinal Wolsey in a remark reminiscent of the proverb "Fair face, foul heart.")

[3] The evil that men do lives after them. *Julius Caesar,* III,ii,77. (More at JULIUS CAESAR.)

[4] Wisdom and goodness to the vile seem vile. *King Lear,* IV,ii,38.

[5] Something wicked this way comes. *Macbeth* IV,i,45. (The Second Witch sensing the approach of Macbeth.)

[6] *Macbeth.* How now, you secret, black, and midnight hags!
What is it you do?
Witches. A deed without a name. *Macbeth,* IV,i,47.

[7]   Bloody,
Luxurious, avaricious, false, deceitful,
Sudden, malicious, smacking of every sin
That has a name. *Macbeth,* IV,iii,57. (Malcolm on Macbeth. *Luxurious* means "lecherous"; *sudden* means "impulsive," "violent.")

[8]   Unnatural deeds
Do breed unnatural troubles. *Macbeth,* V,i,75.

[9]   They that touch pitch will be defiled. *Much Ado About Nothing,* III,iii,58. (Proverbial.)

[10] Knavery's plain face is never seen till used. *Othello,* II,i,312.

[11] On horror's head horrors accumulate;
Do deeds to make heaven weep, all earth amazed. *Othello,* III,iii,367.

[12] Lilies that fester smell far worse than weeds. *Sonnet 94,* 14. (More at VIRTUE.)

[13]   I have done a thousand dreadful things
As willingly as one would kill a fly,
And nothing grieves me heartily indeed,
But that I cannot do ten thousand more. *Titus Andronicus,* V,i,141. (Aaron prefigures Iago, and outdoes him in viciousness. In the nineteenth century, the African-American actor Ira Aldridge was famous for his portrayals of Othello and Aaron in English productions. He also played Lear and Macbeth. Anthony Quayle did the role in Peter Brook's 1955 production at Stratford-upon-Avon, with Laurence Olivier as Titus.)

¹ If one good deed in all my life I did,
I do repent it from my very soul. *Titus Andronicus* V,iii,189. (Aaron—see above—defiantly facing execution.)

² Her life was beastly and devoid of pity. *Titus Andronicus,* V,iii,199. (Said of Tamora, queen of the Goths.)

See also CRIME; DANGER; DANGEROUS PEOPLE; DEVIL; LIES AND DECEIT; REVENGE; RUTHLESSNESS; WILD AND WANTON PEOPLE.

EXCESS

³   That was laid on with a trowel. *As You Like It,* I,ii,100.

⁴ To gild refinèd gold, to paint the lily,
To throw a perfume on the violet,
To smooth the ice, or add another hue
Unto the rainbow, or with taper-light
To seek the beauteous eye of heaven to garnish,
Is wasteful and ridiculous excess. *King John,* IV,ii,11.

EXCITEMENT.   See EAGERNESS.

EXCUSES

⁵ Lay not that flattering unction to your soul. *Hamlet,* III,iv,146. (The next line is "That not your trespass but my madness speaks." Hamlet is speaking to his mother.)

⁶ I must be cruel only to be kind. *Hamlet,* III,iv,179.

⁷   'Tis my vocation, Hal. 'Tis no sin for a man to labor in his vocation. *Henry IV, Part One,* I,ii,108. (Falstaff arguing that God himself has called him to purse-taking.)

⁸ Company, villainous company, hath been the spoil of me. *Henry IV, Part One,* III,iii,10. (Falstaff blaming bad companions for his failings. Later, when the Chief Justice calls him old and refers to his broken voice, Falstaff, who counts himself among the young—see YOUNG IN SPIRIT, THE—replies: "For my voice, I have lost it with hallowing and singing of anthems," *Henry IV, Part Two,* I,ii,196. *Hallowing* refers to hallooing, or shouting, to hounds.)

⁹ And oftentimes excusing of a fault
Doth make the fault the worse by the excuse. *King John,* IV,ii,30.

¹⁰   This is the excellent foppery of the world, that when we are sick in fortune, often the surfeits of our own behavior, we make guilty of

our disasters the sun, the moon, and stars; as if we were villains on necessity; fools by heavenly compulsion; knaves, thieves, and treachers by spherical predominance; drunkards, liars, and adulterers by an enforced obedience of planetary influence; and all that we are evil in, by a divine thrusting on. An admirable evasion of whoremaster man, to lay his goatish disposition on the charge of a star. My father compounded with my mother under the Dragon's Tail, and my nativity was under Ursa Major, so that it follows I am rough and lecherous. *King Lear,* I,ii,128. (The opening words translate: This is the foolishness of the world, that when we meet misfortune, often because of our own excesses of behavior, we blame the sun . . . and so on. Shakespeare's plays include numerous omens and prophecies that appear to have a degree of validity, but his attitude toward them is ambiguous. All in all, he seems to have agreed with Edmund here that astrological portents are no excuse for failure, or explanation of good fortune. As Cassius put it, "The fault, dear Brutus, is not in our stars, / But in ourselves that we are underlings"; see RESPONSIBILITY. See also FATE; FORTUNE; OCCULT, THE.)

[1] I have a strange infirmity, which is nothing
To those that know me. *Macbeth,* III,iv,87. (Macbeth excusing himself to his guests for his strange behavior—caused by seeing Banquo's ghost at the table.)

[2] I humbly do beseech you of your pardon
For too much loving you. *Othello,* III,iii,212. (Iago to Othello, laying it on thick.)

EXILE. See BANISHMENT AND EXILE; SEPARATION.

EXPECTATIONS

[3] To mock the expectation of the world. *Henry IV, Part Two,* V,ii,126. (Cited by Norman Holland of MIT as the key to this play, this line is part of a speech in which the ne'er-do-well young prince, having just become king, vows to surprise those who expect the worst of him. The passage continues: "To frustrate prophecies, and to raze out / Rotten opinion, who hath writ me down / After my seeming.")

[4] For now sits Expectation in the air. *Henry V,* II,Chorus,8.

EXPEDIENCE. See ENDS AND MEANS; RUTHLESSNESS; SELF-INTEREST.

EXPERIENCE

1   To have seen much and to have nothing is to have rich eyes and poor hands. *As You Like It,* IV,i,22.

2   I had rather have a fool to make me merry than experience to make me sad. *As You Like It,* IV,i,25.

3 We are yet but young in deed. *Macbeth,* III,iv,145. (Macbeth here refers to brutal deeds.)

4 Experience is by industry achieved,
And perfected by the swift course of time. *The Two Gentlemen of Verona,* I,iii,22.

5 His years but young, but his experience old. *The Two Gentlemen of Verona,* II,iv,68.

See also LIFE; MATURITY; TRAVEL.

F

FAILINGS

1   Every one fault seeming monstrous until his fellow fault came to match it. *As You Like It,* III,ii,349. (Rosalind, disguised as a man, is speaking of the many faults of women, testing the sentiments of Orlando.)

2   These men,
Carrying, I say, the stamp of one defect,
. . .
Shall in the general censure take corruption
From that particular fault. *Hamlet,* I,iv,30,35.

3   All his faults observed,
Set in a notebook, learned and conned by rote. *Julius Caesar,* IV,iii,96. (Cassius is speaking of himself in the third person. Being constantly criticized, as he sees it, makes life not worth living.)

4 Do you smell a fault? *King Lear,* I,i,16.

5 He wants the natural touch. *Macbeth,* IV,ii,9. (The natural touch lacking is affection for wife and children. Lady Macduff is criticizing her husband.)

6 They say, best men are molded out of faults;
And, for the most, become much more the better
For being a little bad. *Measure for Measure,* V,i,442.

7   I am slow of study. *A Midsummer Night's Dream,* I,ii,68.

8 But men are men; the best sometimes forget. *Othello,* II,iii,240.

[1] Roses have thorns, and silver fountains mud,
Clouds and eclipses stain both moon and sun,
And loathsome canker lives in sweetest bud.
All men make faults. *Sonnet 35, 2.*

See also FAINT PRAISE; FATNESS; FOOLS AND FOOLISHNESS; GULLIBILITY; INSULTS; MISTAKES; WEAKNESS; YOUNG IN SPIRIT, THE.

FAILURE

[2]   The attempt and not the deed
Confounds us. *Macbeth,* II,ii,10. (To attempt the murder of Duncan and not succeed means ruin.)

See also COURAGE (*Macbeth,* I,vii,58); DECLINE; RUIN.

FAINT PRAISE

[3]   She's good, being gone. *Antony and Cleopatra,* I,ii,127. (Antony, upon hearing of the death of his wife, briefly regrets her passing.)

[4] God made him, and therefore let him pass for a man. *The Merchant of Venice,* I,ii,55. (Portia's comment on her French suitor, M. Le Bon.)

[5] My meaning in saying he is a good man, is to have you understand me that he is sufficient. *The Merchant of Venice,* I,iii,15. (Shylock on Antonio. *Sufficient* means "adequate" or "financially responsible.")

[6] He doth indeed show some sparks that are like wit. *Much Ado About Nothing,* II,iii,185.

FAIRIES

[7] Over hill, over dale,
Thorough bush, thorough brier,
Over park, over pale,
Thorough flood, thorough fire,
I do wander everywhere,
Swifter than the moon's sphere;
And I serve the Fairy Queen,
To dew her orbs upon the green.
The cowslips tall her pensioners be:
In their gold coats spots you see;
Those be rubies, fairy favors,
In those freckles live their savors.
I must go seek some dewdrops here,
And hang a pearl in every cowslip's ear. *A Midsummer Night's Dream,* II,i,2.

(A *pale* is enclosed land; *her orbs* are fairy rings. This is a fairy speaking, otherwise unidentified. Puck speaks below.)

[1] I am that merry wanderer of the night. *A Midsummer Night's Dream,* II,i,43.

[2] I know a bank where the wild thyme blows,
Where oxlips and the nodding violet grows,
Quite overcanopied with luscious woodbine,
With sweet musk roses, and with eglantine.
There sleeps Titania sometime of the night,
Lulled in these flowers with dances and delight;
And there the snake throws her enameled skin,
Weed wide enough to wrap a fairy in. *A Midsummer Night's Dream,* II,i,249. (*Weed* here refers to a garment. *Titania,* of course, is the queen of the fairies.)

[3] Come, now a roundel and a fairy song;
Then for the third part of a minute, hence:
Some to kill cankers in the musk-rose buds,
Some war with reremice for their leathern wings
To make my small elves coats, and some keep back
The clamorous owl, that nightly hoots and wonders
At our quaint spirits. Sing me now asleep.
Then to your offices, and let me rest. *A Midsummer Night's Dream,* II,ii,3. (Titania speaks. The first verse of the fairies' song follows below. *Canker* refers to a cankerworm; *reremice* are bats.)

[4] You spotted snakes with double tongue,
Thorny hedgehogs, be not seen;
Newts and blindworms, do no wrong,
Come not near our Fairy Queen. *A Midsummer Night's Dream,* II,ii,9. (A *blindworm* is a legless lizard.)

[5] O, then I see Queen Mab hath been with you.
She is the fairies' midwife, and she comes
In shape no bigger than an agate stone
On the forefinger of an alderman,
Drawn with a team of little atomies
Over men's noses as they lie asleep;
Her wagon spokes made of long spinners' legs,
The cover, of the wings of grasshoppers;
Her traces, of the smallest spider web;
Her collars, of the moonshine's watery beams;
Her whip, of cricket's bone; the lash, of film;

Her wagoner, a small gray-coated gnat,
Not half so big as a round little worm
Pricked from the lazy finger of a maid;
Her chariot is an empty hazelnut,
Made by the joiner squirrel or old grub,
Time out o' mind the fairies' coachmakers.
And in this state she gallops night by night
Through lovers' brains, and then they dream of love. *Romeo and Juliet,*
I,iv,53. (*Atomies* are tiny creatures. The reference to the *lazy finger of a
maid* reflects the folk notion that lazy young women had worms breeding
in their fingers. Spoken by Mercutio.)

1   To fly,
To swim, to dive into the fire, to ride
On the curled clouds. *The Tempest,* I,ii,190. (Ariel announcing what he is
prepared to do if Prospero so orders.)

2 I will be correspondent to command
And do my spriting gently. *The Tempest,* I,ii,297. (Ariel to Prospero.
Correspondent to means "obedient to.")

3   Elves of hills, brooks, standing lakes, and groves. *The Tempest,* V,i,33.
(Those interested in the lore of elves should consult this passage in the
play. It is closely based on Medea's speech in Ovid's *Metamorphoses.*)

4 Where the bee sucks, there suck I;
In a cowslip's bell I lie;
There I couch when owls do cry.
On the bat's back I do fly
After summer merrily.
Merrily, merrily shall I live now
Under the blossom that hangs on the bough. *The Tempest,* V,i,88. (A song
by Ariel.)

See also OCCULT, THE.

FAITH

5   Welcome home again discarded faith. *King John,* V,iv,12.

6 He wears his faith but as the fashion of his hat. *Much Ado About Nothing,*
I,i,71. (Here *faith* is similar to "allegiance.")

See also GOD; PRAYER; RELIGION; TRUST.

FALSTAFF

7 If sack and sugar be a fault, God help the wicked! If to be old and merry
be a sin, then many an old host that I know is damned. *Henry IV, Part One,*
II,iv,470. (Falstaff in eloquent defense of himself. The original Sir John

Falstaff, a friend of Henry V named Sir John Oldcastle, became later in life, through marriage, Lord Cobham. He was evidently a serious civilian and military leader, eventually executed as an adherent of Lollardry and a rebel against the king. This upright man was transformed into Jockey Oldcastle, a buffoonish character in the anonymous play *Famous Victories*—the caricature may have been based on the minority view, expressed by Catholic chroniclers, that Cobham was a drinker and a ruffian. At any rate, he was enlarged in all senses of the word by Shakespeare to the immortal Falstaff, called by John Dryden the "best of Comical Characters." It is surmised that protests from the distinguished Oldham family led to the name change, apparently some time after the play was first performed.)

[1]   Banish plump Jack, and banish all the world! *Henry IV, Part One,* II,iv,479. (Falstaff, taking the role of Prince Hal, pleads in his own behalf—a joke that prefigures Hal's ultimate painful rejection of his mischievous old friend. See under *Henry IV, Part Two* below.)

[2] I could have better spared a better man. *Henry IV, Part One,* V,iv,103. (The prince's spontaneous epitaph for the apparently dead Falstaff at the Battle of Shrewsbury.)

[3] I know thee not, old man. Fall to thy prayers.
How ill white hairs becomes a fool and jester! *Henry IV, Part Two,* V,v,48. (Hal, now Henry V, turns away from his old friend Falstaff. The phrase "I know thee not" may come from *Matthew* 25:10, the parable of the wise and foolish virgins. The shock of the rejection is rooted in the father-son relationship between Falstaff and Hal, a theme well developed by J.I.M. Stewart in *Character and Motive in Shakespeare* and by Philip Williams in "The Birth and Death of Falstaff Reconsidered," *Shakespeare Quarterly,* VIII, 1957.)

[4] Nay sure, he's not in hell! He's in Arthur's bosom, if ever man went to Arthur's bosom. *Henry V,* II,iii,9. (Hostess Quickly announcing the death of Falstaff; more at DEATH. Audiences wanted more, however, and a softened Falstaff reappeared in *The Merry Wives of Windsor*. In the 1709 edition of Shakespeare's works, Nicholas Rowe wrote that Elizabeth I "was so well pleased with that admirable character of Falstaff . . . that she commanded him [Shakespeare] to continue it for one play more, and to show him in love.")

See also Falstaff quotes under EXCUSES; FATNESS; INSULTS; OLD AGE; VIRTUE; YOUNG IN SPIRIT, THE.

FAME

[5]   Too famous to live long! *Henry VI, Part One,* I,i,6. (The reference is to Henry V, who died at age thirty-nine in 1422.)

¹ Glory is like a circle in the water,
Which never ceaseth to enlarge itself
Till by broad spreading it disperse to nought. *Henry VI, Part One,* I,ii,133.

² The painful warrior famousèd for might,
After a thousand victories once foiled,
Is from the book of honor rasèd quite,
And all the rest forgot for which he toiled. *Sonnet 25,* 9.

See also GLORY; GREATNESS; HIGH POSITION; HONOR; MEDIA AND MESSAGES; MORTALITY.

FAMILY

³ My soul, yet I know not why, hates nothing more than he. *As You Like It,* I,i,157. (Classic sibling rivalry, expressed here by Oliver against his younger brother, the attractive Orlando.)

⁴ A little more than kin, and less than kind! *Hamlet,* I,ii,65. (Hamlet to his new stepfather, Claudius.)

⁵ She that herself will sliver and disbranch
From her material sap, perforce must wither
And come to deadly use. *King Lear,* IV,ii,34. (Albany, Goneril's husband, on the dangers of cutting oneself off from one's father. *Material sap* is the essential sap, as in a plant.)

⁶ What, will the line stretch out to the crack of doom? *Macbeth,* IV,i,117. (Macbeth exclaiming at the apparition of Banquo and the line of kings descended from him.)

⁷ Wife and child,
Those precious motives, those strong knots of love. *Macbeth,* IV,iii,26.

⁸ All my pretty ones?
Did you say all? Oh hell-kite! All?
What, all my pretty chickens and their dam
At one fell swoop? *Macbeth,* IV,iii,216. (Macduff upon learning of the murder of his children and wife. *Hell-kite* refers to a kite from hell, a kite being a bird of the hawk family, a carrion-eater.)

⁹ The sins of the father are to be laid upon the children. *The Merchant of Venice,* III,v,1. (Borrowed from *Exodus* 20:5.)

¹⁰ When I shun Scylla your father, I fall into Charybdis your mother. *The Merchant of Venice,* III,v,15.

See also CHILDREN; GENERATIONS; PARENTS.

FAREWELLS

1 Our separation so abides and flies
That thou residing here goes yet with me,
And I hence fleeing here remain with thee. *Antony and Cleopatra,* I,iii,102.
(Antony bidding farewell to Cleopatra.)

2 Come, my coach! Good night, ladies, good night. Sweet ladies,
good night, good night. *Hamlet,* IV,v,72.

3 Sweets to the sweet! Farewell. *Hamlet,* V,i,245. (The queen scattering
flowers on Ophelia's grave. She continues, "I thought thy bride bed to
have decked, sweet maid, / And not have strewed thy grave," l.247.)

4 Good night, sweet Prince. *Hamlet,* V,ii,360. (More at HAMLET.)

5 So part we sadly in this troublous world,
To meet with joy in sweet Jerusalem. *Henry VI, Part Three,* V,v,7.

6 Farewell! A long farewell to all my greatness! *Henry VIII,* III,ii,351. (For
more, see GREATNESS.)

7 Forever, and forever, farewell, Cassius!
If we do meet again, why, we shall smile;
If not, why then this parting was well made. *Julius Caesar,* V,i,116. (Brutus
before the battle at Philippi.)

8 Good night, good night! As sweet repose and rest
Come to thy heart as that within my breast! *Romeo and Juliet,* II,ii,123.

9 Good night, good night! Parting is such sweet sorrow
That I shall say good night till it be morrow. *Romeo and Juliet,* II,ii,184.

10 Farewell, thou art too dear for my possessing,
And like enough thou knowest thy estimate. *Sonnet 87,* 1.

11 As many farewells as be stars in heaven. *Troilus and Cressida,* IV,iv,44.

See also SEPARATION.

FASHION

12 Costly thy habit as thy purse can buy,
But not expressed in fancy; rich, not gaudy,
For the apparel oft proclaims the man. *Hamlet,* I,iii,70. (More at WISDOM,
WORDS OF.)

13 The glass of fashion, and the mold of form,
The observed of all observers. *Hamlet,* III,i,156. (The first line translates:
the mirror of fashion and the standard of manners and behavior. More at
HAMLET.)

[1] Through tattered clothes small vices do appear;
Robes and furred gowns hide all. *King Lear,* IV,vi,166.

[2]   The cunning livery of hell. *Measure for Measure,* III,i,95.

[3]   The fashion is the fashion. *Much Ado About Nothing,* III,iii,122.

[4]   What a deformed thief this fashion is. *Much Ado About Nothing,* III,iii,131.

[5]   The fashion wears out more apparel than the man. *Much Ado About Nothing,* III,iii,140.

[6] See where she comes, appareled like the spring. *Pericles,* I,i,13.

[7] Old fashions please me best. *The Taming of the Shrew,* III,i,78.

[8] Our purses shall be proud, our garments poor. *The Taming of the Shrew,* IV,iii,169. (Petruchio maintaining that it is not worthwhile to buy new clothes. More at VIRTUE.)

[9]   The fashion of the time is changed. *The Two Gentlemen of Verona,* III,i,86.

See also EFFETENESS; HABIT AND CUSTOM; ITALY AND ITALIANS; MANNERS; NOVELTY.

FATE

[10] Our wills and fates do so contrary run
That our devices still are overthrown;
Our thoughts are ours, their ends none of our own. *Hamlet,* III,ii,217.

[11] Let Hercules himself do what he may,
The cat will mew, and dog will have his day. *Hamlet,* V,i,293. (The adage is also in George Borrow's *Lavengro,* 1851: "Youth will be served, every dog has his day, and mine has been a fine one." See, too, Charles Kingsley's *The Water-Babies,* "Young blood must have its course, lad, / And every dog his day.")

[12] There's a divinity that shapes our ends,
Rough-hew them how we will. *Hamlet,* V,ii,10.

[13] There is special providence in the fall of a sparrow. If it be now, 'tis not to come; if it be not to come, it will be now; if it be not now, yet it will come. The readiness is all. *Hamlet,* V,ii,220. (Hamlet preparing to begin his fatal duel with Laertes. The speech is remarkable for its short plain words, especially in contrast with the linguistic flourishes in the preceding scene, in which Hamlet fences verbally with the young courtier Osric.)

¹ O God, that one might read the book of fate. *Henry IV, Part Two*, III,i,45. (But such a gift, the king concludes, would lead to despair. See below.)

²   O, if this were seen,
The happiest youth, viewing his progress through,
What perils past, what crosses to ensue,
Would shut the book, and sit him down and die. *Henry IV, Part Two*, III,i,53. (*This* in the first line refers to the book of fate.)

³ We are in God's hand, brother, not in theirs. *Henry V*, III,vi,177. (The king to his brother, the duke of Gloucester, just before the battle of Agincourt. *Theirs* refers to the French armies.)

⁴ What fates impose, that men must needs abide;
It boots not to resist both wind and tide. *Henry VI, Part Three*, IV,iii,58.

⁵ Men at some time are masters of their fates. *Julius Caesar*, I,ii,139. (More at RESPONSIBILITY.)

⁶   It is the stars,
The stars above us, govern our conditions. *King Lear*, IV,iii,33.

⁷ The wheel is come full circle. *King Lear*, V,iii,176.

⁸ Who can control his fate? *Othello*, V,ii,262.

See also CHANCE; FORTUNE; PROVIDENCE.

FATHERS.   See PARENTS.

FATNESS

⁹ Sweep on, you fat and greasy citizens. *As You Like It*, II,i,55. (Melancholy Jaques addressing a herd of deer who ignore a wounded fellow.)

¹⁰ Falstaff sweats to death and lards the lean earth as he walks along. *Henry IV, Part One*, II,iii,108.

¹¹   I have more flesh than another man, and therefore more frailty. *Henry IV, Part One*, III,iii,172. (Falstaff, of course.)

¹²   The grave doth gape
For thee thrice wider than for other men. *Henry IV, Part Two*, V,v,54. (King Henry V to his old and very fat friend Falstaff. A crude but true comment.)

¹³ Let me have men about me that are fat,
Sleek-headed men, and such as sleep a-nights. *Julius Caesar*, I,ii,192. (Caesar, prefacing the observation that Cassius has a "lean and hungry look";

see DANGEROUS PEOPLE. Antony claims that Cassius is "not dangerous," is "a noble Roman," but Caesar responds, "Would he were fatter!" 1.198.)

See also THINNESS.

FAULTS.   See FAILINGS.

FEAR

1   To be furious
Is to be frighted out of fear. *Antony and Cleopatra,* III,xiii,195. (Enobarbus explaining Antony's psychological preparation for battle. Antony has just vowed to fight death itself.)

2   It harrows me with fear and wonder. *Hamlet,* I,i,44.

3   Distilled
Almost to jelly with the act of fear. *Hamlet,* I,ii,204. (Here *act* means "action.")

4 Be wary then; best safety lies in fear. *Hamlet,* I,iii,43.

5 I could a tale unfold whose lightest word
Would harrow up thy soul, freeze thy young blood,
Make thy two eyes like stars start from their spheres,
Thy knotted and combinèd locks to part,
And each particular hair to stand an end
Like quills upon the fearful porpentine. *Hamlet,* I,v,15. (A *porpentine* is a porcupine. The speaker is the ghost of Hamlet's father.)

6 A plague of all cowards! *Henry IV, Part One,* II,iv,117. (Uttered by that lovable coward Falstaff. Not knowing that his own fearfulness has been revealed in a practical joke, he accuses a companion who arranged the trick, "You are straight enough in the shoulders; you care not who sees your back. Call you that backing of your friends? A plague upon such backing," 1.148.)

7 Of all base passions, fear is most accursed. *Henry VI, Part One,* V,ii,18. (Joan of Arc speaking.)

8 Cowards die many times before their deaths. *Julius Caesar,* II,ii,32. (More at DEATH.)

9   I am sick and capable of fears,
Oppressed with wrongs, and therefore full of fears,
A widow, husbandless, subject to fears,
A woman naturally born to fears. *King John,* II,ii,12. (Constance of Brittany, wronged but irritating. William M. Matchett, in an introduction to

this play, notes that to earlier generations, Constance was a major and sympathetic character because of her devotion to her son Arthur. Professor Matchett adds, however, that in these early productions of the play, Constance's "screeching exchanges" with Queen Elinor were usually omitted.)

[1] But as I travailed hither through the land,
I find the people strangely fantasied,
Possessed with rumors, full of idle dreams,
Not knowing what they fear, but full of fear. *King John,* IV,ii,143. (The exact date is uncertain, but this portrait of an anxious nation may reflect England when the Spanish invasions were imminent: The great Armada sailed in 1588 and another armada captured Calais in 1596. An immediate source for the passage is Raphael Holinshed's *Chronicles,* from 1587, in which Holinshed described the mood in England after the people heard of the death of the young Duke Arthur, apparently murdered on orders from his uncle, King John: "For the space of fifteen days this rumor incessantly ran through both the realms of England and France, and there was ringing for him through the towns and villages as it had been for a funeral.")

[2]   *Albany.* You may fear too far.
Goneril. Safer than trust too far. *King Lear,* I,iv,335.

[3]   Present fears
Are less than horrible imaginings. *Macbeth,* I,iii,137. (See also TEMPTATION and IMAGINATION.)

[4]   Wouldst thou . . .
Live a coward in thine own esteem,
Letting "I dare not" wait upon "I would,"
Like the poor cat in the adage? *Macbeth,* I,vii,41,43. (The cat in the adage wanted to eat fish, but not get its feet wet.)

[5]   Now I am cabined, cribbed, confined, bound in
To saucy doubts and fears. *Macbeth,* III,iv,25.

[6]   When our actions do not,
Our fears do make us traitors. *Macbeth,* IV,ii,3.

[7]   Extreme fear can neither fight nor fly,
But coward-like with trembling terror die. *The Rape of Lucrece,* 230. (Shakespeare did not know the physiology of this reaction, as we do, but he accurately states the effects.)

[8]   *Ratcliffe.* Be not afraid of shadows.
King Richard. By the apostle Paul, shadows tonight

Have struck more terror to the soul of Richard
Than can the substance of ten thousand soldiers. *Richard III,* V,iii,216.
(The shadows are the ghosts of Richard's victims.)

¹ Fears make devils of cherubins; they never see truly. *Troilus and Cressida,*
III,ii,70.

² To fear the worst oft cures the worse. *Troilus and Cressida,* III,ii,74. (The
conclusion of Cressida's response to Troilus's dismissal of her fears; see
above. Fear guided by reason, she argues, is wiser than "blind reason
stumbling without fear," l.73.)

See also SELF-DOUBT.

FEELINGS.   See EMOTIONS.

FLAGS

³   Banners flout the sky. *Macbeth,* I,ii,49.

⁴ Hang out our banners on the outward walls. *Macbeth,* V,v,1. (More at
WAR.)

FLATTERY AND SYCOPHANCY

⁵   The sweet breath of flattery conquers strife. *The Comedy of Errors,*
III,ii,28.

⁶   Praises sauced with lies. *Coriolanus,* I,ix,53.

⁷   Let the candied tongue lick absurd pomp,
And crook the pregnant hinges of the knee
Where thrift may follow fawning. *Hamlet,* III,ii,62. (*Pregnant* means both
"pliant" and "full of promise." For *thrift* read "profit.")

⁸ *Hamlet.* Do you see yonder cloud that's almost in shape of a camel?
Polonius. By th' mass and 'tis, like a camel indeed.
Hamlet. Methinks it is like a weasel.
Polonius. It is backed like a weasel.
Hamlet. Or like a whale.
Polonius. Very like a whale.
Hamlet. Then I will come to my mother by and by. *Hamlet,* III,ii,384.
(Polonius cannot bring himself to disagree with a prince.)

⁹ Why, what a candy deal of courtesy
The fawning greyhound then did proffer me! *Henry IV, Part One,* I,iii,248.
(*Candy deal* means "a portion of candy.")

¹⁰   When the lion fawns upon the lamb,
The lamb will never cease to follow him. *Henry VI, Part Three,* IV,viii,49.

[1] To dance attendance on their lordships' pleasures. *Henry VIII,* V,ii,31.

[2]   You play the spaniel,
And think with wagging of your tongue to win me. *Henry VIII,* V,iii,126.

[3]   When I tell him he hates flatterers,
He says he does, being then most flatterèd. *Julius Caesar,* II,i,207. (Decius Brutus speaking of Caesar.)

[4] Sweet, sweet, sweet poison. *King John,* I,i,213.

[5] Further I will not flatter you, my lord. *King John,* II,i,516.

[6]   The painted flourish of your praise. *Love's Labor's Lost,* II,i,14. (More at BEAUTY.)

[7] For flattery is the bellows blows up sin. *Pericles,* I,ii,40. (For *blows up* read "fans the flames of.")

[8] A thousand flatterers sit within thy crown,
Whose compass is no bigger than thy head. *Richard II,* II,i,100.

[9]   He does me double wrong
That wounds me with the flatteries of his tongue. *Richard II,* III,ii,215.

[10] He that loves to be flattered is worthy of the flatterer. *Timon of Athens,* I,i,229. (The speaker is the worldly-wise Apemantus. See also below.)

[11] O that men's ears should be
To counsel deaf, but not to flattery. *Timon of Athens,* I,ii,260. (Apemantus bemoaning the universal susceptibility to flattery. See also above.)

[12] Flatter and praise, commend, extol their graces;
. . .
That man that hath a tongue, I say, is no man,
If with his tongue he cannot win a woman. *The Two Gentlemen of Verona,* III,i,102. (Shakespeare had a ribald turn of mind, so a double meaning is a distinct possibility.)

See also PRAISE.

FLOWERS.   See GARDENS; PLANTS AND FLOWERS.

FOOD AND EATING

[13]   Epicurean cooks
Sharpen with cloyless sauce his appetite. *Antony and Cleopatra,* II,i,24.

[14]   The taste of sweetness, whereof a little
More than a little is by much too much. *Henry IV, Part One,* III,ii,72. (More at POLITICS.)

[1] He hath eaten me out of house and home. *Henry IV, Part Two,* II,i,75. (Hostess Quickly referring to Falstaff.)

[2] If you can mock a leek, you can eat a leek. *Henry V,* V,i,38. (Captain Fluellen to Pistol, whom he is force-feeding a raw leek. "It is good for your green wound, and your ploody coxcomb," the captain promises, l.43. Leeks are the floral emblem of Wales, Fluellen's homeland, and, along with their cousin garlic and others in the onion family, have always had a reputation for healing powers. Today garlic and leeks are believed to lower blood pressure and bolster the immune system.)

[3] The sixth hour; when beasts most graze, birds best peck, and men sit down to that nourishment which is called supper. *Love's Labor's Lost,* I,i,233.

[4] Now good digestion wait on appetite,
And health on both! *Macbeth,* III,iv,38. (A secular blessing to start off a meal.)

[5] Great with child; and longing . . . for stewed prunes. *Measure for Measure,* II,i,88.

[6] A surfeit of the sweetest things
The deepest loathing to the stomach brings. *A Midsummer Night's Dream,* II,ii,137.

[7] Truly, a peck of provender. I could munch your good dry oats. Methinks I have a great desire to a bottle of hay. Good hay, sweet hay, hath no fellow. *A Midsummer Night's Dream,* IV,i,34. (Bottom, now sporting an ass's head, has developed new tastes but still tends to misspeak. By *bottle* he means "bundle.")

[8] Most dear actors, eat no onions nor garlic, for we are to utter sweet breath. *A Midsummer Night's Dream,* IV,ii,42.

[9] A very valiant trencherman; he hath an excellent stomach. *Much Ado About Nothing,* I,i,49.

[10] The food that to him now is as luscious as locusts shall be to him shortly as bitter as coloquintida. *Othello,* I,iii,344. (*Coloquintida* is a purgative made from a fruit called "bitter apple." *Locusts* refers to an unidentified fruit.)

[11] The daintiest last, to make the end most sweet. *Richard II,* I,iii,68.

[12] Things sweet to taste prove in digestion sour. *Richard II,* I,iii,235. (There are an unusual number of references in this play to sweets and sweetness, as well as to things that are sour and sourness. Note also "The last taste of sweets is sweetest last," II,i,13—more at DEATHBED STATEMENTS.)

¹ With eager feeding, food doth choke the feeder. *Richard II,* II,i,37.

²   I am a great eater of beef, and I believe that does harm to my wit. *Twelfth Night,* I,iii,84.

³   No more cakes and ale. *Twelfth Night,* II,iii,115. (More at VIRTUE.)

FOOLS

⁴ I met a fool in the forest,
A motley fool! *As You Like It,* II,vii,12. (*Motley* refers to the costume of professional fools, which was multicolored or made up of patches. The speaker is "melancholy Jaques," the worldly-wise, cynical courtier. The fool in the forest is his invention, his alter ego. The relation between the foolish wise man and the wise fool is a prominent theme here and, of course, in *King Lear.*

    "O noble fool, / A worthy fool! Motley's the only wear," Jaques concludes, l.33.)

⁵ "The fool doth think he is wise, but the wise man knows himself to be a fool." *As You Like It,* V,i,30. (The wise fool Touchstone, quoting a proverb. Touchstone was originally played by the sophisticated Robert Armin, probably in 1600, following the retirement of the rowdier Will Kempe, who created Dogberry and similar roles. Mr. Kempe dropped from history's view about 1602, a couple of years after he accomplished the strange feat of doing a morris dance over the one hundred miles from Norwich to London. A morris dance is a popular traditional English folk dance dating back to the 15th century. Related to the morisca, or Moorish dance, its characters are a hero [St. George or Robin Hood], a man dressed as a woman, an animal [hobbyhorse, dragon, bull], and a fool. Sometimes done as a sword dance, it contains mythic elements involving the killing of an animal or character representing evil or winter. In the past, the dancers went from house to house and sometimes town to town, accompanied by a piper. The story of Mr. Kempe's marathon dance, done as a wager, is related in *Jack Drum's Entertainment,* published in 1600, and other contemporary sources.)

⁶ Here comes a pair of very strange beasts, which in all tongues are called fools. *As You Like It,* V,iv,36.

⁷ He was but as the cuckoo is in June,
Heard, not regarded. *Henry IV, Part One,* III,ii,75. (Henry IV talking about Richard II. More at POLITICS.)

⁸ *Lear.* Dost thou call me fool, boy?
Fool. All thy other titles thou hast given away; that thou wast born with. *King Lear,* I,iv,152.

[1] A madman so long, now a fool. *Timon of Athens,* IV,iii,222. (The reference is to Timon of Athens, the classical model of a misanthrope. Timon, like Lear, is a man given to extremes, fatally lacking common sense.)

[2] Better a witty fool than a foolish wit. *Twelfth Night,* I,v,35.

[3] Foolery, sir, does walk about the orb like the sun; it shines everywhere. *Twelfth Night,* III,i,39.

[4] This fellow is wise enough to play the fool,
And to do that well craves a kind of wit. *Twelfth Night,* III,i,61. (For the passage that follows on the talents of the professional comedian, see under THEATER.)

See also INSULTS.

FORGIVENESS

[5]   I as free forgive you
As I would be forgiven. I forgive all. *Henry VIII,* II,i,82. (Buckingham just prior to his execution. He adds, "No black envy [malice] / Shall mark my grave," l.85. Another quote from this scene is at LAW AND LAWYERS.)

[6] Pray you now, forget and forgive. *King Lear,* IV,vii,84. (Proverbial. For the context see the *Lear* quotes from this scene at OLD AGE.)

[7] When thou dost ask me blessing, I'll kneel down
And ask of thee forgiveness. *King Lear,* V,iii,10. (Lear to Cordelia. More at HAPPINESS.)

[8] Forget, forgive, conclude, and be agreed. *Richard II,* I,i,156.

See also MERCY.

FORTUNE

[9]   Men's judgments are
A parcel of their fortunes, and things outward
Do draw the inward quality after them
To suffer all alike. *Antony and Cleopatra,* III,xiii,31. (Enobarbus speaks. The meaning is that judgment and chance, character and events, are inextricably linked. *To suffer all alike* means "to endure the same fate together.")

[10]   He's but Fortune's knave. *Antony and Cleopatra,* V,ii,3. (Cleopatra speaking of Caesar. She means that Caesar's greatness depends on the will of Fortune.)

[11]   Fortune reigns in the gifts of the world. *As You Like It,* I,ii,40. (Rosalind excepts from Fortune's rule "the lineaments of Nature": virtue and intelligence.)

¹ Fortune brings in some boats that are not steered. *Cymbeline*, IV,iii,46. (As Webster put it in *The White Devil*, " 'Tis better to be fortunate than wise.")

² The slings and arrows of outrageous fortune. *Hamlet*, III,i,58. (More at SUICIDE.)

³ A man that Fortune's buffets and rewards
Hath taken with equal thanks. *Hamlet*, III,ii,69.

⁴ Blest are those
. . .
That they are not a pipe for Fortune's finger
To sound what stop she please. *Hamlet*, III,ii,70,72. (As part of the same thought, Hamlet appreciates those who are not slaves of passion; see PASSION.)

⁵ Yield not thy neck
To Fortune's yoke. *Henry VI, Part III*, III,iii,16.

⁶ Ill blows the wind that profits nobody. *Henry VI, Part Three*, II,v,55. (Proverbial.)

⁷ That strumpet fortune. *King John*, II,ii,61.

⁸ A good man's fortune may grow out at heels. *King Lear*, II,ii,160. (*Grow out at heels* means "become threadbare.")

⁹ Fortune, good night;
Smile once more, turn thy wheel. *King Lear*, II,ii,175.

¹⁰ I bear a charmèd life. *Macbeth*, V,viii,12. (Macbeth, shortly before his death in battle with Macduff. See WAR.)

¹¹ O you gods!
Why do you make us love your goodly gifts,
And snatch them straight away? *Pericles*, III,i,22.

¹² The giddy round of Fortune's wheel. *The Rape of Lucrece*, 952.

¹³ O, I am fortune's fool! *Romeo and Juliet*, III,i,138. (Romeo in horror after killing Tybalt and realizing he must flee the city. The meaning is "I am fortune's plaything.")

¹⁴ You fools of fortune. *Timon of Athens*, III,vi,97. (The reference is to people who blindly follow the rich and famous, in other words the fortunate. More at INSULTS.)

See also ADVERSITY; CHANCE; FATE; OPPORTUNITY; SUCCESS.

FRANCE AND THE FRENCH

¹⁵ Done like a Frenchman: turn and turn again! *Henry VI, Part One*, III,iii, 85. (Joan of Arc's comment on her colleagues in arms—an unlikely

line, certainly not one that would appear in a French account of the events.)

[1]   Remember where we are:
In France, amongst a fickle wavering nation. *Henry VI, Part One,* IV,i,137. (Henry VI, sounding like a tired tourist.)

[2]   He can speak French; and therefore he is a traitor. *Henry VI, Part Two,* IV,ii,164. (Finally, anti-French sentiment is challenged, the response being "O gross and miserable ignorance!" The first speaker is Jack Cade, the peasant revolutionary, with whom Shakespeare had no sympathy. He is answered by Sir William Stafford.)

FRANKNESS.   See HONESTY; TALK, PLAIN AND FANCY.

FREEDOM

[3]   I must have liberty
Withal, as large a charter as the wind,
To blow on whom I please. *As You Like It,* II,vii,47. (Spoken by the cynical Jaques, an eloquent but uncommitted character with whom Shakespeare has only moderate sympathy.)

[4] Why, headstrong liberty is lashed with woe.
There's nothing situate under heaven's eye
But hath his bound, in earth, in sea, in sky. *The Comedy of Errors,* II,i,15. (In general, Shakespeare valued order above freedom. Here Luciana lectures her hotheaded sister on the importance of knowing one's place, especially if one is a woman. With many such passages, this play is reminiscent of *The Taming of the Shrew,* in which subordination to a husband is the key to feminine happiness.)

[5] I had as lief not be as live to be
In awe of such a thing as I myself.
I was born free. *Julius Caesar,* I,ii,95. (*Such a thing as I myself* refers to Julius Caesar. Cassius would rather die in revolt against Caesar than live under his rule.)

[6] Who is here so base, that would be a bondman? *Julius Caesar,* III,ii,29.

[7] And Liberty plucks Justice by the nose. *Measure for Measure,* I,iii,29.

[8] 'Ban, 'Ban, Ca—Caliban
Has a new master. Get a new man! *The Tempest,* II,ii,192. (Caliban singing in joy at the prospect of escaping Prospero's rule. But the plot against Prospero fails. "This thing of darkness I / Acknowledge mine," says Prospero, V,i,275.)

See also REVOLUTION.

FREE WILL.   See WILL.

FRENCH, THE.   See FRANCE AND THE FRENCH.

FRIENDS

1   Keep thy friend
Under thy own life's key. *All's Well That Ends Well,* I,i,70. (More at
WISDOM, WORDS OF.)

2 Those friends thou hast, and their adoption tried,
Grapple them unto thy soul with hoops of steel. *Hamlet,* I,iii,62. (More at
WISDOM, WORDS OF.)

3 There is flattery in friendship. *Henry V,* III,vii,119. (From the proverbs
contest. See WISDOM, WORDS OF.)

4   We were but hollow friends. *Henry VI, Part Two,* III,ii,66.

5 A friend should bear his friend's infirmities. *Julius Caesar* IV,iii,85. (Cassius is speaking. He adds: "But Brutus makes mine greater than they are."
Infirmities here means "faults.")

6 That sir, which serves and seeks for gain,
And follows but for form,
Will pack, when it begins to rain,
And leave thee in the storm. *King Lear,* II,iv,77. (A description of fair-
weather friends.)

7   So we grew together,
Like to a double cherry, seeming parted,
But yet an union in partition;
Two lovely berries molded on one stem. *A Midsummer Night's Dream,*
III,ii,208.

8 Friendship is constant in all other things
Save in the office and affairs of love. *Much Ado About Nothing,* II,i,173.
(*Office* means "business.")

9 I count myself in nothing else so happy
As in a soul remembering my good friends. *Richard II,* II,iii,46.

10   If the while I think on thee, dear friend,
All losses are restored and sorrows end. *Sonnet 30,* 13.

11 To me, fair friend, you never can be old. *Sonnet 104,* 1. (More at LOVE,
EXPRESSIONS OF.)

12   Friendship's full of dregs. *Timon of Athens,* I,ii,244.

See also ALLIES.

FUN AND FUN PEOPLE

[1]   Come,
Let's have one other gaudy night: call to me
All my sad captains; fill our bowls once more;
Let's mock the midnight bell. *Antony and Cleopatra,* III,xiii,182. (Antony
before his death. *Gaudy Night* was used as a title by Dorothy Sayers in her
Lord Peter Wimsey mystery series. It refers to the gaudy night celebration
at Oxford University, with *gaudy* meaning "joyful." The student song
"Gaudeamus igitur" is related to the festival.)

[2] A truant disposition. *Hamlet,* I,ii,169. (Horatio's explanation for why he
has left his studies in Wittenberg.)

[3]   A merrier man,
Within the limit of becoming mirth,
I never spent an hour's talk withal. *Love's Labor's Lost,* II,i,66. (The
speaker is Rosaline, who, according to A. L. Rowse, is modeled on the
"dark lady" of the sonnets. The man she refers to, Berowne, is modeled
on Shakespeare himself.)

[4] Why should a man whose blood is warm within
Sit like his grandsire, cut in alabaster? *The Merchant of Venice,* I,i,83.

[5] Awake the pert and nimble spirit of mirth. *A Midsummer Night's Dream,*
I,i,13.

[6]   From the crown of his head to the sole of his foot, he is all mirth.
Much Ado About Nothing, III,ii,8.

[7] We make ourselves fools to disport ourselves. *Timon of Athens,* I,ii,138.

See also FALSTAFF; HAPPINESS; PLEASURE.

FUTILITY

[8]   All the yarn she spun in Ulysses' absence did but fill Ithaca full of
moths. *Coriolanus,* I,iii,87. (The reference is to Penelope, wife of Ulysses,
who put off suitors, saying that she was weaving a shawl and could not
consider marriage until she was finished.)

[9]   The task he undertakes
Is numbering sands, and drinking oceans dry. *Richard II,* II,ii,144. (Sir
Henry Green, speaking of a hopeless undertaking, in this case, the
duke of York's resistance to the advance of his nephew Bolingbroke.
"Where one on his side fights, thousands will fly," l.146, Sir Henry
concludes.)

FUTURE

1   We know what we are, but we know not what we may be. *Hamlet,* IV,v,43.

2   We defy augury. *Hamlet,* V,ii,220. (Hamlet's comment when Horatio asks him if he would like to postpone his duel with Laertes.)

3   O, that a man might know
The end of this day's business ere it come! *Julius Caesar,* V,i,122.

4 If you can look into the seeds of time,
And say which grain will grow and which will not,
Speak then to me. *Macbeth,* I,iii,58.

5   Tomorrow is a busy day. *Richard III,* V,iii,18. (More at ACTION, PROMPT.)

6 Not mine own fears nor the prophetic soul
Of the wide world dreaming on things to come. *Sonnet 107,* 1. (More at LOVE AND LOVERS.)

7   The sad augurs mock their own presage. *Sonnet 107,* 6. (The future turned out well; gloomy prophets had to admit they were wrong.)

See also HISTORY; OMENS; TIME.

GARDENS

1   'Tis an unweeded garden
That grows to seed. Things rank and gross in nature
Possess it merely. *Hamlet*, I,ii,135. (*Merely* means "entirely." See also below.)

2 Now 'tis the spring, and weeds are shallow-rooted;
Suffer them now, and they'll o'ergrow the garden. *Henry VI, Part Two*, III,i,31.

3   Adam was a gardener. *Henry VI, Part Two*, IV,ii,131.

See also NATURE; PLANTS AND FLOWERS.

GENERATIONS

4 The younger rises when the old doth fall. *King Lear*, III,iii,26.

5 The oldest hath borne most: we that are young
Shall never see so much, nor live so long. *King Lear*, V,iii,327. (The final lines of the play.)

6 Crabbèd age and youth cannot live together:
Youth is full of pleasance, age is full of care;
Youth like summer morn, age like winter weather;
Youth like summer brave, age like winter bare.
Youth is full of sport, age's breath is short;

Youth is nimble, age is lame;
Youth is hot and bold, age is weak and cold;
Youth is wild, and age is tame.
Age, I do abhor thee; youth, I do adore thee:
O, my love, my love is young! *The Passionate Pilgrim,* stanza xii.

[1] The old bees die, the young possess their hive. *The Rape of Lucrece,* 1769.

See also CHILDREN; PARENTS.

GENEROSITY.   See GIVING.

GENTLENESS.   See KINDNESS.

GHOSTS.   See APPARITIONS; OCCULT, THE.

GIVING

[2]   Thou makest a testament
As worldlings do, giving thy sum of more
To that which had too much. *As You Like It,* II,i,47. (An elaborate
comment on a wounded stag weeping tears into a forest stream. The line
is similar to *Matthew* 25:29: "Unto every one that hath shall be given.")

[3]   To the noble mind
Rich gifts wax poor when givers prove unkind. *Hamlet,* III,i,100. (Ophelia
to Hamlet.)

[4] An old man broken with the storms of state
Is come to lay his weary bones among ye;
Give him a little earth for charity. *Henry VIII,* IV,ii,21. (The broken man
is Cardinal Wolsey.)

[5]   My good will is great, though the gift small. *Pericles,* III,iv,17.

[6] I am not in the giving vein today. *Richard III,* IV,ii,115. (Richard speaks.
It is an extraordinary understatement.)

[7]   There's none
Can truly say he gives, if he receives. *Timon of Athens,* I,ii,10. (Timon's
imprudent generosity, reflected in these lines, provokes contempt and
leads to his ruin. Shakespeare evidently adhered to Aristotle's position in
the *Nicomachaean Ethics:* "The liberal man will give to the right people, the
right amounts, and at the right time. . . . Nor will he neglect his own
property. . . . He who exceeds is prodigal.")

[8]   He's the very soul of bounty. *Timon of Athens,* I,ii,215.

[1] Hate all, curse all, show charity to none,
But let the famished flesh slide from the bone
Ere thou relieve the beggar. *Timon of Athens,* IV,iii,536. (Here the embittered, once-generous Timon rejects kindness in any form. In the ancient world, Timon was the model of extreme, absurd misanthropy. In Shakespeare's works, he is similar to Lear: arrogant, imprudent, and irrational in his virtues as well as his faults.)

[2] Out of my lean and low ability
I'll lend you something. *Twelfth Night,* III,iv,356.

See also HELP; HOSPITALITY; KINDNESS.

GLORY. See FAME; GREATNESS; HONOR; POWER; RICH, THE; SUCCESS.

GOD

[3] God is our fortress. *Henry VI, Part One,* II,i,26. (The image of God as a fortress was popular in this period. Martin Luther's hymn "Ein' feste burg ist unser Gott," "A mighty fortress is our God," was written in 1529 and translated into English by Frederick Henry Hedge. Shakespeare's line was written in 1599. Thomas Quarles used a similar figure of speech in *Divine Poems,* 1592–1644. In the King James translation of the Bible, we find "The Lord is my rock, and my fortress, and my deliverer" at *II Samuel* 22:2, and "He is my refuge and my fortress" at *Psalms* 91:2. Both biblical passages are spoken by the warrior-king David.)

[4]   God shall be my hope,
My stay, my guide and lanthorn to my feet. *Henry VI, Part Two,* II,iii,24. (The king, alluding to Psalm 119: "Thy word is a lamp unto my feet, and a light unto my path.")

[5] Now, God be praised, that to believing souls
Gives light in darkness, comfort in despair! *Henry VI, Part Two,* II,i,66. (The king is speaking.)

[6]   God defend the right! *Henry VI, Part Two,* II,iii,55. (The king again. Relatively pious but almost completely ineffectual, this young man needed more help from God than he got.)

[7] Heaven is above all yet; there sits a judge
That no king can corrupt. *Henry VIII,* III,i,100.

See also PRAYER; PRAYERS; PROVIDENCE; RELIGION.

GOODNESS.   See GIVING; JUSTICE; KINDNESS; MERCY; VIRTUE.

GOOD TIMES.   See HAPPINESS; PEACE.

GOVERNMENT

1   Wert thou regent of the world,
It were a shame to let this land by lease;
. . .
Landlord of England art thou now, not king. *Richard II,* II,i,109. (A speech that recalls our own debates on how public land and natural resources should be used. John of Gaunt is rebuking his nephew Richard.)

2 Woe to that land that's governed by a child! *Richard III,* II,iii,11.

See also CENSORSHIP; HIGH POSITION; POLITICS; POWER; TAXES; UTOPIA.

GRACE

3   Happy is your Grace
That can translate the stubbornness of fortune
Into so quiet and so sweet a style. *As You Like It,* II,i,18. (A courtier in exile complimenting the rightful duke on what we would call grace under pressure.)

4 See what a grace was seated on this brow. *Hamlet,* III,iv,56. (Hamlet speaking of a portrait of his father. More of the quote below.)

5 A combination and a form indeed
Where every god did seem to set his seal
To give the world assurance of a man. *Hamlet,* III,iv,61. (Again, Hamlet speaking of his father; see above.)

6 He hath a daily beauty in his life. *Othello,* V,i,19.

7 O momentary grace of mortal men,
Which we more hunt for than the grace of God! *Richard III,* III,iv,95. (*Grace* here is used in the sense of the favor or kindness of a prince.)

8 Holy, fair, and wise is she;
The heaven such grace did lend her,
That she might admirèd be. *The Two Gentlemen of Verona,* IV,ii,40. (From the song "Silvia." More at LOVE, EXPRESSIONS OF.)

See also BEAUTY; VIRTUE.

GRATITUDE.   See INGRATITUDE.

GREATNESS

1   I have
Immortal longings in me. *Antony and Cleopatra,* V,ii,280. (Cleopatra preparing to die. See also CLEOPATRA.)

2 Then there's hope a great man's memory may outlive his life half a year.
Hamlet, III,ii,135. (More at DEATH AND GRIEF.)

3   Greatness knows itself. *Henry IV, Part One,* IV,iii,74.

4 O, give me the spare men, and spare me the great ones. *Henry IV, Part
Two,* III,ii,278. (Falstaff on the subject of the superiority of thin men over
large men in battle, with obvious emphasis on the double meaning of
great.)

5 How soon this mightiness meets misery. *Henry VIII,* Prologue, 30. (Many
scholars believe that John Fletcher wrote parts of this play, including the
Prologue. In any case, the brevity of fortune's favor is a major theme
throughout.)

6 I have touched the highest point of all my greatness. *Henry VIII,* III,ii,223.
(Cardinal Wolsey speaks. More at RUIN, and see below.)

7 Farewell! A long farewell to all my greatness!
This is the state of man: today he puts forth
The tender leaves of hopes; tomorrow blossoms,
And bears his blushing honors thick upon him.
The third day comes a frost, a killing frost,
And, when he thinks, good easy man, full surely
His greatness is aripening, nips his root,
And then he falls, as I do. I have ventured,
Like little wanton boys that swim on bladders,
This many summers in a sea of glory,
But far beyond my depth. My high-blown pride
At length broke under me and now has left me,
Weary and old with service, to the mercy
Of a rude stream that must forever hide me.
Vain pomp and glory of this world, I hate ye. *Henry VIII,* III,ii,351. (The
conclusion of this speech—Wolsey's farewell to greatness—is at HIGH
POSITION.)

8 Wherever the bright sun of heaven shall shine,
His honor and the greatness of his name
Shall be, and make new nations. *Henry VIII,* V,v,50. (The reference is to

James I. *Henry VIII* was written to celebrate the marriage of James's daughter Elizabeth to the Elector Palatine.)

¹   This man
Is now become a god. *Julius Caesar*, I,ii,115. (A bitter comment by Cassius on the success of Caesar.)

²   He doth bestride the narrow world
Like a Colossus, and we petty men
Walk under his huge legs and peep about
To find ourselves dishonorable graves. *Julius Caesar*, I,ii,135. (Again, Cassius on Caesar. *Colossus* is a general term for any large statue, the most famous being the Colossus of Rhodes, one of the seven wonders of the ancient world. This bronze statue of Apollo was evidently more than one hundred feet high. Legend held that its legs spanned the entrance to the harbor at Rhodes. To return to reality, it was located on a hill overlooking the harbor, and was destroyed by an earthquake about 224 B.C.)

³ When beggars die, there are no comets seen;
The heavens themselves blaze forth the death of princes. *Julius Caesar*, II,ii,30. (Calphurnia to Caesar.)

⁴   Packs and sects of great ones
That ebb and flow by the moon. *King Lear*, V,iii,18. (Lear's description of the mighty in this world. These are the last lines in the speech that begins "Come, let's away to prison." See HAPPINESS.)

⁵   Spirits are not finely touched
But to fine issues. *Measure for Measure*, I,i,35. (Souls are made great only to deal with great issues.)

⁶   Be not afraid of greatness. Some are born great, some achieve greatness, and some have greatness thrust upon 'em. *Twelfth Night*, II,v,143.

See also AMBITION; CLEOPATRA; ELITE; ELIZABETH I; EPITAPHS; FAME; HENRY V; HIGH POSITION: HONOR; JULIUS CAESAR; NOBILITY; POWER; RUIN; SUCCESS; VANITY; VIRTUE; WOLSEY, CARDINAL.

GREED

⁷   Didst thou never hear
That things ill got had ever bad success?
And happy always was it for that son
Whose father for his hoarding went to hell? *Henry VI, Part Three*, II,ii,45.

⁸ Those that much covet are with gain so fond
That what they have not, that which they possess

They scatter and unloose it from their bond,
And so by hoping more they have but less. *The Rape of Lucrece,* 134.

See also ENVY; SELF-INTEREST.

GRIEF.   See DEATH AND GRIEF; SORROW AND SADNESS.

GUESTS
1   Unbidden guests
Are often welcomest when they are gone. *Henry VI, Part One,* II,ii,55.

GUILE.   See CRAFTINESS; DECEPTIVENESS; EVIL; HYPOCRISY;
LIES AND DECEIT.

GUILT
2 And then it started, like a guilty thing
Upon a fearful summons. *Hamlet,* I,i,148. (*It* refers to the ghost of Hamlet's father. *Started* means "jumped." What startled the spirit was the crowing of a cock.)

3   There is a kind of confession in your looks, which your modesties have not craft enough to color. *Hamlet,* II,ii,286.

4 The lady doth protest too much, methinks. *Hamlet,* III,ii,236. (Queen Gertrude's comment on the Player Queen, her counterpart in the play written by Hamlet to trick Gertrude and his uncle into revealing the truth concerning his father's death. The Player Queen has repeatedly stated her devotion to her husband.)

5 So full of artless jealousy is guilt
It spills itself in fearing to be spilt. *Hamlet,* IV,v,19. (*Jealousy* here means "suspicion.")

6   We know enough if we know we are the King's subjects: if his cause be wrong, our obedience to the King wipes the crime of it out of us. *Henry V,* IV,i,132. (The traditional "we were following orders" excuse. During the battle of Agincourt, Henry V ordered the mass execution of prisoners, fearing an attack from behind his lines. John Keegan in *The Face of Battle* notes that some wounded prisoners apparently were burned to death in cottages where they had been taken. Nobles, worth large ransoms, were generally spared. The order was revoked after the French were in irreversible retreat.)

7 All offenses, my lord, come from the heart. *Henry V,* IV,viii,46. (The meaning is that one must intend an offense for it to be truly an offense.)

[1] Suspicion always haunts the guilty mind;
The thief doth fear each bush an officer. *Henry VI, Part Three,* V,vi,11.

[2] Will all great Neptune's ocean wash this blood
Clean from my hand? *Macbeth,* II,ii,59. (Macbeth to his wife. She tries to
bring him back to practical considerations: "A little water clears us of this
deed: / How easy is it then!" l.66. Ironically, it is she who ends mad,
compulsively scrubbing her hands. See two quotes below.)

[3] Thou canst not say I did it. Never shake
Thy gory locks at me. *Macbeth,* III,iv,51. (Macbeth to the ghost of Banquo.)

[4] Out, damned spot! Out, I say! *Macbeth,* V,i,38. (Lady Macbeth sleepwalking. See also two quotes above. In her correspondence with Thornton
Wilder, actress Ruth Gordon relayed a comment from Dame Edith Evans
on why she had not played this great tragic role: "I could never reconcile
the part of Lady Macbeth with the Scottish sense of hospitality.")

[5] Here's the smell of the blood still. All the perfumes of Arabia will not
sweeten this little hand. *Macbeth,* V,i,53.

[6] Condemn the fault, and not the actor of it?
Why, every fault's condemned ere it be done. *Measure for Measure,* II,ii,37.
(Cold-blooded Angelo—"a man of stricture and firm abstinence,"
I,iii,12—sees only guilt or innocence, black or white. The guilty one in this
case is Claudio, who got his fiancée pregnant. The punishment is death.)

[7] That would hang us, every mother's son. *A Midsummer Night's Dream,*
I,ii,78.

[8] Masters, it is proved already that you are little better than false knaves.
Much Ado About Nothing, IV,ii,20.

[9] Few love to hear the sins they love to act. *Pericles,* I,i,93. (This may not
be by Shakespeare. Scholars differ on how much of this play he wrote
himself.)

See also APPEARANCES; CONSCIENCE; CRIME; SCAPEGOATS.

GULLIBILITY

[10] The Moor is of a free and open nature
And thinks men honest that but seem to be so. *Othello,* I,iii,390.

[11] They'll take suggestion as a cat laps milk. *The Tempest,* II,i,292.

HABIT AND CUSTOM

[1]   Though I am native here
And to the manner born, it is a custom
More honored in the breach than the observance. *Hamlet,* I,iv,14. (What
Hamlet means is that there is more honor in breaking than observing the
custom, which is to drain a goblet of wine in a single gulp when making
a toast. He finds his country's reputation for drunkenness embarrassing.
The quote is commonly misused to refer to a custom more often ignored
than followed.)

[2]   Refrain tonight,
And that shall lend a kind of easiness
To the next abstinence; the next more easy;
For use almost can change the stamp of nature. *Hamlet,* III,iv,166. (Hamlet to his mother. *Use* means "habit" or "practice.")

[3] How use doth breed a habit in a man! *The Two Gentlemen of Verona,*
V,iv,1. (For *use* read "custom" or "what one is used to.")

See also FASHION; MANNERS.

HALLUCINATIONS.   See APPARITIONS.

HAMLET

[4] O what a noble mind is here o'erthrown!
The courtier's, soldier's, scholar's, eye, tongue, sword,

The expectancy and rose of the fair state,
The glass of fashion, and the mold of form,
The observed of all observers, quite, quite down! *Hamlet,* III,i,153. (Ophelia speaks. See also MADNESS.)

[1] Now cracks a noble heart. Good night, sweet Prince,
And flights of angels sing thee to thy rest. *Hamlet,* V,ii,360. (The speaker is Horatio.)

HAPPINESS

[2] Your heart's desires be with you! *As You Like It,* I,ii,188.

[3] O, how bitter a thing it is to look into happiness through another man's eyes! *As You Like It,* V,ii,42.

[4] My crown is in my heart, not on my head;
Not decked with diamonds and Indian stones,
Nor to be seen. My crown is called content.
A crown it is that seldom kings enjoy. *Henry VI, Part Three,* III,i,62. (In the same period, Robert Greene wrote, "A mind content both crown and kingdom is," *Farewell to Folly,* 1591.)

[5]   'Tis better to be lowly born
And range with humble livers in content
Than to be perked up in a glistering grief
And wear a golden sorrow. *Henry VIII,* II,iii,19.

[6] Nought's had, all's spent,
Where our desire is got without content. *Macbeth,* III,ii,4. (Lady Macbeth speaks. They have gained the throne, but without happiness or contentment.)

[7]   Happy man be his dole. *The Merry Wives of Windsor,* III,iv,63. (The quote means "May it be his lot to be a happy man." Proverbial. Also at *The Winter's Tale,* I,ii,163.)

[8]   As merry as the day is long. *Much Ado About Nothing,* II,i,49.

[9] Silence is the perfectest herald of joy. I were but little happy if I could say how much. *Much Ado About Nothing,* II,i,303.

[10]   There was a star danced, and under that was I born. *Much Ado About Nothing,* II,i,331. (Beatrice is speaking of her gift for happiness.)

[11] I am not merry; but I do beguile
The thing I am by seeming otherwise. *Othello,* II,i,120.

[12]   Our loves and comforts should increase
Even as our days do grow. *Othello,* II,i,192.

¹ Poor and content is rich, and rich enough. *Othello,* III,iii,172.

²   Joy delights in joy. *Sonnet 8, 2.*

³   Laugh yourselves into stitches. *Twelfth Night,* III,ii,68.

⁴ Jog on, jog on, the footpath way,
And merrily hent the stile-a;
A merry heart goes all the day,
Your sad tires in a mile-a. *The Winter's Tale,* IV,iii,127. (*Hent the stile* means "take" or "jump" the fence.)

See also FUN AND FUN PEOPLE; HAPPINESS, EXPRESSIONS OF; LEISURE; PLEASURE; SORROW AND SADNESS.

HAPPINESS, EXPRESSIONS OF

⁵ O wonderful, wonderful, and most wonderful wonderful, and yet again wonderful, and after that, out of all hooping! *As You Like It,* III,ii,190.

⁶   They threw their caps
As they would hang them on the horns of the moon. *Coriolanus,* I,i,213.

⁷ We two alone will sing like birds i' the cage:
When thou dost ask me blessing, I'll kneel down
And ask of thee forgiveness: so we'll live,
And pray, and sing, and tell old tales, and laugh
At gilded butterflies, and hear poor rogues
Talk of court news; and we'll talk with them too,
Who loses and who wins, who's in, who's out;
And take upon's the mystery of things,
As if we were God's spies: and we'll wear out,
In a walled prison, packs and sects of great ones
That ebb and flow by the moon. *King Lear,* V,iii,9. (Lear to Cordelia as they enter prison. She is murdered before the day is out.)

HASTE.   See CAREFULNESS; IMPULSIVITY; SPEED.

HATE

⁸ Curses not loud but deep. *Macbeth,* V,iii,27.

⁹ He hates our sacred nation . . .
    . . .
    Cursèd be my tribe
If I forgive him. *The Merchant of Venice,* I,iii,45,48. (Shylock speaking of Antonio.)

[1] Deep malice makes too deep incision. *Richard II,* I,i,155.

[2] See what a scourge is laid upon your hate,
That heaven finds means to kill your joys with love. *Romeo and Juliet,*
V,iii,292.

[3] I am Misanthropos and hate mankind. *Timon of Athens,* IV,iii,54. (Said by
Timon of Athens. See also below.)

[4] Hate all, curse all, show charity to none. *Timon of Athens,* IV,iii,536. (More
at GIVING.)

See also ANGER; DESPAIR AND RAGE; ENEMIES AND ENMITY; ENVY; EVIL.

HAVES AND HAVE-NOTS.   See RICH AND POOR.

HEALTH

[5] Unquiet meals make ill digestions. *The Comedy of Errors,* V,i,74.

[6]   I'll purge, and leave sack, and live cleanly, as a nobleman should do.
Henry IV, Part One, V,iv,162. (Falstaff in one of his many promises to
reform. By *purge* is meant "repent." Sack was a popular white wine made
in Spain and the Canary Islands. Its name derives from *sec,* French for
"dry"—the wine was dry.)

[7]   Is Brutus sick,
And will he steal out of his wholesome bed,
To dare the vile contagion of the night? *Julius Caesar,* II,i,263. (Portia
challenges her husband's claim that ill health accounts for his moodiness.
The belief that the night air is harmful was common, possibly based on the
greater nighttime prevalence of disease-carrying mosquitos.)

See also DOCTORS; FATNESS; MADNESS; MEDICINE; SICKNESS.

HEAVENS, THE

[8]   This most excellent canopy, the air, . . . this brave o'erhanging
firmament, this majestical roof fretted with golden fire. *Hamlet,* II,ii,307.
(More at DEPRESSION.)

[9]   Look how the floor of heaven
Is thick inlaid with patens of bright gold.
There's not the smallest orb which thou behold'st
But in his motion like an angel sings. *The Merchant of Venice,* V,i,58.
(Lorenzo is speaking of the music of the spheres, believed to be music
produced by the motion of heavenly bodies, a music inaudible to human
ears. The phrase "music from the spheres" appears in *Twelfth Night,*
III,i,112. More at MUSIC.)

See also MOON, THE; STARS.

HEIGHTS

1   The dreadful summit of the cliff
That beetles o'er his base into the sea. *Hamlet,* I,iv,70. (*Beetles* means "juts
out," as in "beetle-browed.")

2   Hills whose heads touch heaven. *Othello,* I,iii,140.

See also DOVER CLIFFS.

HELP

3 'Tis not enough to help the feeble up,
But to support him after. *Timon of Athens,* I,i,107.

See also COMFORT; GIVING.

HENRY V

4 I know you all, and will awhile uphold
The unyoked humor of your idleness.
Yet herein will I imitate the sun,
Who doth permit the base contagious clouds
To smother up his beauty from the world,
That, when he please again to be himself,
Being wanted, he may be more wondered at
By breaking through the foul and ugly mists
Of vapors that did seem to strangle him.
If all the year were playing holidays,
To sport would be as tedious as to work. *Henry IV, Part One,* I,ii,199.
(Prince Hal in a speech forecasting his eventual rejection of his drinking
companions. See FALSTAFF.)

5   A Corinthian, a lad of mettle, a good boy. *Henry IV, Part One,*
II,iv,12. (Prince Hal, joking about the compliments paid him by drinking
companions. "A good boy" is probably not the way we would describe this
charming but wild teenager. *A Corinthian* means a high-spirited, usually
wealthy young man, so-called after the people of ancient Corinth, reputed
lovers of luxury.)

6 I saw young Harry with his beaver on. *Henry IV, Part One,* IV,i,103. (From
a passage describing the prince in arms before the battle of Shrewsbury.
See also SOLDIERS. A *beaver* is the lower part of a helmet's face guard.)

7   The mirror of all Christian kings. *Henry V,* II,Chorus,6.

8 The royal captain of this ruined band
Walking from watch to watch, from tent to tent. *Henry V,* IV,Chorus, 29.

(Henry V encouraging his army the night before the battle of Agincourt. "With cheerful semblance and sweet majesty," 1.40, he conveys comfort and confidence. See also below and under WAR.)

[1] A little touch of Harry in the night. *Henry V,* IV, Chorus, 47. (From the Chorus passage describing the young king among his troops on the night before the battle of Agincourt. See also above and WAR.)

HIGH POSITION

[2] So excellent a king. *Hamlet,* I,ii,139. (More at MARRIAGE.)

[3]   His will is not his own.
For he himself is subject to his birth.
He may not, as unvalued persons do,
Carve for himself; for on his choice depends
The safety and health of this whole state. *Hamlet,* I,iii,17. (Laertes warning Ophelia that Hamlet, because he is king, is not free to marry whom he pleases.)

[4] There's such divinity doth hedge a king
That treason can but peep to what it would. *Hamlet,* IV,v,123. (Claudius pompously reassuring Gertrude that no harm will come to him. The second line means that a person thinking of treason cannot even approach the throne, can only glimpse it from a distance.)

[5] Uneasy lies the head that wears a crown. *Henry IV, Part Two,* III,i,31. (The king, troubled by insomnia. Later his son Hal speaks of the crown as a "polished perturbation" and a "golden care." See ANXIETY AND WORRY.)

[6]   What infinite heart's-ease
Must kings neglect that private men enjoy!
And what have kings that privates have not too,
Save ceremony, save general ceremony?
And what art thou, thou idol Ceremony?
What kind of god art thou, that suffer'st more
Of mortal griefs than do thy worshippers?
What are thy rents? What are thy comings-in?
O Ceremony, show me but thy worth! *Henry V,* IV,i,241. (The king is speaking. More below.)

[7] 'Tis not the balm, the scepter, and the ball,
The sword, the mace, the crown imperial,
The intertissued robe of gold and pearl,
The farcèd title running fore the king,
The throne he sits on, nor the tide of pomp

That beats upon the high shore of this world—
No, not all these, thrice-gorgeous ceremony,
Not all these, laid in bed majestical,
Can sleep so soundly as the wretched slave,
Who, with a body filled, and vacant mind,
Gets him to rest, crammed with distressful bread;
Never sees horrid night, the child of hell. *Henry V,* IV,i,265. (The king, like his father before him, sleeps little. See *Henry IV, Part Two* above. *Farced* means "stuffed," "puffed up." *Distressful bread* is bread earned by hard labor.)

1   Nice customs cursy to great kings. *Henry V,* V,ii,281. (For *cursy* read "curtsy." More at MANNERS.)

2 How sweet a thing it is to wear a crown,
Within whose circuit is Elysium
And all that poets feign of bliss and joy. *Henry VI, Part Three,* I,ii,29. (The future Richard III to his father, the duke of York.)

3   I would not be a queen
For all the world. *Henry VIII,* II,iii,45. (Said by Anne Bullen [Boleyn].)

4   My crown is called content.
A crown it is that seldom kings enjoy. *Henry VI, Part Three,* III,i,64. (More at HAPPINESS.)

5   O, how wretched
Is that poor man that hangs on princes' favors!
There is betwixt that smile we would aspire to,
That sweet aspect of princes, and their ruin,
More pangs and fears than wars or women have.
And when he falls, he falls like Lucifer,
Never to hope again. *Henry VIII,* III,ii,366. (The conclusion of Cardinal Wolsey's farewell to greatness; see GREATNESS.)

6   He would be crowned.
How that might change his nature, there's the question. *Julius Caesar,* II,i,12.

7   Ay, every inch a king. *King Lear,* IV,vi,109. (Thus Lear, wandering and draped in wild flowers, describes himself.)

8   To be King
Stands not within the prospect of belief. *Macbeth,* I,iii,73. (Macbeth to the witches. But the seed of belief has been planted.)

9 For princes are the glass, the school, the book,
Wherein subjects' eyes do learn, do read, do look. *The Rape of Lucrece,* 615.

1   Greatest scandal waits on greatest state. *The Rape of Lucrece,* 1006.

2 We were not born to sue, but to command. *Richard II,* I,i,196. (Richard was crowned at age ten in the most magnificent secular ceremony ever seen up to that time in England.)

3 Not all the water in the rough rude sea
Can wash the balm off from an anointed king. *Richard II,* III,ii,54. (Shakespeare strongly advocated stability in government, and most Elizabethans accepted the divine right of kings as the keystone of social stability. Yet Richard here presumes too much.)

4 For God's sake let us sit upon the ground
And tell sad stories of the death of kings:
How some have been deposed, some slain in war,
Some haunted by the ghosts they have deposed,
Some poisoned by their wives, some sleeping killed,
All murdered—for within the hollow crown
That rounds the mortal temples of a king
Keeps Death his court. *Richard II,* III,ii,155.

5 The name of a king? a God's name, let it go.
I'll give my jewels for a set of beads;
My gorgeous palace for a hermitage;
My gay apparel for an almsman's gown;
My figured goblets for a dish of wood;
My scepter for a palmer's walking-staff;
My subjects for a pair of carvèd saints;
And my large kingdom for a little grave,
A little, little grave, an obscure grave. *Richard II,* III,iii,145. (In line 1, for *a God's name* read "in God's name." In line 2, *beads* refers to a rosary.)

6 Now is this golden crown like a deep well
That owes two buckets, filling one another,
The emptier ever dancing in the air,
The other down, unseen, and full of water.
That bucket down and full of tears am I,
Drinking my griefs, whilst you mount up on high. *Richard II,* IV,i,183. (For *owes* in line 2, read "owns" or "has." Richard is handing over his crown to Bolingbroke.)

7 O, that I were a mockery king of snow,
. . .
To melt myself away in water drops! *Richard II,* IV,i,259.

8 Is the chair empty? Is the sword unswayed?
Is the King dead, the empire unpossessed? *Richard III,* IV,iv,469. (Rich-

ard's sarcastic questions are provoked by the news that the earl of Richmond—the future Henry VII—intends to claim the crown.)

1   The King's name is a tower of strength. *Richard III,* V,iii,12.

2 The Emperor's court is like the House of Fame,
The palace full of tongues, of eyes, and ears. *Titus Andronicus,* II,i,126.
(Fame is a personification of what is talked about, of gossip and rumor. The House of Fame is the subject of poems by Chaucer and Ovid.)

See also CLEOPATRA; ELIZABETH I; GOVERNMENT; GREATNESS; HENRY V; JULIUS CAESAR; LEADERS; POWER.

HISTORY

3 There is a history in all men's lives,
Figuring the nature of the times deceased,
The which observed, a man may prophesy,
With a near aim, of the main chance of things
As yet not come to life. *Henry IV, Part Two,* III,i,80. (Warwick speaking. In other words, study of the past, of times deceased, makes one better able to predict the future.)

4   The chronicle of wasted time. *Sonnet 106,* 1. (More at BEAUTY.)

5 *Duke.* And what's her history?
Viola. A blank, my lord. *Twelfth Night,* II,iv,110. (More at LOVE AND LOVERS.)

See also PAST, THE.

HOLY LAND

6   Those holy fields
Over whose acres walked those blessèd feet
Which fourteen hundred years ago were nailed
For our advantage on the bitter cross. *Henry IV, Part One,* I,i,24.

HOME

7 Ay, now am I in Arden, the more fool I. When I was at home, I was in a better place, but travelers must be content. *As You Like It,* II,iv,15. (Touchstone upon arriving in the Forest of Arden.)

8 Home-keeping youth have ever homely wits. *The Two Gentlemen of Verona,* I,i,2.

See also EXPERIENCE; TRAVEL.

HONESTY

1 Rich honesty dwells like a miser, sir, in a poor house, as your pearl in your foul oyster. *As You Like It,* V,iv,60.

2   Would you have me
False to my nature? Rather say I play
The man I am. *Coriolanus,* III,ii,14. (Coriolanus speaking. Like Timon of Athens—see below—he carried honesty rather too far.)

3   Armed so strong in honesty. *Julius Caesar* IV,iii,67. (From a rather pompous speech by Brutus: "There is no terror, Cassius, in your threats; / For I am armed so strong in honesty / That they pass by me as the idle wind.")

4 The weight of this sad time we must obey,
Speak what we feel, not what we ought to say. *King Lear,* V,iii,325.

5 He hath a heart as sound as a bell; and his tongue is the clapper, for what his heart thinks, his tongue speaks. *Much Ado About Nothing,* III,ii,12.

6 Men should be what they seem. *Othello,* III,iii,128. (Iago to Othello; see also below.)

7   Take note, take note, O world,
To be direct and honest is not safe. *Othello,* III,iii,374. (Iago speaks.)

8 Every man has his fault, and honesty is his. *Timon of Athens,* III,i,29.

9 Methinks thou art more honest now than wise. *Timon of Athens,* IV,iii,511.

10   What a fool Honesty is! *The Winter's Tale,* IV,iv,599.

See also DISHONESTY; PROMISES.

HONEYBEES.   See ANIMALS.

HONOR

11   If I lose mine honor,
I lose myself. *Antony and Cleopatra,* III,iv,22. (Antony speaks.)

12   Rightly to be great
Is not to stir without great argument,
But greatly to find quarrel in a straw
When honor's at stake. *Hamlet,* IV,iv,53.

13 By heaven, methinks it were an easy leap
To pluck bright honor from the pale-faced moon. *Henry IV, Part One,* I,iii,199. (Hotspur, imagining the great exploits he will perform.)

¹ What is honor? A word. What is in that word honor? What is that honor? Air—a trim reckoning! Who hath it? He that died a Wednesday. *Henry IV, Part One,* V,i,134. (Falstaff resolving to stay out of trouble during the battle of Shrewsbury. *Trim* means "fine.")

² The fewer men, the greater share of honor. *Henry V,* IV,iii,22. (The king finding a silver lining in a desperate situation. His army is outnumbered five to one. More below.)

³ But if it be a sin to covet honor,
I am the most offending soul alive. *Henry V,* IV,iii,28. (The king again. See above.)

⁴ A load would sink a navy—too much honor. *Henry VIII,* III,ii,383. (*Honor* here means "success" or "prestige." For the opening phrase, read "a load that would sink a navy.")

⁵   I love
The name of honor more than I fear death. *Julius Caesar,* I,ii,88.

⁶   Honor is the subject of my story. *Julius Caesar,* I,ii,92.

⁷   Brutus is an honorable man,
So are they all, all honorable men. *Julius Caesar,* III,ii,84. (From Mark Antony's funeral speech for Caesar.)

⁸ That honor which shall
. . . make us heirs of all eternity. *Love's Labor's Lost,* I,i,6. (The king of Navarre referring to the honor inherent in a life of learning and contemplation.)

⁹ An honorable murderer, if you will;
For naught I did in hate, but all in honor. *Othello,* V,ii,290. (Othello's characterization of himself.)

¹⁰ Mine honor is my life, both grow in one;
Take honor from me, and my life is done. *Richard II,* I,i,182.

¹¹   Honor travels in a strait so narrow
Where one but goes abreast. Keep, then, the path. *Troilus and Cressida,* III,iii,154.

¹² Life every man holds dear; but the dear man
Holds honor far more precious-dear than life. *Troilus and Cressida,* V,iii,27. (A *dear man* is a worthy man.)

See also ELITE, THE; FAME; GREATNESS; NOBILITY; REPUTATION.

HOPE

1   Who lined himself with hope,
Eating the air and promise of supply. *Henry IV, Part Two*, I,iii,27. (The reference is to Hotspur, killed by Prince Hal at the battle of Shrewsbury. He *lined himself with hope* means that he reinforced himself with hope only; *reinforcement* and *lining* have a similar meaning in tailoring and less specifically in the military, where reinforcements back up the line. See also PLANNING.)

2 *Si fortuna me tormenta, spero contenta. Henry IV, Part Two*, V,v,97. (A proverb: "If fortune torments me, hope contents me.")

3   The world may laugh again. *Henry VI, Part Two*, II,iv,82.

4 The miserable have no other medicine
But only hope. *Measure for Measure*, III,i,2.

5   Hope: he is a flatterer,
A parasite. *Richard II*, II,ii,69. (More at SICKNESS.)

6 True hope is swift and flies with swallow's wings;
Kings it makes gods, and meaner creatures kings. *Richard III*, V,ii,23.

HORSES.   See ANIMALS; RIDING.

HOSPITALITY

7 Small cheer and great welcome makes a merry feast. *The Comedy of Errors*, III,i,26. (*Cheer* means "entertainment, provisions." The statement represents a hope, not a fact.)

8 You pay a great deal too dear for what's given freely. *The Winter's Tale*, I,i,18. (A lord of Sicily is assuring a lord of Bohemia that there is no need of extravagant entertainment to win Sicily's respect.)

See also GUESTS; MANNERS.

HUMAN NATURE AND HUMANKIND

9   The indifferent children of the earth. *Hamlet*, II,ii,230. (*Indifferent* means "ordinary.")

10 What a piece of work is a man, how noble in reason, how infinite in faculties, in form and moving how express and admirable, in action how like an angel, in apprehension how like a god: the beauty of the world, the paragon of animals. *Hamlet*, II,ii,312. (Hamlet to Rosencrantz and Guildenstern. For the conclusion—"Man delights not me"—see DEPRESSION.)

¹ What should such fellows as I do crawling between earth and heaven? We are arrant knaves all; believe none of us. *Hamlet,* III,i,128. (Hamlet to Ophelia.)

² What is a man,
If his chief good and market of his time
Be but to sleep and feed? A beast, no more.
Sure he that made us with such large discourse,
Looking before and after, gave us not
That capability and godlike reason
To fust in us unused. *Hamlet,* IV,iv,33. (*Market,* in the second line, means "profit." *To fust* means "to molder.")

³ Is man no more than this? *King Lear,* III,iv,105.

⁴ Unaccommodated man is no more but such a poor, bare, forked animal as thou art. *King Lear,* III,iv,109. (*Unaccommodated* means "uncivilized" or "without the trappings of culture and fashion.")

⁵ Men
Are as the time is. *King Lear,* V,iii,31. (People are shaped by the demands of the moment.)

⁶ But man, proud man,
Dressed in a little brief authority,
Most ignorant of what he's most assured,
His glassy essence, like an angry ape,
Plays such fantastic tricks before high heaven
As makes the angels weep. *Measure for Measure,* II,ii,117. (*Glassy essence* probably refers to the mirrorlike surface shine and showiness, as well as the fragility, of man's nature.)

⁷ O, what may man within him hide,
Though angel on the outward side! *Measure for Measure,* III,ii,274.

⁸ Lord, what fools these mortals be! *A Midsummer Night's Dream,* III,ii,115.

⁹ Man is a giddy thing. *Much Ado About Nothing,* V,iv,107. (This could equally well be filed under MEN. Benedick is referring to his decision to marry after his many vows to remain a bachelor.)

¹⁰ Nor I, nor any man that but man is,
With nothing shall be pleased, till he be eased
With being nothing. *Richard II,* V,v,39.

¹¹ We are such stuff
As dreams are made on, and our little life
Is rounded with a sleep. *The Tempest,* IV,i,156. (More at THEATER.)

[1] How many goodly creatures are there here!
How beauteous mankind is! O brave new world
That has such people in it! *The Tempest,* V,i,182.

[2] I wonder men dare trust themselves with men. *Timon of Athens,* I,ii,43.

[3] One touch of nature makes the whole world kin. *Troilus and Cressida,* III,iii,174. (Often quoted, but seldom with Shakespeare's meaning. The "touch of nature" common to us all is the tendency to praise whatever is new at the expense of the old; see NOVELTY. For more of Ulysses' great speech on the way of the world, see TIME.)

See also LIFE; MEN; MORTALITY; WORLD.

HUMILITY

[4] The blessedness of being little. *Henry VIII,* IV,ii,66.

[5] Shall I bend low, and in a bondman's key,
With bated breath, and whispering humbleness,
Say this [?] *The Merchant of Venice,* I,iii,120. (Shylock to Antonio, asking whether Antonio expects a humble offer of a loan after having publicly spat upon Shylock and called him a dog.)

See also SMALL PEOPLE.

HUMOR.   See JOKES; WIT.

HUNGER

[6] Famine and no other hath slain me. *Henry VI, Part Two,* IV,x,62. (The dying revolutionary Jack Cade makes this excuse for having recklessly picked the fight that led to a mortal wound. Shakespeare, no friend of revolution, is consistently hard on Cade, who actually died resisting arrest.)

HURRY.   See CAREFULNESS; SPEED.

HYPOCRISY

[7] With devotion's visage
And pious action, we do sugar o'er
The devil himself. *Hamlet,* III,i,47. (In John Webster's *The Duchess of Malfi,* 1614, there is the line "Thus the devil / Candies all sins o'er.")

[8] The devil can cite Scripture for his purpose. *The Merchant of Venice,* I,iii,95.

[9] A goodly apple rotten at the heart.
O what a goodly outside falsehood hath! *The Merchant of Venice,* I,iii,98.

1   Some of you, with Pilate, wash your hands,
Showing an outward pity. *Richard II,* IV,i,238.

2   I clothe my naked villainy
With odd old ends stolen forth of holy writ,
And seem a saint when most I play the devil. *Richard III,* I,iii,335.

See also DECEPTIVENESS; LIES AND DECEIT.

I

IDEAS.　　　　See IMAGINATION; INSPIRATION; MIND; THOUGHT.

IDENTITY

[1]　　I am I, howe'er I was begot. *King John,* I,i,175. (The speaker is the Bastard, an illegitimate son of Richard I—a character invented by Shakespeare.)

[2]　　A man of my kidney. *The Merry Wives of Windsor,* III,v,113. (For *kidney* read "temperament.")

[3] Thus play I in one person many people,
And none contented. *Richard II,* V,v,31.

[4]　　I am that I am. *Sonnet 121,* 9. (From *Exodus* 3:14, "And God said unto Moses, I AM THAT I AM.")

[5]　　What I was, I am. *The Winter's Tale,* IV,iv,468. (Prince Florizel, his royalty revealed, asserts that he is the same person as before, his love for Perdita is no less than before.)

See also SELF.

IGNORANCE

[6]　　Ignorance is the curse of God. *Henry VI, Part Two,* IV,vii,75.

[7] That unlettered small-knowing soul. *Love's Labor's Lost,* I,i,248. (From a letter by Don Adriano de Armado referring to the jester Costard—his rival for the love of Jaquenetta.)

[1] O thou monster Ignorance. *Love's Labor's Lost,* IV,ii,23.

[2]   There is no darkness but ignorance. *Twelfth Night,* IV,ii,43.

See also EDUCATION; KNOWLEDGE.

IMAGINATION

[3]   Chewing the food of sweet and bitter fancy. *As You Like It,*
IV,iii,102. (Oliver describing the mood of lovelorn Orlando.)

[4]   My imaginations are as foul
As Vulcan's stithy. *Hamlet,* III,ii,85.

[5]   Present fears
Are less than horrible imaginings.
My thought, whose murder yet is but fantastical,
Shakes so my single state of man that function
Is smothered in surmise, and nothing is
But what is not. *Macbeth,* I,iii,137. (Macbeth seems to be one of those
people whose imagination and fantasies are so strong as to overwhelm
reality and ordinary life. Banquo refers to him here as "rapt," l.143.
Macbeth expresses horror that the witches' prediction that he will become
king has stimulated vivid thoughts of murder. *Single state of man* means
"man alone, unaided, frail." See also TEMPTATION and FEAR.)

[6] Lovers and madmen have such seething brains,
Such shaping fantasies, that apprehend
More than cool reason ever comprehends.
The lunatic, the lover and the poet
Are of imagination all compact.
One sees more devils than vast hell can hold,
That is the madman. The lover, all as frantic,
Sees Helen's beauty in a brow of Egypt.
The poet's eye, in a fine frenzy rolling,
Doth glance from heaven to earth, from earth to heaven;
And as imagination bodies forth
The forms of things unknown, the poet's pen
Turns them to shapes, and gives to airy nothing
A local habitation and a name.
Such tricks hath strong imagination,
That, if it would but apprehend some joy,
It comprehends some bringer of that joy;
Or in the night, imagining some fear,
How easy is a bush supposed a bear! *A Midsummer Night's Dream,* V,i,4.
(*Of imagination all compact* means "composed of imagination"; *brow of
Egypt* means "the face of a gypsy.")

See also INSPIRATION; LOVE AND LOVERS (*Twelfth Night,* I,i,14.); STORIES; THEATER; THOUGHT.

IMPROVEMENTS

[1] Striving to better, oft we mar what's well. *King Lear,* I,iv,353.

IMPULSIVITY

[2] He's sudden if a thing comes in his head. *Henry VI, Part Three,* V,v,86. (Said of the future king Richard III, a violent, duplicitous man.)

[3] I have no joy of this contract tonight.
It is too rash, too unadvised, too sudden;
Too like the lightning, which doth cease to be
Ere one can say it lightens. *Romeo and Juliet,* II,ii,117. (Juliet speaking of the vows of love which she and Romeo have exchanged within hours of their first meeting.)

See also BOLDNESS; DANGEROUS PEOPLE; EMOTIONS; PASSION.

INACTION. See ACTION, PROMPT; DELAY; THOUGHT (*Hamlet,* III,i,83).

INGRATITUDE

[4] Blow, blow, thou winter wind,
Thou art not so unkind
As man's ingratitude. *As You Like It,* II,vii,174. (This play treats lightly themes that reappear darkly in *King Lear.* Compare this to Lear's "Blow winds, and crack your cheeks! rage! blow!" at DESPAIR AND RAGE. See also the quotes from *King Lear* below.)

[5] Ingratitude is monstrous. *Coriolanus,* II,iii,9.

[6] Beggar that I am, I am even poor in thanks. *Hamlet,* II,ii,278. (An ironic remark by Hamlet to Rosencrantz and Guildenstern.)

[7] Ingratitude! thou marble-hearted fiend. *King Lear,* I,iv,266. (More at CHILDREN, along with the condemnation of the thankless child, who is sharper than a serpent's tooth.)

[8] Crack Nature's molds, all germains spill at once,
That makes ingrateful man. *King Lear,* III,ii,8. (The first line refers to molds in which creatures are formed. *Germaines* are the seeds of life. The whole passage is given at DESPAIR AND RAGE.)

[9] I hate ingratitude more in a man
Than lying, vainness, babbling, drunkenness,
Or any taint of vice whose strong corruption
Inhabits our frail blood. *Twelfth Night,* III,iv,366.

INJUSTICE

[1] The patient dies while the physician sleeps;
The orphan pines while the oppressor feeds;
Justice is feasting while the widow weeps. *The Rape of Lucrece,* 904.

See also JUSTICE; POVERTY; RICH AND POOR; TYRANNY.

INNOCENCE

[2] Some innocents 'scape not the thunderbolt. *Antony and Cleopatra,* II,v,77.

[3] The trust I have is in mine innocence,
And therefore am I bold and resolute. *Henry VI, Part Two,* IV,iv,59. (The
trust was imprudent. See TRUST.)

[4]   I am a man
More sinned against than sinning. *King Lear,* III,ii,59. (Lear speaks,
whether accurately or not is one of the play's interesting questions.)

[5] In maiden meditation, fancy-free. *A Midsummer Night's Dream,* II,i,164.
(*Fancy-free* means "free of thoughts of love.")

[6] A maiden never bold,
Of spirit so still and quiet that her motion
Blushed at herself. *Othello,* I,iii,94.

[7] We were as twinned lambs, that did frisk in the sun,
And bleat the one at the other; what we changed
Was innocence for innocence; we knew not
The doctrine of ill-doing, nor dreamed
That any did. *The Winter's Tale,* I,ii,67. (In the second line, *changed* means
"exchanged." See also YOUTH.)

[8] The silence often of pure innocence
Persuades, when speaking fails. *The Winter's Tale,* II,ii,40.

[9]   Innocence shall make
False Accusation blush, and Tyranny
Tremble at Patience. *The Winter's Tale,* III,ii,29.

See also GULLIBILITY; VIRTUE; YOUTH.

INSANITY.   See MADNESS.

INSPIRATION

[10] O for a Muse of fire, that would ascend
The brightest heaven of invention. *Henry V,* Prologue, 1. (More at
THEATER.)

[1] Be thou the tenth Muse. *Sonnet 38,* 9.

See also IMAGINATION.

INSULTS

[2] I do desire we may be better strangers. *As You Like It,* III,ii,256.

[3] He is deformèd, crookèd, old and sere,
Ill-faced, worse bodied, shapeless everywhere:
Vicious, ungentle, foolish, blunt, unkind,
Stigmatical in making, worse in mind. *The Comedy of Errors,* IV,ii,19.
(Adriana on the subject of her husband. Obviously she loves the guy.)

[4]   One Pinch, a hungry lean-faced villain;
A mere anatomy, a mountebank,
A threadbare juggler and a fortune-teller,
A needy-hollow-eyed-sharp-looking wretch;
A living dead man. *The Comedy of Errors,* V,i,238. (Shakespeare was suspicious of thin people. See Caesar's comment on Cassius under DANGEROUS PEOPLE.)

[5]   This Triton of the minnows? *Coriolanus,* III,i,89.

[6]   So much for him. *Hamlet,* I,ii,25.

[7] *Polonius.* Do you know me, my lord?
Hamlet. Excellent well. You are a fishmonger. *Hamlet,* II,ii,173. (The double meaning of *fishmonger* is pimp, or procurer. The term may also be a reference to Lord Burghley's efforts, when England's treasurer, to promote the fish trade. Burghley was most probably the model for Polonius.)

[8] These tedious old fools! *Hamlet,* II,ii,221.

[9] Who calls me villain? Breaks my pate across?
Plucks off my beard and blows it in my face? *Hamlet,* II,ii,583.

[10] Thou wretched, rash, intruding fool, farewell!
I took thee for thy better. *Hamlet,* III,iv,32. (Hamlet to Polonius, whom he has just slain. Hamlet, stabbing through a curtain, hoped to kill the king.)

[11] There's neither honesty, manhood, nor good fellowship in thee. *Henry IV, Part One,* I,ii,143. (Falstaff to Prince Hal—affectionately.)

[12]   *Prince.* this bed-presser, this horseback-breaker, this huge
hill of flesh—
Falstaff. 'Sblood, you starveling, you eel-skin, you dried neat's-tongue, you bull's pizzle, you stockfish—O, for breath to utter what is like thee!—you

tailor's yard, you sheath, you bowcase, you vile standing tuck! *Henry IV, Part One,* II,iv,242. (Prince Hal and Falstaff having at each other. Hal is thin. Falstaff calls him a dried ox tongue [*neat's tongue*], a dried codfish [*stockfish*], and an upright rapier [*standing tuck*], among other names. Later Hal returns to the subject: "How long is't ago, Jack, since thou sawest thine own knee?")

1   Such a man, so faint, so spiritless,
So dull, so dead in look, so woebegone. *Henry IV, Part Two,* I,i,70.

2 Away, you scullion! You rampallian! You fustilarian. I'll tickle your catastrophe. *Henry IV, Part Two,* II,i,60. (Shakespeare punning and having fun. A *catastrophe* signifies an ending, with a pun on *ass* and *cat.* The apparently made-up term *fustilarian* probably refers to *fustilugs,* a term for a gross, fat woman. *Rampallion* is related to *rampant* and *ramp,* the latter referring to a bold, vulgar woman. A *scullion* is a kitchen maid.)

3 You blocks, you stones, you worse than senseless things! *Julius Caesar,* I,i,38.

4 You are dull, Casca. *Julius Caesar,* I,iii,57.

5 This is a slight unmeritable man,
Meet to be sent on errands. *Julius Caesar,* IV,i,12. (Lepidus is remembered as much for this insult by Mark Antony as for his accomplishments. He was part of the triumvirate established in 43 B.C. that included Antony and Octavius.)

6 I had rather be a dog, and bay the moon,
Than such a Roman. *Julius Caesar,* IV,iii,27.

7 Away, slight man! *Julius Caesar,* IV,iii,37. (Brutus to Cassius, his co-conspirator and brother-in-law.)

8 I'll use you for my mirth, yea, for my laughter. *Julius Caesar,* IV,iii,49. (Brutus again.)

9 Thou wear a lion's hide! Doff it for shame,
And hang a calfskin on those recreant limbs. *King John,* III,i,54. (Constance assaulting the duke of Austria. *Lion's hide* refers to Richard Coeur de Lion, who, in this play, is killed by the duke. Shakespeare took liberty with history. Richard was imprisoned and held for ransom in Austria, but was killed by an archer during a siege of a small castle in France.)

10   The son and heir of a mongrel bitch. *King Lear,* II,ii,22. (The climax of a cascade of insults.)

11 I have seen better faces in my time. *King Lear,* II,ii,95.

¹ Some carry-tale, some please-man, some slight zany,
Some mumble-news, some trencher-knight, some Dick. *Love's Labor's
Lost,* V,ii,464. (A *please-man* is a yes-man. A *trencher-knight* is a knight of
the dinner table. *Dick* means "guy" or "fellow.")

² Let me take you a buttonhole lower. *Love's Labor's Lost,* V,ii,700.

³ *First Murderer.* We are men, my liege.
Macbeth. Ay, in the catalogue ye go for men. *Macbeth,* III,i,91. (*Go for*
means "pass for.")

⁴ The devil damn thee black, thou cream-faced loon!
Where got'st thou that goose look? *Macbeth,* V,iii,11. (There are two kinds
of loons in the world, crazy and stupid; Shakespeare had the latter in mind
here; see Hugh Rawson's *Wicked Words* [Crown, 1989]. Macbeth here is
berating a servant for bringing him news of the enemy's advance. Sir
William Davenant "improved" *Macbeth* in a number of strange ways,
including puffing out Lady Macduff's role and changing this robust insult
to "Now friend, what means thy change of countenance?" Macbeth also
called the servant "lily-livered"; see below.)

⁵ Thou lily-livered boy. *Macbeth,* V,iii,15. (This traditional insult was based
on the theory that the liver is the source of the passions. A liver deficient
in blood would indicate cowardice.)

⁶ When he is best he is a little worse than a man, and when he is worst he
is little better than a beast. *The Merchant of Venice,* I,ii,86. (Portia on the
subject of a drunken German suitor. In fact, the entire group of suitors is
unsatisfactory. "There is not one among them," she confides, "but I dote
on his very absence," l.108. See also FAINT PRAISE.)

⁷ Thou call'dst me dog before thou hadst a cause,
But since I am a dog, beware my fangs. *The Merchant of Venice,* III,iii,6.
(Shylock to Antonio. A buffoon and a dangerous enemy, Shylock is too
large a figure to fit comfortably into this light romance.)

⁸ You Banbury cheese! *The Merry Wives of Windsor,* I,i,127. (A thin kind of
cheese. The remark is directed at Slender.)

⁹   Egregiously an ass. *Othello,* II,i,309.

¹⁰   A lunatic, lean-witted fool,
Presuming on an ague's privilege. *Richard II,* II,i,115. (Richard insulting
the dying John of Gaunt.)

¹¹   Thou toad, thou toad. *Richard III,* IV,iv,145. (Richard is called much
worse, but this is to the point.)

1   *Petruchio.* Come sit on me.
Kate. Asses are made to bear and so are you.
Petruchio. Women are made to bear and so are you. *The Taming of the Shrew,* II,i,198.

2   Such an injury [insult] would vex a very saint. *The Taming of the Shrew,* III,ii,28.

3 Thou deboshed fish thou. *The Tempest,* III,ii,27. (Trinculo to Caliban. *Deboshed* means "debauched," "drunk." Poor Caliban has just been called a "mooncalf" twice by Stephano, ll.22–23.)

4   Live loathed and long,
Most smiling, smooth, detested parasites,
Courteous destroyers, affable wolves, meek bears,
You fools of fortune, trencher-friends, time's flies. *Timon of Athens,* III, vi,94. (*Fools of fortune* are people who blindly follow the rich and successful; see also FORTUNE. *Trencher-friends* are friends only as long as they can get a free meal. *Time's flies* are fair-weather insects.)

5   Ajax, who wears his wit in his belly and his guts in his head. *Troilus and Cressida,* II,i,76. (Ajax, a king and hero in Homer's *Iliad,* is a thick-skulled braggart in *Troilus and Cressida.* Shakespeare was only one among many writers to contribute to this demotion. In *Troilus,* Ajax is often said to portray Ben Jonson. Incidentally, the speaker, Thersites, is a world-class master of invective, and scholars have suggested various contemporary figures as his model. He is, in any case, the ideal Chorus for this sour comedy.)

See also FATNESS; FOOLS AND FOOLISHNESS; WOMEN.

INTEGRITY.   See HONESTY; PROMISES; SELF; VIRTUE.

INTELLIGENCE.   See COMMON SENSE; CRAFTINESS;
                                          WISDOM; WIT.

INTERPRETATION
6   Men may construe things after their fashion. *Julius Caesar,* I,iii,34.

ITALY AND ITALIANS
7 Those girls of Italy, take heed of them.
They say our French lack language to deny
If they demand. *All's Well That Ends Well,* II,i,19.

8 Report of fashions in proud Italy
Whose manners still our tardy-apish nation

Limps after in base imitation. *Richard II,* II,i,21. (Italy's fashions were still copied two hundred years later, when English dandies were called "macaronis," and English soldiers derided American colonists as macaronis and Yankee doodle dandies—only to have to live with American acceptance of the designation, and with the sound of the song "Yankee Doodle" sung in victory.)

[1] I think we do know the sweet Roman hand. *Twelfth Night,* III,iv,28. (Malvolio is speaking of an elegant cursive style of handwriting.)

JEALOUSY

[1] How many fond fools serve mad jealousy! *The Comedy of Errors,* II,i,116.

[2] The venom clamors of a jealous woman
Poisons more deadly than a mad dog's tooth. *The Comedy of Errors,* V,i,69.
(For *venom* read "venomous.")

[3]   Green-eyed jealousy. *The Merchant of Venice,* III,ii,110. (See also below.)

[4] O, beware, my lord, of jealousy!
It is the green-eyed monster, which doth mock
The meat it feeds on. That cuckold lives in bliss
Who, certain of his fate, loves not his wronger;
But O, what damnèd minutes tells he o'er
Who dotes, yet doubts—suspects, yet fondly loves! *Othello,* III,iii,165.
(Iago to Othello. *Tell* means "counts.")

[5] Think'st thou I'd make a life of jealousy,
To follow still the changes of the moon
With fresh suspicions? No! To be once in doubt
Is to be resolved. *Othello,* III,iii,177. (Othello's response to Iago; see above. Having determined not to live with jealous doubt but to resolve the issue absolutely, Othello is well caught on Iago's hook.)

[6]   O curse of marriage,
That we can call these delicate creatures ours,

And not their appetites! I had rather be a toad
And live upon the vapor of a dungeon
Than keep a corner in the thing I love
For others' uses. *Othello,* III,iii,267. (Othello, working himself into a dangerous state.)

1   Trifles light as air
Are to the jealous confirmations strong
As proofs of Holy Writ. *Othello,* III,iii,319. (Iago sees that Othello is now ready to fall for the trick with the handkerchief.)

2 I must dance barefoot on her wedding day,
And, for your love to her, lead apes in hell. *The Taming of the Shrew,* II,i,33. (Kate accusing her father of favoring her sister, Bianca, arranging a marriage for her, while leaving Kate as a single spinster, leading apes in hell. This traditional fate of the spinster is also referred to in *Much Ado About Nothing,* II,i,41.)

JESUS.   See CHRISTMAS; HOLY LAND.

JEWS AND JUDAISM

3 For sufferance is the badge of all our tribe.
You call me misbeliever, cutthroat dog,
And spit upon my Jewish gaberdine. *The Merchant of Venice,* I,iii,107. (Shylock to Antonio. See also HATE and RELIGION. *Gaberdine* refers to the gown traditionally worn by Jews.)

4 I am a Jew. Hath not a Jew eyes? Hath not a Jew hands, organs, dimensions, senses, affections, passions?—fed with the same food, hurt with the same weapons, subject to the same diseases, healed by the same means, warmed and cooled by the same winter and summer as a Christian is? If you prick us, do we not bleed? If you tickle us, do we not laugh? If you poison us, do we not die? And if you wrong us, shall we not revenge? If we are like you in the rest, we will resemble you in that. *The Merchant of Venice,* III,i,55.

JOKES

5 It would be argument for a week, laughter for a month, and a good jest forever. *Henry IV, Part One,* II,ii,95. (Prince Hal contemplating a practical joke on Falstaff. For *argument* read "gossip" or "discussion.")

6 He jests at scars that never felt a wound. *Romeo and Juliet,* II,ii,1.

7 O jest unseen, inscrutable, invisible,
As a nose on a man's face, or a weathercock on a steeple! *The Two*

Gentlemen of Verona, II,i,132. (The servant Speed, exasperated with his master's inability to see the humor in a totally absurd situation.)

See also WIT.

JOY. See HAPPINESS.

JUDGES

1   The justice,
In fair round belly with good capon lined,
With eyes severe and beard of formal cut,
Full of wise saws and modern instances. *As You Like It,* II,vii,153. (From "the seven ages of man" speech. See LIFE.)

2   See how yond justice rails upon yond simple thief. Hark, in thine ear: change places, and, handy-dandy, which is the justice, which is the thief? *King Lear,* IV,vi,153.

3 A Daniel come to judgment! Yea, a Daniel! *The Merchant of Venice,* IV,i,222. (Shylock in praise of Portia—before she points to the flaw that voids his pound-of-flesh contract; see CONTRACTS. After that, it is Gratiano who exclaims, "A Daniel still say I, a second Daniel!" l.339. More below.)

4   You are a worthy judge;
You know the law, your exposition
Hath been most sound. *The Merchant of Venice,* IV,i,235.

5 An upright judge, a learnèd judge! *The Merchant of Venice,* IV,i,322.

See also JUSTICE; LAW AND LAWYERS; PUNISHMENT.

JUDGING OTHERS

6 Forbear to judge, for we are sinners all. *Henry VI, Part Two,* III,iii,31.

7 Why, all the souls that were forfeit once;
And He that might the vantage best have took
Found out the remedy. How would you be,
If He, which is the top of judgment, should
But judge you as you are? *Measure for Measure,* II,ii,73. (Isabella imploring Angelo to be less judgmental and more merciful in the spirit of Jesus, who died to save the souls of sinners.)

See also JUSTICE; MERCY; PUNISHMENT.

JULIET. See ROMEO AND JULIET.

JULIUS CAESAR

¹ Upon what meat doth this our Caesar feed,
    That he is grown so great? *Julius Caesar*, I,ii,149. (A bitter question, posed
by Cassius.)

² Caesar must bleed for it. *Julius Caesar*, II,i,171. (Brutus concluding that
there is no way to kill Caesar's spirit, a spirit of tyranny, other than by
killing him. Curiously, one of history's most famous assassins, John Wilkes
Booth, played the role of Mark Antony, who so eloquently condemns the
conspirators. This was in a benefit production at the Winter Garden in
New York in 1864 to raise money for a statue of Shakespeare in Central
Park. Junius Brutus Booth played Cassius. Edwin Booth played Brutus.)

³ O mighty Caesar! Dost thou lie so low?
    Are all thy conquests, glories, triumphs, spoils,
    Shrunk to this little measure? *Julius Caesar*, III,i,148.

⁴ O pardon me, thou bleeding piece of earth,
    That I am meek and gentle with these butchers!
    Thou art the ruins of the noblest man
    That ever livèd in the tide of times. *Julius Caesar*, III,i,254. (Antony to the
corpse of Caesar. Antony has just negotiated the right to speak at Caesar's
funeral. See below.)

⁵ Friends, Romans, countrymen, lend me your ears;
    I come to bury Caesar, not to praise him.
    The evil that men do lives after them,
    The good is oft interrèd with their bones. *Julius Caesar*, III,ii,75. (Mark
Antony, at the outset of his funeral speech for Caesar.)

⁶ When that the poor have cried, Caesar hath wept. *Julius Caesar*, III,ii,93.

⁷   Great Caesar fell.
    O, what a fall was there, my countrymen!
    Then I, and you, and all of us fell down,
    Whilst bloody treason flourished over us. *Julius Caesar*, III,ii,191.

⁸ O Julius Caesar, thou art mighty yet! *Julius Caesar*, V,iii,94. (Brutus is
speaking. The murder of Caesar has accomplished nothing. Cassius and
Brutus both die by suicide.)

See also CRIME; GREATNESS.

JUSTICE

⁹ Use every man after his desert, and who shall scape whipping? *Hamlet*,
II,ii,540. (Translation: Treat every person as he deserves, and who shall
escape being whipped? More at MANNERS.)

[1] For 'tis the sport to have the enginer
Hoist with his own petar. *Hamlet*, III,iv,207. (A *petar* is an explosive device for creating holes in fortress gates and walls. It misfired often enough for *hoist with one's own petard* to become a metaphor for being caught in a trap of one's own making. The word *petard* comes from an explosion of another sort, deriving from the French *péter*, "to fart," and ultimately the Latin *pedere*, with the same low meaning.)

[2] Thrice is he armed that hath his quarrel just,
And he but naked, though locked up in steel,
Whose conscience with injustice is corrupted. *Henry VI, Part Two*, III,ii,233. (The king asserting that justice is a better defense than is armor. The king, unfortunately, is incompetent.)

[3] Be just, and fear not. *Henry VIII*, III,ii,446. (More at VIRTUE.)

[4] The gods are just. *King Lear*, V,iii,172. (More at PLEASURE.)

[5] This judgment of the heavens, that makes us tremble,
Touches us not with pity. *King Lear*, V,iii,233. (The duke of Albany reacting to the violent death of his wife, Goneril, and her sister Regan.)

[6] This even-handed justice
Commends the ingredients of our poisoned chalice
To our own lips. *Macbeth*, I,vii,10.

[7] Haste still pays haste, and leisure answers leisure;
Like doth quit like, and Measure still for Measure. *Measure for Measure*, V,i,413. (*Quits* means "pays." The reference is to *Matthew* 7:1–2, "Judge not, that ye be not judged. For with what judgment ye judge, ye shall be judged; and with what measure ye mete, it shall be measured to you again.")

[8] In the course of justice, none of us
Should see salvation. *The Merchant of Venice*, IV,i,198. (More at MERCY.)

[9] Thus hath the course of justice whirled about
And left thee but a very prey to time. *Richard III*, IV,iv,105.

See also INJUSTICE; JUDGES; JUDGING OTHERS; LAW AND LAWYERS; MERCY.

K

KINDNESS

[1]　　But whate'er you are
That in this desert inaccessible,
Under the shade of melancholy boughs,
Lose and neglect the creeping hours of time;
If ever you have looked on better days,
If ever been where bells have knolled to church,
If ever sat at any good man's feast,
If ever from your eyelids wiped a tear
And know what 'tis to pity and be pitied,
Let gentleness my strong enforcement be. *As You Like It,* II,vii,109. (Orlando, abandoning an attempt to steal food by force of arms, accepts, with this eloquent apology, the duke's invitation to sit and eat. The scene is the Forest of Arden.)

[2] Kindness, nobler ever than revenge. *As You Like It,* IV,iii,129.

[3] Yet hath a woman's kindness overruled. *Henry VI, Part One,* II,ii,50. (More at MEN AND WOMEN.)

[4] I thank them for their tender loving care. *Henry VI, Part Two,* III,ii,280.

[5]　　Yet do I fear thy nature;
Is too full of the milk of human kindness. *Macbeth,* I,v,17.

[6] A kind heart he hath. A woman would run through fire and water for such a kind heart. *The Merry Wives of Windsor,* III,iv,100.

¹ Kindness in women, not their beauteous looks,
Shall win my love. *The Taming of the Shrew,* IV,ii,41.

² He is so kind that he now pays interest for it. *Timon of Athens,* I,ii,205.
(Said of the imprudently generous Timon, who is on the road to ruin. See
also GIVING.)

³ Poor honest lord, brought low by his own heart,
Undone by goodness. *Timon of Athens,* IV,ii,37.

⁴ Is she kind as she is fair?
For beauty lives with kindness. *The Two Gentlemen of Verona,* IV,ii,43.
(From the song "Silvia." More at LOVE, EXPRESSIONS OF.)

See also COMFORT; GIVING; HELP; MERCY; VIRTUE.

KINGS.   See HIGH POSITION.

KNOWLEDGE.   See EDUCATION; IGNORANCE.

LANGUAGE.   See EDUCATION; NAMES; TALK; TALK, PLAIN AND FANCY; WORDS.

LATENESS

1   Better three hours too soon than a minute too late. *The Merry Wives of Windsor,* II,ii,311.

2 Pray God we may make haste and come too late! *Richard II,* I,iv,64. (Richard, hoping to arrive too late to attend upon the dying John of Gaunt.)

LAW AND LAWYERS

3 Why may not that be the skull of a lawyer? Where be his quiddities now, his quillities, his cases, his tenures, and his tricks? *Hamlet,* V,i,99. (Hamlet in the gravedigging scene. Shakespeare loved the eccentricity of legal language. *Quiddities* are legal arguments, the term deriving from the Latin *quidditas,* "essence" or "whatness." *Quillities* are fine distinctions. *Tenures* refers to tenure of property.)

4   Old father Antic the law? *Henry IV, Part One,* I,ii,63. (Shakespeare's familiarity with the law has led to speculation that he may have studied in this profession. Richard Posner in *Law and Literature* notes that the many legal references in Shakespeare's plays have been used as evidence by those who argue that Francis Bacon, a lawyer, was the true author of some or all of the plays.)

1   A rotten case abides no handling. *Henry IV, Part Two*, IV,i,159. (A proverb with a double meaning. A rotten case could be a box or trunk that is falling apart from age. In context here, the earl of Westmoreland is arguing against the position taken by Lord Mowbray, who is unwilling to accept an offer of peace from the king.)

2   An honest man, sir, is able to speak for himself, when a knave is not. *Henry IV, Part Two*, V,i,45. (A traditional and deep-rooted view that always comes into play when a defendant does not take the stand.)

3   These nice sharp quillets of the law. *Henry VI, Part One*, II,iv,17. (A lovely phrase denoting subtle legal distinctions. The speaker, the earl of Warwick, claims to have some degree of judgment, "But in these nice sharp quillets of the law," he says, "Good faith I am no wiser than a daw." *Daw* is a shortening of *jackdaw*, and means a "simpleton.")

4   The first thing we do, let's kill all the lawyers. *Henry VI, Part Two*, IV,ii,75. (Neither the fact that Shakespeare was unsympathetic to the speaker, Dick the Butcher, nor that lawyers here represent order and justice has prevented this from becoming one of the most popular of all Shakespearean quotes.)

5   Is not this a lamentable thing, that of the skin of an innocent lamb should be made parchment? That parchment, being scribbled over, should undo a man? *Henry VI, Part Two*, IV,ii,76. (Parchment was used for legal documents. The revolutionary leader Jack Cade is speaking.)

6   And what makes robbers bold but too much lenity? *Henry VI, Part Three*, II,vi,22.

7   The law I bear no malice for my death:
It has done, upon the premises, but justice.
But those that sought it I could wish more Christians. *Henry VIII*, II,i,62. (The duke of Buckingham forgives those who have engineered his execution, but adds, "Yet let them look they glory not in mischief / Nor build their evils [toilets] on the graves of great men," 1.66.)

8   His own opinion was his law. *Henry VIII*, IV,ii,37. (The reference is to Cardinal Wolsey.)

9   When law can do no right,
Let it be lawful that law bar no wrong! *King John*, III,i,111. (Roughly, if the law is corrupt, then let there be anarchy.)

10 Adultery?
Thou shalt not die: die for adultery! No. *King Lear*, IV,vi,112. (The half-demented king still has the wit to see that laws against adultery are not worth enforcing. More at SEX.)

[1] We have strict statutes and most biting laws. *Measure for Measure*, I,iii,19.

[2] We must not make a scarecrow of the law,
Setting it up to fear the birds of prey,
And let it keep one shape, till custom make it
Their perch and not their terror. *Measure for Measure*, II,i,1.

[3] The jury, passing on the prisoner's life,
May in the sworn twelve have a thief or two
Guiltier than him they try. *Measure for Measure*, II,i,19.

[4] The law hath not been dead, though it hath slept. *Measure for Measure*, II,ii,90.

[5] In law, what plea so tainted and corrupt,
But being seasoned with a gracious voice,
Obscures the show of evil? *The Merchant of Venice*, III,ii,75.

[6] I will make a Star-chamber matter of it. *The Merry Wives of Windsor*, I,i,1.
(Justice Shallow referring to Falstaff's poaching deer. The Star Chamber, named for a room in Westminster Palace with painted stars on its ceiling, was the court run by the monarch and the royal council, as distinct from the common law courts. It had jurisdiction in various serious crimes, such as riot and forgery. Scholars believe that the model for Shallow was either Sir Thomas Lucy, who may have prosecuted the young Shakespeare for deer poaching, or William Gardiner, a corrupt justice of the peace, who unfairly required Shakespeare to post a bond in about the year 1596.)

[7]   The bloody book of law
You shall yourself read in the bitter letter
After your own sense. *Othello*, I,iii,67.

[8] Justice is feasting while the widow weeps. *The Rape of Lucrece*, 906. (More at INJUSTICE.)

[9] Let's choose executors and talk of wills. *Richard II*, III,ii,148. (More at DEATH.)

[10]   Do as adversaries do in law,
Strive mightily but eat and drink as friends. *The Taming of the Shrew*, I,ii,277.

[11]   Pity is the virtue of the law. *Timon of Athens*, III,v,8. (Meaning: Pity, or mercy, is the characteristic virtue of law.)

[12]   As she hath
Been publicly accused, so shall she have
A just and open trial. *The Winter's Tale*, II,iii,201.

See also CONTRACTS; CRIME; GUILT; JUSTICE; NEGOTIATION; PROFESSIONS; PUNISHMENT.

LAZINESS

¹ I were better to be eaten to death with a rust than to be scoured to nothing with perpetual motion. *Henry IV, Part Two,* I,ii,228. (Falstaff to the Chief Justice.)

²   Fie, you slugabed. *Romeo and Juliet,* IV,v,2.

LEADERS

³   He was indeed the glass
Wherein the noble youth did dress themselves. *Henry IV, Part Two,* II,iii,21. (The young widow of Harry Percy [Hotspur] describing his leadership among England's young lords. The *glass* refers to a mirror. For a similar quote, see HAMLET.)

⁴   What though the mast be now blown overboard,
The cable broke, the holding-anchor lost,
And half our sailors swallowed in the flood?
Yet lives our pilot still. *Henry VI, Part Three,* V,iv,3.

⁵ Those he commands move only in command,
Nothing in love. Now does he feel his title
Hang loose about him, like a giant's robe
Upon a dwarfish thief. *Macbeth,* V,ii,19.

⁶ We cannot all be masters. *Othello,* I,i,40.

See also HIGH POSITION.

LEARNING.   See EDUCATION; PHILOSOPHY; SCIENCE.

LEISURE

⁷   Many young gentlemen flock to him every day, and fleet the time carelessly as they did in the golden world. *As You Like It,* I,i,113. (The "golden world" is the mythical golden age. The passage here refers to the idle and idyllic life lived in the forest of Arden by the circle of gentlemen surrounding the rightful duke. The forest is named for Ardennes in France, as well as after the forest of Arden near Stratford—the Ardens were Shakespeare's maternal ancestors. The name also suggests Eden, a place for innocent, pastoral pleasures. See also COUNTRY LIFE.)

⁸ If all the year were playing holidays,
To sport would be as tedious as to work. *Henry IV, Part One,* I,ii,208.

LIBERTY.

See FREEDOM.

LIES AND DECEIT

1   If I tell thee a lie, spit in my face, call me a horse. *Henry IV, Part One*, II,iv,192. (Spoken by that grand liar Flastaff.)

2 Lord, Lord, how this world is given to lying. *Henry IV, Part One*, V,iv,143. (Falstaff again.)

3   You lie in your throat. *Henry IV, Part Two*, I,ii,88.

4 He would say untruths and be ever double
Both in his words and meaning. *Henry VIII*, IV,ii,38. (Katherine of Aragon remembering Cardinal Wolsey.)

5   Falsehood falsehood cures. *King John*, III,i,203. (Sometimes deceit is necessary to cope with deceit. Perhaps true, uttered by one of Shakespeare's slimiest characters, Cardinal Pandulph.)

6   I want that glib and oily art
To speak and purpose not. *King Lear*, I,i,226. (For *I want* read "I lack." Cordelia is speaking. As for her dishonest sisters, she predicts: "Time shall unfold what plighted cunning hides, / Who covers faults, at last shame them derides," l.282.)

7 Away, and mock the time with fairest show:
False face must hide what the false heart doth know. *Macbeth*, I,vii,81. (*Mock the time* means "deceive the world.")

8 To show an unfelt sorrow is an office
Which the false man does easy. *Macbeth*, II,iii,138.

9 O what a goodly outside falsehood hath! *The Merchant of Venice*, I,iii,99. (More at HYPOCRISY.)

10 O, what authority and show of truth
Can cunning sin cover itself withal! *Much Ado About Nothing*, IV,i,34.

11 They have committed false report; moreover, they have spoken untruths; secondarily, they are slanders; sixth and lastly, they have belied a lady; thirdly, they have verified unjust things; and to conclude, they are lying knaves. *Much Ado About Nothing*, V,i,214.

12 She was false as water. *Othello*, V,ii,133. (Othello speaking of Desdemona.)

13 False creeping craft and perjury. *The Rape of Lucrece*, 1517.

¹ Was ever book containing such vile matter
So fairly bound? O, that deceit should dwell
In such a gorgeous palace! *Romeo and Juliet,* III,ii,83.

²   Some virtuous lie. *Sonnet 72,* 5.

See also APPEARANCES; DECEPTIVENESS; DISHONESTY; EVIL; HYPOCRISY.

LIFE

³ The web of our life is of a mingled yarn, good and ill together. *All's Well That Ends Well,* IV,iii,74.

⁴ I love long life better than figs. *Antony and Cleopatra,* I,ii,32. (The term *fig* has a sexual meaning going back to ancient times, as witness these lines from Aristophanes' *The Peace:* "Now live splendidly together, / Free from adversity / Pick your figs. May his be large and hard. / May hers be sweet.")

⁵ And so, from hour to hour, we ripe and ripe,
And then, from hour to hour, we rot and rot;
And thereby hangs a tale. *As You Like It,* II,vii,26. (More at TIME.)

⁶ All the world's a stage,
And all the men and women merely players;
They have their exits and their entrances,
And one man in his time plays many parts,
His acts being seven ages. At first, the infant,
Mewling and puking in the nurse's arms.
Then the whining schoolboy, with his satchel
And shining morning face, creeping like snail
Unwillingly to school. And then the lover,
Sighing like furnace, with a woeful ballad
Made to his mistress' eyebrow. Then a soldier,
Full of strange oaths and bearded like the pard,
Jealous in honor, sudden and quick in quarrel,
Seeking the bubble reputation
Even in the cannon's mouth. And then the justice,
In fair round belly with good capon lined,
With eyes severe and beard of formal cut,
Full of wise saws and modern instances;
And so he plays his part. The sixth age shifts
Into the lean and slippered pantaloon,
With spectacles on nose and pouch on side;
His youthful hose, well saved, a world too wide
For his shrunk shank, and his big manly voice,

Turning again toward childish treble, pipes
And whistles in his sound. Last scene of all,
That ends this strange eventful history,
Is second childishness and mere oblivion,
Sans teeth, sans eyes, sans taste, sans everything. *As You Like It,* II,vii,139.
(Spoken by "melancholy Jaques," whose bitter view of life is rejected in
this joyous play. *As You Like It* is the comic counterpart of *King Lear,* in
which the world is truly a "stage of fools." See WORLD. The name Jaques,
by the way, was pronounced with two syllables: "jay-kees" or "jay-
kwees.")

[1] I do not set my life at a pin's fee. *Hamlet,* I,iv,65. (More at SOUL.)

[2]   The time of life is short!
To spend that shortness basely were too long. *Henry IV, Part One,* V,ii,81.
(Hotspur about to enter mortal combat with Hal—the future Henry V.)

[3] Thus sometimes hath the brightest day a cloud;
And after summer evermore succeeds
Barren winter with his wrathful nipping cold:
So cares and joys abound, as seasons fleet. *Henry VI, Part Two,* II,iv,1.

[4] Life is as tedious as a twice-told tale,
Vexing the dull ear of a drowsy man. *King John,* III,iii,108. (The entire
passage is: "There's nothing in this world can make me joy; / Life is as
tedious as a twice-told tale, / Vexing the dull ear of a drowsy man, / And
bitter shame hath spoiled the sweet words' taste, / That it yields nought
but shame and bitterness." In some versions, "the sweet words' taste" is
rendered "the sweet world's taste." The speech belongs to a minor character, the dauphin of France.)

[5] As flies to wanton boys, are we to the gods,
They kill us for their sport. *King Lear,* IV,i,36.

[6] The wine of life is drawn. *Macbeth,* II,iii,97. (More at RUIN.)

[7] Tomorrow, and tomorrow, and tomorrow
Creeps in this petty pace from day to day,
To the last syllable of recorded time;
And all our yesterdays have lighted fools
The way to dusty death. Out, out, brief candle!
Life's but a walking shadow, a poor player
That struts and frets his hour upon the stage
And then is heard no more. It is a tale
Told by an idiot, full of sound and fury
Signifying nothing. *Macbeth,* V,v,19.

1   Thou hast nor youth nor age,
But, as it were, an after-dinner's sleep,
Dreaming on both; for all thy blessèd youth
Becomes as agèd, and doth beg the alms
Of palsied eld, and when thou art old and rich,
Thou hast neither heat, affection, limb, nor beauty,
To make thy riches pleasant. *Measure for Measure,* III,i,32. (The duke,
Vincentio, describing life led in the shadow of the fear of death. See also
DEATH. *Eld* means "old age.")

2 The weariest and most loathèd wordly life
That age, ache, penury, and imprisonment
Can lay on nature is a paradise
To what we fear of death. *Measure for Measure,* III,i,129.

3   The music of men's lives. *Richard II,* V,v,44. (More at MUSIC.)

4   We are such stuff
As dreams are made on, and our little life
Is rounded with a sleep. *The Tempest,* IV,i,156. (More at THEATER.)

5   Life's uncertain voyage. *Timon of Athens,* V,i,203.

See also EXPERIENCE; WORLD.

LIKES AND DISLIKES

6 Some men there are love not a gaping pig,
Some that are mad if they behold a cat,
And others, when the bagpipe sings in the nose,
Cannot contain their urine. *The Merchant of Venice,* IV,i,47.

7 I see, lady, the gentleman is not in your books. *Much Ado About Nothing,*
I,i,74. (Meaning: The gentleman is not in your favor. The lady is Beatrice
and the gentleman is Benedick. Her first words to him are, "I wonder that
you will still be talking, Signior Benedick; nobody marks you," l.112. His
response is "What, my dear Lady Disdain! Are you yet living?" l.114.)

LIMITS

8   Tempt us not to bear above our power! *King John,* V,vi,38.

LISTENING

9 Give every man thine ear, but few thy voice. *Hamlet,* I,iii,68. (More at
WISDOM, WORDS OF.)

10   It is the disease of not listening, the malady of not marking, that I am
troubled withal. *Henry IV, Part Two,* I,ii,126. (Falstaff impertinently in-

forming the Chief Justice that he can hear what the man is saying, but is choosing not to listen.)

See also TALK.

LONDON.   See CITIES.

LONELINESS

1   I tell my sorrows to the stones. *Titus Andronicus,* III,i,37.

2 For now I stand as one upon a rock,
Environed with a wilderness of sea. *Titus Andronicus,* III,i,93.

See also DEPRESSION; SEPARATION.

LOVE AND LOVERS

3   'Twere all one
That I should love a bright particular star,
And think to wed it, he is so above me. *All's Well That Ends Well,* I,i,91.
(Helena speaking of her love for Bertram, who is not so wonderful as she believes. *'Twere all one / That I should love* means "It is as if I were to love.")

4 The hind that would be mated by the lion
Must die for love. *All's Well That Ends Well,* I,i,97.

5   Love that comes too late,
Like a remorseful pardon slowly carried. *All's Well That Ends Well,* V,iii,57.

6   All impediments in fancy's course
Are motives of more fancy. *All's Well That Ends Well,* V,iii,214. (*Fancy* means "love"—or at least attraction.)

7 There's beggary in the love that can be reckoned. *Antony and Cleopatra,* I,i,14. (Antony's answer to Cleopatra's question "If it be love indeed, tell me how much," l.13.)

8 Eternity was in our lips and eyes,
Bliss in our brows' bent. *Antony and Cleopatra,* I,iii,35. (Cleopatra to Antony.)

9   What think you of falling in love? *As You Like It,* I,ii,24. (Rosalind to her cousin Celia. Contemplating the possibility of love leads quickly to the experience.)

10 If thou rememb'rest not the slightest folly
That ever love did make thee run into,
Thou hast not loved. *As You Like It,* II,iv,32.

[1] We that are true lovers run into strange capers; but as all is mortal in nature, so is all nature in love mortal in folly. *As You Like It*, II,iv,51.

[2]   And then the lover,
Sighing like furnace, with a woeful ballad
Made to his mistress' eyebrow. *As You Like It*, II,vii,147. (From "the seven ages of man" speech. See LIFE.)

[3] The worst fault you have is to be in love. *As You Like It*, III,ii,279.

[4] The sight of lovers feedeth those in love. *As You Like It*, III,iv,54.

[5]   The wounds invisible
That love's keen arrows make. *As You Like It*, III,v,30.

[6]   'Tis such fools as you
That makes the world full of ill-favored children. *As You Like It*, III,v,52. (Rosalind urging the infatuated shepherd Silvius to open his eyes and get a grip on himself. See also the quote below.)

[7]   Down on your knees,
And thank heaven, fasting, for a good man's love. *As You Like It*, III,v,57. (Rosalind to Phebe, who is loved by Silvius. See above.)

[8] Who ever loved that loved not at first sight? *As You Like It*, III,v,82. (Shakespeare here pays tribute to Christopher Marlowe with a direct quote from Marlowe's *Hero and Leander*. The preceding line reads, "Dead shepherd, now I find thy saw [saying] of might . . ."; Marlowe, age twenty-nine, was killed in a fight in 1593, about six years before this play was written.)

[9] Men have died from time to time, and worms have eaten them, but not for love. *As You Like It*, IV,i,101. (Rosalind, in disguise, to Orlando. He protests, "Her frown [Rosalind's] might kill me." Similarly, Henry V tells the French princess Katherine that if she turns him down, it is true to say that he will die—but not for love; see SOLDIERS, *Henry V*, V,ii,154 [note].)

[10] My affection hath an unknown bottom, like the Bay of Portugal. *As You Like It*, IV,1,198.

[11]   Love hath made thee a tame snake. *As You Like It*, IV,iii,71.

[12] Your brother and my sister no sooner met but they looked; no sooner looked but they loved; no sooner loved but they sighed; no sooner sighed but they asked one another the reason; no sooner knew the reason but they sought the remedy. *As You Like It*, V,ii,31.

[13] Ere I learn love, I'll practice to obey. *The Comedy of Errors*, II,i,29. (The right attitude for a young Elizabethan woman looking forward to marriage.

This is perhaps the earliest of Shakespeare's plays, but his views on this issue did not change much.)

¹ O, a kiss
Long as my exile, sweet as my revenge! *Coriolanus,* V,iii,44.

² These fellows of infinite tongue, that can rhyme themselves into ladies' favors, they do always reason themselves out again. *Henry V,* V,ii,160. (Henry claims to be a simple soldier, unable to rhyme himself into a lady's favor, but he points out that he has a good heart—see VIRTUE—as well as a kingdom, of course.)

³ This is the very ecstasy of love. *Hamlet,* II,i,102.

⁴ *Ophelia.* 'Tis brief, my lord.
Hamlet. As woman's love. *Hamlet,* III,ii,158.

⁵ Where love is great, the littlest doubts are fear;
Where little fears grow great, great love grows there. *Hamlet,* III,ii,177. (Not quite up to Shakespeare's usual standard—it is from the play written by Hamlet to trap the king.)

⁶ There lives within the very flame of love
A kind of wick or snuff that will abate it. *Hamlet,* IV,vii,114. (The *snuff* is burned wick, which dims a flame.)

⁷ This word "love," which graybeards call divine. *Henry VI, Part Three,* V,vi,81. (The speaker is a bad character indeed: Richard, the future King Richard III. More at CRIME.)

⁸ Though last, not least in love. *Julius Caesar,* III,i,189.

⁹ When love begins to sicken and decay
It useth an enforcèd ceremony.
There are no tricks in plain and simple faith. *Julius Caesar,* IV,ii,20.

¹⁰ You may think my love was crafty love,
And call it cunning. *King John,* IV,i,53. (Young Arthur, King John's nephew, pleading with Hubert not to blind him, reminding Hubert how he has loved him, challenging Hubert to dismiss this love as craftiness if he can.)

¹¹ Love, and be silent. *King Lear,* I,i,64. (Cordelia's instructions to herself in response to her father's demand that she prove her love of him. See also below.)

¹² My love's
More ponderous than my tongue. *King Lear,* I,i,79. (*Ponderous* means "serious" or "weighty." In other versions the quote reads, "My love's /

More richer than my tongue." The point is that Cordelia chooses not to devalue love by boasting of it to curry favor. See also above.)

[1] Love is a familiar; Love is a devil. There is no evil angel but Love. *Love's Labor's Lost,* I,ii,170. (A *familiar* is a familiar spirit.)

[2] Adieu, valor; rust, rapier; be still, drum; for your manager is in love. *Love's Labor's Lost,* I,ii,179.

[3] This wimpled, whining, purblind, wayward boy,
This senior-junior, giant-dwarf, Dan Cupid,
Regent of love-rhymes, lord of folded arms,
The anointed sovereign of sighs and groans,
Liege of all loiterers and malcontents,
Dread prince of plackets, king of codpieces,
Sole imperator and great general
Of trotting paritors. *Love's Labor's Lost,* III,i,181. (Berowne, railing against love. Before being smitten himself, he was, as he says, "love's whip, / A very beadle to a humorous sigh," l.176. *Humorous* here means "moody" or "dreamy." For *Dan Cupid* read "Don Cupid" or "Lord Cupid." A *placket* is a slit in a petticoat; a *paritor* was an officer of the ecclesiastical court, charged with enforcing sexual rules.)

[4] By heaven, I do love, and it hath taught me to rhyme, and to be melancholy. *Love's Labor's Lost,* IV,iii,12.

[5] Love, first learnèd in a lady's eyes,
Lives not alone immurèd in the brain,
But with the motion of all elements,
Courses as swift as thought in every power,
And gives to every power a double power. *Love's Labor's Lost,* IV,iii,326. (See quotes below.)

[6] It adds a precious seeing to the eye. *Love's Labor's Lost,* IV,iii,332. (*It* refers to love. The passage begins above.)

[7] [Love is] as sweet and musical
As bright Apollo's lute, strung with his hair.
And when Love speaks, the voice of all the gods
Make heaven drowsy with the harmony. *Love's Labor's Lost,* IV,iii,341. (From the same passage as the quotes above.)

[8] Charity itself fulfils the law,
And who can sever love from charity? *Love's Labor's Lost,* IV,iii,363. (Here Shakespeare alludes to the biblical precept "He that loveth another hath fulfilled the law," *Romans* 13:8. And in a lighthearted spirit he raises an issue that has embarrassed theologians, the difficulty of distinguishing

between sacred love [charity] and profane love [romantic, or sexual, love].)

¹   Love is full of unbefitting strains,
All wanton as a child, skipping and vain. *Love's Labor's Lost,* V,ii,761. (When writing this play, Shakespeare had recently been through a difficult affair with the "dark lady" of the sonnets—she apparently betrayed him with his patron, the earl of Southampton. The playwright thus was well aware of the "unbefitting strains" of love.)

²   Lovers ever run before the clock. *The Merchant of Venice,* II,vi,4.

³   Love is blind, and lovers cannot see
The pretty follies that themselves commit. *The Merchant of Venice,* II,vi,36. ("Love is blind" is a proverbial saying, also used by Chaucer in "The Merchant's Tale." See also below, *A Midsummer Night's Dream,* I,i,234.)

⁴ Tell me where is fancy bred,
Or in the heart, or in the head?
How begot, how nourishèd?
Reply, reply. *The Merchant of Venice,* III,ii,63.

⁵ In love the heavens themselves do guide the state;
Money buys lands, and wives are sold by fate. *The Merry Wives of Windsor,* V,v,233. (A comment on the impossibility of forcing love and marriage into the service of rational, financially sound matchmaking.)

⁶   For aught that I could ever read,
Could ever hear by tale or history,
The course of true love never did run smooth. *A Midsummer Night's Dream,* I,i,132.

⁷   Momentary as a sound,
Swift as a shadow, short as any dream,
Brief as the lightning in the collied night,
That, in a spleen, unfolds both heaven and earth,
And ere a man hath power to say "Behold!"
The jaws of darkness do devour it up:
So quick bright things come to confusion. *A Midsummer Night's Dream,* I,i,143. (*Collied* means "dark," and *in a spleen* means "in a flash.")

⁸ Love looks not with the eyes, but with the mind,
And therefore is winged Cupid painted blind. *A Midsummer Night's Dream,* I,i,234. (See above, *The Merchant of Venice,* II,vi,36.)

⁹ We cannot fight for love, as men may do;
We should be wooed, and were not made to woo. *A Midsummer Night's*

Dream, II,i,241. (Helena speaks. In fact, she has been wooing Demetrius with unbounded enthusiasm.)

[1] Cupid is a knavish lad,
Thus to make poor females mad. *A Midsummer Night's Dream,* III,ii,440.

[2] My Oberon, what visions I have seen!
Methought I was enamored of an ass. *A Midsummer Night's Dream,* IV,i,79. (Titania expressing a not uncommon distress at recalling a love no longer felt.)

[3] Lovers and madmen have such seething brains,
Such shaping fantasies, that apprehend
More than cool reason ever comprehends. *A Midsummer Night's Dream,* V,i,4. (More at IMAGINATION.)

[4] I had rather hear my dog bark at a crow than a man swear he loves me. *Much Ado About Nothing,* I,i,127.

[5] Speak low if you speak love. *Much Ado About Nothing,* II,i,98.

[6]   All hearts in love use their own tongues;
Let every eye negotiate for itself
And trust no agent; for beauty is a witch
Against whose charms faith melteth into blood. *Much Ado About Nothing,* II,i,175. (The sense is: Plead your own case in love, do not trust a friend, for beauty will destroy loyalty, and passion will take its place.)

[7]   Love may transform me to an oyster. *Much Ado About Nothing,* II,iii,24.

[8] Some Cupid kills with arrows, some with traps. *Much Ado About Nothing,* III,i,106.

[9]   My story being done,
She gave me for my pains a world of kisses.
She swore in faith 'twas strange, 'twas passing strange;
'Twas pitiful, 'twas wondrous pitiful.
She wished she had not heard it; yet she wished
That heaven had made her such a man. She thanked me,
And bade me, if I had a friend that loved her,
I should but teach him how to tell my story,
And that would woo her. Upon this hint I spake.
She loved me for the dangers I had passed,
And I loved her that she did pity them.
This only is the witchcraft I have used. *Othello,* I,iii,157. (Othello explaining how Desdemona fell in love with him.)

1   Base men being in love have then a nobility in their natures more than is native to them. *Othello,* II,i,213.

2 I know a lady in Venice would have walked barefoot to Palestine for a touch of his nether lip. *Othello,* IV,iii,39. (Emilia speaking of Lodovico.)

3   One that loved not wisely, but too well. *Othello,* V,ii,340. (More at DEATHBED STATEMENTS.)

4 A pair of star-crossed lovers. *Romeo and Juliet,* Prologue,6.

5 Love is a smoke made with the fume of sighs. *Romeo and Juliet,* I,i,193. (A slightly affected comment by Romeo, before he has met Juliet.)

6 *Benvolio.* Blind is his love and best befits the dark.
Mercutio. If love be blind, love cannot hit the mark. *Romeo and Juliet,* II,i,32. (They are speaking of their friend Romeo. Mercutio's jest is a little naughty.)

7   Stony limits cannot hold love out. *Romeo and Juliet,* II,ii,67.

8   What love can do, that dares love attempt. *Romeo and Juliet,* II,ii,68.

9   If thou swearest,
Thou mayst prove false. At lovers' perjuries,
They say Jove laughs. *Romeo and Juliet,* II,ii,91. (A comment dating at least to Roman times. Thus, Ovid in *Ars Amatoria* and Albius Tibullus in his *Elegies* have the same line: *Periuria ridet amantum Iupiter,* "Jupiter laughs at the perjuries of lovers." Dryden put it, "Jove but laughs at lovers' perjury," using the line in *Palamon and Arcite,* 1680, and in *Amphitryon,* 1690. See also PROMISES.)

10 This bud of love, by summer's ripening breath,
May prove a beauteous flower when next we meet. *Romeo and Juliet,* II,ii,121.

11 Love goes toward love as schoolboys from their books;
But love from love, toward school with heavy looks. *Romeo and Juliet,* II,ii,156.

12 How silver-sweet sound lovers' tongues by night,
Like softest music to attending ears! *Romeo and Juliet,* II,ii,165.

13   Young men's love then lies
Not truly in their hearts, but in their eyes. *Romeo and Juliet,* II,iii,67.

14   Love moderately: long love doth so;
Too swift arrives as tardy as too slow. *Romeo and Juliet,* II,vi,14. (Friar Lawrence to Romeo. A perfectly useless remark to make to a teenager.)

[1] O, learn to read what silent love hath writ. *Sonnet 23, 13.*

[2]   Thy sweet love remembered such wealth brings,
That then I scorn to change my state with kings. *Sonnet 29, 13.*

[3] When love, converted from the thing it was,
Shall reasons find of settled gravity. *Sonnet 49, 7.* (When love must be justified by grave reasons, the poet admits he can press no further claims, "Since why to love I can allege no cause," 1.14.)

[4] Not mine own fears nor the prophetic soul
Of the wide world dreaming on things to come
Can yet the lease of my true love control. *Sonnet 107, 1.*

[5] Let me not to the marriage of true minds
Admit impediments; love is not love
Which alters when it alteration finds,
Or bends with the remover to remove.
O, no, it is an ever-fixèd mark
That looks on tempests and is never shaken;
It is the star to every wand'ring bark,
Whose worth's unknown, although his height be taken.
Love's not Time's fool, though rosy lips and cheeks
Within his bending sickle's compass come;
Love alters not with his brief hours and weeks,
But bears it out even to the edge of doom.
If this be error and upon me proved,
I never writ, nor no man ever loved. *Sonnet 116.* (The mention of *impediments* in the second line is a reference to the Book of Common Prayer marriage service, "If any of you know cause or just impediment. . . ." This is probably the most famous of Shakespeare's sonnets. Speaking of the sonnet form, Wordsworth wrote, "With this key / Shakespeare unlocked his heart," "Scorn Not the Sonnet," 1827.)

[6] And ruined love, when it is built anew,
Grows fairer than at first, more strong, far greater. *Sonnet 119, 11.*

[7] When my love swears that she is made of truth,
I do believe her though I know she lies. *Sonnet 138, 1.*

[8] Love is too young to know what conscience is. *Sonnet 151, 1.*

[9]   These lovers will not keep the peace. *Titus Andronicus,* II,i,37.

[10]   This love will undo us all. *Troilus and Cressida,* III,i,111.

[11]   Hot blood begets hot thoughts, and hot thoughts beget hot deeds, and hot deeds is love. *Troilus and Cressida,* III,i,128. (Paris defines love.

Shakespeare's view of the prince's life-style is reflected in Paris's vulgar grammar.)

[1] Is love a generation of vipers? *Troilus and Cressida,* III,i,132. (In *Matthew* 3:7, 12:34, and 23:33 Pharisees and others are called a generation of vipers.)

[2] They say all. lovers swear more performance than they are able, and yet reserve an ability that they never perform, vowing more than the perfection of ten and discharging less than the tenth part of one. *Troilus and Cressida,* III,ii,86. (See also SEX, *Troilus and Cressida,* III,ii,82.)

[3] To be wise and love
Exceeds man's might; that dwells with gods above. *Troilus and Cressida,* III,ii,157.

[4] O spirit of love, how quick and fresh art thou. *Twelfth Night,* I,i,9. (From the opening speech of the play, which begins "If music be the food of love, play on"; see MUSIC.)

[5] So full of shapes is fancy
That it alone is high fantastical. *Twelfth Night,* I,i,14. (Translation: So full of fantasies is love that it alone is the highest form of imagination.)

[6] What is love? 'Tis not hereafter;
Present mirth hath present laughter;
What's to come is still unsure:
In delay there lies no plenty;
Then come kiss me, sweet, and twenty,
Youth's a stuff will not endure. *Twelfth Night,* II,iii,48.

[7] Such as I am all true lovers are,
Unstaid and skittish in all motions else
Save in the constant image of the creature
That is beloved. *Twelfth Night,* II,iv,17. (*Motions* refers to emotions.)

[8] Let thy love be younger than thyself,
Or thy affection cannot hold the bent;
For women are as roses, whose fair flower,
Being once displayed, doth fall that very hour. *Twelfth Night,* II,iv,36. (The duke to Viola, who is disguised as a boy. For more on why he thinks men should marry younger women, see MEN AND WOMEN. The duke is also responsible for the quote just above.)

[9] *Duke.* And what's her history?
Viola. A blank, my lord. She never told her love,
But let concealment, like a worm i' th' bud,

Feed on her damask cheek. She pined in thought;
And, with a green and yellow melancholy,
She sat like Patience on a monument,
Smiling at grief. Was not this love indeed?
We men may say more, swear more; but indeed
Our shows are more than will; for still we prove
Much in our vows but little in our love. *Twelfth Night,* II,iv,110. (Viola, dressed as a man, makes a few points concerning the depth of love in men and women. She claims to be telling a story about her sister.)

[1] I may command where I adore. *Twelfth Night,* II,v,116.

[2] Love sought is good, but given unsought is better. *Twelfth Night,* III,i,158.

[3] He after honor hunts, I after love. *The Two Gentlemen of Verona,* I,i,63.

[4] *Julia.* They do not love that do not show their love.
Lucetta. O, they love least that let men know their love. *The Two Gentlemen of Verona,* I,ii,31.

[5] O, how this spring of love resembleth
The uncertain glory of an April day,
Which now shows all the beauty of the sun,
And by and by a cloud takes all away! *The Two Gentlemen of Verona,* I,iii,84.

[6]   Love will creep in service where it cannot go. *The Two Gentlemen of Verona,* IV,ii,19. (*Where it cannot go* means "where it cannot go walking upright." The saying is proverbial.)

[7] Alas, how love can trifle with itself! *The Two Gentlemen of Verona,* IV,iv,183.

[8]   She cannot choose but love. *Venus and Adonis,* 79.

[9] Love is a spirit all compact of fire,
Not gross to sink, but light and will aspire. *Venus and Adonis,* 149.

[10] O, what a war of looks was then between them. *Venus and Adonis,* 355.

[11] Love comforteth like sunshine after rain,
But Lust's effect is tempest after sun.
Love's gentle spring doth always fresh remain;
Lust's winter comes ere summer half be done. *Venus and Adonis,* 799. (See also under SEX, Sonnet 129, "the lust sonnet.")

[12] I think there is not half a kiss to choose
Who loves another best. *The Winter's Tale,* IV,iv,175. (The shepherd commenting on the young lovers Florizel and Perdita. For *another* read "the other.")

[1] I
am heir to my affection. *The Winter's Tale,* IV,iv,484. (Prince Florizel, renouncing his father and royal right of succession in order to live with Perdita, whom he believes to be a shepherdess.)

[2] Prosperity's the very bond of love. *The Winter's Tale,* IV,iv,577.

See also JEALOUSY; LOVE, EXPRESSIONS OF; MARRIAGE; MEN AND WOMEN; PASSION; ROMEO AND JULIET; SEPARATION; SEX; WOMEN.

LOVE, EXPRESSIONS OF

[3] My house, mine honor, yea, my life be thine. *All's Well That Ends Well,* IV,ii,52.

[4]   Is he on his horse?
O happy horse, to bear the weight of Antony! *Antony and Cleopatra,* I,v,20. (Cleopatra speaks. She goes on to call Antony "the demi-Atlas of this earth, the arm / And burgonet of men," l.23. A *burgonet* is a visored helmet.)

[5]   Heavenly Rosalind! *As You Like It,* I,ii,279. (Orlando stricken by love "at first sight"; see LOVE AND LOVERS above.)

[6] *Jaques.* What stature is she of?
Orlando. Just as high as my heart. *As You Like It,* III,ii,266.

[7] Doubt thou the stars are fire,
Doubt that the sun doth move;
Doubt truth to be a liar,
But never doubt I love. *Hamlet,* II,ii,116. (From a letter written by Hamlet to Ophelia, in part to provoke her father.)

[8] I loved Ophelia. Forty thousand brothers
Could not with all their quantity of love
Make up my sum. *Hamlet,* V,i,271. (Hamlet to Laertes.)

[9] I know no ways to mince it in love, but directly to say, "I love you." *Henry V,* V,ii,128. (The king courting the French princess Katherine. See also below and SOLDIERS.)

[10] You have witchcraft in your lips, Kate. *Henry V,* V,ii,288.

[11]   Where thou art, there is the world itself. *Henry VI, Part Two,* III,ii,362.

[12] Take, O, take those lips away,
That so sweetly were forsworn;
And those eyes, the break of day,
Lights that do mislead the morn;

But my kisses bring again, bring again;
Seals of love, but sealed in vain, sealed in vain. *Measure for Measure,* IV,i,1.

¹ What's mine is yours, and what is yours is mine. *Measure for Measure,* V,i,540.

² For you in my respect are all the world.
Then how can it be said I am alone,
When all the world is here to look on me? *A Midsummer Night's Dream,* II,i,224. (*Respect* means "regard" or "view.")

³   I will wear my heart upon my sleeve. *Othello,* I,i,61.

⁴ Excellent wretch! Perdition catch my soul
But I do love thee! And when I love thee not,
Chaos is come again. *Othello,* III,iii,90. (The idea of chaos entering when love is gone appears also in *Venus and Adonis;* see DEATH AND GRIEF.)

⁵   Unkindness may do much,
And his unkindness may defeat my life,
But never taint my love. *Othello,* IV,ii,158. (Desdemona speaking of Othello.)

⁶ Whither he goes, thither let me go. *Richard II,* V,i,85. (Queen Isabel asking permission to accompany Richard into exile. The line recalls *Ruth* 1:16, "Whither thou goest, I will go; and where thou lodgest, I will lodge." There is a similar line in *Henry IV, Part One,* spoken by Hotspur to his wife: "Whither I go, thither shall you go too," II,iii,115.)

⁷   O, it is my love!
O, that she knew she were! *Romeo and Juliet,* II,ii,10. (Romeo in the balcony scene. See also ROMEO AND JULIET.)

⁸ See how she leans her cheek upon her hand!
O, that I were a glove upon that hand,
That I might touch that cheek! *Romeo and Juliet,* II,ii,23.

⁹   I'll prove more true
Than those that have the cunning to be strange. *Romeo and Juliet,* II,ii,100. (Juliet promising that her love although quickly given is not lightly given. *Strange* refers to acting as a stranger, keeping a distance, playing hard to get.)

¹⁰   When I shall die,
Take him and cut him out in little stars,
And he will make the face of heaven so fine
That all the world will be in love with night
And pay no worship to the garish sun. *Romeo and Juliet,* III,ii,21. (Juliet

speaking of Romeo. In some editions the first line reads, "When he shall die.")

[1] Who is it that says most, which can say more
Than this rich praise, that you alone are you. *Sonnet 84,* 1.

[2] To me, fair friend, you never can be old,
For as you were when first your eye I eyed,
Such seems your beauty still. *Sonnet 104,* 1.

[3] That is my home of love; if I have ranged,
Like him that travels, I return again. *Sonnet 109, 5.* (*That* refers to "in thy breast.")

[4]   Kiss me, Kate, "We will be married a Sunday." *The Taming of the Shrew,* II,i,317. (Used as the title of the great 1949 Cole Porter musical *Kiss Me, Kate!* The line is from a ballad. The phrase appears again at the end of the play, V,ii,180.)

[5] If I be false or swerve a hair from truth,
When time is old and hath forgot itself,
When waterdrops have worn the stones of Troy,
And blind oblivion swallowed cities up,
And mighty states characterless are grated
To dusty nothing, yet let memory,
From false to false among false maids in love,
Upbraid my falsehood! When they've said, "As false
As air, as water, wind or sandy earth,
As fox to lamb, as wolf to heifer's calf,
Pard to the hind, or stepdame to her son,"
Yea, let them say, to stick the heart of falsehood,
"As false as Cressid." *Troilus and Cressida,* III,ii,185. (Cressida indeed became a byword for wantonness and treachery, eventually punished, in some stories, by the affliction of leprosy. This harsh view of her was a rather late development, however. In Chaucer, she is more victim than harlot. In Shakespeare, she is not so much evil as shallow and willful. The role is notoriously thankless, the motivation being very unclear.)

[6] Make me a willow cabin at your gate
And call upon my soul within the house;
Write loyal cantons of contemnèd love
And sing them loud even in the dead of night;
Hallo your name to the reverberate hills
And make the babbling gossip of the air
Cry out "Olivia!" *Twelfth Night,* I,v,269. (Viola, who is disguised as a man, describes to Olivia how she would press her love if she were Orsino.)

¹ What light is light, if Silvia be not seen?
What joy is joy, if Silvia be not by? *The Two Gentlemen of Verona,* III,i,174.

² Except I be by Silvia in the night,
There is no music in the nightingale. *The Two Gentlemen of Verona,*
III,i,178.

³ Who is Silvia, what is she,
That all our swains commend her?
Holy, fair, and wise is she;
That heaven such grace did lend her,
That she might admirèd be.

Is she kind as she is fair?
For beauty lives with kindness. *The Two Gentlemen of Verona,* IV,ii,38.

⁴   I'll smother thee with kisses. *Venus and Adonis,* 18.

⁵   For I cannot be
Mine own, nor anything to any, if
I be not thine. *The Winter's Tale,* IV,iv,43. (The speaker is Florizel, prince
of Bohemia. His love, whom he believes to be a shepherdess, is by birth
Perdita, princess of Sicily.)

See also LOVE AND LOVERS; MEN AND WOMEN; ROMEO AND JULIET; WOMEN.

LOYALTY

⁶   He that can endure
To follow with allegiance a fallen lord
Does conquer him that did his master conquer
And earns a place in the story. *Antony and Cleopatra,* III,xiii,43.

⁷ O, where is faith? O, where is loyalty? *Henry VI, Part Two,* V,i,166.

⁸ One for all, or all for one we gage. *The Rape of Lucrece,* 144. (*Gage* means
"pledge.")

See also ALLIES.

LUCK.   See CHANCE; FATE; FORTUNE.

LUXURY

⁹   Our basest beggars
Are in the poorest thing superfluous.
Allow not nature more than nature needs,
Man's life is cheap as beast's. *King Lear,* II,iv,263. (Translation: Our

poorest beggars have at least some little superfluous possession. If humans cannot have more than the mere necessities of survival, their lives are no different than a beast's.)

[1]   The devil Luxury, with his fat rump and potato finger. *Troilus and Cressida,* V,ii,53.

See also CONSPICUOUS CONSUMPTION; MONEY; RICH, THE; RICH AND POOR.

M

MACBETH

[1] Laugh to scorn
The power of man, for none of woman born
Shall harm Macbeth. *Macbeth,* IV,i,79. (Macduff, who eventually kills
Macbeth, was not "born" of woman; he was delivered surgically, "from his
mother's womb / Untimely ripped," V,viii,15. Macbeth's bad karma
seems to have affected actors playing the part. According to Kathryn
Forbush in the theater department at the Taft School, in a 1934 Old Vic
production, four actors were needed in a single week. [One got laryngitis,
one caught a fever, and one was fired.] Add to this the death of the boy
playing Lady Macbeth in the original production in 1606, and any number
of accidents involving falls and fires, and one opening-night death, and no
wonder the play is considered bad luck. Some have avoided saying its
name, using instead circumlocutions such as "the Scottish play.")

[2] Macbeth shall never vanquished be until
Great Birnam Wood to high Dunsinane Hill
Shall come against him. *Macbeth,* IV,i,92. (Macbeth takes the prophecy
literally, saying, "That will never be," l.94. But the prophecy is fulfilled when
Malcolm orders, "Let every soldier hew him down a bough / And bear it
before him." Thus camouflaged, they advance on Macbeth's castle.)

MADNESS

[3] That he's mad, 'tis true: 'tis true 'tis pity,
And pity 'tis 'tis true. *Hamlet,* II,ii,97. (Polonius speaking of Hamlet. The

prince, however, is acting. There's a method in his madness; see CRAFTI-
NESS and the second quote below).

[1] O what a noble mind is here o'erthrown! *Hamlet,* III,i,153. (More at
HAMLET and below.)

[2] Now see that noble and most sovereign reason
Like sweet bells jangled, out of time and harsh. *Hamlet,* III,i,160. (Ophelia
speaks. In filmed interviews with a half-dozen of the leading Hamlets of
our age, shown on the Arts and Entertainment television network in
December 1990 as "To Be Hamlet," all of the actors agreed that while
Hamlet began by pretending to be mad, the pretense at some point gave
way to real madness, at least for a time. On the relationship between the
sensitive mind and madness, Dryden wrote: "Great wits are sure to
madness near allied," *Absalom and Achitophel.*)

[3] Madness in great ones must not unwatched go. *Hamlet,* III,i,191.

[4] His madness is poor Hamlet's enemy. *Hamlet,* V,ii,240. (Hamlet speaks.)

[5]   My wits begin to turn. *King Lear,* III,ii,67.

[6] O, that way madness lies; let me shun that.
No more of that. *King Lear,* III,iv,21. (Lear speaks. *That way* refers to
thoughts of the cruelty and ingratitude of his daughters Goneril and
Regan.)

[7] Or have we eaten on the insane root
That takes the reason prisoner? *Macbeth,* I,iii,84. (One root widely alleged
to cause insanity was the mandrake root, which sometimes is shaped
vaguely like a human being. The narcotic effects of mandrake, a plant in
the nightshade family, probably were intensified by the many superstitions
surrounding it. When pulled from the ground, it was said to scream so
horribly as to cause madness or death.)

[8] Is this a dagger which I see before me? *Macbeth,* II,i,33. (More at APPARI-
TIONS. Macbeth asks himself whether he is hallucinating the dagger as a
result of mental disturbance: "Art thou but / A dagger of the mind, a false
creation, / Proceeding from the heat-oppressèd brain?" l.37. But Samuel
Johnson argued that his bustling, normal behavior just prior to the vision
seems to belie madness as a cause. On the other side of the issue, one
might cite Macbeth's calling Banquo's ghost an "unreal mockery,"
III,iv,108; see APPARITIONS. The scenes can be interpreted effectively either
way.)

[9] These deeds must not be thought
After these ways; so, it will make us mad. *Macbeth,* II,ii,32. (Lady Macbeth
foresees that if she and her husband dwell on the murder of Duncan, they

will become mad. Macbeth, too, senses the trauma they have inflicted on themselves. He tells her, "Methought I heard a voice cry 'Sleep no more!' " l.34. See SLEEP.)

[1] The Thane of Fife had a wife. Where is she now? *Macbeth,* V,i,45. (The sleepwalking, distraught Lady Macbeth.)

[2] Canst thou not minister to a mind diseased? *Macbeth,* V,iii,40. (More at MEDICINE.)

[3] Lovers and madmen have such seething brains,
Such shaping fantasies, that apprehend
More than cool reason ever comprehends. *A Midsummer Night's Dream,*
V,i,4. (More at IMAGINATION.)

[4] Why, this is very midsummer madness. *Twelfth Night,* III,iv,58.

[5]   As mad as a march hare. *The Two Noble Kinsmen,* III,v,74. (This traditional metaphor apparently derives from the mating behavior of hares in the spring.)

MAGIC.   See FAIRIES; OCCULT, THE.

MAN.   See HUMAN NATURE AND HUMANKIND; MEN.

MANIPULATION

[6]   Do you think I am easier to be played on than a pipe? *Hamlet,* III,ii,377.

[7]   She, poor soul,
Knows not which way to stand, to look, to speak,
And sits as one new-risen from a dream. *The Taming of the Shrew,* IV,i,178. (The reference is to Kate, numbed by Petruchio's brainwashing techniques, including deprivation of sleep and food, with exposure to a heavy dose of unpredictable noise and abuse. Petruchio likens his method to the training of a falcon. "I'll curb her mad and headstrong humor," he promises, l.203, adding in recognition of the harshness of his method, "He that knows better how to tame a shrew, / Now let him speak—'tis charity to show," l.204. See also MARRIAGE and ARGUMENTS.)

MANNERS

[8] Be thou familiar, but by no means vulgar. *Hamlet,* I,iii,61. (More at WISDOM, WORDS OF.)

[9]   I am native here
And to the manner born. *Hamlet,* I,iv,14. (More at HABIT AND CUSTOM.)

¹ *Polonius.* My lord, I will use them according to their desert.
Hamlet. God's bodkin, man, much better! Use every man after his desert, and who shall scape whipping? Use them after your own honor and dignity. The less they deserve, the more merit is in your bounty. *Hamlet,* II,ii,538. (The speakers are discussing the hospitality to be shown the troupe of actors.)

² Nice customs cursy to great kings. Dear Kate, you and I cannot be confined within the weak list of a country's fashion: we are the makers of manners. *Henry V,* V,ii,281. (For *cursy* read "curtsy"; for *list,* "limits.")

³ Two women placed together makes cold weather. *Henry VIII,* I,iv,22. (Comment by the Lord Chamberlain as he seats a gentleman—Lord Sands—between Anne Bullen [Boleyn] and another lady of the court.)

⁴ Buckingham,
The mirror of all courtesy. *Henry VIII,* II,i,52.

⁵ I never stood on ceremonies. *Julius Caesar,* II,ii,13. (The sense of the phrase has changed. Calphurnia is saying that she has never paid attention to prophecies or omens.)

⁶ A proper man as one shall see in a summer's day; a most lovely, gentlemanlike man. *A Midsummer Night's Dream,* I,ii,86.

⁷ I am the very pink of courtesy. *Romeo and Juliet,* II,iv,61.

⁸ Keep a good tongue in your head. *The Tempest,* III,ii,37.

⁹ We must be gentle, now we are gentlemen. *The Winter's Tale,* V,ii,162.

¹⁰ There's magic in thy majesty. *The Winter's Tale,* V,iii,39.

See also CEREMONY; EFFETENESS; FASHION; HABIT AND CUSTOM; HOSPITALITY; ITALY AND ITALIANS; MANNERS, BAD; TALK; TALK, PLAIN AND FANCY.

MANNERS, BAD

¹¹ New-made honor doth forget men's names. *King John,* I,i,187. (The newly honored, or elevated, person makes a point of forgetting humble people's names. To call an ordinary person by his correct name would be "too respective and too sociable," l.188.)

MARRIAGE

¹² Get thee a good husband, and use him as he uses thee. *All's Well That Ends Well,* I,i,221.

¹ I have been, madam, a wicked creature. . . . I do marry that I may repent. *All's Well That Ends Well*, I,iii,35. (Spoken by the clever Clown; see also below.)

² If men could be contented to be what they are, there were no fear in marriage. *All's Well That Ends Well*, I,iii,51. (An insight from the Clown. It comes in the midst of a bawdy acknowledgment of the probability of being cuckolded in marriage.)

³ A young man married is a man that's marred. *All's Well That Ends Well*, II,iii,301.

⁴ Octavia . . . whose beauty claims
No worse a husband than the best of men. *Antony and Cleopatra*, II,ii,133. (Agrippa suggesting a marriage between Octavia, Caesar's sister, and Mark Antony.)

⁵ Men are April when they woo, December when they wed. Maids are May when they are maids, but the sky changes when they are wives. *As You Like It*, IV,i,140.

⁶ Thou art an elm, my husband, I a vine,
Whose weakness, married to thy stronger state,
Makes me with thy strength to communicate. *The Comedy of Errors*, II,ii,175. (This clinging vine—Adriana—is actually the more liberated, or shrewish, of two sisters. She has just been given a lecture on the virtue of womanly subservience by her sister, Luciana, which she appears to have taken to heart. The sentiments expressed here are honed to perfection in *The Taming of the Shrew*.)

⁷ So excellent a king, that was to this
Hyperion to a satyr, so loving to my mother
That he might not beteem the winds of heaven
Visit her face too roughly. Heaven and earth,
Must I remember? Why, she would hang on him
As if increase of appetite had grown
By what it fed on; and yet within a month—
Let me not think on it; frailty thy name is woman. *Hamlet*, I,ii,139. (*Hyperion* is the sun god—Hamlet is comparing his father to his wicked uncle. *Beteem* means "allow." Hamlet cannot credit that despite this excellent marriage, his mother could so quickly forget her late husband and marry his brother. See below.)

⁸ Thrift, thrift, Horatio. The funeral baked meats
Did coldly furnish forth the marriage tables. *Hamlet*, I,ii,180. (Hamlet's ironic comment on the rush to marriage by his mother and his uncle,

Claudius, following the death of Hamlet's father. Hamlet concludes, "Would I had met my dearest foe in heaven / Or ever I had seen that day," l.182.")

¹   What is wedlock forcèd but a hell,
An age of discord and continual strife?
Whereas the contrary bringeth bliss,
And is a pattern of celestial peace. *Henry VI, Part One,* V,v,62. (The earl of Suffolk unctuously promoting the politically disastrous match between Henry VI and the beautiful Margaret of Anjou. As for "celestial bliss," Suffolk hopes to share the queen's affections.)

²   Hasty marriage seldom proveth well. *Henry VI, Part Three,* IV,i,18.

³ He counsels a divorce. *Henry VIII,* II,ii,30. (*He* is Cardinal Wolsey.)

⁴   Dwell I but in the suburbs
Of your good pleasure? If it be no more,
Portia is Brutus' harlot, not his wife. *Julius Caesar,* II,i,285. (Portia asking Brutus not to keep secrets from her. In the suburbs of London prostitutes plied their trade, so Shakespeare's audience would have found the figure of speech very apt.)

⁵ You are my true and honorable wife. *Julius Caesar,* II,i,288. (Brutus to Portia.)

⁶ Render me worthy of this noble wife! *Julius Caesar,* II,i,303.

⁷ He is the half part of a blessèd man,
Left to be finishèd by such as she,
And she a fair divided excellence,
Whose fullness of perfection lies in him. *King John,* II,i,437. (This exquisite portrait of bride and bridegroom refers to Blanch of Spain and the French dauphin, two young people forced into marriage for political reasons.)

⁸ Hanging and wiving goes by destiny. *The Merchant of Venice,* II,ix,82. (Proverbial.)

⁹   A light wife doth make a heavy husband. *The Merchant of Venice,* V,i,130.

¹⁰ Shall I never see a bachelor of threescore again? *Much Ado About Nothing,* I,i,192. (In other words: Is every man going to get married?)

¹¹ "In time the savage bull doth bear the yoke." *Much Ado About Nothing,* I,i,252. (Don Pedro delivers this adage in response to Benedick's assertion that he will remain a bachelor. Benedick then says that the yoke may be borne by the bull, but that if he ever weds, people can paint a sign on him:

"Here is good horse to hire. . . . Here you may see Benedick the married man," I.256.)

[1] Time goes on crutches till Love have all his rites. *Much Ado About Nothing,* II,i,352. (Time goes slowly before a wedding.)

[2] Thou art sad; get thee a wife, get thee a wife! *Much Ado About Nothing,* V,iv,122. (Not that Benedick assumes this leads to happiness ever after. His next line is "There is no staff so reverend as one tipped with horn"—that is, the horns of a cuckold.)

[3] A fellow almost damned in a fair wife. *Othello,* I,i,18.

[4] O curse of marriage,
That we can call these delicate creatures ours,
And not their appetites. *Othello,* III,iii,267. (More at JEALOUSY.)

[5] I come to wive it wealthily in Padua;
If wealthily, then happily in Padua. *The Taming of the Shrew,* I,ii,74. (Petruchio's lines here became the basis of Alfred Drake's opening number as Petruchio in the 1949 Cole Porter musical *Kiss Me Kate.* The book, by Bella and Samuel Spewack, is a play within a play, in which a production of *The Taming of the Shrew* is the setting for a stormy romance between the stage director and his ex-wife, the play's star. Shakespeare's *The Taming of the Shrew* is also a play within a play, thus the musical is a three-layer theatrical confection.)

[6] Who wooed in haste and means to wed at leisure. *The Taming of the Shrew,* III,ii,11.

[7] This is a way to kill a wife with kindness. *The Taming of the Shrew,* IV,i,202. (Petruchio refers to a proverb about how to ruin a wife with indulgence. His "kindness" consists in constantly finding things wrong with the meals brought to Kate or the way the bed is made, so that she has no chance either to eat or to sleep. See also MANIPULATION.)

[8] Thy husband is thy lord, thy life, thy keeper,
Thy head, thy sovereign—one that cares for thee. *The Taming of the Shrew,* V,ii,146. (A newly docile Kate speaks. Shakespeare appears to have been essentially serious here, although the play is a comedy and therefore not to be taken completely literally. As a fairly conservative man of his time, Shakespeare feared disorder and chaos. He believed that order in a marriage depends on the wife accepting the rule of the husband, and the husband accepting the responsibility to care for his family. See below.)

[9] Such duty as the subject owes the prince,
Even such a woman oweth to her husband. *The Taming of the Shrew,* V,ii,155.

¹ Honor, riches, marriage blessing,
Long continuance, and increasing,
Hourly joys be still upon you! *The Tempest,* IV,i,106. (Juno's blessing upon Ferdinand and Miranda.)

² What nearer debt in all humanity
Than wife is to the husband? *Troilus and Cressida,* II,ii,175. (Hector, stating a proposition that Shakespeare supported: By the laws of nature and society, a wife owes fidelity to her husband.)

³ Many a good hanging prevents a bad marriage. *Twelfth Night,* I,v,19.

⁴ Fools are as like husbands as pilchers are to herrings—the husband's the bigger. *Twelfth Night,* III,i,35. (A *pilcher* is a small herring.)

⁵ One feast, one house, one mutual happiness. *The Two Gentlemen of Verona,* V,iv,173. (The last line of the play.)

See also CHILDREN; FAMILY; LOVE AND LOVERS; MEN AND WOMEN; WOMEN.

MATHEMATICS

⁶   There is divinity in odd numbers. *The Merry Wives of Windsor,* V,i,3. (More at OCCULT, THE.)

MATURITY

⁷ Consideration like an angel came
And whipped the offending Adam out of him. *Henry V,* I,i,28. (The reference is to Henry V's sudden conversion to decent behavior following the death of his father. *Consideration* denotes "care" or "thoughtfulness." *Adam* stands for original sin.)

⁸ Ripeness is all. *King Lear,* V,ii,11.

See also EXPERIENCE; MIDDLE AGE.

MEANS.   See ENDS AND MEANS.

MEDIA AND MESSAGES

⁹   Being daily swallowed by men's eyes. *Henry IV, Part One,* III,ii,70. (A reference to the dangers of overexposure. More at POLITICS.)

¹⁰ To see sad sights moves more than hear them told. *The Rape of Lucrece,* 1324. (A picture's worth a thousand words.)

¹¹   Things in motion sooner catch the eye
Than what stirs not. *Troilus and Cressida,* III,iii,182.

1   I love a ballad in print, a-life, for then we are sure they are true. *The Winter's Tale,* IV,iv,261. (*A-life* just means "dearly." This must be one of the earliest references to people's tending to believe what they see in print.)

See also NEWS; PUBLIC RELATIONS.

MEDICINE

2 I have seen a medicine
That's able to breathe life into a stone. *All's Well That Ends Well,* II,i,74.

3   Now remains
That we find out the cause of this effect,
Or rather say the cause of this defect,
For this effect defective comes by cause. *Hamlet,* II,ii,101. (Polonius suggesting that it is time to investigate the cause of Hamlet's madness—which the audience knows is only feigned, at least so far. See MADNESS.)

4   Diseases desperate grown
By desperate appliance are relieved,
Or not at all. *Hamlet,* IV,iii,9.

5 If the rascal hath not given me medicines to make me love him, I'll be hanged. *Henry IV, Part One,* II,ii,18. (Falstaff joking that he may have been given a love potion. Until modern times, the distinctions between medicines, magic potions, and poisons were vague at best.)

6   Tender loving care. *Henry VI, Part Two,* III,ii,280. (The best medicine. Now sometimes abbreviated to TLC.)

7 Give me an ounce of civet; good apothecary, sweeten my imagination. *King Lear,* IV,vi,132. (From the scent gland of the civet, a musklike substance was derived and used in perfume.)

8 This disease is beyond my practice. *Macbeth,* V,i,62. (The doctor speaking of Lady Macbeth's sleepwalking and mental agony.)

9 *Macbeth.* Canst thou not minister to a mind diseased,
Pluck from the memory a rooted sorrow,
Raze out the written troubles of the brain,
And with some sweet oblivious antidote
Cleanse the stuffed bosom of that perilous stuff
Which weighs upon the heart?
Doctor. Therein the patient
Must minister to himself.
Macbeth. Throw physic to the dogs, I'll none of it. *Macbeth,* V,iii,40. (*Raze out* means "erase"; *oblivious* means "bringing oblivion"; *physic* is medicine.)

[1]   O true apothecary!
Thy drugs are quick. *Romeo and Juliet,* V,iii,119. (Romeo as he takes poison.)

See also DOCTORS; HEALTH; SICKNESS.

MEDIOCRITY

[2] "So so" is good, very good, very excellent good; and yet it is not, it is but so. *As You Like It,* V,i,26.

[3] Happy in that we are not overhappy.
On Fortune's cap we are not the very button. *Hamlet,* II,ii,231. (Guildenstern describing the relative contentment felt by himself and his friend Rosencrantz.)

See also FAINT PRAISE.

MEMORY

[4] The memory be green. *Hamlet,* I,ii,2.

[5] 'Tis in my memory locked,
And you yourself shall keep the key of it. *Hamlet,* I,iii,85.

[6]   Remember thee?
Ay, thou poor ghost, whiles memory holds a seat
In this distracted globe. Remember thee?
Yea, from the table of my memory
I'll wipe away all trivial fond records,
. . .
And thy commandment all alone shall live
Within the book and volume of my brain. *Hamlet,* I,v,97,102.

[7] There's rosemary, that's for remembrance. *Hamlet,* IV,v,174. (More at PLANTS AND FLOWERS.)

[8] I'll note you in my book of memory. *Henry VI, Part One,* II,iv,101.

[9]   Memory, the warder of the brain. *Macbeth,* I,vii,65.

[10] I cannot but remember such things were,
That were most precious to me. *Macbeth,* IV,iii,222. (Macduff, while vowing to take revenge for the murder of his wife and children, still cannot put grief and memory aside. More at EMOTIONS.)

[11] I summon up remembrance of things past. *Sonnet 30,* 2. (More at PAST, THE.)

¹ Let us not burden our remembrance with
A heaviness that's gone. *The Tempest,* V,i,199.

See also PAST, THE.

MEN

² Think you there was or might be such a man
As this I dreamt of? *Antony and Cleopatra,* V,ii,93. (Cleopatra concluding her impassioned epitaph to Antony; see EPITAPHS.)

³ We'll have a swashing and a martial outside,
As many other mannish cowards have. *As You Like It,* I,iii,118. (Rosalind, counting on a male disguise and a bold manner to see her and her cousin safely through the Forest of Arden.)

⁴ You a man! You lack a man's heart. *As You Like It,* IV,iii,164. (Oliver to the disguised Rosalind. She readily confesses to this failing.)

⁵ Man, more divine, the master of all these,
Lord of the wide world and wild watery seas. *The Comedy of Errors,* II,i,20. (*These* in the first line refers to the world's creatures. In context it seems that by *man* Shakespeare does not mean mankind including women. Four lines later, he adds "masters to their females, and their lords.")

⁶   A man's life is a tedious one. *Cymbeline,* III,vi,1.

⁷ He was a man, take him for all in all,
I shall not look upon his like again. *Hamlet,* I,ii,187. (Hamlet speaking of his dead father.)

⁸ If it be man's work, I'll do it. *King Lear,* V,iii,40. (The captain agreeing to murder Cordelia.)

⁹ Sigh no more, ladies, sigh no more,
Men were deceivers ever,
One foot in sea, and one on shore,
To one thing constant never. *Much Ado About Nothing,* II,iii,62.

¹⁰ What a pretty thing man is when he goes in his doublet and hose and leaves off his wit! *Much Ado About Nothing,* V,i,198.

¹¹   There's no trust,
No faith, no honesty in men; all perjured,
All forsworn, all naught, all dissemblers. *Romeo and Juliet,* III,ii,85. (Juliet's nurse speaks. Her feelings toward men are somewhat confused. Her next lines are "Ah, where's my man? Give me some *aqua vitae.* / These griefs, these woes, these sorrows make me old." The warm if muddleheaded

character of the nurse is not in the earliest sources of the play, which date at least as far back as a story by Masuccio Salernitano, written in 1476. The nurse was added in *The Tragicall Historeye of Romeus and Juliet,* a poem by Arthur Brooke, or Broke, published in 1562. Brooke's nurse was very much the same sort of person as the nurse in Shakespeare's version.)

¹   Were man
But constant, he were perfect! *The Two Gentlemen of Verona,* V,iv,110. (In this context, *constant* means "faithful" in love.)

See also HUMAN NATURE; MARRIAGE; MEN AND WOMEN; SOLDIERS.

MEN AND WOMEN

² I must comfort the weaker vessel, as doublet and hose ought to show itself courageous to petticoat. *As You Like It,* II,iv,5. (Rosalind, disguised as a man, comforts her cousin Celia.)

³ Men's vows are women's traitors! *Cymbeline,* III,iv,54.

⁴ Be something scanter of your maiden presence. *Hamlet,* I,iii,121. (Polonius warning his daughter, Ophelia, to stay away from Hamlet. "With a larger tether may he walk / Than may be given you," Polonius explains, l.125.)

⁵   When a world of men
Could not prevail with all their oratory,
Yet hath a woman's kindness overruled. *Henry VI, Part One,* II,ii,48.

⁶ Would it not grieve a woman to be overmastered with a piece of valiant dust? To make an account of her life to a clod of wayward marl? *Much Ado About Nothing,* II,i,60. (*Marl* means "earth." Beatrice is making the point that a man is in no way so special that a woman should have to answer to him.)

⁷   Have not we affections?
Desires for sport? and frailty? as men have?
Then let them use us well; else let them know,
The ills we do, their ills instruct us so. *Othello,* IV,iii,103. (Emilia speaks. Her husband is Iago.)

⁸ Women may fall when there's no strength in men. *Romeo and Juliet,* II,iii,80.

⁹ I will be master of what is mine own.
She is my goods, my chattels; she is my house,
My household stuff, my field, my barn,
My horse, my ox, my ass, my anything. *The Taming of the Shrew,* III,ii,229.

(Petruchio stating with a touch of farcical exaggeration the relative status of man and wife. See also quotes for *The Taming of the Shrew* under MARRIAGE.)

[1] I am ashamed that women are so simple
To offer war where they should kneel for peace,
Or seek for rule, supremacy, and sway,
When they are bound to serve, love, and obey. *The Taming of the Shrew,*
V,ii,161. (Lines like these have made it very difficult to produce this play
in recent years. See also MARRIAGE.)

[2]   Let still the woman take
An elder than herself: so wears she to him,
So sways she level in her husband's heart;
For, boy, however we do praise ourselves,
Our fancies are more giddy and unfirm,
More longing, wavering, sooner lost and worn,
Than women's are. *Twelfth Night,* II,iv,29. (The duke to Viola, who is
dressed as a boy. He is saying, "Let a woman always marry an older man.
Thus she will adapt to him and remain loved." Some editions use *won*
instead of *worn* in the next to last line.)

See also LOVE AND LOVERS; MARRIAGE; MEN; REJECTION; SEX; WOMEN.

MERCY

[3] No ceremony that to great ones 'longs,
Nor the king's crown, nor the deputed sword,
The marshal's truncheon, nor the judge's robe,
Become them with one half so good a grace
As mercy does. *Measure for Measure,* II,ii,59.

[4] How shalt thou hope for mercy, rendering none? *The Merchant of Venice,*
IV,i,88. (The duke of Venice to Shylock.)

[5] The quality of mercy is not strained;
It droppeth as the gentle rain from heaven
Upon the place beneath. It is twice blest;
It blesseth him that gives and him that takes.
'Tis mightiest in the mightiest; it becomes
The thronèd monarch better than his crown.
His scepter shows the force of temporal power,
The attribute to awe and majesty,
Wherein doth sit the dread and fear of kings;
But mercy is above this sceptered sway;
It is enthronèd in the hearts of kings,

It is an attribute to God himself,
And earthly power doth then show likest God's
When mercy seasons justice. *The Merchant of Venice,* IV,i,183. (In the first
line, *strained* means "forced," "compelled." This is Portia pleading for the
life of Antonio, in one of the best-known passages in world literature.)

1   We do pray for mercy,
And that same prayer doth teach us all to render
The deeds of mercy. *The Merchant of Venice,* IV,i,199. (From Portia's great
speech on the quality of mercy. See above.)

2 Mercy but murders, pardoning those that kill. *Romeo and Juliet,* III,i,199.

3 Nothing emboldens sin so much as mercy. *Timon of Athens,* III,v,3. (Spoken by an unpleasant Athenian senator. Alcibiades quickly responds, "Pity is the virtue of the law," l.8.)

4 Sweet mercy is nobility's true badge. *Titus Andronicus,* I,i,119.

See also FORGIVENESS; KINDNESS; PUNISHMENT.

MIDDLE AGE

5 You cannot call it love, for at your age
The heyday in the blood is tame, it's humble,
It waits upon the judgment. *Hamlet,* III,iv,69. (Hamlet to his mother.)

6 Your lordship, though not clean past your youth, hath yet some smack of
an age in you, some relish of the saltness of time in you. *Henry IV, Part
Two,* I,ii,99. (A cheeky remark by Falstaff to the Chief Justice.)

7   I am declined
Into the vale of years. *Othello,* III,iii,264. (Othello speaks.)

8   Tis not hard, I think,
For men as old as we to keep the peace. *Romeo and Juliet,* I,ii,2. (Capulet
speaks.)

9 When forty winters shall besiege thy brow,
And dig deep trenches in thy beauty's field,
Thy youth's proud livery, so gazed on now,
Will be a tottered weed of small worth held. *Sonnet 2,* 1.

See also EXPERIENCE; MATURITY; OLD AGE.

MILITARY, THE.   See DEFENSE; SOLDIERS; WAR.

MIND

1   Men's judgments are
A parcel of their fortunes. *Antony and Cleopatra*, III,iii,31. (One's judgment is part of one's fate, or fortune. More at FORTUNE.)

2 In my mind's eye, Horatio. *Hamlet*, I,ii,185.

3 All things are ready, if our minds be so. *Henry V*, IV,iii,71. (The king at the outset of the battle of Agincourt.)

4   The tempest in my mind
Doth from my senses take all feeling else,
Save what beats there. *King Lear*, III,iv,12. (Lear, tormented by mental pain, scarcely perceives the heavy wind and rain buffeting him. He is aware only of the storm within.)

5 These are begot in the ventricle of memory, nourished in the womb of *pia mater*, and delivered upon the mellowing of occasion. *Love's Labor's Lost*, IV,ii,69. (*These*—the subject—refers to ideas and fancies in the mind of the speaker, Holofernes. The *ventricle of memory* was supposed to be a part of the brain; the *pia mater* is the membrane around the brain.)

6   'Tis the mind that makes the body rich. *The Taming of the Shrew*, IV,iii,170. (More at VIRTUE.)

7 In nature there's no blemish but the mind. *Twelfth Night*, III,iv,379. (More at VIRTUE.)

See also BRAIN; IMAGINATION; INSPIRATION; MADNESS; THOUGHT.

MIRACLES

8 They say miracles are past. *All's Well That Ends Well*, II,iii,1. (Thomas Carlyle, however, exclaimed, "The Age of Miracles is forever here!" in his *History of the French Revolution*, 1837.)

MISANTHROPY.   See HATE.

MISFORTUNE.   See ADVERSITY; FORTUNE; HUNGER; INJUSTICE; POVERTY; TYRANNY.

MISTAKES

9   This must be patched
With cloth of any color. *Coriolanus*, III,i,251.

10 O hateful Error. *Julius Caesar*, V,iii,67.

¹ It is not so; thou hast misspoke, misheard. *King John,* II,ii,4. (Misspeaking: a disorder that afflicts public figures.)

² Like a fair house built on another man's ground. *The Merry Wives of Windsor,* II,ii,216. (An enterprise doomed from the beginning.)

³ Alas, 'tis true I have gone here and there
And made myself a motley to the view,
Gored my own thoughts, sold cheap what is most dear,
Made old offenses of affections new. *Sonnet 110,* 1. (*Motley* is a clown's costume.)

See also FAILINGS.

MONEY

⁴   He that wants money, means, and content is without three good friends. *As You Like It,* III,ii,24.

⁵   'Tis gold
Which buys admittance. *Cymbeline,* II,iii,69. (The passage concludes, "What / Can it not do and undo," l.74.)

⁶ Thrift, thrift, Horatio. *Hamlet,* I,ii,180. (More at MARRIAGE.)

⁷ Neither a borrower nor a lender be. *Hamlet,* I,iii,75. (More at WISDOM, WORDS OF.)

⁸   In the fatness of these pursy times
Virtue itself of vice must pardon beg. *Hamlet,* III,iv,154. (*Pursy* means "bloated.")

⁹ I can get no remedy against this consumption of the purse.
Borrowing only lingers and lingers it out, but the disease is
incurable. *Henry IV, Part Two,* I,ii,246. (Falstaff bemoaning his chronic lack of funds.)

¹⁰ How quickly nature falls into revolt
When gold becomes her object! *Henry IV, Part Two,* IV,v,65. (The king referring to what he imagines to be his son Hal's intention to depose him; see also CHILDREN.)

¹¹ Bell, book, and candle shall not drive me back
When gold and silver becks me to come on. *King John,* III,ii,22. (Bell, book, and candle were used in the ceremony of excommunication. Closing the book signified death. The candle, representing the soul, was extinguished by throwing it to the ground. The bell was tolled as if a person had died.)

1   Distribution should undo excess,
And each man have enough. *King Lear*, IV,i,72.

2   Superfluity comes sooner by white hairs, but competency lives longer.
The Merchant of Venice, I,ii,8. (*Superfluity* means "great wealth." *Competency* means "adequate wealth.")

3 My daughter! O my ducats! O my daughter!
Fled with a Christian! O my Christian ducats!
Justice! The law! My ducats and my daughter!
A sealèd bag, two sealèd bags of ducats,
Of double ducats, stolen from me by my daughter! *The Merchant of Venice*,
II,viii,15. (Shylock discovering the elopement of his daughter, Jessica.
Similar to the passage in Christopher Marlowe's *The Jew of Malta*, when
Barabas's daughter, Abigail, throws money to him from his secret horde:
"O girl! O gold! O beauty! O my bliss!")

4 You take my house, when you do take the prop
That doth sustain my house. You take my life
When you do take the means whereby I live. *The Merchant of Venice*,
IV,i,374. (Shylock commenting on the proposed confiscation of his savings. Without money, of course, he could not continue in the business of
making loans.)

5 Seven hundred pounds and possibilities is goot [good] gifts. *The Merry
Wives of Windsor*, I,i,62. (Evans speaking of Mistress Page's fiscal appeal.)

6 O, what a world of vile ill-favored faults
Looks handsome in three hundred pounds a year. *The Merry Wives of
Windsor*, III,iv,32. (Mistress Page speaking slightingly of Slender, a young
man chosen for her by her father.)

7 Put money in thy purse. *Othello*, I,iii,335. (Iago's advice.)

8   Saint-seducing gold. *Romeo and Juliet*, I,i,217.

9   Nothing comes amiss so money comes withal. *The Taming of the
Shrew*, I,ii,80. (Grumio agreeing with Petruchio's determination to "wive
it wealthily in Padua," l.74; see MARRIAGE. *Withal* means "with it.")

10   The dog coins gold. *Timon of Athens*, II,i,6.

11   The learned pate
Ducks to the golden fool. *Timon of Athens*, IV,iii,17.

12   We'll do anything for gold. *Timon of Athens*, IV,iii,151. (Admitted by
a frank "brace of harlots," l.81.)

13 Win her with gifts, if she respect not words. *The Two Gentlemen of Verona*,
III,i,89.

[1] This is fairy gold, boy, and 'twill prove so. *The Winter's Tale,* III,iii,122. (The reference is to the gold hoarded by fairies, which must be kept secret. The shepherd who speaks has found the gold left with an infant, whom he calls a "changeling," fairies being reputed to steal children and leave lesser substitutes in their place. The child is Perdita, the daughter of the king and queen of Sicily.)

See also BUSINESS; CONSPICUOUS CONSUMPTION; LUXURY; POVERTY; RICH, THE; RICH AND POOR; SELF-INTEREST; SUCCESS.

MOON, THE

[2]   The moist star,
Upon whose influence Neptune's empire stands,
Was sick almost to doomsday with eclipse. *Hamlet,* I,i,118. (From a passage in which Horatio speaks of the portents preceding Caesar's death. See OMENS, the note on *Hamlet,*I,i,112.)

[3] How sweet the moonlight sleeps upon this bank! *The Merchant of Venice,* V,i,55. (The quote continues at MUSIC.)

[4] Ill met by moonlight, proud Titania. *A Midsummer Night's Dream,* II,i,60.

[5] A calendar, a calendar! Look in the almanac; find out moonshine, find out moonshine. *A Midsummer Night's Dream,* III,i,53. (Bottom in answer to Quince's question as to whether the moon will shine the night that they put on their play.)

[6]   It is the very error of the moon.
She comes more nearer earth than she was wont
And makes men mad. *Othello,* V,ii,108. (Othello, on the verge of murdering Desdemona, reacts to news of a fatal duel. The *error of the moon* is a wandering from its course closer to earth.)

[7] O, swear not by the moon, the inconstant moon,
That monthly changes in her circle orb. *Romeo and Juliet,* II,ii,109. (More at PROMISES.)

[8]   The moon's an arrant thief,
And her pale fire she snatches from the sun. *Timon of Athens,* IV,iii,444. (Shakespeare drew on astronomy often for images. The novelist Vladimir Nabokov used this Shakespearean passage in the title *Pale Fire.*)

See also NIGHT.

MORALITY

[9] Virtue itself turns vice, being misapplied,
And vice sometime by action dignified. *Romeo and Juliet,* II,iii,21.

¹   These moral laws
Of nature and of nations speak aloud. *Troilus and Cressida,* II,ii,184.

See also CONSCIENCE; ENDS AND MEANS; EVIL; VIRTUE.

MORNING

² Hark, hark, the lark at heaven's gate sings,
And Phoebus gins arise,
His steeds to water at those springs
On chaliced flowers that lies;
And winking Mary-buds begin
To ope their golden eyes.
With every thing that pretty is,
My lady sweet, arise. *Cymbeline,* II,iii,20. (*Phoebus* is Phoebus Apollo, the
sun god. He drives the chariot of the sun across the sky. *Winking Mary-buds* are closed marigolds.)

³ But look, the morn in russet mantle clad
Walks o'er the dew of yon high eastward hill. *Hamlet,* I,i,166.

⁴ The glowworm shows the matin to be near. *Hamlet,* I,v,89.

⁵ The country cocks do crow, the clocks do toll. *Henry V,* IV,Chorus,15.

⁶ It was the lark, the herald of the morn. *Romeo and Juliet,* III,v,6. (Juliet has
tried to persuade Romeo that the bird call they have just heard is of a
nightingale and thus he can stay longer in her bed. But here he tells her
it was a lark. The quote continues below.)

⁷   What envious streaks
Do lace the severing clouds in yonder East.
Night's candles are burnt out, and jocund day
Stands tiptoe on the misty mountaintops. *Romeo and Juliet,* III,v,7. (It is
undeniably day; see above. Romeo must flee or be killed. "More light and
light it grows," Juliet admits, l.35, and he answers, "More light and
light—more dark and dark our woes," l.36.)

⁸ Full many a glorious morning have I seen
Flatter the mountain tops with sovereign eye,
Kissing with golden face the meadows green,
Gilding pale streams with heavenly alchemy. *Sonnet 33,* 1.

⁹ The hunt is up, the morn is bright and gray,
The fields are fragrant, and the woods are green. *Titus Andronicus,* II,ii,1.

MORTALITY

¹ A man may fish with the worm that hath eat of a king, and eat of the fish that hath fed of that worm. *Hamlet,* IV,iii,27.

²   Alas, poor Yorick! I knew him, Horatio, a fellow of infinite jest, of most excellent fancy. He hath borne me on his back a thousand times. And now how abhorred in my imagination it is! My gorge rises at it. Here hung those lips that I have kissed I know not how oft. Where be your gibes now? Your gambols, your songs, your flashes of merriment that were wont to set the table on a roar? Not one now to mock your own grinning? Quite chapfallen? *Hamlet,* V,i,185. (*Chapfallen* means "down in the mouth." In these few affectionate lines, Shakespeare created here a memorable character. Yorick is said to have been modeled on the famous actor Richard Tarlton, the clown of the Queen's Men company. After this speech, Hamlet continues to contemplate death, asking Horatio, "Dost thou think Alexander [the Great] looked of this fashion in the earth?" l.199. Horatio answers, "Even so." "And smelt so? Pah!" "Even so, my lord." Then see below.)

³ To what base uses we may return, Horatio!
Why may not the imagination trace the noble dust of
Alexander till 'a find it stopping a bunghole? *Hamlet,* V,i,204.

⁴ Imperious Caesar, dead and turned to clay,
Might stop a hole to keep the wind away. *Hamlet,* V,i,215.

⁵ We cannot hold mortality's strong hand. *King John,* IV,ii,82. (For *hold* read "hold back," or "restrain.")

⁶   It smells of mortality. *King Lear,* IV,vi,135. (Thus Lear explains wiping his hand before giving it to Gloucester to kiss.)

⁷   Everything that grows
Holds in perfection but a little moment. *Sonnet 15,* 1.

⁸ Shall I compare thee to a summer's day?
Thou art more lovely and more temperate.
Rough winds do shake the darling buds of May,
And summer's lease hath all too short a date. *Sonnet 18,* 1. (Shakespeare is urging his friend and patron, usually identified as the earl of Southampton—a fair, almost pretty young man—to remember that beauty fades quickly. "But thy eternal summer shall not fade," Shakespeare promises, l.9—it will live through Shakespeare's verse and, if Southampton marries, through his children.)

See also DEATH; DECLINE; ENTROPY; LIFE; NATURE.

MURDER.   See CRIME; EVIL; VIOLENCE.

MUSIC

[1] Give me some music: music, moody food
Of us that trade in love. *Antony and Cleopatra,* II, v,1.

[2] I can suck melancholy out of a song as a weasel sucks eggs. *As You Like It,* II,v,10. (Said by "melancholy Jaques," a character who makes much of world-weariness. See also DANCE.)

[3] Beat thou the drum, that it speak mournfully. *Coriolanus,* V,vi,150. (The funeral march ending the play.)

[4] *Lady Percy.* Lie still, ye thief, and hear the lady sing in Welsh.
Hotspur. I had rather hear Lady, my brach, howl in Irish. *Henry IV, Part One,* III,i,236. (Banter between Hotspur and his wife. *Brach* means "female dog," "bitch.")

[5] Orpheus with his lute made trees,
And the mountain tops that freeze,
Bow themselves when he did sing. *Henry VIII,* III,i,3. (Shakespeare loved music. A. L. Rowse identified the "dark lady" of the sonnets as a member of a family of court musicians, and as an accomplished player on the virginal. See also below, the second quote from *Love's Labor's Lost.*)

[6] Warble, child, make passionate my sense of hearing. *Love's Labor's Lost,* III,i,1.

[7]   As sweet and musical
As bright Apollo's lute, strung with his hair. *Love's Labor's Lost,* IV,iii,341. (The metaphor describes love. A. L. Rowse maintains that the character who speaks here, Berowne, is modeled on Shakespeare himself, and Berowne's love, Rosaline, is based on the "dark lady" of the sonnets. She was, according to Rowse, the daughter of an Italian musician in the English court, and also a musician herself. More of this passage is given under LOVE.)

[8] The words of Mercury are harsh after the songs of Apollo. *Love's Labor's Lost,* V,ii,931. (Clever words are not welcome after sweet music. The last line of the play. More at TALK.)

[9]   Music oft hath such a charm
To make bad good, and good provoke to harm. *Measure for Measure,* IV,i,14.

[10]   The vile squealing of the wry-necked fife. *The Merchant of Venice,* II,v,30. (The *wry-necked fife* may refer to the musician, with his head

twisted to one side, or to the instrument, which at this time was made with
its mouthpiece set at an angle.)

1   A swanlike end,
Fading in music. *The Merchant of Venice,* III,ii,44. (The swan was reputed
not to sing until its death.)

2   Dulcet sounds in break of day. *The Merchant of Venice,* III,ii,51.

3 How sweet the moonlight sleeps upon this bank!
Here will we sit and let the sounds of music
Creep in our ears; soft stillness and the night
Become the touches of sweet harmony.
Sit, Jessica. Look how the floor of heaven
Is thick inlaid with patens of bright gold.
There's not the smallest orb which thou behold'st
But in his motion like an angel sings,
Still quiring to the young-eyed cherubins;
Such harmony is in immortal souls,
But whilst this muddy vesture of decay
Doth grossly close it in, we cannot hear it. *The Merchant of Venice,* V,i,55.
(Lorenzo and his beloved Jessica prepare to listen to music on a moonlit
night. While waiting for the performers to appear, Lorenzo speaks of the
music of the spheres, believed to be created by the motion of heavenly
bodies, and to be audible to angels and the immortal souls of the dead.
Touches of sweet harmony would be harmonious notes produced by touching, or plucking, an instrument; *patens* are metal plates or tiles; *quiring* is
making music.)

4 I am never merry when I hear sweet music. *The Merchant of Venice,* V,i,69.
(Shakespeare, a lover of music, understood its paradoxical effects.)

5 The man that hath no music in himself,
Nor is not moved with concord of sweet sounds,
Is fit for treasons, strategems, and spoils;
. . .
Let no such man be trusted. *The Merchant of Venice,* V,i,83.

6   Once I sat upon a promontory,
And heard a mermaid, on a dolphin's back,
Uttering such dulcet and harmonious breath,
That the rude sea grew civil at her song,
And certain stars shot madly from their spheres,
To hear the sea maid's music. *A Midsummer Night's Dream,* II,i,149.

[1] I have a reasonable good ear in music. Let's have the tongs and the bones. *A Midsummer Night's Dream,* IV,i,31. (Bottom to Titania. *Tongs* and *bones* are folk percussion instruments.)

[2]   I never heard
So musical a discord, such sweet thunder. *A Midsummer Night's Dream,* IV,i,120.

[3] An admirable musician. O, she will sing the savageness out of a bear! *Othello,* IV,i,190. (Othello speaking of Desdemona.)

[4]   How sour sweet music is
When time is broke, and no proportion kept;
So is it in the music of men's lives. *Richard II,* V,v,42. (For *time* read "tempo." The antonyms *sour* and *sweet* recur frequently in *Richard II;* see FOOD AND EATING.)

[5] This music mads me: let it sound no more. *Richard II,* V,v,61.

[6]   The lascivious pleasing of a lute. *Richard III,* I,i,13. (More at WAR AND PEACE.)

[7] This music crept by me upon the waters,
Allaying both their fury and my passion
With its sweet air. *The Tempest,* I,ii,392. (The music is Ariel's singing. The speaker is Ferdinand. *Passion* here means "suffering," in particular, Ferdinand's grief that his father has apparently drowned.)

[8]   The isle is full of noises,
Sounds and sweet airs that give delight and hurt not. *The Tempest,* III,ii,140. (Caliban speaking of the music made by Ariel. Although Caliban is uncivilized and dangerous, he is sensitive to this music.)

[9] Feast your ears with the music awhile. *Timon of Athens,* III,vi,33.

[10] If music be the food of love, play on,
Give me excess of it, that, surfeiting,
The appetite may sicken, and so die.
That strain again! It had a dying fall;
O, it came o'er my ear like the sweet sound
That breathes upon a bank of violets,
Stealing and giving odor. *Twelfth Night,* I,i,1.

N

NAMES

[1] I cannot tell what the dickens his name is. *The Merry Wives of Windsor,* III,ii,16.

[2] What's in a name? That which we call a rose
By any other word would smell as sweet. *Romeo and Juliet,* II,ii,43. (See also ROMEO AND JULIET.)

See also MANNERS, BAD; WORDS.

NATURE

[3] In Nature's infinite book of secrecy
A little I can read. *Antony and Cleopatra,* I,ii,9.

[4]   These trees shall be my books. *As You Like It,* III,ii,5. (In isolation the lines seem to express a sentiment similar to that of Saint Bernard's observation in Epistle 106: "What I know of the divine science and Holy Scripture I learnt in woods and fields." But in fact, Orlando intends to carve Arden's tree trunks with love poems to Rosalind. He also attaches notes to the trees—which is far better for the poor trees.)

[5]   Nature her custom holds,
Let shame say what it will. *Hamlet,* IV,vii,187. (Laertes commenting on his inability to hold back tears when he learns of the death of Ophelia.)

[6] Diseasèd nature oftentimes breaks forth
In strange eruptions. *Henry IV, Part One,* III,i,26. (Hotspur rejecting

Glendower's claim that comets and earthquakes at the time of Glendower's birth were miraculous signs of his special importance.)

[1] Nature's above art in that respect. *King Lear*, IV,vi,86. (The king, wandering and half demented, states that by birth he is above laws made to apply to most men. In particular, *that respect* refers to laws against minting coins.)

[2] To shallow rivers, to whose falls
Melodious birds sings madrigals;
There will we make our peds of roses,
And a thousand fragrant posies. *The Merry Wives of Windsor*, III,i,16. (This song is almost a direct quote from a song in *The Jew of Malta* by Christopher Marlowe, a poet and playwright to whom Shakespeare paid tribute throughout his life. For *peds* read "beds.")

[3] O, mickle is the powerful grace that lies
In plants, herbs, stones, and their true qualities;
For naught so vile that on the earth doth live
But to the earth some special good doth give. *Romeo and Juliet*, II,iii,15. (Friar Lawrence, an herbalist, speaks.)

[4]   I have seen the hungry ocean gain
Advantage on the kingdom of the shore,
And the firm soil win of the watery main,
Increasing store with loss and loss with store. *Sonnet 64*, 5. (A reference to a changing shoreline.)

[5] Methought the billows spoke and told me of it;
The winds did sing it to me; and the thunder,
. . . pronounced
The name of Prosper. *The Tempest*, III,iii,96. (Nature and the music of Ariel reveal to the king of Naples the depth of his guilt in conspiring to murder Prospero.)

[6] Though the seas threaten, they are merciful. *The Tempest*, V,i,178.

[7] He makes sweet music with the enameled stones. *The Two Gentlemen of Verona*, II,vii,28. (*He* refers to a brook.)

[8]   Thou met'st with things dying, I with things new born. *The Winter's Tale*, III,iii,112. (One character, Antigonus, has been killed by a bear. But almost simultaneously the shepherd who speaks here finds an abandoned baby girl. Unbeknownst to him, she is the princess of Sicilia. In this pastoral setting, nature's cycle, taking and giving life, dominates the plans and plots of mortals.)

[9] Yet Nature is made better by no mean
But Nature makes that mean; so over that art,

Which you say adds to Nature, is an art,
That Nature makes. *The Winter's Tale,* IV,iv,89. (For *mean* read "way" or
"means." Polixenes in a classic debate argues that one can change nature,
but only through nature. Specifically he is speaking of creating new varie-
ties through horticulture. "This is an art / ," he says, "Which does mend
nature . . . but / The art itself is nature." See also GARDENS.)

¹ The art itself is Nature. *The Winter's Tale,* IV,iv,97. (For the meaning see
above.)

²   What fine chisel
Could ever yet cut breath? *The Winter's Tale,* V,iii,78. (Art cannot create
life.)

See also COUNTRY LIFE; ENVIRONMENT; GARDENS; HUMAN NATURE; MORTAL-
ITY; PLANTS AND FLOWERS.

NECESSITY

³ Sink, or swim! *Henry IV, Part One,* I,iii,192. (In context this refers not to
the necessity to swim—as the phrase usually is used—but to a hopeless
situation in which one is done for whether one sinks or swims.)

⁴ We see which way the stream of time doth run,
And are enforced from our most quiet there
By the rough torrent of occasion. *Henry IV, Part Two,* IV,i,70. (Similar to
the "tide in the affairs of men" passage from *Julius Caesar;* see OPPORTU-
NITY. Here the Archbishop of York, né Richard Scroop, is making a case
for war against the king. The force of events, or "rough torrent of occasion," he argues unctuously, is pushing him to take up arms.)

⁵   Nature must obey necessity. *Julius Caesar,* IV,iii,226. (The necessity
to which Brutus refers is to get some sleep.)

⁶   Necessity's sharp pinch. *King Lear,* II,iv,210.

⁷ The art of our necessities is strange,
That can make vile things precious. *King Lear,* III,ii,70. (The vile thing
that now seems precious is a bed of straw in a hovel.)

⁸ There is no virtue like necessity. *Richard II,* I,iii,277. (John of Gaunt
advising his son Henry Bolingbroke to make the best of his banishment.
He recommends a positive attitude: "Think not the king did banish thee,
/ But thou the king," l.278. For Bolingbroke's impatient reaction, see
THOUGHT.)

⁹ Are you content . . .
To make a virtue of necessity? *The Two Gentlemen of Verona,* IV,i,61. (The
idea of making a virtue of necessity expressed here and just above dates

back to antiquity, e.g., "We give to necessity the praise of virtue," Quintilian, *De Institutione Oratoria.* Bartlett also cites quotes from Chaucer and Erasmus.)

NEED.   See NECESSITY; POVERTY.

NEGOTIATION

1   This offer,
. . . proceeds from policy, not love. *Henry IV, Part Two,* IV,i,145. (*Policy* refers to political and military considerations. Lord Mowbray is expressing doubt as to the good faith of an offer conveyed by the king. Defending the offer, the earl of Westmoreland asserts, "This offer comes from mercy, not from fear," l.148.)

2 I like not fair terms and a villain's mind. *The Merchant of Venice,* I,iii,176. (Bassanio expressing distaste for Shylock's bargain with Antonio; see CONTRACTS.)

NEWS

3 The nature of bad news infects the teller. *Antony and Cleopatra,* I,ii,96. (A recurring theme in Shakespeare's works.)

4 Though it be honest, it is never good
To bring bad news. *Antony and Cleopatra,* II,v,85.

5   I am dead;
Thou livest; report me and my cause aright. *Hamlet,* V,ii,339. (The dying Hamlet to Horatio. More of this final plea below.)

6 O God, Horatio, what a wounded name,
Things standing thus unknown, shall live behind me!
If thou didst ever hold me in thy heart,
Absent thee from felicity awhile,
And in this harsh world draw thy breath in pain,
To tell my story. *Hamlet,* V,ii,345.

7   Let me tell the world. *Henry IV, Part One,* V,ii,65. (Sir Richard Vernon, looking forward to announcing to the world the valor and, he hopes, success of the Prince of Wales—the future Henry V—on the battlefield of Shrewsbury.)

8   The first bringer of unwelcome news
Hath but a losing office, and his tongue
Sounds ever after as a sullen bell,
Remembered tolling a departing friend. *Henry IV, Part Two,* I,i,100. (In

Antigone, Sophocles put it, "Nobody likes the man who brings bad news.")

[1] *Constance.* Fellow, be gone! I cannot brook thy sight.
This news hath made thee a most ugly man.
Salisbury. What other harm have I, good lady, done,
But spoke the harm that is by others done? *King John,* II,ii,36.

[2]   If you be afeard to hear the worst,
Then let the worst unheard fall on your head. *King John,* IV,ii,135. (The Bastard, son of Richard I, to King John, who is complaining about the "ill tidings" and "ill news" the Bastard has brought.)

[3]   News fitting to the night,
Black, fearful, comfortless, and horrible. *King John,* V,vi,19.

[4] This news is old enough, yet it is every day's news. *Measure for Measure,* III,ii,232.

[5] What news on the Rialto? *The Merchant of Venice,* I,iii,35. (The Rialto is a bridge in Venice, formerly a commercial center. The same question appears in III,i,1.)

[6] Here are a few of the unpleasantest words
That ever blotted paper! *The Merchant of Venice,* III,ii,251.

[7] Thy honesty and love doth mince this matter. *Othello,* II,iii,246. (Othello assumes that Iago, out of loyalty to Cassio, is mincing the matter, that is, not reporting the whole truth of a brawl involving Cassio.)

[8] Speak of me as I am. Nothing extenuate,
Nor set down aught in malice. *Othello,* V,ii,338. (Othello, preparing for suicide, hopes to influence the news reports to follow. More at DEATHBED STATEMENTS.)

[9] What great ones do, the less will prattle of. *Twelfth Night,* I,ii,33.

See also MEDIA; RUMOR.

NIGHT

[10] In the dead waste and middle of the night. *Hamlet,* I,ii,198.

[11] 'Tis now the very witching time of night,
When churchyards yawn, and hell itself breathes out
Contagion to this world. *Hamlet,* III,ii,396.

[12]   The horrid night, the child of hell. *Henry V,* IV,i,276. (More at HIGH POSITION.)

¹ Deep night, dark night, the silent of the night,
The time of night when Troy was set on fire,
The time when screech-owls cry, and ban-dogs howl
And spirits walk, and ghosts break up their graves—
That time best fits the work we have in hand. *Henry VI, Part Two,* I,iv,17.
(The work in hand is a bit of witchcraft. It is difficult now to imagine the
fearful emotions associated with night when there were no electric lights,
no television, no means to call the police, no police, in fact, to call.)

² The gaudy, blabbing and remorseful day
Is crept into the bosom of the sea. *Henry VI, Part Two,* IV,i,1.

³ The moon is down. *Macbeth,* II,i,2.

⁴ There's husbandry in heaven.
Their candles are all out. *Macbeth,* II,i,4. (*Husbandry* means "thrift." The
reference is to the darkness of the night. See also above.)

⁵   Now o'er the one half-world
Nature seems dead, and wicked dreams abuse
The curtained sleep; witchcraft celebrates
Pale Hecate's offerings. *Macbeth,* II,i,49. (*Hecate* is the goddess of sor-
cery.)

⁶ 'Twas a rough night. *Macbeth,* II,iii,63. (An actor has to be careful not to
get a laugh with this line. It is said by Macbeth on the morning after he
has murdered Duncan. The body has not yet been found. Lennox is going
on about what a stormy night it was, full of strange sounds and eerie
portents.)

⁷ I must become a borrower of the night
For a dark hour or twain. *Macbeth,* III,i,26. (Banquo means he will not
complete his trip before nightfall.)

⁸ Come, seeling night,
Scarf up the tender eye of pitiful day,
And with thy bloody and invisible hand
Cancel and tear to pieces that great bond
Which keeps me pale! Light thickens, and the crow
Makes wing to th' rooky wood.
Good things of day begin to droop and drowse,
Whiles night's black agents to their preys do rouse. *Macbeth,* III,ii,46.
(Macbeth calling upon night to come and the murder of Banquo and his
son to be accomplished. *Night's black agents* are the murderers he has hired,
as well as beasts of prey in general. *Seeling* means "closing the eyes"; *scarf
up* means "blindfold." The reference to the *great bond* is unclear; it is

possibly Banquo's bond to life, or the bond of fate, as announced by the witches, or the bond between Macbeth and Banquo.)

[1] The moon shines bright. In such a night as this,
When the sweet wind did gently kiss the trees
And they did make no noise, in such a night
Troilus methinks mounted the Troyan walls,
And sighed his soul toward the Grecian tents
Where Cressid lay that night. *The Merchant of Venice,* V,i,1. (The first of several verses, with which Lorenzo and Jessica compete in talking of love.)

[2] The iron tongue of midnight hath told twelve.
Lovers, to bed; 'tis almost fairy time. *A Midsummer Night's Dream,* V,i,365.

[3]   The mask of night is on my face. *Romeo and Juliet,* II,ii,85. (Juliet to Romeo. See also below.)

[4] Spread thy close curtain, love-performing night. *Romeo and Juliet,* III,ii,5. (Juliet speaks. See also ROMEO AND JULIET.)

See also MOON, THE; STARS.

NOBILITY

[5] It is well done, and fitting for a princess
Descended of so many royal kings. *Antony and Cleopatra,* V,ii,326. (Charmian, herself on the verge of death, speaking of Cleopatra's suicide. She is answering one of Caesar's men who asked, "What work is here! Charmian, is this well done?" The dialogue is almost word for word from Plutarch's *Lives.*)

[6] His nature is too noble for the world. *Coriolanus,* III,i,254. (Menenius, speaking with distinct impatience of Coriolanus.)

[7] True nobility is exempt from fear. *Henry VI, Part Two,* IV,i,129.

[8] This was the noblest Roman of them all. *Julius Caesar,* V,v,68. (Antony speaking of Brutus. The passage continues at VIRTUE.)

[9] For he was great of heart. *Othello,* V,ii,357. (Cassio on Othello after Othello's suicide.)

See also GREATNESS; VIRTUE.

NOISE

[10] Silence that dreadful bell! It frights the isle
From her propriety. *Othello,* II,iii,174.

NONSENSE

1 Skimble-skamble stuff. *Henry IV, Part One,* III,i,153.

2 The eye of man hath not heard, the ear of man hath not seen, man's hand is not able to taste, his tongue to conceive, nor his heart to report, what my dream was. *A Midsummer Night's Dream,* IV,i,214. (Bottom tends to scramble his words. He seems to have in mind *I Corinthians* 2:9, "Eye hath not seen, nor ear heard, neither have entered into the heart of man the things which God hath prepared for them that love him.")

3 Thou wilt be condemned into everlasting redemption for this. *Much Ado About Nothing,* IV,ii,55. (Like Bottom—see above—Dogberry has a weakness for malapropisms.)

NOVELTY

4 All with one consent praise new borne gauds,
Though they are made and molded of things past,
And give to dust that is a little gilt
More laud than gilt o'erdusted. *Troilus and Cressida,* III,iii,175. (This tendency to overvalue the new and fashionable is the "touch of nature" common to all people; see HUMAN NATURE.)

See also ENNUI.

OATHS

[1] I call the gods to witness. *Timon of Athens,* I,i,137. (A traditional oath.)

See also PROMISES; TALK, PLAIN AND FANCY.

OCCULT, THE

[2] It faded on the crowing of the cock.
Some say that ever 'gainst that season comes
Wherein our Savior's birth is celebrated,
This bird of dawning singeth all night long,
And then, they say, no spirit dare stir abroad,
The nights are wholesome, then no planets strike,
No fairy takes, nor witch hath power to charm:
So hallowed and so gracious is that time. *Hamlet,* I,i,157. (*It* refers to the ghost of Hamlet's father. The rest is a charming Christmas legend. *Strike* here means "exert an evil influence"; *takes* means "bewitches.")

[3] *Glendower.* I can call spirits from the vasty deep.
Hotspur. Why, so can I, or so can any man;
But will they come when you do call for them? *Henry IV, Part One,* III,i,52.

[4]   How much he wrongs his fame,
. . .
To join with witches and the help of hell. *Henry VI, Part One,* II,i,16,18. (The duke of Bedford dismisses alliance with witches as shameful. The reference is to the dauphin's accepting aid from Joan of Arc.)

[1] The weïrd sisters, hand in hand,
Posters of the sea and land,
Thus do go about, about:
Thrice to thine, and thrice to mine,
And thrice again, to make up nine.
Peace! The charm's wound up. *Macbeth,* I,iii,32. (*Weird* here is marked with a diacritical mark over the "i," indicating that the word is pronounced in two syllables. *Weird* originally meant "fate," and the witches in the story were once the Fates. Shakespeare revived this almost extinct term. See Hugh Rawson's *Wicked Words* [Crown, 1989] for the relationship to *weirdo*.

This charm incidentally reflects real superstitions, with three and nine considered magic numbers. Samuel Johnson, for example, referred to an old Irish practice of turning three times to the right and digging a hole if one has taken a fall. The idea is that there is a bad spirit in the ground there. For more on numbers, see the quote from *The Merry Wives of Windsor* below. For ailments caused by *Macbeth*'s witches, see SICKNESS.)

[2] *First Witch.* Round about the caldron go;
In the poisoned entrails throw.
Toad, that under cold stone
Days and nights has thirty-one
Swelt'red venom sleeping got,
Boil thou first i' th' charmèd pot.
All. Double, double, toil and trouble;
Fire burn and caldron bubble.
Second Witch. Fillet of a fenny snake,
In the caldron boil and bake;
Eye of newt and toe of frog,
Wool of bat and tongue of dog,
Adder's fork and blindworm's sting,
Lizard's leg and howlet's wing,
For a charm of powerful trouble,
Like a hell-broth boil and bubble. *Macbeth,* IV,i,4. (*Sweltered venom,* etc. refers to venom sweated out during sleep; a *fenny snake* is a swamp snake; the next ingredients are the forked tongue of an adder and the sting of a legless lizard; a *howlet* is an owlet.)

[3] Show his eyes and grieve his heart;
Come like shadows, so depart! *Macbeth,* IV,i,110. (The witches summoning up Banquo and the kings of his family.)

[4] This is the third time; I hope good luck lies in odd numbers. . . . They say there is divinity in odd numbers, either in nativity, chance, or death.

The Merry Wives of Windsor, V,i,2. (An ancient notion, expressed, for example, by Pliny the Elder in his *Natural History:* "Why is it that we entertain the belief that for every purpose odd numbers are the most effectual?" Also by Virgil in his *Eclogues:* "The god delights in an odd number.")

[1] How now, mad spirit! *A Midsummer Night's Dream,* III,ii,4. (Oberon to Puck.)

[2]   I have bedimmed
The noontide sun, called forth the mutinous winds,
And 'twixt the green sea and the azured vault
Set roaring war. *The Tempest,* V,i,41. (From Prospero's farewell to his magic, "my so potent art," l.50. More below.)

[3]   This rough magic
I here abjure. *The Tempest,* V,i,50.

[4]   I'll break my staff,
Bury it certain fathoms in the earth,
And deeper than did ever plummet sound
I'll drown my book. *The Tempest,* V,i,54. (*The Tempest* was written near the end of Shakespeare's life, and many readers feel that here the playwright is bidding farewell to his own almost magical powers.)

[5] These are not natural events; they strengthen
From strange to stranger. *The Tempest,* V,i,227.

[6] Now my charms are all o'erthrown,
And what strength I have's mine own. *The Tempest,* Epilogue,1.

See also ANIMALS (*Macbeth,* I,i,8); APPARITIONS; FAIRIES; NIGHT; OMENS.

OCEANS.   See NATURE; SHIPS AND SAILING.

OLD AGE

[7] For we are old, and on our quickest decrees
The inaudible and noiseless foot of Time
Steals ere we can effect them. *All's Well That Ends Well,* V,iii,40.

[8] Wrinkles forbid! *Antony and Cleopatra,* I,ii,19.

[9]   Unregarded age in corners thrown. *As You Like It,* II,iii,42.

[10]   He that doth the ravens feed,
Yea, providently caters for the sparrow,
Be comfort to my age. *As You Like It,* II,iii,43. (The aged Adam, after

offering his life's savings to his young master, Orlando. He is referring to the Lord, who "giveth . . . to the young ravens which cry," *Psalms* 147:9, and who cares for the sparrow: "Are not five sparrows sold for two farthings, and not one of them is forgotten before God?" *Luke* 12:6.)

¹ Though I look old, yet I am strong and lusty. *As You Like It,* II,iii,47. (Adam speaks. More at DRINKING.)

² My age is as a lusty winter,
Frosty, but kindly. *As You Like It,* II,iii,52. (Adam again; see also above. He attributes his health in old age to abstaining from liquors in his youth.)

³ Oppressed with two weak evils, age and hunger. *As You Like It,* II,vii,132. (*Weak evils* means "evils causing weakness.")

⁴ Last scene of all,
That ends this strange eventful history,
Is second childishness and mere oblivion,
Sans teeth, sans eyes, sans taste, sans everything. *As You Like It,* II,vii,163. (From the "seven ages of man" speech; see LIFE.)

⁵ By misfortunes was my life prolonged
To tell sad stories of my own mishaps. *The Comedy of Errors,* I,i,119.

⁶ They say an old man is twice a child. *Hamlet,* II,ii,394. (A proverbial saying, which dates back at least as far as Aristophanes: "Old men are children for a second time," *The Clouds.*)

⁷ What doth gravity out of his bed at midnight? *Henry IV, Part One,* II,iv,295. (*Gravity* refers to a grave, old person.)

⁸ That reverend vice, that gray iniquity, that father ruffian, that vanity in years? *Henry IV, Part One,* II,iv,452. (From a string of insults laughingly directed at Falstaff by his good friend Hal, the Prince of Wales. *Vice, iniquity, and vanity* are evils all the worse in a person old enough to know better. Of course, his incorrigibility in old age is one of the man's most appealing qualities. See below and under FALSTAFF.)

⁹ If to be old and merry be a sin, then many an old host that I know is damned. *Henry IV, Part One,* II,iv,471.

¹⁰ How ill white hairs becomes a fool and jester! *Henry IV, Part Two,* V,v,49. (Hal, now Henry V, harshly dismissing his old friend Falstaff. See FALSTAFF.)

¹¹ I could be well content
To entertain the lag-end of my life
With quiet hours. *Henry IV, Part One,* V,i,23.

[1] My comfort is that old age, that ill layer-up of beauty, can do no more spoil upon my face. *Henry V,* V,ii,238. (Henry, courting Katherine, explains that he will look better as he gets older—he is just twenty-seven. *Layer-up* means "preserver.")

[2] 'Tis the infirmity of his age. *King Lear,* I,i,295. (Regan referring to her father's poor judgment. Yet she adds that he was never very wise: "He hath ever but slenderly known himself," l.295.)

[3] Sir, I am too old to learn. *King Lear,* II,ii,129. (Said ironically by Kent, who, unlike Lear, does have his wits about him.)

[4]   O, sir, you are old,
Nature in you stands on the very verge
Of his confine. You should be ruled, and led
By some discretion that discerns your state
Better than you yourself. *King Lear,* II,iv,145. (Horrible Regan to her father.)

[5]   A poor old man,
As full of grief as age. *King Lear,* II,iv,271. (Lear speaking of himself.)

[6]   Here I stand your slave,
A poor, infirm, weak, and despised old man. *King Lear,* III,ii,19.

[7] I am a very foolish fond old man,
Fourscore and upward, not an hour more nor less;
And, to deal plainly,
I fear I am not in my perfect mind. *King Lear,* IV,vii,60. (Lear to Cordelia. *Fond* means "foolish" or "simpleminded." A few moments later, he begs her, "Pray you now, forget and forgive. I am old and foolish," l.84. Lear's reluctant realization that he is old and unwise is a heartbreaking moment, for Goethe wrote, *"Ein alter Mann ist stets ein Konig Lear"*—"An old man is always a King Lear.")

[8] Ripeness is all. *King Lear,* V,ii,11. (In the summer of 1990, John R. Silber, president of Boston University, in a campaign speech for the Democratic gubernatorial nomination, startled voters with the statement: "Shakespeare was right when he said 'Ripeness is all.' When you've had a long life and you're ripe, then it's time to go." More at DEATH.)

[9] A good old man, sir; he will be talking. As they say, "When the age is in, the wit is out." *Much Ado About Nothing,* III,v,32.

[10] Hath love in thy old blood no living fire? *Richard II,* I,ii,10.

[11]   You and I are past our dancing days. *Romeo and Juliet,* I,v,33.

¹ Care keeps his watch in every old man's eye,
And where care lodges, sleep will never lie. *Romeo and Juliet,* II,iii,35.

² That time of year thou mayest in me behold
When yellow leaves, or none, or few, do hang
Upon those boughs which shake against the cold,
Bare ruined choirs where late the sweet birds sang. *Sonnet 73,* 1. (Shakespeare was about thirty when he penned these grim lines. Byron used a similar image in "On My Thirty-sixth Year" [!]—"My days are in the yellow leaf; / The flowers and fruits of love are gone; / The worm, the canker, and the grief / Are mine alone!")

³   I, an old turtle,
Will wing me to some withered bough, and there
My mate, that's never to be found again,
Lament till I am lost. *The Winter's Tale,* V,iii,132. (A *turtle* is a turtle dove. The widowed Paulina speaks.)

See also DECLINE; GENERATIONS; MIDDLE AGE; YOUNG IN SPIRIT, THE.

OMENS

⁴ This bodes some strange eruption to our state. *Hamlet,* I,i,69. (Horatio's reaction to the appearance of the king's ghost on the battlements.)

⁵ A mote it is to trouble the mind's eye. *Hamlet,* I,i,112. (Another reference to the king's ghost; see above. Horatio then goes on to describe omens before the death of Caesar: "A little ere the mightiest Julius fell, / The graves stood tenantless, and the sheeted dead / Did squeak and gibber in the Roman streets; / As stars with trains of fire and dews of blood, / Disasters in the sun; and the moist star, / Upon whose influence Neptune's empire stands, / Was sick almost to doomsday with eclipse," l.114.)

⁶ For many men that stumble at the threshold
Are well foretold that danger lurks within. *Henry VI, Part Three,* IV,vii,11. (Most of the omens in Shakespeare relate to comets, eclipses, and so on, for which we now have other explanations. But this is more of a commonsense observation that when something is wrong, we may be subconsciously aware of it. Or conversely, when we are slightly off-form, we are at risk. Carl Jung cites an African observation that if one trips leaving one's hut, one should best go back to bed.)

⁷ A falcon, towering in her pride of place,
Was by a mousing owl hawked at and killed. *Macbeth,* II,iv,12. (*Towering in her pride of place* means "soaring in the high regions that are her territory." A very explicit omen of the murder of Duncan. For a prescient owl, see ANIMALS, *Macbeth,* II,ii,3.)

[1] By the pricking of my thumbs,
Something wicked this way comes:
Open, locks,
Whoever knocks! *Macbeth,* IV,i,44. (The Second Witch speaks. The one
who comes is Macbeth.)

See also BAD TIMES (quote from *Richard II*); DANGER; FUTURE; OCCULT, THE.

OMISSION

[2]   Omittance is no quittance. *As You Like It,* III,v,133. (Failure to do
something is not a surrender of the right to do it later.)

OPINION OF OTHERS

[3] You have too much respect upon the world;
They lose it that do buy it with much care. *The Merchant of Venice,* I,i,74.
(Translation: You have too much regard for the world's opinion. You lose
the good opinion of others if you care too much about winning it.)

[4]   Fish not with this melancholy bait
For this fool gudgeon, this opinion. *The Merchant of Venice,* I,i,101. (The
speaker is Gratiano, who is also responsible for the quote above. Translated, his point is: Do not cultivate a melancholy speechlessness in order
to gain a reputation for silent wisdom. A *gudgeon* is a proverbially stupid
fish.)

[5] Opinion's but a fool that makes us scan
The outward habit for the inward man. *Pericles,* II,ii,55.

See also APPEARANCES; FASHION; PUBLIC, THE; REPUTATION.

OPPORTUNISM.   See SELF-INTEREST.

OPPORTUNITY

[6] Who seeks, and will not take when once 'tis offered,
Shall never find it more. *Antony and Cleopatra,* II,vii,85.

[7] Now might I do it pat. *Hamlet,* III,iii,73. (Hamlet comes upon Claudius
kneeling in prayer, and sees his chance to kill him. But he decides against
it, ostensibly because he does not want to give Claudius a chance to die
penitent and thus attain salvation.)

[8] There is a tide in the affairs of men
Which, taken at the flood, leads on to fortune;
Omitted, all the voyage of their life
Is bound in shallows and in miseries.

On such a full sea are we now afloat,
And we must take the current when it serves,
Or lose our ventures. *Julius Caesar,* IV,iii,217. (Brutus to Cassius, arguing that the enemy should be met at Philippi. Brutus won the argument, but lost the war. For a similar passage, see under NECESSITY, the "stream of time" speech from *Henry IV, Part Two,* IV,i,70.)

See also ADVERSITY; BOLDNESS; CHANCE; DECISION, MOMENT OF; FORTUNE; SUCCESS.

OPTIMISM AND PESSIMISM

[1] Against ill chances men are ever merry,
But heaviness foreruns the good event. *Henry IV, Part Two,* IV,ii,81. (The sententious bishop of York. The earl of Westmoreland comments, "Therefore be merry, coz, since sudden sorrow / Serves to say thus, 'Some good thing comes tomorrow,' " l.83.)

[2] Receive what cheer you may.
The night is long that never finds the day. *Macbeth,* IV,iii,239. (There is light at the end of the tunnel.)

[3] All may be well; but if God sort it so,
'Tis more than we deserve or I expect. *Richard III,* II,iii,36.

See also HOPE; THOUGHT.

ORDER

[4] Therefore doth heaven divide
The state of man in divers functions,
Setting endeavor in continual motion;
To which is fixèd, as an aim or butt,
Obedience; for so work the honeybees,
Creatures that by a rule in nature teach
The act of order to a peopled kingdom. *Henry V,* I,ii,183. (The *state of man* means "the kingdom of man." This passage continues with a portrait of a bee colony that is remarkable; a few more lines are given at ANIMALS.)

[5] The heavens themselves, the planets, and this center
Observe degree, priority, and place,
Insisture, course, proportion, season, form,
Office, and custom, in all line of order. *Troilus and Cressida,* I,iii,85. (*Insisture* means "regularity of position." This great speech by Ulysses reflects Shakespeare's own deep feeling that order, rank, and authority are necessary to the well-being of communities; see also below.)

[1]   Oh, when degree is shaked,
Which is the ladder to all high designs,
The enterprise is sick. *Troilus and Cressida,* I,iii,101. (*Degree* refers to rank,
authority, order.)

[2] Take but degree away, untune that string,
And hark what discord follows. *Troilus and Cressida,* I,iii,109.

See also ORGANIZATION; PLANNING.

ORGANIZATION

[3]   Many things, having full reference
To one consent, may work contrariously;
As many arrows loosèd several ways
Come to one mark, as many ways meet in one town,
As many fresh streams meet in one salt sea,
As many lines close in the dial's center,
So may a thousand actions, once afoot,
End in one purpose, and be all well borne
Without defeat. *Henry V,* I,ii,205.

See also ORDER; PLANNING.

ORIENT.   See EAST, THE.

OTHELLO

[4] Is this the noble Moor whom our full Senate
Call all in all sufficient? Is this the nature
Whom passion could not shake? whose solid virtue
The shot of accident nor dart of chance
Could neither graze nor pierce? *Othello,* IV,i,264. (Jealousy has destroyed
Othello. For more on Othello, see under LOVE AND LOVERS and DEATHBED
STATEMENTS.)

OTHERS, JUDGING.   See JUDGING OTHERS.

OTHERS, OPINION OF.   See OPINION OF OTHERS.

P

PARADOX

[1] Fair is foul, and foul is fair.
Hover through the fog and filthy air. *Macbeth,* I,i,10. (The witches speak in paradoxes. See also OCCULT, THE.)

PARENTS

[2]   The foolish overcareful fathers
Have broke their sleep with thoughts,
Their brains with care, their bones with industry. *Henry IV, Part Two,* IV,v,67.

[3]   'Tis prize enough to be his son. *Henry VI, Part Three,* II,i,20. (The future Richard III, in praise of his father, the rebellious duke of York.)

[4]   This is my true-begotten father. *The Merchant of Venice,* II,ii,35.

[5] It is a wise father that knows his own child. *The Merchant of Venice,* II,ii,76.

[6]   Be advised, fair maid.
To you your father should be as a god. *A Midsummer Night's Dream,* I,i,46. (See below for the daughter's response.)

[7] I would my father looked but with my eyes. *A Midsummer Night's Dream,* I,i,56.

[8] Thou art thy mother's glass, and she in thee
Calls back the lovely April of her prime. *Sonnet 3,* 9.

[1] Do not give dalliance too much the rein. *The Tempest,* IV,i,51. (Prospero to Ferdinand, whom he would like to have as a son-in-law, but still does not entirely trust.)

See also CHILDREN; FAMILY.

PARTIES.
See FUN AND FUN PEOPLE.

PARTNERS.
See ALLIES.

PASSION

[2]   These blazes, daughter,
Giving more light than heat . . .
. . .
You must not take for fire. *Hamlet,* I,iii,117,120. (Polonius warning his daughter, Ophelia, that Hamlet's passion is not likely to endure. The figure of speech is the reverse of the phrase used most commonly today. Shakespeare is referring to a fire of paper or dry kindling that suddenly blazes and quickly dies out. The heat is almost immediately dissipated.)

[3]   Give me that man
That is not passion's slave, and I will wear him
In my heart's core, ay, in my heart of heart,
As I do thee. *Hamlet,* III,ii,73. (Hamlet to Horatio.)

[4] The brain may devise laws for the blood, but a hot temper leaps over a cold decree. *The Merchant of Venice,* I,ii,17.

[5]   Violent fires soon burn out themselves.
Small showers last long, but sudden storms are short. *Richard II,* II,i,34.

[6] These violent delights have violent ends. *Romeo and Juliet,* II,vi,9.

[7] Affection! Thy intention stabs the center.
Thou dost make possible things not so held,
Communicat'st with dreams. *The Winter's Tale,* I,ii,138. (*Affection* means "passion" or "obsession." To paraphrase: Passion, your force goes to the center of things. You make possible things held to be impossible. You deal in dreams and illusions.)

See also AGGRESSION; ANGER; LOVE AND LOVERS; SEX.

PAST, THE

[8]   The golden world. *As You Like It,* I,i,115. (The "golden age.")

[9] We have seen the best of our time. *King Lear,* I,ii,122. (In other words: Our best days are past; bad times lie ahead.)

¹ O, call back yesterday, bid time return. *Richard II,* III,ii,69.

² When to the sessions of sweet silent thought
I summon up remembrance of things past,
I sigh the lack of many a thing I sought,
And with old woes new wail my dear Time's waste. *Sonnet 30,* 1.

³ Where is the life that late I led? *The Taming of the Shrew,* IV,i,134. (Sung by Petruchio—in Shakespeare's play and in Cole Porter's musical.)

⁴   The dark backward and abysm of time? *The Tempest,* I,ii,50.

⁵   What's past is prologue. *The Tempest,* II,i,257.

⁶   I feel
The best is past. *The Tempest,* III,iii,50. (This line and Prospero's farewell to his magical powers [see OCCULT, THE] are especially poignant when one recalls that this play was written toward the end of Shakespeare's life. It is perhaps the last play written completely by him, without a collaborator.)

See also DECLINE; HISTORY; MEMORY; REGRET; TIME.

PATIENCE

⁷ You tread upon my patience. *Henry IV, Part One,* I,iii,4.

⁸ I am as poor as Job, my lord, but not so patient. *Henry IV, Part Two,* I,ii,131. (Falstaff to the Chief Justice.)

⁹ Though patience be a tired mare, yet she will plod. *Henry V,* II,i,25.

¹⁰ Have patience and endure. *Much Ado About Nothing,* IV,i,253.

¹¹ How poor are they that have not patience!
What wound did ever heal but by degrees? *Othello,* II,iii,370.

¹² Patience, thou young and rose-lipped cherubin! *Othello,* IV,ii,62.

¹³ Be patient; for the world is broad and wide. *Romeo and Juliet,* III,iii,16.

¹⁴ She sat like Patience on a monument,
Smiling at grief. *Twelfth Night,* II,iv,115. (More at LOVE AND LOVERS.)

PATRIOTISM

¹⁵ Not that I loved Caesar less, but that I loved Rome more. *Julius Caesar,* III,ii,212. (Brutus explaining his motive in killing Caesar.)

See also BANISHMENT AND EXILE; ENGLAND AND THE ENGLISH; WAR.

PEACE

[1] The time of universal peace is near. *Antony and Cleopatra,* IV,vi,5.

[2] Then is there mirth in heaven
When earthly things made even
Atone together. *As You Like It,* V,iv,108. (*Made even* means "reconciled.")

[3] This peace is nothing but to rust iron, increase tailors, and breed ballad-makers. *Coriolanus,* IV,v,231.

[4]   We have made peace
With no less honor to the Antiates
Than shame to the Romans. *Coriolanus,* V,vi,79. (One of the early connections of the term *peace* with the concept of honor or dishonor. In *Safire's Political Dictionary,* Cicero is credited with the negative "peace with dishonor," dating from 49 B.C. Safire also cites Theobald, count of Champagne, from the twelfth century; Shakespeare, from the sixteenth century; Sir Kenelm Digby in the seventeenth century; Edmund Burke in the eighteenth; and, the most famous instance, Disraeli in the nineteenth. The Antiates, incidentally, were courageous warriors.)

[5] Rest, rest, perturbèd spirit. *Hamlet,* I,v,182.

[6]   The cankers of a calm world and a long peace. *Henry IV, Part One,* IV,ii,30. (Falstaff's scornful description of the ragtag soldiers he has forced into service.)

[7]   Sheathed their swords for lack of argument. *Henry V,* III,i,21. (The peace that arrives at the end of a long day's battle, when the victors sheathe their swords. From the "once more unto the breach" passage; see WAR.)

[8] I would give all my fame for a pot of ale, and safety. *Henry V,* III,ii,12. (An English soldier boy, tired and frightened by the French campaign.)

[9]   The naked, poor, and mangled Peace,
Dear nurse of arts, plenties and joyful births. *Henry V,* V,ii,34.

[10] Expect Saint Martin's summer, halcyon's days. *Henry VI, Part One,* I,ii,131. (The feast of Saint Martin of Tours is on November 11 and thus is associated with the season that we call Indian summer. The *halcyon,* a symbol of peace, is a mythical bird believed to breed on the waves of the sea, which subside for it. The phrase "halcyon days" dates back at least as far as Aristophanes and is used in his play *The Birds.* Edward Gibbon in *Decline and Fall of the Roman Empire* said that the phrase "was applied to a rare and bloodless week of repose.")

[11]   Blessèd are the peacemakers on earth. *Henry VI, Part Two,* II,i,35. (The king drawing on the Sermon on the Mount, *Matthew* 5:9.)

[1] In thy right hand carry gentle peace. *Henry VIII,* III,ii,445.

[2] Every man shall eat in safety
Under his own vine what he plants, and sing
The merry songs of peace to all his neighbors. *Henry VIII,* V,v,33. (This reference to a golden era of peace in the reign of Elizabeth I recalls similar biblical verses, including "They shall sit every man under his vine and under his fig tree; and none shall make them afraid," *Micah* 4:4. The translation is from the King James Version, named for Elizabeth's successor. *Henry VIII* was written to celebrate the marriage of Princess Elizabeth, James's daughter, to Prince Frederick, the Elector Palatinate. The play is believed to have been a collaborative effort, and this passage may have been written by John Fletcher, not Shakespeare. It continues: "Nor shall this peace sleep with her; but as when / The bird of wonder dies, the maiden phoenix, / Her ashes new create another heir / As great in admiration as herself," l.39. See also GREATNESS.)

[3] Keep up your bright swords, for the dew will rust them. *Othello,* I,ii,58. (Othello advising Roderigo and Brabantio to calm down and put away their swords.)

[4] Now is the winter of our discontent
Made glorious summer by this sun of York. *Richard III,* I,i,1. (Opening lines by the future Richard III. The *sun of York* is his brother, Edward IV, whose emblem was the sun. Richard and Edward were sons of Richard Plantagenet, duke of York.)

[5] This weak piping time of peace. *Richard III,* I,i,24. (Richard scorned the pleasures of peace. A *piping time* would be a time that shepherds played their pipes. See also WAR AND PEACE for other quotes from this opening soliloquy.)

[6] Incertainties now crown themselves assured,
And peace proclaims olives of endless age. *Sonnet 107,* 7. (A time of fear and uncertainty has ended.)

[7] The sea being smooth,
How many shallow bauble boats dare sail
Upon her patient breast. *Troilus and Cressida,* I,iii,34.

See also WAR AND PEACE.

PEOPLE. See DANGEROUS PEOPLE; DEMOCRACY; FUN AND FUN PEOPLE; HUMAN NATURE AND HUMANKIND; MEN AND WOMEN; PUBLIC, THE; WILD AND WANTON PEOPLE.

PERCEPTION

[1] Sometime we see a cloud that's dragonish,
A vapor sometime like a bear or lion,
A towered citadel, a pendant rock,
A forkèd mountain, or blue promontory
With trees upon't that nod unto the world
And mock our eyes with air. Thou hast seen these signs:
They are black vesper's pageants. *Antony and Cleopatra,* IV,xiv,2. (Reminiscent of Aristophanes, "Haven't you sometimes seen a cloud that looked like a centaur? / Or a leopard perhaps? Or a wolf? Or a bull?" *The Clouds.* Shakespeare used a similar theme with Hamlet teasing Polonius; see below. But here the mood is somber. Antony's reference to "black vesper's pageants" denotes twilight's mirages, and is identified with death. Antony goes on to say that he is like these mirages: "I . . . cannot hold this visible shape," l.13.)

[2] What error drives our eyes and ears amiss? *Comedy of Errors,* II,ii,185.

[3] *Hamlet.* Do you see yonder cloud that's almost in shape of a camel?
Polonius. By th' mass and 'tis, like a camel indeed.
Hamlet. Methinks it is like a weasel.
Polonius. It is backed like a weasel.
Hamlet. Or like a whale.
Polonius. Very like a whale. *Hamlet,* III,ii,384. (Similar to the passage in *Antony and Cleopatra;* see above.)

[4]   Grief has so wrought on him,
He takes false shadows for true substances. *Titus Andronicus,* III,ii,79. (Shakespeare was fascinated by hallucinations, false perceptions, and quasi-supernatural experiences.)

See also VISION.

PERSEVERANCE

[5]   Stand fast;
We have as many friends as enemies. *Coriolanus,* III,i,230.

[6]   Hold-fast is the only dog, my duck. *Henry V,* II,iii,53. (More at WISDOM, WORDS OF.)

[7]   I am a kind of burr; I shall stick. *Measure for Measure,* IV,iii,181.

[8]   Perseverance, dear my lord,
Keeps honor bright. To have done, is to hang
Quite out of fashion, like a rusty mail
In monumental mockery. *Troilus and Cressida,* III,iii,150.

See also DETERMINATION.

PESSIMISM.   See OPTIMISM AND PESSIMISM.

PHILOSOPHY

[1] Hast any philosophy in thee, shepherd? *As You Like It,* III,ii,21. (Here *philosophy* refers to learning. The shepherd in fact possesses good practical sense, and Touchstone, who posed this question, concludes that the shepherd is "a natural philosopher," l.32.)

[2] There are more things in heaven and earth, Horatio,
Than are dreamt of in your philosophy. *Hamlet,* I,v,166.

[3]   There is something in this more than natural, if philosophy could find it out. *Hamlet,* II,ii,375. (The something that is not quite natural is the way the people of Denmark idolize the new king, whom formerly they scorned.)

[4] Preach some philosophy to make me mad. *King John,* III,iii,51.

[5] To hold opinion with Pythagoras
That souls of animals infuse themselves
Into the trunks of men. *The Merchant of Venice,* IV,i,131. (Also in *Twelfth Night:* "*Clown.* What is the opinion of Pythagoras concerning wild fowl? *Malvolio.* That the soul of our granddam might happily inhabit a bird," IV,ii,51. These passages indicate that Greek philosophy was routinely taught to educated Elizabethans, and that students then, as now, tended to remember the curious doctrine of the transmigration of souls. For a quote on Greek moral philosophy, see under YOUTH, the passage from *Troilus and Cressida.*)

[6] Adversity's sweet milk, philosophy. *Romeo and Juliet,* III,iii,55. (The phrase is from Friar Lawrence. Philosophy proves no comfort at all to Romeo. "Hang up philosophy!" he answers, l.57, "Unless philosophy can make a Juliet.")

[7] How, how, how, how, chopped-logic? *Romeo and Juliet,* III,v,150. (Juliet's father cannot understand a word she is saying.)

[8] To suck the sweets of sweet philosophy. *The Taming of the Shrew,* I,i,28.

[9]   Young men, whom Aristotle thought
Unfit to hear moral philosophy. *Troilus and Cressida,* II,ii,166. (See this quote at YOUTH for an explanatory note.)

PITY

[10] We may pity, though not pardon thee. *The Comedy of Errors,* I,i,97.

[11]   Pity, like a naked newborn babe,
Striding the blast. *Macbeth,* I,vii,21. (More at CRIME.)

[1] But yet the pity of it, Iago. O Iago, the pity of it, Iago. *Othello,* IV,i,197. (Othello just before murdering Desdemona.)

[2] No beast so fierce but knows some touch of pity. *Richard III,* I,ii,71.

PLAIN AND FANCY TALK. See TALK, PLAIN AND FANCY

PLANNING

[3]   When we mean to build,
We first survey the plot, then draw the model.
And when we see the figure of the house,
Then must we rate the cost of the erection,
Which if we find outweighs ability,
What do we then but draw anew the model
In fewer offices, or at least desist
To build at all? *Henry IV, Part Two,* I,iii,41. (In the last two lines, *in fewer offices* means "with fewer kinds of rooms"; *at least desist to build* means "in the worst case, desist to build." The speaker is Lord Bardolph, likening preparation of armed rebellion to careful planning of a building. Nothing is to be left to "conjecture, expectation, and surmise," l.23—above all one must not rely on hope. See also HOPE and another quote from this passage at WAR.)

See also ORDER; ORGANIZATION; PRUDENCE.

PLANTS AND FLOWERS

[4] And winking Mary-buds begin
To ope their golden eyes. *Cymbeline,* II,iii,24. (More at MORNING. *Mary-buds* are marigolds.)

[5] A violet in the youth of primy nature,
Forward, not permanent, sweet, not lasting. *Hamlet,* I,iii,7.

[6] There's rosemary, that's for remembrance. Pray you, love, remember. And there is pansies, that's for thoughts. *Hamlet,* IV,v,174. (The association of rosemary with remembrance may have to do with the way it retains its flavor and scent throughout the winter; see *The Winter's Tale,* below. Also, there was a folk custom in which friends of a bride would give the groom a nosegay of rosemary, bound with gold silk or lace. See *Shakespeare's Flowers* by Jessica Kerr, illustrated by Anne Ophelia Dowden [T. Y. Crowell, 1969]. The pansies here are not the large blooms we know today, but rather Johnny-jump-ups, or heartsease, or love-in-idleness. The name *pansy* comes from the French *pensée,* meaning thought. For more on pansies, see below, *A Midsummer Night's Dream,* II,i,163. See also the next quote.)

[1] There's fennel for you, and columbines. There's rue for you, and here's some for me. We may call it herb of grace o' Sundays. O, you must wear your rue with a difference. There's a daisy. I would give you some violets, but they withered all when my father died. They say 'a made a good end. *Hamlet*, IV,v,179. (More from Ophelia, broken by grief. Fennel was symbolic of flattery and also figures in the proverb "Sow fennel, sow sorrow." Columbine, associated with ingratitude and faithlessness, is the emblem of deceived lovers. Rue is bitter, and is associated with repentance and forgiveness, therefore the reference to grace on Sunday. See also the quote from *Richard II*, below. The term *difference* is used in heraldry to denote coats of arms of different branches of a family. Ophelia here is addressing the king and queen. For some reason daisies, or day's eyes, were associated with dissembling. Ophelia also wore them when she drowned herself; see below. Violets are symbolic of faithfulness; see DEATH AND GRIEF, *Hamlet*, V,i,242.)

[2] Therewith fantastic garlands did she make
Of crowflowers, nettles, daisies, and long purples. *Hamlet*, IV,vii,168.
(*Crowflowers* are probably pink ragged robins, which grow in moist ground and are good for making wreaths. *Long purples* are evidently phallic in appearance, for in the following lines, the queen mentions that maidens call them dead men's fingers, but shepherds use a grosser term.)

[3] Sweets to the sweet! *Hamlet*, V,i,245. (See FAREWELLS.)

[4] Yet marked I where the bolt of Cupid fell.
It fell upon a little western flower,
Before milk-white, now purple with love's wound,
And maidens call it love-in-idleness. *A Midsummer Night's Dream*, II,i,165.
(*Love in idleness* means "love in vain." This is the wild pansy, or Johnny-jump-up, or heartsease, referred to in *Hamlet* as well; see above. It reputedly had aphrodisiac powers, and Oberon explains, "The juice of it on sleeping eyelids laid / Will make or man or woman madly dote / Upon the next live creature that it sees," l.170.)

[5] I know a bank where the wild thyme blows,
Where oxlips and the nodding violet grows,
Quite overcanopied with luscious woodbine,
With sweet musk roses, and with eglantine. *A Midsummer Night's Dream*, II,i,249. (More at FAIRIES.)

[6] So doth the woodbine the sweet honeysuckle
Gently entwist; the female ivy so
Enrings the barky fingers of the elm. *A Midsummer Night's Dream*, IV,i,45.
(Titania describing her caresses of Bottom.)

1   Here in this place
I'll set a bank of rue, sour herb of grace;
Rue, even for ruth, here shortly shall be seen,
In the remembrance of a weeping queen. *Richard II,* III,iv,104. (*Ruth*
means "pity." See also the note above on Ophelia and rue. The weeping
queen here is Isabel, wife of the doomed Richard II.)

2 "Small herbs have grace, great weeds do grow apace." *Richard III,* II,iv,13.
(*Grace* here means "virtue" or "good quality.")

3 Rough winds do shake the darling buds of May. *Sonnet 18,* 3. (More at
MORTALITY.)

4 The summer's flower is to the summer sweet. *Sonnet 94,* 9. (More at
VIRTUE.)

5 For you there's rosemary and rue; these keep
Seeming and savor all the winter long. *The Winter's Tale,* IV,iv,74. (See
also quotes from *Hamlet,* above.)

6   Here's flowers for you.
Hot lavender, mints, savory, marjoram,
The marigold that goes to bed with the sun,
And with him rises, weeping, these are flowers
Of middle summer, and I think they are given
To men of middle age. *The Winter's Tale,* IV,iv,103. (These flowers are all
spices, with a reputed tonic effect. Of course, they would be most common
in an English garden, not one in either Bohemia or Sicily [the locales of
The Winter's Tale]. The marigold mentioned here is the pot marigold, or
calendula, used as a spice and as medicine against small pox and measles.
It closes up at sunset. The phrase *rises weeping* means "rises dewy.")

7   Daffodils,
That come before the swallow dares, and take
The winds of March with beauty. *The Winter's Tale,* IV,iv,118.

See also GARDENS; SPRING.

PLEASURE

8 There's not a minute of our lives should stretch
Without some pleasure now. *Antony and Cleopatra,* I,i,46. (Antony to
Cleopatra.)

9 The gods are just, and of our pleasant vices
Make instruments to plague us. *King Lear,* V,iii,172. (*Pleasant vices* are
pleasurable vices.)

1   All delights are vain. *Love's Labor's Lost,* I,i,72. (More at WORK.)

2   Sweets grown common lose their dear delight. *Sonnet 102,* 12.

3   Sit by my side
And let the world slip. We shall ne'er be younger. *The Taming of the Shrew,*
Induction,ii,142.

4 No profit grows where is no pleasure taken. *The Taming of the Shrew,* I,i,39.
(More at EDUCATION.)

See also DESIRE; FUN AND FUN PEOPLE; HAPPINESS; LEISURE; SEX.

POETRY

5 This is the very false gallop of verses. *As You Like It,* III,ii,113.

6 When a man's verses cannot be understood . . . it strikes a man more dead
than a great reckoning in a little room. *As You Like It,* III,iii,11,13. (For
the implications of *a great reckoning in a little room,* see the quote from the
same passage at DEATH.)

7 Truly, I would the gods had made thee poetical. *As You Like It,* III,iii,14.

8   The truest poetry is the most feigning, and lovers are given to poetry.
As You Like It, III,iii,18. (Touchstone answering the question "Is poetry
a true thing?")

9 I had rather be a kitten and cry mew
Than one of these same meter ballad-mongers. *Henry IV, Part One,*
III,i,128. (*Meter ballad-mongers* were professional singers of doggerel bal-
lads.)

10   Mincing poetry.
'Tis like the forced gait of a shuffling nag. *Henry IV, Part One,* III,i,133.

11 Assist me some extemporal god of rhyme, for I am sure I shall turn sonnet.
Love's Labor's Lost, I,ii,181. (*Turn sonnet* means "write a sonnet.")

12 I had rather than forty shillings I had my Book of Songs and Sonnets here.
The Merry Wives of Windsor, I,i,191. (Said by the insipid Slender as
everyone else is settling down to eat and drink. The book was a popular
anthology published by Richard Tottel.)

13   As imagination bodies forth
The forms of things unknown, the poet's pen
Turns them to shapes, and gives to airy nothing
A local habitation and a name. *A Midsummer Night's Dream,* V,i,14. (More
at IMAGINATION. The phrase ending *a local habitation and a name* is a fine
summary of the creation of a vivid reality from imagined events.)

¹ No, I was not born under a rhyming planet. *Much Ado About Nothing,*
V,ii,40.

² Not marble, nor the gilded monuments
Of princes, shall outlive this powerful rhyme. *Sonnet 55,* 1.

³ Much is the force of heaven-bred poesy. *The Two Gentlemen of Verona,*
III,ii,72.

POLITICS

⁴ Equality of two domestic powers
Breed scrupulous faction. *Antony and Cleopatra,* I,iii,47. (*Scrupulous faction*
refers to fighting over every small issue.)

⁵   This thou shouldst have done,
And not have spoke on it. In me 'tis villainy,
In thee it had been good service. *Antony and Cleopatra,* II,vii,75. (Pompey
explaining the principle of deniability. Menas has just suggested that he,
Menas, murder Octavius Caesar, Antony, and Lepidus. Another basic rule
of politics follows below.)

⁶ Better to leave undone, than by our deed
Acquire too high a fame when him we serve's away. *Antony and Cleopatra,*
III,i,14. (Ventidius declining to pursue the Parthians, reasoning that An-
tony will be more envious of than pleased by a great victory in his absence.
See also AMBITION.)

⁷   You speak of the people
As if you were a god, to punish, not
A man of their infirmity. *Coriolanus,* III,i,80. (The *you* refers to Coriolanus,
a great warrior [see SOLDIERS] but a hopeless politician.)

⁸ This might be the pate of a politician, . . . one that would circumvent God.
Hamlet, V,i,79. (Hamlet speaking, in the gravedigging scene.)

⁹   This vile politician. *Henry IV, Part One,* I,iii,239. (The reference is to
Henry Bolingbroke, that is, Henry IV.)

¹⁰   Being daily swallowed by men's eyes,
They surfeited with honey and began
To loathe the taste of sweetness, whereof a little
More than a little is by much too much.
So, when he had occasion to be seen,
He was but as the cuckoo is in June,
Heard, not regarded. *Henry IV, Part One,* III,ii,70. (A warning on the
dangers of overexposure. Henry IV is reminding his scapegrace son, Hal,

that mixing with the common people and being constantly visible and accessible contributed to the downfall of Richard II.)

1 Be it thy course to busy giddy minds
With foreign quarrels. *Henry IV, Part Two,* IV,v,213. (Clever advice from the dying king to his son, the future Henry V.)

2 Hear him debate of commonwealth affairs,
You would say it hath been all in all in his study. *Henry V,* I,i,41. (The Archbishop of Canterbury wisely discerns brilliance in the new king. He continues, "Turn him to any cause of policy, [any matter of politics] / The Gordian knot of it he will unloose," l.45. King Gordias of Gordium, according to legend, tied the Gordian knot; the one who untied it was to rule Asia.)

3 Civil dissension is a viperous worm
That gnaws the bowels of the commonwealth. *Henry VI, Part One,* III,i,72.

4 Thou setter up and plucker down of kings. *Henry VI, Part Three,* II,iii,37. (The reference is to Richard Nevil, earl of Warwick, called historically the Kingmaker. There is another reference at III,iii,157: "Proud setter up and puller down of kings!" The American "kingmaker" was Mark Hanna, the Ohio industrialist who dominated Republican politics in the 1890s. William McKinley was one of his protégés.)

5   How can tyrants safely govern home,
Unless abroad they purchase great alliance? *Henry VI, Part Three,* III,iii,69. (For *purchase,* the precise translation is "obtain" or "arrange" by any means.)

6   When the lion fawns upon the lamb,
The lamb will never cease to follow him. *Henry VI, Part Three,* IV,viii,49.

7 Those that with haste will make a mighty fire
Begin it with weak straws. *Julius Caesar,* I,iii,107. (The "weak straws" are the people of Rome, easily incited to follow one strong man after another.)

8   You yourself
Are much condemned to have an itching palm,
To sell and mart your offices for gold
To undeservers. *Julius Caesar,* IV,iii,9. (Brutus bickering with his brother-in-law Cassius.)

9   Duty shall have dread to speak
When power to flattery bows? *King Lear,* I,i,149. (This is posed as a question: "Thinkest thou that duty shall have dread to speak . . ." etc. The speaker, Kent, goes on to explain that honor requires frankness even in

speaking to the powerful: "To plainness honor's bound / When majesty falls to folly," l.150.)

¹   Get thee glass eyes,
And, like a scurvy politician, seem
To see things thou dost not. *King Lear,* IV,vi,172. (*Glass eyes* are eyeglasses. There is another anachronistic reference to eyeglasses at I,ii,36; see under SHAKESPEAREAN SLIPS.)

² The caterpillars of the commonwealth,
Which I have sworn to weed and pluck away. *Richard II,* II,iii,165. (*Caterpillar* was a common term of abuse in Elizabethan times, as might be expected in a nation of gardeners.)

³   Banish me?
Banish your dotage, banish usury,
That makes the senate ugly. *Timon of Athens,* III,v,97. (Alcibiades' response when banished by the Athenian senate.)

See also BRIBERY; GOVERNMENT; HIGH POSITION: POWER; PUBLIC, THE; TAXES.

POOR, THE.   See POVERTY; RICH AND POOR.

POSITIVE THINKING.   See HOPE; OPTIMISM AND PESSIMISM; THOUGHT.

POSSESSIONS

⁴ An ill-favored thing, sir, but mine own. *As You Like It,* V,iv,59. (Touchstone referring to his bride-to-be, Audrey. In requesting a duke's permission to wed, it was prudent to understate the charms of one's intended. Nevertheless, Audrey's reputed homeliness is usually taken at face value, so to speak. Traditionally actresses in the role have been asked to eat—or at least nibble on—a turnip to project the appropriate earthy quality.)

⁵   Having nothing, nothing can he lose. *Henry VI, Part Three,* III,iii,152.

See also CONSPICUOUS CONSUMPTION; LUXURY; POVERTY; RICH AND POOR; VALUE.

POVERTY

⁶   Poor but honest. *All's Well That Ends Well,* I,iii,197. (Thus Helena describes her family.)

⁷   He that wants money, means, and content is without three good friends. *As You Like It,* III,ii,24.

¹ A king of shreds and patches. *Hamlet,* III,iv,103. (Hamlet refers to the ghost of his father. Sir William Gilbert's wandering minstrel describes himself as a "thing of shreds and patches," *The Mikado.*)

² I am as poor as Job, my lord, but not so patient. *Henry IV, Part Two,* I,ii,131. (Falstaff to the Chief Justice.)

³   Beggars mounted run their horse to death. *Henry VI, Part Three,* I,iv,127. (Identified as an adage. It is in fact one that takes less censorious forms. Note, for example, the German proverb "Set a beggar on horseback and he'll outride the devil." Also, from Robert Burton's *Anatomy of Melancholy,* "Set a beggar on horseback and he will ride a gallop.")

⁴   Prayers and wishes
Are all I can return. *Henry VIII,* II,iii,69. (Anne Bullen [Boleyn] referring to gifts given her by the king.)

⁵ Poor naked wretches, wheresoe'er you are,
That bide the pelting of this pitiless storm,
How shall your houseless heads and unfed sides,
Your looped and windowed raggedness, defend you
From seasons such as these? O, I have ta'en
Too little care of this! Take physic, pomp;
Expose thyself to feel what wretches feel. *King Lear,* III,iv,28. (Lear, abandoned and impoverished, realizes how little the powerful understand the suffering of the poor and homeless. *Take physic, pomp* means "take medicine to remedy your lack of understanding, you great and wealthy people.")

⁶ The naked truth of it is, I have no shirt. *Love's Labor's Lost,* V,ii,710. (The speaker is wearing wool underclothing for penance—or so he says—rather than a shirt.)

⁷   An honest exceeding poor man. *The Merchant of Venice,* II,ii,52.

⁸ Steeped me in poverty to the very lips. *Othello,* IV,ii,49.

⁹ Evermore thank's the exchequer of the poor. *Richard II,* II,iii,65. (Thanks are all that the poor have to offer.)

¹⁰ The world is not thy friend, nor the world's law;
The world affords no law to make thee rich. *Romeo and Juliet,* V,i,72. (Romeo to the needy apothecary, who, while selling Romeo poison, excuses himself, "My poverty but not my will consents," l.75. Romeo answers, "I pay thy poverty and not thy will.")

¹¹   He's poor, and that's revenge enough. *Timon of Athens,* III,iv,61.

¹ What an alteration of honor has desperate want made! *Timon of Athens,* IV,iii,470.

See also HUNGER; MONEY; POSSESSIONS; RICH AND POOR.

POWER

² Let Rome in the Tiber melt, and the wide arch
Of the ranged empire fall! Here is my space,
Kingdoms are clay. *Antony and Cleopatra,* I,i,33. (Antony renouncing imperial power to remain with Cleopatra.)

³ Small curs are not regarded when they grin,
But great men tremble when the lion roars. *Henry VI, Part Two,* III,i,18. (To *grin* is to bare one's teeth.)

⁴ You put sharp weapons in a madman's hands. *Henry VI, Part Two,* III,i,347. (Richard Plantagenet, duke of York, who recognizes that his ambition verges on madness, commenting on his good luck in having been handed an army for an Irish campaign.)

⁵ Why, what is pomp, rule, reign, but earth and dust?
And, live we how we can, yet die we must. *Henry VI, Part Three,* V,ii,27.

⁶   He's revengeful, and I know his sword
Hath a sharp edge. It's long and it may be said
It reaches far. *Henry VIII,* I,i,109. (The duke of Norfolk speaking of Cardinal Wolsey.)

⁷ The hearts of princes kiss obedience,
So much they love it; but to stubborn spirits
They swell, and grow as terrible as storms. *Henry VIII,* III,i,162.

⁸ The abuse of greatness is when it disjoins
Remorse from power. *Julius Caesar,* II,i,18.

⁹ A scepter snatched with an unruly hand
Must be as boisterously maintained as gained,
And he that stands upon a slipp'ry place
Makes nice of no vile hold to stay him up. *King John,* III,iii,135.

¹⁰   O, it is excellent
To have a giant's strength; but it is tyrannous
To use it like a giant. *Measure for Measure,* II,ii,107.

¹¹   Lions make leopards tame. *Richard II,* I,i,174.

¹² They that have the power to hurt and will do none. *Sonnet 94,* 1. (More at VIRTUE.)

[1] The eagle suffers little birds to sing
And is not careful what they mean thereby,
Knowing that with the shadow of his wings
He can at pleasure stint their melody. *Titus Andronicus,* IV,iv,84.

See also AMBITION; GREATNESS; HIGH POSITION; POLITICS; SUCCESS; TYR-ANNY.

PRACTICAL JOKES.   See JOKES.

PRAISE

[2] I will praise any man that will praise me. *Antony and Cleopatra,* II,vi,88. (Said by Enobarbus, a soldier and a plain speaker.)

[3]   Worse than the sun in March,
This praise doth nourish agues. *Henry IV, Part One,* IV,i,110. (Hotspur unhappy with Sir Richard Vernon's glowing description of the young Prince Hal, Hotspur's rival. The figure of speech is based on the belief that the spring sun fostered flu symptoms. In spring in fifteenth-century England, people probably did suffer from lowered resistance, because of a limited and meager winter diet.)

[4] Our praises are our wages. *The Winter's Tale,* I,ii,94. (Hermione speaking of the importance of kindness in winning loyalty.)

See also FLATTERY.

PRAISE, FAINT.   See FAINT PRAISE.

PRAYER

[5]   We, ignorant of ourselves,
Beg often our own harms, which the wise powers
Deny us for our good; so find we profit
By losing of our prayers. *Antony and Cleopatra,* II,i,5.

[6] My words fly up, my thoughts remain below.
Words without thoughts never to heaven go. *Hamlet,* III,iii,97. (Claudius, unable to pray. Macbeth also finds he cannot pray; see below.)

[7] Watch tonight, pray tomorrow. *Henry IV, Part One,* II,iv,278. (Falstaff is alluding to *Matthew* 26:41, "Watch and pray, that ye enter not into temptation." Falstaff would never willingly endure a night without temptation.)

[8] I had most need of blessing, and "Amen"
Stuck in my throat. *Macbeth,* II,ii,31. (Another Shakespearean king—Claudius—also found that he could not pray. See *Hamlet* above.)

¹ His worst fault is that he is given to prayer; he is something peevish that way. *The Merry Wives of Windsor,* I,iv,12.

PRAYERS

² Angels and ministers of grace defend us! *Hamlet,* I,iv,39. (More at APPARI-TIONS.)

³   Nymph, in thy orisons
Be all my sins remembered. *Hamlet,* III,i,89. (Hamlet speaking; the nymph is Ophelia.)

⁴   Flights of angels sing thee to thy rest. *Hamlet,* V,ii,361. (More at HAMLET.)

⁵ O God of battles, steel my soldiers' hearts. *Henry V,* IV,i,294. (More at SOLDIERS.)

⁶ Pardon me, God! I knew not what I did. *Henry VI, Part Three,* II,v,69. (The prayer of a son who has accidentally killed his own father in battle.)

⁷ Go with me like good angels to my end;
And as the long divorce of steel falls on me,
Make of your prayers one sweet sacrifice,
And lift my soul to heaven. *Henry VIII,* II,i,75. (Buckingham as he is led to execution.)

⁸ To thee [God] I do commend my watchful soul
Ere I let fall the windows of mine eyes.
Sleeping and waking, O defend me still! *Richard III,* V,iii,116.

⁹ From all such devils, good Lord deliver us! *The Taming of the Shrew,* I,i,66.

¹⁰ Immortal gods, I crave no pelf;
I pray for no man but myself.
Grant I may never prove so fond,
To trust man on his oath or bond. *Timon of Athens,* I,ii,62. (*Pelf* means "property"; *fond* means "foolish.")

See also RELIGION.

PRESENT, THE

¹¹   We, which now behold these present days,
Have eyes to wonder, but lack tongues to praise. *Sonnet 106,* 13.

¹²   These most brisk and giddy-pacèd times. *Twelfth Night,* II,iv,6.

¹³   Every present time doth boast itself
Above a better, gone. *The Winter's Tale,* V,i,96.

See also TIME.

PRESS.   See MEDIA AND MESSAGES; NEWS.

PRIDE

[1] My pride fell with my fortunes. *As You Like It,* I,ii,242.

[2]   And yet his pride becomes him.
He'll make a proper man. *As You Like It,* III,v,114.

[3] Small things make base men proud. *Henry VI, Part Two,* IV,i,106.

[4]   He will never follow anything
That other men begin. *Julius Caesar,* II,i,151. (Brutus dismissing the suggestion that Cicero be asked to join the conspiracy against Caesar.)

[5] Your wisdom is consumed in confidence. *Julius Caesar,* II,ii,49. (Calphurnia reacting to Caesar's claim that he is stronger than danger itself.)

[6]   I can see his pride
Peep through each part of him. *Henry VIII,* I,i,68. (Lord Abergavenny speaking of Cardinal Wolsey.)

[7]   My high-blown pride
At length broke under me. *Henry VIII,* III,ii,361. (From Wolsey's farewell to greatness; see GREATNESS.)

[8] A falcon, towering in her pride of place. *Macbeth,* II,iv,12. (More at OMENS.)

[9] He that is proud eats up himself. Pride is his own glass, his own trumpet, his own chronicle. *Troilus and Cressida,* II,iii,156.

[10] He will be the physician that should be the patient. *Troilus and Cressida,* II,iii,215.

See also VANITY.

PRISON.   See PUNISHMENT.

PROCRASTINATION.   See ACTION, PROMPT; DELAY.

PROFESSIONS

[11] I had thought to let in some of all professions that go the primrose way to the everlasting bonfire. *Macbeth,* II,iii,18. (The porter posing as the porter to hell. The professions he has already admitted are a farmer who hoarded produce and then committed suicide when the harvest was good; an equivocator, i.e., a Jesuit; and a thieving English tailor.)

1   Good counselors lack no clients. *Measure for Measure,* I,ii,109.

2   There is boundless theft
In limited professions. *Timon of Athens,* IV,iii,435. (The reference is to
professions in which one must qualify to be a member. In Shakespeare's
time, the guilds controlled many occupations.)

See also DOCTORS; LAW AND LAWYERS; MEDICINE.

PROMISES

3 'Tis not the many oaths that makes the truth,
But the plain single vow that is vowed true. *All's Well That Ends Well,*
IV,ii,21.

4 Read not my blemishes in the world's report:
I have not kept my square, but that to come
Shall all be done by the rule. *Antony and Cleopatra,* II,iii,5. (Antony prom-
ising Octavia that he will reform his ways.)

5   Falser than vows made in wine. *As You Like It,* III,v,73.

6   Springes to catch woodcocks. I do know,
When the blood burns, how prodigal the soul
Lends the tongue vows. *Hamlet,* I,iii,115. (Polonius warning his daughter,
Ophelia, not to credit Hamlet's vows of love. A *springe* is a trap, made with
a noose and a bent branch that acts as a spring.)

7 "By and by" is easily said. *Hamlet,* III,ii,395.

8   Marriage vows
As false as dicers' oaths. *Hamlet,* III,iv,45.

9 He will give the devil his due. *Henry IV, Part One,* I,ii,123. (Said of a man
who will always keep a bargain, even with the devil. See also the proverb
contest in *Henry V,* under WISDOM, WORDS OF.)

10 His promises were, as he then was, mighty,
But his performance, as he is now, nothing. *Henry VIII,* IV,ii,41. (Katherine of Aragon taking aim at an old enemy, Cardinal Wolsey, now dead.)

11 And be these juggling fiends no more believed,
That palter with us in a double sense;
That keep the word of promise to our ear,
And break it to our hope. *Macbeth,* V,viii,19. (Macbeth speaking of the
witches' prophecies, which seemed to promise absolute protection, but
were simply word tricks.)

¹   If thou swearest,
Thou mayst prove false. *Romeo and Juliet,* II,ii,91. (Juliet to Romeo. More at LOVE AND LOVERS. See also below.)

² O, swear not by the moon, the inconstant moon. *Romeo and Juliet,* II,ii,109. (Romeo then asks Juliet, "What shall I swear by?" l.112. Her answer is below.)

³ Do not swear at all;
Or if thou wilt, swear by thy gracious self,
Which is the god of my idolatry. *Romeo and Juliet,* II,ii,112. (Idolatry, because in Christian theology it is a sin to love anyone or anything as much as God.)

⁴ His promises fly so beyond his state
That what he speaks is all in debt; he owes for every word. *Timon of Athens,* I,ii,203. (*State* means "estate" or "assets.")

⁵ His words are bonds. *The Two Gentlemen of Verona,* II,vii,75.

See also CONTRACTS; TRUST.

PROOF

⁶ Be sure of it; give me the ocular proof. *Othello,* III,iii,357. (Othello, like most of us, unduly trusts eyewitness evidence. He is thus easily gulled. See also DOUBT.)

PROVERBS.   See WISDOM, WORDS OF.

PROVIDENCE

⁷ There is special providence in the fall of a sparrow. *Hamlet,* V,ii,220. (Hamlet refers to *Matthew* 10:29: "Are not two sparrows sold for a farthing? and one of them shall not fall to the ground without your Father." More at FATE.)

⁸   If angels fight,
Weak men must fall, for heaven still guards the right. *Richard II,* III,ii,61. (Richard predicting that because he is the rightful king, God will aid him in battle with Bolingbroke.)

See also GOD.

PRUDENCE

⁹ My ventures are not in one bottom trusted. *The Merchant of Venice,* I,i,42. (For *bottom* read "ship.")

See also CAREFULNESS; DISCRETION; PLANNING; RISK; SECURITY; WISDOM, WORDS OF.

PRYING

1   You would pluck out the heart of my mystery. *Hamlet,* III,ii,373. (Hamlet to Guildenstern.)

See also INSULTS (Hamlet's farewell to Polonius).

PSYCHOPATHS.   See CRIME; DANGEROUS PEOPLE.

PUBLIC, THE

2   Our slippery people,
Whose love is never linked to the deserver
Till his deserts are past. *Antony and Cleopatra,* I,ii,187. (Antony on the Roman people.)

3   The many-headed multitude. *Coriolanus,* II,iii,16. (The image of the populace as a many-headed beast dates back to Horace and Plato and appears fairly often in Renaissance literature. Shakespeare used the image again later in this play—"The beast / With many heads butts me away," IV,i,2—and in *Henry IV, Part Two,;* see under RUMOR.)

4   The mutable, rank-scented many. *Coriolanus,* III,i,66. (Coriolanus, the world's worst politician, speaking of the citizens of Rome. See also CLEANLINESS.)

5 Was ever feather so lightly blown to and fro as this multitude? *Henry VI, Part Two,* IV,viii,56.

6   The body public be
A horse whereon the governor doth ride. *Measure for Measure,* I,ii,162.

7   The fool multitude that choose by show. *The Merchant of Venice,* II,ix,25.

See also DEMOCRACY; OPINION OF OTHERS; POLITICS.

PUBLIC RELATIONS

8 Let's write "good angel" on the devil's horn. *Measure for Measure,* II,iv,16.

9   Therefore is it most expedient for the wise . . . to be the trumpet of his own virtues. *Much Ado About Nothing,* V,ii,82.

PUBLIC SPEAKING

¹ I'll rant as well as thou. *Hamlet,* V,i,286. (Hamlet to Laertes.)

² Hear me for my cause, and be silent, that you may hear. *Julius Caesar,* III,ii,13.

³ I come not, friends, to steal away your hearts,
I am no orator, as Brutus is;
But (as you know me all) a plain blunt man. *Julius Caesar,* III,ii,218. (Here Antony uses a venerable ploy: pretending to be a simple, ordinary person.)

⁴ It is not enough to speak, but to speak true. *A Midsummer Night's Dream,* V,i,121. (Here *true* represents a play on words. It means "well," "clearly," "precisely," as well as "truthfully." The reference is to an actor who runs on ignoring the "stops" or, in other words, the punctuation, the periods. A musician who does not know the stops will not play true.)

⁵   Little shall I grace my cause
In speaking for myself. *Othello,* I,iii,88. (Othello excusing his blunt, soldierly speech.)

⁶ The text is old, the orator too green. *Venus and Adonis,* 806.

See also TALK, PLAIN AND FANCY.

PUNISHMENT

⁷ *Coriolanus.* Let them hang.
Volumnia. Ay, and burn too. *Coriolanus,* III,ii,23. (*They* are the citizens of Rome.)

⁸ They'll give him death by inches. *Coriolanus,* V,iv,41.

⁹   Leave her to heaven
And to those thorns that in her bosom lodge
To prick and sting her. *Hamlet,* I,v,86. (The ghost of Hamlet's father urging Hamlet not to try to punish his mother for her hasty remarriage to his brother, Hamlet's uncle. By the standards of the time, such a marriage would be incestuous, apart from the issue of what knowledge she may have had of her husband's murder.)

¹⁰   Where the offense is, let the great ax fall. *Hamlet,* IV,v,216. (Claudius speaks, even though, by this standard, his own head should be the first to fall.)

¹¹   Put him to execution; for discipline ought to be used. *Henry V,* III,vi,57.

¹ Come, let's away to prison:
We two alone will sing like birds in the cage. *King Lear,* V,iii,8. (Lear to
Cordelia in a moment of happiness that will end with her murder. More
at HAPPINESS.)

² He who the sword of heaven will bear
Should be as holy as severe. *Measure for Measure,* III,ii,264.

³ Wouldst thou have a serpent sting thee twice? *The Merchant of Venice,*
IV,i,69. (Shylock is speaking. The idea is that instant punishment—or
death—will prevent that second sting.)

⁴ Some of us will smart for it. *Much Ado About Nothing,* V,i,109.

⁵ Some base notorious knave, some scurvy fellow.
O heavens, that such companions thou'dst unfold,
And put in every honest hand a whip
To lash the rascals naked through the world. *Othello,* IV,ii,139. (Emilia
calling for punishment of whoever it is who has persuaded Othello that
Desdemona has been unfaithful. The villain, of course, is her own hus-
band, Iago.)

⁶ Off with his head! *Richard III,* III,iv,75. (Richard in action. Thanks to
Lewis Carroll, this line could not be written seriously today.)

⁷ Friend or brother,
He forfeits his own blood that spills another. *Timon of Athens,* III,v,87.
(Shakespeare is not sympathetic to the speaker, an unpleasant, narrow-
minded Athenian senator.)

⁸ It is an heretic that makes the fire,
Not she which burns in't. *The Winter's Tale,* II,iii,113.

See also LAW AND LAWYERS; MERCY; SCAPEGOATS.

PUNS.   See WIT.

PURITY.   See INNOCENCE; SEX; VIRTUE.

QUARRELS.   See ARGUMENTS.

QUEENS.   See CLEOPATRA; ELIZABETH I; HIGH POSITION.

QUIET

[1] Not a mouse stirring. *Hamlet,* I,i,10.

R

RAGE.   See ANGER; DESPAIR AND RAGE.

READING

[1] *Polonius.* What do you read, my lord?
Hamlet. Words, words, words. *Hamlet,* II,ii,192.

[2]   My library
Was dukedom large enough. *The Tempest,* I,ii,109. (Prospero speaking of
his love of books; see also below. After Prospero is deposed as duke of
Milan by his wicked brother, a loyal courtier, Gonzalo, gives him some
of his possessions to take into his exile: "Knowing I loved my books, he
furnished me / From mine own library with volumes that / I prize above
my dukedom," l.166. The intent of those who sent him into exile was that
he would die at sea; see SHIPS AND SAILING.)

See also EDUCATION; STORIES.

REASON

[3]   In the why and wherefore is neither rhyme nor reason? *The Comedy
of Errors,* II,ii,48. (See, too, the quote from this play under REASONS below.
"Neither rhyme nor reason" also appears in *As You Like It,* III,ii,389,
when Orlando maintains that neither rhyme nor reason can express how
much he is in love. In *The Merry Wives of Windsor,* V,v,128, Falstaff uses
the phrase "of the teeth of all rhyme and reason." The coupling of rhyme
and reason predates Shakespeare. In *Brush Up Your Shakespeare,* Michael

Macrone traces it to a 1520s verse by John Skelton: "For reason can I none find / Nor good rhyme in your matter." Thomas Fuller in *Worthies of England* [1662] quotes Edmund Spenser [1522–1599] on the subject of a promised pension: "I was promised on a time, / To have reason for my rhyme; / From that time unto this season, / I received nor rhyme nor reason.")

[1] O judgment, thou art fled to brutish beasts,
And men have lost their reason! *Julius Caesar,* III,ii,106.

[2] The will of man is by his reason swayed. *A Midsummer Night's Dream,* II,ii,115.

REASONS

[3] The why is plain as way to parish church. *As You Like It,* II,vii,52.

[4]   Every why hath a wherefore. *The Comedy of Errors,* II,ii,43. (See also REASON, the note on the quote from this play.)

[5] If reasons were as plentiful as blackberries, I would give no man a reason upon compulsion. *Henry IV, Part One,* II,iv,238. (Falstaff, caught out in a lie, announcing that he will not be pushed into further explanation.)

[6] There is occasions and causes why and wherefore in all things. *Henry V,* V,i,3.

[7] Gratiano speaks an infinite deal of nothing. . . . His reasons are as two grains of wheat hid in two bushels of chaff: you shall seek all day ere you find them, and when you have them they are not worth the search. *The Merchant of Venice,* I,i,114.

See also ARGUMENTS; CONCLUSIONS.

REBELLION

[8] Rebellion lay in his way, and he found it. *Henry IV, Part One,* V,i,28. (Falstaff's scornful comment on the earl of Worcester's claim that he did not really want to rebel against the king. The king's own comment on Worcester's lengthy justification is that rebellion has never needed excuses: "Never yet did insurrection want / Such water colors to impaint his cause," l.79.)

[9] The smallest worm will turn, being trodden on. *Henry VI, Part Three,* II,ii,17.

[10] Flout 'em and scout 'em
And scout 'em and flout 'em!

Thought is free. *The Tempest*, III,ii,126. (*Scout* means "jeer at." The lines are sung by Stephano for Caliban in anticipation of his liberation from Prospero.)

See also FREEDOM; RESISTANCE; REVOLUTION.

REGRET

1   Praising what is lost
Makes the remembrance dear. *All's Well That Ends Well*, V,iii,19.

2   Things without all remedy
Should be without regard: what's done is done. *Macbeth*, III,ii,11.

3 To mourn a mischief that is past and gone
Is the next way to draw new mischief on. *Othello*, I,iii,201.

4 Things past redress are now with me past care. *Richard II*, II,iii,170.

5 I sigh the lack of many a thing I sought,
And with old woes new wail my dear Time's waste. *Sonnet 30, 3*. (More at PAST, THE.)

6   What's gone and what's past help
Should be past grief. *The Winter's Tale*, III,ii,220.

See also PAST, THE; REPENTANCE; TIME.

REJECTION

7 Get thee to a nunnery. *Hamlet*, III,i,121. (Hamlet to Ophelia.)

8 Stand not upon the order of your going,
But go at once. *Macbeth*, III,iv,120.

9   If I do prove her haggard,
Though that her jesses were my dear heartstrings,
I'd whistle her off and let her down the wind
To prey at fortune. *Othello*, III,iii,259. (Othello, using the language of falconry, is saying that if Desdemona is *haggard,* that is, only half tamed, then he will release the strap that holds her, the *jesses,* and set her flying free.)

10   She sent him away cold as a snowball; saying his prayers too. *Pericles*, IV,vi,145.

11 Do not . . .
Come in the rearward of a conquered woe;
Give not a windy night a rainy morrow,

To linger out a purposed overthrow.
If thou wilt leave me, do not leave me last,
When other petty griefs have done their spite,
But in the onset come; so shall I taste
At first the very worst of fortune's might,
And other strains of woe, which now seem woe,
Compared with loss of thee will not seem so. *Sonnet 90, 5.*

1   Let them hang themselves in their own straps. *Twelfth Night,* I,iii,12.

RELIGION

2   I tell thee, churlish priest,
A ministering angel shall my sister be
When thou liest howling. *Hamlet,* V,i,242. (Laertes to the priest who refused to perform a full burial service for Ophelia on the grounds that her death was "doubtful," i.e., possibly a suicide.)

3   I have not forgotten what the inside of a church is made of. *Henry IV, Part One,* III,iii,7. (Falstaff claiming that he is still capable of changing his ways.)

4 They should be good men, their affairs as righteous;
But all hoods make not monks. *Henry VIII,* III,i,22. (Queen Katherine speaking of Cardinal Wolsey and Cardinal Campeius.)

5 Had I but served my God with half the zeal
I served my King, he would not in mine age
Have left me naked to mine enemies. *Henry VIII,* III,ii,455. (Cardinal Wolsey, ruined and near death. The lines may be by John Fletcher rather than Shakespeare.)

6   This meddling priest. *King John,* III,i,89. (A reference to the pope. King John's excommunication by Pope Innocent III was probably, to an Elizabethan audience, his chief virtue. He also quarreled with his own barons, who eventually forced him to sign the Magna Carta. John's irritation with "this meddling priest" recalls the plea of his father, Henry II, to be rid of "this turbulent priest"—Thomas à Becket.)

7 Yes, to smell pork, to eat of the habitation which your prophet the Nazarite conjured the devil into! I will buy with you, sell with you, talk with you, walk with you, and so following; but I will not eat with you, drink with you, nor pray with you. *The Merchant of Venice,* I,iii,31. (Shylock's response to a dinner invitation from Bassanio. Shakespeare could have known few if any Jews or other non-Christians—Jews were banished from England from 1290 to 1655. But he had a quick imagination for what

Christianity might look like to an outsider. In *Mark* and *Luke,* the story of the devils forced into the bodies of the Gadarene swine is rather odd if taken literally.)

[1]   How like a fawning publican he looks.
I hate him for he is a Christian. *The Merchant of Venice,* I,iii,38. (*Publican* may refer to a Roman tax collector or an inn or keeper, or as we might say a "pub" keeper. Shylock is referring to Antonio. In this play, Shakespeare presents religious hatred as a commonplace. A few lines later, Shylock says of Antonio, undoubtedly correctly, "He hates our sacred nation," l.45.)

[2] The devil can cite Scripture for his purpose. *The Merchant of Venice,* I,iii,95.

[3]   'Tis mad idolatry
To make the service greater than the god. *Troilus and Cressida,* II,ii,56.

[4] It is a heretic that makes the fire,
Not she which burns in it. *The Winter's Tale,* II,iii,113.

See also CHRISTIANS; CONVERSIONS; FAITH; HOLY LAND; HYPOCRISY; JEWS AND JUDAISM; PRAYER; PRAYERS.

REMEDIES

[5]   Diseases desperate grown
By desperate appliance are relieved,
Or not at all. *Hamlet,* IV,iii,9.

[6]   Things without all remedy
Should be without regard: what's done is done. *Macbeth,* III,ii,11.

See also COMFORT; MEDICINE.

REMORSE.   See REGRET; REPENTANCE.

REPENTANCE

[7]   Confess yourself to heaven,
Repent what's past, avoid what is to come. *Hamlet,* III,iv,150. (Hamlet to his mother.)

[8] Woe, that too late repents. *King Lear,* I,iv,264.

REPUTATION

[9] Be thou as chaste as ice, as pure as snow, thou shalt not escape calumny. *Hamlet,* III,i,137.

1   What a wounded name,
Things standing thus unknown, shall live behind me! *Hamlet,* V,ii,345.
(The dying Hamlet realizes that unless the full story is told, his reputation
will be shameful. He begs Horatio to bring the true story forward. See
NEWS.)

2 I would to God thou and I knew where a commodity of good names were
to be bought. *Henry IV, Part One,* I,ii,85. (Falstaff to Hal.)

3 My credit now stands on such slippery ground. *Julius Caesar,* III,i,191.

4   I have bought
Golden opinions from all sorts of people. *Macbeth,* I,vii,32. (*Opinions*
translates as "reputation.")

5 Reputation, reputation, reputation! O, I have lost my reputation! I have
lost the immortal part of myself, and what remains is bestial. *Othello,*
II,iii,261. (Cassio speaks. Iago, who had secretly arranged the brawl that
led to Cassio's demotion, answers below.)

6 Reputation is an idle and most false imposition, oft got without merit and
lost without deserving. *Othello,* II,iii,267. (Iago speaks out of the other side
of his mouth when talking to Othello; see below.)

7 Good name in man and woman, dear my lord,
Is the immediate jewel of their souls.
Who steals my purse steals trash; 'tis something, nothing;
'Twas mine, 'tis his, and has been slave to thousands;
But he that filches from me my good name
Robs me of that which not enriches him
And makes me poor indeed. *Othello,* III,iii,155. (Iago speaks.)

8 Yea, though I die, the scandal will survive. *The Rape of Lucrece,* 204.

9 The purest treasure mortal times afford
Is spotless reputation. *Richard II,* I,i,177.

10 'Tis better to be vile than vile esteemed
When not to be receives reproach of being. *Sonnet 121,* 1. (The second line
means "when one is reproached with being vile even when not being so
at all.")

11 I see my reputation is at stake. *Troilus and Cressida,* III,iii,227. (Achilles is
speaking.)

See also FAME; HONOR; OPINION OF OTHERS; RUMOR; SLANDER.

RESIGNATION

[1]   I will sit as quiet as a lamb. *King John,* IV,i,79. (The young Duke Arthur, promising Hubert that he will submit to being blinded if Hubert will send away the other guards.)

RESISTANCE

[2] Stand for your own, unwind your bloody flag. *Henry V,* I,ii,101.

[3]   Yield not thy neck
To Fortune's yoke. *Henry VI, Part Three,* III,iii,16.

[4] It boots not to resist both wind and tide. *Henry VI, Part Three,* IV,iii,59.

[5] Yet, countrymen, O, yet hold up your heads! *Julius Caesar,* V,iv,1. (Brutus during the battle at Philippi.)

[6] Prevent it, resist it, let it not be so. *Richard II,* IV,i,148.

[7] I'll not budge an inch. *The Taming of the Shrew,* Induction, I,i,14.

See also DEFENSE; DETERMINATION; PERSEVERANCE; REVOLUTION; WAR.

RESPECT

[8] I hold you as a thing enskied and sainted. *Measure for Measure,* I,iv,34. (*Enskied* means "heavenly.")

[9] Is there no respect of place, persons, nor time in you? *Twelfth Night,* II,iii,92.

RESPONSIBILITY

[10] Men at some time are masters of their fates:
The fault, dear Brutus, is not in our stars,
But in ourselves, that we are underlings. *Julius Caesar,* I,ii,139.

See also EXCUSES; GUILT.

RETREAT

[11]   Let us make an honorable retreat. *As You Like It,* III,ii,160. (Said by the clown Touchstone, with the light conclusion ". . . though not with bag and baggage, yet with scrip and scrippage." The latter are a shepherd's pouch and its contents.)

[12]   I would ne'er have fled,
But that they left me 'midst my enemies. *Henry VI, Part One,* I,ii,23. (The dauphin makes this comical excuse for a rapid if prudent retreat. *They* refers to the men who went into battle—briefly—with him. Shakespeare,

of course, was partisan with respect to England's traditional enemy; see also FRANCE AND THE FRENCH.)

REVENGE

1   Kindness, nobler ever than revenge. *As You Like It,* IV,iii,129.

2 How all occasions do inform against me
And spur my dull revenge! *Hamlet,* IV,iv,32.

3 Revenge should have no bounds. *Hamlet,* IV,vii,128. (Claudius to Laertes.)

4   He's revengeful, and I know his sword
Hath a sharp edge. *Henry VIII,* I,i,109. (More at POWER.)

5 I will have such revenges on you both
That all the world shall—I will do such things—
What they are, yet I know not; but they shall be
The terrors of the earth. *King Lear,* II,iv,278. (A broken Lear attempting to frighten his daughters Goneril and Regan.)

6   Blood will have blood. *Macbeth,* III,iv,123. (More at CRIME.)

7 Let's make us medicines of our great revenge,
To cure this deadly grief. *Macbeth,* IV,iii,214.

8 If I can catch him once upon the hip,
I will feed fat the ancient grudge I bear him. *The Merchant of Venice,* I,iii,43. (Shylock speaking of Antonio. Catching someone on the hip is a wrestling move that gives an advantage.)

9   My bloody thoughts, with violent pace,
Shall never look back, never ebb to humble love,
Till that a capable and wide revenge
Swallow them up. *Othello,* III,iii,454.

10 Can vengeance be pursued further than death? *Romeo and Juliet,* V,iii,55.

11 Vengeance is in my heart, death in my hand,
Blood and revenge are hammering in my head. *Titus Andronicus,* II,iii,38. (The speaker is the monstrously vicious Aaron.)

See also EVIL; PUNISHMENT.

REVOLUTION

12 We shall be called purgers, not murderers. *Julius Caesar,* II,i,180. (Brutus making a distinction that has been made many times since, most famously by Stalin.)

¹ Liberty! Freedom! Tyranny is dead!
Run hence, proclaim, cry it about the streets. *Julius Caesar,* III,i,78. (Cinna
trying to inspire a general uprising just after the assassination of Caesar.
Cassius follows, with "Some to the common pulpits, and cry out, / "Liberty, freedom, and enfranchisement!" l.80.)

² Let's all cry "Peace, freedom, and liberty!" *Julius Caesar,* III,i,110. (Brutus
to his fellow conspirators. The illusion that peace and liberty have been
won through the death of Caesar is quickly destroyed.)

See also BAD TIMES; EDUCATION (the anti-education quotes from *Henry VI,
Part Two*); REBELLION; RESISTANCE; WAR.

RICH, THE

³   Rich men deal gifts,
Expecting in return twenty for one? *Timon of Athens,* IV,iii,518.

See also MONEY; RICH AND POOR; SUCCESS.

RICH AND POOR

⁴   To have seen much and to have nothing is to have rich eyes and poor
hands. *As You Like It,* IV,i,22.

⁵   The gods sent not
Corn for the rich men only. *Coriolanus,* I,i,208.

⁶   Whiles I am a beggar, I will rail
And say there is no sin but to be rich;
And being rich, my virtue then shall be
To say there is no vice but beggary. *King John,* II,i,593.

⁷ The orphan pines while the oppressor feeds. *The Rape of Lucrece,* 905.

See also MONEY; INJUSTICE; POVERTY; RICH, THE.

RIDING

⁸   Witch the world with noble horsemanship. *Henry IV, Part One,*
IV,i,109.

⁹ When I bestride him, I soar, I am a hawk; he trots the air; the earth sings
when he touches it. *Henry V,* III,vii,15. (The dauphin praising his horse.)

See also ANIMALS.

RISK

¹⁰   Were it good
To set the exact wealth of all our states

All at one cast? To set so rich a main
On the nice hazard of one doubtful hour?
It were not good. *Henry IV, Part One,* IV,i,45. (Paraphrase: Is it a good
idea to risk all our wealth on one cast of the dice? To set so rich a stake
on the precarious chance of one doubtful hour? No, it is not a good idea.)

[1]   Men that hazard all
Do it in hope of fair advantages. *The Merchant of Venice,* II,vii,18.

[2] I have set my life upon a cast,
And I will stand the hazard of the die. *Richard III,* V,iv,9. (The king at the
battle of Bosworth Field.)

See also BOLDNESS; CHANCE; DANGER; DECISION, MOMENT OF; PRUDENCE.

ROME.   See CITIES.

ROMEO AND JULIET

[3] My only love, sprung from my only hate!
Too early seen unknown, and known too late! *Romeo and Juliet,* I,v,140.
(Juliet's response after realizing that the man with whom she has just fallen
in love is Romeo, a Montague. They are indeed "a pair of star-crossed
lovers," Prologue,6.)

[4] But soft! What light through yonder window breaks?
It is the East, and Juliet is the sun!
Arise, fair sun, and kill the envious moon,
Who is already sick and pale with grief
That thou her maid art far more fair than she. *Romeo and Juliet,* II,ii,2.
(Romeo speaks as Juliet appears at her window.)

[5] O Romeo, Romeo! Wherefore art thou Romeo?
Deny thy father and refuse thy name;
Or, if thou wilt not, be but sworn my love,
And I'll no longer be a Capulet. *Romeo and Juliet,* II,ii,33. (Juliet speaking
aloud on her balcony, not knowing that Romeo is hidden in the garden
below. Quite naturally, he is inclined to listen a little longer: "Shall I hear
more, or shall I speak at this?" 1.37. Juliet's lines are so famous that they
are a challenge for an actress to get past. Henry Fielding parodied the
passage in his *Life and Death of Tom Thumb the Great:* "O Tom Thumb!
Tom Thumb! wherefore art thou Tom Thumb?")

[6] In truth, fair Montague, I am too fond. *Romeo and Juliet,* II,ii,98. (But
Juliet goes on to say that although her love was given quickly, it will
endure. See LOVE, EXPRESSIONS OF.)

[1] Come, night; come, Romeo. *Romeo and Juliet,* III,ii,17. (Juliet, eagerly awaiting nightfall and the arrival of Romeo. See also NIGHT. In the same passage are the lines "When he shall die, / Take him and cut him out in little stars . . ."; see LOVE, EXPRESSIONS OF.)

[2] For never was a story of more woe
Than this of Juliet and her Romeo. *Romeo and Juliet,* V,iii,309. (The last lines in the play.)

See also BEAUTY; LOVE AND LOVERS; LOVE, EXPRESSIONS OF.

RUIN

[3]   We have kissed away
Kingdoms and provinces. *Antony and Cleopatra,* III,x,7. (Scarus, a friend of Antony, at the battle of Actium.)

[4]   No pity,
No friends, no hope; no kindred weep for me;
Almost no grave allowed me. *Henry VIII,* III,i,149. (Queen Katherine—Catherine of Aragon—to Cardinal Wolsey.)

[5] I have touched the highest point of all my greatness,
And from that full meridian of my glory
I haste now to my setting. I shall fall
Like a bright exhalation in the evening,
And no man see me more. *Henry VIII,* III,ii,223. (Cardinal Wolsey speaks. *Exhalation* refers to a meteor. The notion was that clouds and other vaporous forms were exhalations of the earth; similarly meteors and comets were thought to be made of inflammable gases, or exhalations, in the outer sky. Shakespeare uses similar images in *Richard II*—see below—and elsewhere.)

[6] Farewell! A long farewell to all my greatness! *Henry VIII,* III,ii,351. (More at GREATNESS.)

[7]   When he falls, he falls like Lucifer,
Never to hope again. *Henry VIII,* III,ii,371. (The end of Cardinal Wolsey's farewell to greatness; see GREATNESS and HIGH POSITION.)

[8] Thou lowest and most dejected thing of fortune. *King Lear,* IV,i,3.

[9] O ruined piece of nature! *King Lear,* IV,vi,136. (Gloucester, speaking to and of Lear. More at ENTROPY.)

[10] Had I but died an hour before this chance,
I had lived a blessèd time; for from this instant
There's nothing serious in mortality:

All is but toys. Renown and grace is dead,
The wine of life is drawn, and the mere lees
Is left this vault to brag of. *Macbeth,* II,iii,93. (Macbeth in the morning
when Duncan's body is found. The middle lines mean "There's nothing
of value in this mortal life, only trifles.")

[1] I have lived long enough. My way of life
Is fallen into the sear, the yellow leaf,
And that which should accompany old age,
As honor, love, obedience, troops of friends,
I must not look to have. *Macbeth,* V,iii,22. (*Fallen into the sear* means
"shriveled." Byron used the same image: "My days are in the yellow leaf;
/ The flowers and fruits of love are gone," in the poem "On My Thirty-
sixth Year.")

[2] Then yield thee, coward,
And live to be the show and gaze of the time. *Macbeth,* V,viii,23. (Macduff
to Macbeth. Macbeth decides to fight. See WAR.)

[3] The fixèd figure for the time of scorn
To point his slow and moving finger at. *Othello,* IV,ii,53. (Othello imagining how it would feel to be the object of public scorn.)

[4] I see thy glory like a shooting star
Fall to the base earth from the firmament. *Richard II,* II,iv,19. (Salisbury
predicting the ruin of Richard in an image reminiscent of the fall of Lucifer;
see *Henry VIII,* III,ii,371, above.)

[5]   O, that I were as great
As is my grief, or lesser than my name!
Or that I could forget what I have been!
Or not remember what I must be now! *Richard II,* III,iii,135.

[6] When, in disgrace with Fortune and men's eyes,
I all alone beweep my outcast state,
And trouble deaf heaven with my bootless cries,
And look upon myself and curse my fate. *Sonnet 29,* 1. (The sonnet
concludes on a happier note: thoughts of his dear friend's love bring a
wealth of happiness.)

[7]   Contempt and clamor
Will be my knell. *The Winter's Tale,* I,ii,189.

See also ADVERSITY; DEATH; DECLINE.

RULERS. See CLEOPATRA; ELIZABETH I; GREATNESS; HENRY V; HIGH
POSITION; JULIUS CAESAR; LEADERS.

RUMOR

[1] Open your ears, for which of you will stop
The vent of hearing when loud Rumor speaks? *Henry IV, Part Two,*
Induction,i. (As for those people who are especially good at picking up
rumors, Shakespeare might have applied the old quip "Pitchers have
ears," *Richard III,* II,iv,37.)

[2]   Rumor is a pipe
Blown by surmises, jealousies, conjectures,
And of so easy and so plain a stop
That the blunt monster with uncounted heads,
The still-discordant wav'ring multitude,
Can play upon it. *Henry IV, Part Two,* Induction,15. (On the image of the
people as a many-headed monster, see also the quote from *Coriolanus*
under PUBLIC, THE.)

[3] Rumor doth double, like the voice and echo,
The numbers of the feared. *Henry IV, Part Two,* III,i,97.

[4] I find the people strangely fantasied,
Possessed with rumors. *King John,* IV,ii,144. (More, with a note, at FEAR.)

RUTHLESSNESS

[5] There is no more mercy in him than there is milk in a male tiger. *Coriolanus,* V,iv,28.

[6] Henceforth I will not have to do with pity:
. . .
In cruelty will I seek out my fame. *Henry VI, Part Two,* V,ii,56,60. (From
the famous speech by the embittered young Clifford, standing over the
body of his father slain in combat.)

[7]   Think him as a serpent's egg
. . .
And kill him in the shell. *Julius Caesar,* II,i,32,34.

[8] Is there any cause in nature that make these hard hearts? *King Lear,*
III,vi,76. (Lear speaking of his daughters Goneril and Regan.)

[9] The raven himself is hoarse
That croaks the fatal entrance of Duncan
Under my battlements. Come, you spirits
That tend on mortal thoughts, unsex me here,
And fill me, from the crown to the toe, top-full
Of direst cruelty! Make thick my blood,

Stop up th' access and passage to remorse,
That no compunctious visitings of nature
Shake my fell purpose, nor keep peace between
Th' effect and it! Come to my woman's breasts,
And take my milk for gall, you murd'ring ministers,
Wherever in your sightless substances
You wait on nature's mischief! Come, thick night,
And pall thee in the dunnest smoke of hell,
That my keen knife see not the wound it makes,
Nor heaven peep through the blanket of the dark,
To cry "Hold, hold!" *Macbeth,* I,v,39. (Lady Macbeth. *Take my milk for gall* means "exchange my milk for gall." *Sightless* means "invisible." *Pall thee,* etc. means "enshroud thyself in the darkest smoke of hell." See also below.)

[1]   I have given suck, and know
How tender 'tis to love the babe that milks me:
I would, while it was smiling in my face,
Have plucked my nipple from his boneless gums,
And dashed the brains out, had I so sworn as you
Have done to this. *Macbeth,* I,vii,54. (Lady Macbeth trying to steel her husband to murder Duncan. Whether she could actually kill a baby is questionable. She does not murder Duncan when she has the opportunity, and her mind soon breaks. See GUILT AND MADNESS.)

[2] Men must learn now with pity to dispense,
For policy sits above conscience. *Timon of Athens,* III,ii,91.

[3] That what you cannot as you would achieve,
You must perforce accomplish as you may. *Titus Andronicus,* II,i,106. (In other words, if you cannot do something the nice way—the way that you would like to do it—then do it any way you can. Aaron, a remarkable villain, similar to Iago, is recommending rape.)

See also CRIME; DANGEROUS PEOPLE; EVIL; VIOLENCE; WAR.

SACRIFICES

[1] Upon such sacrifices, my Cordelia,
The gods themselves throw incense. *King Lear,* V,iii,20.

SADNESS.   See SORROW AND SADNESS.

SCAPEGOATS

[2] A staff is quickly found to beat a dog. *Henry VI, Part Two,* III,i,171.
(Identified as an "ancient proverb.")

SCIENCE

[3]   Our houses, and ourselves, and children,
Have lost, or do not learn for want of time,
The sciences that should become our country. *Henry V,* V,ii,56. (The duke
of Burgundy refers particularly to the decline of agriculture in wartime.)

[4] He that is giddy thinks the world turns round. *The Taming of the Shrew,*
V,ii,20.

See also EDUCATION; MATHEMATICS; MEDICINE; PHILOSOPHY; STARS.

SCRUPLES

[5]   Some craven scruple
Of thinking too precisely on the event. *Hamlet,* IV,iv,40. (*Event* means
"result.")

SEAS, THE. See NATURE; SHIPS AND SAILING.

SEASONS

[1] At Christmas I no more desire a rose
Than wish a snow in May's new-fangled shows,
But like of each thing that in season grows. *Love's Labor's Lost,* I,1,105.

[2] How many things by season, seasoned are
To their right praise and true perfection! *The Merchant of Venice,* V,i,107.

See also SPRING; SUMMER; WINTER.

SECRECY

[3]   We have done but greenly
In huggermugger to inter him. *Hamlet,* IV,v,83. (Translation: We have acted foolishly to bury him in secret and in haste. The king speaks of the burial of Polonius, whose death is the subject of widespread rumors.)

[4] Wherefore are these things hid? *Twelfth Night,* I,iii,121.

See also PRYING; SECURITY.

SECURITY

[5] Thou wilt not utter what thou dost not know,
And so far will I trust thee. *Henry IV, Part One,* II,iii,111. (Hotspur declining to tell his wife his plans for armed rebellion.)

[6]   *Albany.* You may fear too far.
Goneril. Safer than trust too far. *King Lear,* I,iv,335.

[7] To be thus is nothing, but to be safely thus. *Macbeth,* III,i,48. (Macbeth has no sooner become king than he begins to worry about who may assassinate or dethrone him. He is preparing to order the murder of Banquo, whom he fears.)

[8] Fast bind, fast find,
A proverb never stale in thrifty mind. *The Merchant of Venice,* II,v,53. (Shylock instructing his daughter to lock up the house to protect their money.)

See also CONSPIRACY; DEFENSE; SECRECY.

SELF

[9] This above all, to thine own self be true. *Hamlet,* I,iii,78. (More at WISDOM, WORDS OF.)

¹ Self-love, my liege, is not so vile a sin
As self-neglecting. *Henry V,* II,iv,74.

²   Be to yourself
As you would to your friend. *Henry VIII,* I,i,135.

³   I do see the very book indeed,
Where all my sins are writ, and that's myself. *Richard II,* IV,i,273.

⁴ I to myself am dearer than a friend. *The Two Gentlemen of Verona,* II,vi,23.

See also IDENTITY; SELF-INTEREST; SOUL.

SELF-CONTROL

⁵ Season your admiration for a while. *Hamlet,* I,ii,192. (Translation: Control your amazement for a while.)

⁶ They that have power to hurt and will do none. *Sonnet 94,* 1. (More at VIRTUE.)

See also EMOTIONS; WEEPING.

SELF-CRITICISM

⁷ O, what a rogue and peasant slave am I! *Hamlet,* II,ii,560. (The prince berating himself for not taking action to avenge his father. He continues with "I am pigeon-livered and lack gall / To make oppression bitter," l.588, and "Why, what an ass am I!" l.594.)

SELF-DETERMINATION.   See FREEDOM; RESPONSIBILITY.

SELF-DOUBT

⁸   Our doubts are traitors,
And make us lose the good we oft might win,
By fearing to attempt. *Measure for Measure,* I,iv,77.

See also FEAR.

SELF-INTEREST

⁹ Love thyself last; cherish those hearts that hate thee. *Henry VIII,* III,ii,443. (Cardinal Wolsey warning from experience not to use high office to pursue one's self-interest.)

¹⁰ That smooth-faced gentleman, tickling commodity,
Commodity, the bias of the world. *King John,* II,i,573. (*Commodity* means, roughly, "self-interest." Harold C. Goddard in *The Meaning of Shakespeare*

comments that *commodity* is similar to William James's "bitch goddess, Success"; other names for it are Mammon and the Main Chance. In this scene, the character called the Bastard, an illegitimate son of Richard I, realizes that commodity runs the world; see also WORLD.)

¹   This same bias, this commodity,
This bawd, this broker. *King John,* II,i,581. (A continuation of the monologue above. The use of *commodity* in this passage is one of several indications that Shakespeare turned to Raphael Holingshed's *Chronicles* as a source. In the same context, Holingshed describes the French king as choosing what was "commodious" to him. The passage is even stronger if one knows that in Shakespeare's day *commodity* was also used to refer to a woman's private parts.)

² Since kings break faith upon commodity,
Gain, be my lord, for I will worship thee! *King John,* II,i,597. (The conclusion of the famous monologue that begins "Mad world! Mad kings!"—see WORLD—and includes the two quotes above.)

³ In following him, I follow but myself. *Othello,* I,i,55. (Iago explaining that it is in his own interest to follow Othello, or appear to do so.)

⁴ Every way makes my gain. *Othello,* V,i,14. (Iago again.)

⁵   'Tis an ill cook that cannot lick his own fingers. *Romeo and Juliet,* IV,ii,6.

See also SELF.

SELF-KNOWLEDGE

⁶   The eye sees not itself
But by reflection, by some other things. *Julius Caesar,* I,ii,52. (The point is that we cannot know ourselves directly, only as we are reflected in the perceptions of others.)

⁷ Who is it that can tell me who I am? *King Lear,* I,iv,236. (Asked half ironically, half seriously by Lear, who is beginning to sense that things are going very wrong. Lear at his best never had much insight into himself or others. "He hath ever but slenderly known himself," his daughter Regan comments, I,i,295.)

⁸ I do begin to perceive that I am made an ass. *The Merry Wives of Windsor,* V,v,122.

SEPARATION

⁹   This must my comfort be,
That sun that warms you here shall shine on me. *Richard II,* I,iii,144.

¹ How like a winter hath my absence been
From thee. *Sonnet 97*, 1.

See also BANISHMENT AND EXILE; FAREWELLS; LONELINESS; SPRING *(Sonnet 98)*.

SERIOUSNESS

² He was disposed to mirth; but on the sudden
A Roman thought hath struck him. *Antony and Cleopatra*, I,ii,83. (Cleopatra making fun of Roman propriety. This was early in Rome's history, of course.)

³ I fear he will prove the weeping philosopher when he grows old, being so full of unmannerly sadness in his youth. *The Merchant of Venice*, I,ii,47. *(Sadness* here means "seriousness.")

SEX

⁴   Virginity is peevish, proud, idle, made of self-love. *All's Well That Ends Well*, I,i,151. (Parolles, a great talker, trying to persuade Helena that virginity is not worth preserving. "The longer kept," he argues, "the less worth," l.161.)

⁵ The triple pillar of the world transformed
Into a strumpet's fool. *Antony and Cleopatra*, I,i,12. (Philo's bitter comment on Antony's relationship with Cleopatra. The phrase *the triple pillar of the world* refers to the triumvirate that ruled Rome after the death of Julius Caesar: Mark Antony, Augustus Caesar, and Lepidus. See under POWER for Antony's readiness to renounce the empire for love.)

⁶   A lover's pinch,
Which hurts, and is desired. *Antony and Cleopatra*, V,ii,295. (At the moment of death, Cleopatra speaks in sexual terms. Referring to the asp she uses to commit suicide, she says, "Dost thou not see the baby at my breast, / That sucks the nurse asleep?" l.309. See also CLEOPATRA and DEATH.)

⁷ Take thou no scorn to wear the horn,
It was a crest ere thou wast born,
Thy father's father wore it,
And thy father bore it.
The horn, the horn, the lusty horn,
Is not a thing to laugh to scorn. *As You Like It*, IV,ii,14. (Forester's song, referring to a deer's horns to be worn as a trophy—and of course to cuckoldry. Sylvan Barnet, in the Signet edition of *As You Like It*, relates that in 1879, in the opening season of the Shakespeare Memorial Theatre in Stratford-on-Avon in England, a stag was killed as a stage prop for the

scene in which the foresters sing this song. The animal was selected from Charlecot, where Shakespeare is supposed to have poached deer. The stag was thereafter stuffed and used in pastoral scenes in numerous productions of this and other plays. Audiences were quite offended when in 1919, Nigel Playfair, in a modernistic *As You Like It*, left the stag in storage.)

1   Chaste as the icicle
That's curdied by the frost from purest snow. *Coriolanus,* V,iii,65. (*Curdied* means "hardened." From Coriolanus, this is a compliment to the woman he is describing.)

2   I thought her
As chaste as unsunned snow. *Cymbeline,* II,v,12.

3 Why, she would hang on him
As if increase of appetite had grown
By what it fed on. *Hamlet,* I,ii,143. (Hamlet remembering his mother's passion for his father. More at MARRIAGE.)

4   The primrose path of dalliance. *Hamlet,* I,iii,50. (More at ADVICE.)

5 But virtue, as it never will be moved,
Though lewdness court it in a shape of heaven,
So lust, though to a radiant angel linked,
Will sate itself in a celestial bed
And prey on garbage. *Hamlet,* I,v,53.

6 O shame, where is thy blush? Rebellious hell,
If thou canst mutine in a matron's bones,
To flaming youth let virtue be as wax
And melt in her own fire. Proclaim no shame
When the compulsive ardor gives the charge,
Since frost itself as actively doth burn,
And reason panders will. *Hamlet,* III,iv,83. (Hamlet scandalized by his mother's behavior; see also MIDDLE AGE. The last phrase means "Reason panders to desire.")

7 I understand thy kisses, and thou mine. *Henry IV, Part One,* III,i,204.

8   Sweetheart,
I were unmannerly to take you out
And not to kiss you. *Henry VIII,* I,iv,94. (The king making a quick move on Anne Bullen [Boleyn].)

9   Why brand they us
With base? With baseness? Bastardy? Base? Base?
Who, in the lusty stealth of nature, take

More composition and fierce quality
Than doth, within a dull, stale, tired bed,
Go to the creating a whole tribe of fops. *King Lear,* I,ii,9. (Said by the
ambitious Edmund, illegitimate son of the earl of Gloucester. He concludes, "Now, gods, stand up for bastards," l.22.)

[1] Adultery?
Thou shalt not die: die for adultery! No:
The wren goes to it, and the small gilded fly
Doth lecher in my sight.
Let copulation thrive. *King Lear,* IV,vi,112. (Lear, although wandering in
mind, still has the sense to see that adultery cannot be outlawed. For his
view of women and sex, see below.)

[2] Beneath is all the fiend's.
There's hell, there's darkness, there is the sulphurous pit,
Burning, scalding, stench, consumption; fie, fie, fie! *King Lear,* IV,vi,129.
(*Beneath* means "below the waist." Lear is speaking of lascivious women,
his two vicious daughters in particular.)

[3] The cuckoo then, on every tree,
Mocks married men; for thus sings he, "Cuckoo!
Cuckoo, cuckoo!" O word of fear,
Unpleasing to a married ear! *Love's Labor's Lost,* V,ii,899. (Sometimes an
unlucky married man would be teased by calls of "cuckoo." See also
SPRING.)

[4] How shall I be revenged on him? I think the best way were to entertain
him with hope till the wicked fire of lust have melted him in his own
grease. *The Merry Wives of Windsor,* II,i,64. (Mistress Page speaking of
Falstaff.)

[5] Fie on sinful fantasy!
Fie on lust and luxury! *The Merry Wives of Windsor,* V,v,96. (A fake fairy
song sung to Falstaff in the course of an elaborate practical joke.)

[6]   Earthlier happy is the rose distilled,
Than that which, withering on the virgin thorn,
Grows, lives, and dies in single blessedness. *A Midsummer Night's Dream,*
I,i,76. (A *rose distilled* is one made into perfume.)

[7]   An old black ram
Is tupping your white ewe. *Othello,* I,i,85. (Iago to Desdemona's father;
see also below.)

[8] Your daughter and the Moor are making the beast with two backs.
Othello, I,i,113.

[1] He hath a person and a smooth dispose
To be suspected—framed to make women false. *Othello,* I,iii,388. (Iago on
Roderigo. He means: He is the kind of person and has the smooth manner
to warrant suspicion, he is shaped to seduce women.)

[2] 'Tis the strumpet's plague
To beguile many and be beguiled by one. *Othello,* IV,i,98. (And therefore
we have the profession of pimp.)

[3] I do think it is their husbands' faults
If wives do fall. *Othello,* IV,iii,89. (Emilia to Desdemona.)

[4] Touches so soft still conquer chastity. *The Passionate Pilgrim,* iv,8. (*Still*
means "always.")

[5] Were kisses all the joys in bed,
One woman would another wed. *The Passionate Pilgrim,* xviii,47.

[6] A dream, a breath, a froth of fleeting joy. *The Rape of Lucrece,* 212.
(Tarquin's characterization of sexual conquest. See also VALUE.)

[7] He capers nimbly in a lady's chamber
To the lascivious pleasing of a lute. *Richard III,* I,i,12. (More at WAR AND
PEACE.)

[8] Was ever woman in this humor wooed?
Was ever woman in this humor won?
I'll have her, but I will not keep her long. *Richard III,* I,ii,228. (Richard in
the midst of his fantastic courtship of Lady Anne, whose husband and
father-in-law he has murdered. She knows what he is, but marries him.
For similar quotes, see WOMEN [*Titus Andronicus*].)

[9] So shall I live, supposing thou art true,
Like a deceivèd husband; so love's face
May still seem love to me, though altered new,
Thy looks with me, thy heart in other place. *Sonnet 93,* 1. (Shakespeare's
beloved "dark lady" evidently was unfaithful, apparently with his friend
Southampton, according to A. L. Rowse. That she was probably also
married was of much less account. See *Sonnet 136* under SHAKESPEARE.)

[10] The expense of spirit in a waste of shame
Is lust in action; and, till action, lust
Is perjured, murd'rous, bloody, full of blame,
Savage, extreme, rude, cruel, not to trust;
Enjoyed no sooner but despisèd straight;
Past reason hunted, and no sooner had,
Past reason hated as a swallowed bait

On purpose laid to make the taker mad;
Made in pursuit, and in possession so;
Had, having, and in quest to have, extreme;
A bliss in proof, and proved, a very woe,
Before, a joy proposed; behind, a dream.
All this the world well knows, yet none knows well
To shun the heaven that leads men to this hell. *Sonnet 129.* (Sometimes
called "the lust sonnet." For a comparison of love and lust, see under LOVE
AND LOVERS, the quote from *Venus and Adonis,* l.799.)

[1] For I have sworn thee fair, and thought thee bright,
Who art as black as hell, as dark as night. *Sonnet 147,* 13. (Here and above,
Shakespeare is in despair over the infidelity of the "dark lady" and his
inability to govern his desires.)

[2] Be a whore still; they love thee not that use thee. *Timon of Athens,* IV,iii,84.

[3]   Women are angels wooing;
Things won are done, joy's soul lies in the doing. *Troilus and Cressida,*
I,ii,298.

[4] This is the monstruosity [sic] in love, lady, that the will is infinite and the
execution confined; that the desire is boundless and the act a slave to limit.
Troilus and Cressida, III,ii,82.

[5] The kiss you take is better than you give. *Troilus and Cressida,* IV,v,38.

[6] There's language in her eye, her cheek, her lip;
Nay, her foot speaks. Her wanton spirits look out
At every joint and motive of her body. *Troilus and Cressida,* IV,v,55.
(Ulysses interpreting Cressida's body language. *Motive* means "moving
part.")

[7] Lechery, lechery; still wars and lechery; nothing else holds fashion. *Troilus
and Cressida,* V,ii,192. (Thersites in Shakespeare's most bitter comedy. See
also WAR, *Troilus and Cressida,* II,iii,77.)

[8] Pearls are fair; and the old saying is, Black men are pearls in beauteous
ladies' eyes. *The Two Gentlemen of Verona,* V,ii,11.

[9]   Paddling palms and pinching fingers. *The Winter's Tale,* I,ii,115.
(Flirtatious touching that the jealous king of Sicily, Leontes, believes he
detects between his wife and his friend King Polixenes of Bohemia.)

[10] It is a bawdy planet. *The Winter's Tale,* I,ii,201.

See also CLEOPATRA; DESIRE; LOVE AND LOVERS; MARRIAGE; MEN AND
WOMEN; PLEASURE; WILD AND WANTON PEOPLE; WOMEN.

SHAKESPEARE

(Here follow quotes on Shakespeare.)

[1] I acknowledge Shakespeare to be the world's greatest dramatic poet, but regret that no parent could place the uncorrected book in the hands of his daughter, and therefore I have prepared the Family Shakespeare. (Thomas Bowdler, preface to *The Family Shakespeare,* 1818. This classic justification for censorship is from the second, enlarged edition of the work that produced the word *bowdlerize.* The first edition, published in 1807, was not prepared by Thomas, but by his sister Henrietta Maria, usually known by her nickname, Harriet. Her name never appeared on the book, however, probably because, as a maiden lady, she did not wish the public to know just how much of Shakespeare's language she really understood.)

[2]   Our myriad-minded Shakespeare. (Samuel Taylor Coleridge, *Biographia Literaria,* 1817.)

[3]   He was the man who of all modern, and perhaps ancient poets, had the largest and most comprehensive soul. (John Dryden, *Essay of Dramatic Poesy,* 1668.)

[4] For there is an upstart crow, beautified with our feathers, that with his tiger's heart wrapped in a player's hide, supposes he is as well able to bumbast out a blank verse as the best of you; and being an absolute *Johannes fac totum,* is in his own conceit the only Shake-scene in a country." (Robert Greene, *The Groatsworth of Wit,* 1592. A famous attack on Shakespeare, a parody of a line describing Margaret of Anjou in *Henry VI, Part Three.* See under WOMEN.)

[5]   Soul of the age!
The applause, delight, the wonder of our stage!
My Shakespeare rise. (Ben Jonson, *To the Memory of My Beloved, the Author, Mr. William Shakespeare,* 1623.)

[6] Thou art a monument without a tomb,
And art alive still while thy book doth live,
And we have wits to read and praise to give. (Ben Jonson, *To the Memory of My Beloved, the Author, Mr. William Shakespeare,* 1623.)

[7] He was not of an age, but for all time. (Ben Jonson, *To the Memory of My Beloved, the Author, Mr. William Shakespeare,* 1623.)

[8]   Sweet Swan of Avon! (Ben Jonson, *To the Memory of My Beloved, the Author, Mr. William Shakespeare,* 1623.)

[9]   The players have often mentioned it as an honor to Shakespeare that in his writing (whatsoever he penned) he never blotted out a line. My

answer hath been, "Would he had blotted a thousand." (Ben Jonson, *Timber; or Discoveries Made upon Men and Matter,* 1640.)

[1]   Sweetest Shakespeare, Fancy's child,
Warbles his native wood-notes wild. (John Milton, *L'Allegro,* 1631.)

[2] Make but my name thy love, and love that still,
And then thou lovest me for my name is *Will. Sonnet 136,* 13. (A complicated, flirtatious pun. In addition to prompting the lady to say "I will," *will* was a slang term for penis. Also, according to A. L. Rowse, the "dark lady" addressed here, whom he identifies as Emilia Bassana, was matched in a marriage of convenience with *Will* Lanier. Both were musicians.)

[3] Good friend, for Jesus' sake forbear
To dig the dust enclosèd here.
Blessed be the man that spares these stones
And cursed be he that moves my bones. (Verse on Shakespeare's gravestone, possibly by the playwright himself.)

[4] With the single exception of Homer, there is no eminent writer, not even Sir Walter Scott, whom I can despise so entirely as I despise Shakespeare when I measure my mind against his. (George Bernard Shaw, *Saturday Review,* September 26, 1896.)

[5] Even when Shakespeare, in his efforts to be a social philosopher, does rise for an instant to the level of a sixth-rate Kingsley, his solemn self-complacency infuriates me. And yet, so wonderful is his art, that it is not easy to disentangle what is unbearable from what is irresistible. (George Bernard Shaw, *Saturday Review,* December 5, 1896. The Rev. Charles Kingsley, 1819–1875, was a novelist, poet, and social reformer, being a reverend, and a Christian one, not to Shaw's liking.)

See also under EDUCATION and FUN AND FUN PEOPLE, quotes from *Love's Labor's Lost.*

SHAKESPEAREAN SLIPS

[6]   I am Saint Jaques' pilgrim, thither gone. *All's Well That Ends Well,* III,iv,4. (Dr. Johnson pounced upon this passage, pointing out that making a pilgrimage to the shrine of St. James at Compostela in Spain was an unlikely detour for Helena, who was traveling from Paris to Florence.)

[7]   Let's to billiards. *Antony and Cleopatra,* II,v,3. (Cleopatra, in the absence of Antony, suggesting a futuristic diversion.)

[8]   Thou hast caused printing to be used, and contrary to the King, his crown and dignity, thou hast built a paper mill. *Henry VI, Part Two,*

IV,vii,37. (Neither printing nor paper mills existed in England in the mid-fifteenth century. The play takes place just about the time that Gutenberg printed the Bible. The anachronisms may have been intended as humor. For more, see EDUCATION.)

[1] *Brutus.* Peace! Count the clock.
Cassius. The clock hath stricken three. *Julius Caesar,* II,i,192. (Mechanical clocks did not exist in ancient times, other than rare water-driven clocks. Weight-driven clocks were invented in the tenth or possibly the ninth century. In 1286, a clock that struck the hours was installed in St. Paul's Cathedral in London.)

[2] O, bravely came we off,
When with a volley of our needless shot,
After such bloody toil, we bid good night
And wound our tott'ring colors clearly up,
Last in the field, and almost lords of it! *King John,* V,v,4. (The French dauphin celebrating a victory over the English. The unnecessary volley of shot, however, would not have been fired early in the thirteenth century, the period in which the play is set. The first military guns in Europe appeared about a century later.)

[3] I shall not need spectacles. *King Lear,* I,ii,36. (Anachronistic spectacles also appear in IV,vi,172; see under POLITICS.)

[4] *Ira furor brevis est. Timon of Athens,* I,ii,28. (A famous quote from Horace's *Epistles,* unlikely to have been uttered by Timon of Athens, who lived a few hundred years earlier. For a similar slip, see YOUTH, the note on *Troilus and Cressida,* II,ii,166).

[5] By mine honesty, welcome to Padua. *The Two Gentlemen of Verona,* II,v,i. (Actually, the characters are in Milan. This is just one of a number of slips in this play. Later, the duke of Milan refers to his country as Verona. Proteus, for another example, evidently forgets that he has met the memorable Silvia, saying only that he has seen a picture of her. Samuel Johnson commented, "The reason for all this confusion seems to be that he took his story from a novel, which sometimes he followed and sometimes forsook, sometimes remembered and sometimes forgot," *The Plays of William Shakespeare.*)

[6] Scene III. [*Bohemia, the seacoast.*] *The Winter's Tale,* III,iii, opening stage note. (Shakespeare's source was Robert Greene's novel *Pandosto, or the Triumph of Time.* But Shakespeare switched the two kingdoms in the story, Sicily and Bohemia, which led to this erroneous attribution of a seacoast to Bohemia. The error has distressed numerous scholars, including Ben Jonson. In a letter to the *New York Times* in 1988, a reader named Jackie

Boyce suggested that in one period in the fourteenth century the Kingdom of Bohemia extended to the Adriatic coast, and further claimed that in the sixteenth century, under Hapsburg rulers, Bohemia was united with the Archduchy of Austria and therefore extended to the coast. This was denied by a subsequent correspondent. It does seem that a simple mixup caused the error. Shakespeare also referred to "the deserts of Bohemia," *The Winter's Tale*, III,iii,2.)

SHAME. See CONSCIENCE; GUILT; RUIN; VIRTUE (*Romeo and Juliet*).

SHIPS AND SAILING

1   Your argosies with portly sail. *The Merchant of Venice*, I,i,9.

2   Ships are but boards, sailors but men; there be land rats and water rats, water thieves and land thieves. *The Merchant of Venice*, I,iii,21. (Shylock on Antonio's argosies.)

3 How like a younger or a prodigal
The scarfèd bark puts from her native bay,
Hugged and embracèd by the strumpet wind!
How like the prodigal doth she return,
With over-weathered ribs and ragged sails,
Lean, rent, and beggared by the strumpet wind! *The Merchant of Venice*, II,vi,14. (Shakespeare used the image of a ship putting out to sea to express eagerness and desire; see also DESIRE. In line 1, a *younger* is a younger son; *scarfèd* is "decorated.")

4 Methoughts I saw a thousand fearful wracks;
A thousand men that fishes gnawed upon. *Richard III*, I,iv,24. (More at DEATH.)

5   Like a drunken sailor on a mast,
Ready with every nod to tumble down
Into the fatal bowels of the deep. *Richard III*, III,iv,98.

6 Now would I give a thousand furlongs of sea for an acre of barren ground.
. . . I would fain die a dry death. *The Tempest*, I,i,64,67. (The aged royal councilor Gonzalo during the tempest and shipwreck at the beginning of this play. Shakespeare probably drew on reports of a shipwreck in a storm off the Bermudas in 1609. In I,ii,229, he refers to the "still-vexed Bermoothes" [Bermudas]. News that crew and passengers had been saved after this storm arrived in England in 1610. The men had survived quite comfortably on a balmy, lush island for nine months. Shakespeare probably began writing *The Tempest* that year. The first production was staged at court in 1611.)

¹ A rotten carcass of a butt, not rigged,
Nor tackle, nor sail, nor mast; the very rats
Instinctively have quit it. *The Tempest,* I,ii,146. (A *butt* is a barrel, a tub.
Prospero and his infant daughter, Miranda, were exiled in this hulk.)

²   He is gone aboard a new ship, to purge melancholy and air himself.
The Winter's Tale, IV,iv,767.

See also NATURE.

SICKNESS

³   The thousand natural shocks
That flesh is heir to! *Hamlet,* III,i,62.

⁴   Who comes here! a grave unto a soul,
Holding the eternal spirit, against her will,
In the vile prison of afflicted breath. *King John,* III,iii,17. (*A grave unto a
soul* means "one lingering on the verge of death.")

⁵ Within me is a hell. *King John,* V,vii,46. (King John is said to be dying of
poison, apparently from food he ate. His symptoms are consistent with
ergotism. He suffers mental derangement, or "strange fantasies," in the
words of his son Prince Henry, l.18. He complains of burning pain and
pleads, "Comfort me with cold . . . I beg cold comfort," l.41. Ergotism,
epidemic in the Middle Ages, is caused by a fungus infection of rye and
other grains used in bread.)

⁶   All the shrouds wherewith my life should sail
Are turnèd to one thread, one little hair:
My heart hath one poor string to stay it by. *King John,* V,vii,53.

⁷ O, how this mother swells up toward my heart!
Hysterica passio, down, thou climbing sorrow,
Thy element's below. *King Lear,* II,iv,55. (A reference to choking in panic.
Mother refers to the contents of the stomach. *Element* means "proper
place.")

⁸ Sleep shall neither night nor day
Hang upon his penthouse lid;
He shall live a man forbid:
Weary sev'nights nine times nine
Shall he dwindle, peak, and pine. *Macbeth,* I,iii,19. (A *penthouse* is a sort
of lean-to and therefore a half-open lid. This is a witch's curse—wasting
diseases were often blamed on witches.)

1   They are as sick that surfeit with too much as they that starve with nothing. *The Merchant of Venice,* I,ii,5.

2   Hope: he is a flatterer,
A parasite, a keeper-back of Death,
Who gently would dissolve the bands of life
Which false Hope lingers in extremity. *Richard II,* II,ii,69. (For *lingers* read "causes to linger.")

3 Unwieldy, slow, heavy and pale as lead. *Romeo and Juliet,* II,v,17. (A description by Juliet's nurse of those "old folks" who seem almost dead.)

See also DOCTORS; HEALTH; MEDICINE.

SILENCE.   See HAPPINESS (*Much Ado About Nothing,* II,i,303); LISTENING; NOISE; TALK.

SIMPLICITY.   See COUNTRY LIFE; TALK, PLAIN AND FANCY.

SIN AND SINNERS.   See CRIME; DANGEROUS PEOPLE; DISHONESTY; EVIL; JUDGING OTHERS; LIES AND DECEIT; TEMPTATION; WILD AND WANTON PEOPLE.

SKEPTICISM.   See DOUBT.

SKY.   See HEAVENS, THE; MOON, THE; STARS.

SLANDER

4 For slander lives upon succession,
For ever housed where it gets possession. *The Comedy of Errors,* III,i,105.

5   Slander,
Whose edge is sharper than the sword, whose tongue
Outvenoms all the worms of Nile, whose breath
Rides on the posting winds and doth belie
All corners of the world. *Cymbeline,* III,iv,34. (*Worms* are snakes. *Posting* means "speeding," and *belie* means "fill with lies.")

6 Done to death by slanderous tongues. *Much Ado About Nothing,* V,iii,3.

7   Slander,
Whose sting is sharper than the sword's. *The Winter's Tale,* II,iii,84.

See also REPUTATION; RUMOR; TALK.

SLEEP AND DREAMS

[1] I have not slept one wink. *Cymbeline,* III,iv,102.

[2]   Weariness
Can snore upon the flint when resty sloth
Finds the down pillow hard. *Cymbeline,* III,vi,33. (For *resty* read "lazy.")

[3] O God, I could be bounded in a nutshell and count myself a king of infinite space, were it not that I have bad dreams. *Hamlet,* II,ii,258.

[4]   To sleep—
To sleep—perchance to dream: ay, there's the rub. *Hamlet,* III,i,64. (More at SUICIDE.)

[5]   O sleep, O gentle sleep,
Nature's soft nurse, how have I frighted thee,
That thou no more wilt weigh my eyelids down
And steep my senses in forgetfulness? *Henry IV, Part Two,* III,i,5. (As befits a king's education, Henry's soliloquy includes a classical allusion: "Sleep, most gentle sleep," Ovid, *Metamorphoses,* Book II. See ANXIETY AND WORRY for Prince Hal's soliloquy on "golden care" that keeps "the ports of slumber open wide.")

[6] Enjoy the honey-heavy dew of slumber. *Julius Caesar,* II,i,230.

[7]   O murderous slumber! *Julius Caesar,* IV,iii,266.

[8] Our foster-nurse of nature is repose. *King Lear,* IV,iv,12.

[9] Sleep shall neither night nor day
Hang upon his penthouse lid. *Macbeth,* I,iii,19. (A witch's curse. More at SICKNESS.)

[10] Methought I heard a voice cry "Sleep no more!
Macbeth does murder sleep"—the innocent sleep,
Sleep that knits up the raveled sleave of care,
The death of each day's life, sore labor's bath,
Balm of hurt minds, great nature's second course,
Chief nourisher in life's feast. *Macbeth,* II,ii,34. (The importance of rest to health well described, about four hundred years before studies of sleep deprivation supplied the physiological details. The *raveled sleave* refers to a filament of silk or other material that unraveled or was pulled out, as from a fabric. The sleave could be woven back in. Nature's first *course* would be nourishment, eating.)

¹ "Glamis hath murdered sleep, and therefore Cawdor
Shall sleep no more: Macbeth shall sleep no more." *Macbeth,* II,ii,41.
(*Glamis* and *Cawdor* are Macbeth's former and present titles.)

² Shake off this downy sleep, death's counterfeit. *Macbeth,* II,iii,78.

³ You lack the season of all natures, sleep. *Macbeth,* III,iv,142.

⁴ I have an exposition of sleep come upon me. *A Midsummer Night's Dream,*
IV,i,42. (A characteristic malapropism from Bottom. By *exposition* he
means "expectation.")

⁵   Not poppy mor mandragora,
Nor all the drowsy syrups of the world,
Shall ever medicine thee to that sweet sleep
Which thou owedst yesterday. *Othello,* III,iii,327. (Sleeping medicines
included opium and mandrake root, of the nightshade family.)

⁶ O, I have passed a miserable night,
So full of fearful dreams, of ugly sights,
That, as I am a Christian faithful man,
I would not spend another such a night
Though 'twere to buy a world of happy days,
So full of dismal terror was the time. *Richard III,* I,iv,2.

⁷   I talk of dreams;
Which are the children of an idle brain. *Romeo and Juliet,* I,iv,96. (This
follows the brilliant description of Queen Mab coursing the night world in
her fairy carriage, bringing dreams. The first part of the speech is given at
FAIRIES, through the reference to her bringing lovers dreams of love. For
the dreams she brings to others, consult the play, I,iv,71.)

⁸ In sleep a king, but waking no such matter. *Sonnet 87,* 14.

⁹   Sits as one new-risen from a dream. *The Taming of the Shrew,* IV,i,180.
(The reference is to Kate. More at MANIPULATION.)

¹⁰   In dreaming,
The clouds methought would open and show riches
Ready to drop upon me, that, when I waked,
I cried to dream again. *The Tempest,* III,ii,145. (Caliban's dream.)

¹¹   I shall sleep like a top. *The Two Noble Kinsmen,* III,iv,26.

See also DREAMERS; FAIRIES (the Queen Mab passage from *Romeo and
Juliet*); HIGH POSITION (*Henry IV, Part Two* and *Henry V*).

SMALL PEOPLE

[1] He that of greatest works is finisher,
Oft does them by the weakest minister. *All's Well That Ends Well,* II,i,137.

[2] You are the hare of whom the proverb goes,
Whose valor plucks dead lions by the beard. *King John,* II,i,137. (The speaker—a fictional bastard son of Richard I—here baits the duke of Austria, Leopold V, who had imprisoned Richard. These lines are believed to refer to Thomas Kyd's *The Spanish Tragedy* [1589], which contains the following verse: "He hunted well that was a lion's death, / Not he that in a garment wore his skin; / So hares may pull dead lions by the beard.")

[3]   A little pot and soon hot. *The Taming of the Shrew,* IV,i,5. (Here the reference is to small stature. One interpretation of this adage is as a description of that common type, the small but feisty male.)

See also HUMILITY.

SMALL THINGS

[4] Dispense with trifles. *The Merry Wives of Windsor,* II,i,46.

[5] "Small herbs have grace, great weeds do grow apace." *Richard III,* II,iv,13. (*Grace* here means "virtue" or "good quality." The young duke of York is quoting a proverb that he learned from his uncle, the future Richard III. The boy adds that he is in no hurry to grow quickly. He senses that the future is dangerous. He and his brother, the Prince of Wales, are murdered by Richard.)

[6]   In such indexes, although small pricks
To their subsequent volumes, there is seen
The baby figure of the giant mass
Of things to come. *Troilus and Cressida,* I,iii,343. (In this metaphor, small signs of things to come are likened to book indexes. In Elizabethan times, the index was more like a table of contents, and printed in the front of the book.)

SOCIAL CLASS.   See WORK (*Hamlet,* V).

SOLDIERS

[7]   Thou, the greatest soldier of the world. *Antony and Cleopatra,* I,iii,38. (Cleopatra to Antony.)

[8]   Ambition
(The soldier's virtue). *Antony and Cleopatra,* III,i,22. (More at AMBITION.)

¹   Call to me
All my sad captains. *Antony and Cleopatra,* III,xiii,183. (Antony before his death. More at FUN AND FUN PEOPLE.)

² O, withered is the garland of the war,
The soldier's pole is fallen. *Antony and Cleopatra,* IV,xv,64. (Cleopatra on the death of Antony. More at DEATH AND GRIEF.)

³   A soldier,
Full of strange oaths and bearded like the pard,
Jealous in honor, sudden and quick in quarrel,
Seeking the bubble reputation
Even in the cannon's mouth. *As You Like It,* II,vii,149. (From the "seven ages of man" speech; see LIFE. *Pard* means "leopard.")

⁴ He was a thing of blood, whose every motion
Was timed with dying cries. *Coriolanus,* II,ii,110. (Coriolanus in action on the battlefield.)

⁵ Not to be other than one thing, not moving
From the casque to the cushion, but commanding peace
Even with the same austerity and garb
As he controlled the war. *Coriolanus,* IV,vii,42. (Coriolanus in peacetime.)

⁶   But for these vile guns,
He would himself have been a soldier. *Henry IV, Part One,* I,iii,62. (From Hotspur's account of remarks by a certain "popinjay" who found war distasteful. Hotspur's account is influenced by the fact that the popinjay was an emissary of the king asking Hotspur to turn over prisoners. See also EFFETENESS.)

⁷   All furnished, all in arms;
. . .
Glittering in golden coats like images;
As full of spirit as the month of May
And gorgeous as the sun at midsummer. *Henry IV, Part One,* IV,i,96,99. (Sir Richard Vernon describing Prince Hal and his comrades in armor at the start of the battle of Shrewsbury.)

⁸   Food for powder, food for powder, they'll fill a pit as well as better. *Henry IV, Part One,* IV,ii,66. (The *powder* is gunpowder. Falstaff is saying that the ragged troops he has forced into service are adequate cannon fodder. Another description of these poor troops is at PEACE.)

⁹   He will maintain his argument as well as any military man in the world. *Henry V,* III,ii,81. (Said by Captain Fluellen, a great admirer of the Roman military methods, of Captain Jamy, who, he believes, shares this enthusiasm.)

¹ O God of battles, steel my soldiers' hearts,
Possess them not with fear! Take from them now
The sense of reckoning, or the opposèd numbers
Pluck their hearts from them. *Henry V,* IV,i,294. (Henry praying before
the battle of Agincourt that God will not let his men realize the full force
of numbers against them for fear they will lose heart. The English army,
once 10,000 strong, was reduced at the time of the battle, October 25,
1415, to about 5,500 archers and 1,000 men-at-arms. The French probably
numbered about 25,000, the majority being men-at-arms. The effective-
ness of the English archers, the relative mobility of the troops, and numerous other factors, including desperation, led to the great victory.)

²   Our houses, and ourselves, and children,
  . . .
. . . grow like savages—as soldiers will,
That nothing do but meditate on blood. *Henry V,* V,ii,56,59. (The duke
of Burgundy on the effects of war. See also SCIENCE.)

³ Will you vouchsafe to teach a soldier terms
Such as will enter at a lady's ear,
And plead his love suit to her gentle heart? *Henry V,* V,ii,99. (The victori-
ous soldier Henry V to Katherine, the French royal princess. See also
LOVE, EXPRESSIONS OF.)

⁴ I speak to thee plain soldier: if thou canst love me for this, take me. *Henry
V,* V,ii,153. (The king again to Katherine; see above. He adds that if she
were to turn him down, "To say to thee that I shall die, is true—but for
thy love, by the Lord, no; yet I love thee too," l.154. Frank and winning,
the speech is reminiscent of Rosalind's remark in *As You Like It,* Act IV,
that men have died from time to time, but not for love; see LOVE AND
LOVERS. See also LOVE, EXPRESSIONS OF.)

⁵ I am a soldier and unapt to weep
Or to exclaim on fortune's fickleness. *Henry VI, Part One,* V,iii,133.

⁶   Let no soldier fly.
He that is truly dedicate to war
Hath no self-love. *Henry VI, Part Two,* V,ii,36.

⁷ Rash, inconsiderate, fiery voluntaries,
  . . .
Have sold their fortunes at their native homes,
Bearing their birthrights proudly on their backs,
To make a hazard of new fortunes here. *King John,* II,i,67. (*Voluntaries*
were English volunteers, soldiers of fortune. They sold off their inheri-
tances to purchase armor to make war against the king of France.)

[1] Fie, my lord, fie! A soldier, and afeared? *Macbeth,* V,i,40. (The sleepwalking Lady Macbeth.)

[2] Your son, my lord, hath paid a soldier's debt. *Macbeth,* V,viii,39. (More at EPITAPHS.)

[3] That in the captain's but a choleric word,
Which in the soldier is flat blasphemy. *Measure for Measure,* II,ii,130. (Isabella, arguing that the severity of an offense may depend on the rank of the offender.)

[4] Horribly stuffed with epithets of war. *Othello,* I,i,13. (Iago's description of Othello's manner of speech.)

[5] A soldier's a man,
O man's life's but a span,
Why then, let a soldier drink. *Othello,* II,iii,68.

[6] You may relish him more in the soldier than in the scholar. *Othello,* II,i,163.

[7] Thou art a soldier, therefore seldom rich. *Timon of Athens,* I,ii,230.

[8] 'Tis honor with most lands to be at odds;
Soldiers should brook as little wrongs as gods. *Timon of Athens,* III,v,115. (Spoken by the proud Alcibiades—a general.)

See also ENGLAND AND THE ENGLISH; WAR.

SORROW AND SADNESS

[9] My heart is heavy and mine age is weak;
Grief would have tears, and sorrow bids me speak. *All's Well That Ends Well,* III,iv,41.

[10]   We are not all alone unhappy. *As You Like It,* II,vii,136. (Translation: We are not the only unhappy people in the world. More at WORLD.)

[11] Some griefs are medicinable. *Cymbeline,* III,ii,33. (In other words, some griefs do good. In this case, the grief of separation keeps love healthy.)

[12]   I have that within which passes show;
These but the trappings and the suits of woe. *Hamlet,* I,ii,85. (Hamlet stating that his black clothes and sorrowful behavior are signs of a sorrow too deep to express in such outward show.)

[13] A countenance more in sorrow than in anger. *Hamlet,* I,ii,232. (The reference is to the ghost of Hamlet's father.)

1   O, woe is me
To have seen what I have seen, see what I see! *Hamlet*, III,i,163. (Ophelia speaking of Hamlet's apparent madness.)

2 When sorrows come, they come not single spies,
But in battalions. *Hamlet*, IV,v,78. (A common thought. Bartlett's *Familiar Quotations* cites parallels in Cervantes, Herrick, and Edward Young. Here the king speaks. Later Gertrude says very much the same thing; see TROUBLE.)

3 I am as melancholy as a gib-cat or a lugged bear. *Henry IV, Part One*, I,ii,76. (Falstaff claims to be as melancholy as a tomcat or a bear tied to a stake and baited by dogs.)

4 A plague of sighing and grief, it blows a man up like a bladder. *Henry IV, Part One*, II,iv,332.

5   A golden sorrow. *Henry VIII*, II,iii,22. (More at HAPPINESS.)

6 What private griefs they have, alas, I know not. *Julius Caesar*,III,ii,215.

7 I will instruct my sorrows to be proud,
For grief is proud and makes his owner stoop. *King John*, II,ii,68.

8 Affliction may one day smile again, and till then sit thee down, sorrow! *Love's Labor's Lost*, I,i,309. (Costard reminding himself that when things aren't going too badly, one might as well be happy.)

9 Give sorrow words. The grief that does not speak
Whispers the o'er-fraught heart, and bids it break. *Macbeth*, IV,iii,209. (In the second line, we might say, "Whispers to the overburdened heart.")

10 What a sigh is there! The heart is sorely charged. *Macbeth*, V,i,56. (The doctor speaking of Lady Macbeth.)

11 I cannot weep, nor answers have I none. *Othello*, IV,ii,102. (Desdemona, crushed and confused by Othello's accusations.)

12 The poor soul sat singing by a sycamore tree,
Sing all a green willow;
Her hand on her bosom, her head on her knee,
Sing willow, willow, willow.
The fresh streams ran by her and murmured her moans;
Sing willow, willow, willow;
Her salt tears fell from her, and soft'ned the stones—
Sing willow, willow, willow. *Othello*, IV,iii,41. (A sad song sung by Desdemona—impossible to hear now without thinking of Gilbert and Sullivan's "Tit Willow.")

¹ The sad companion, dull-eyed melancholy. *Pericles,* I,ii,3.

² Grief makes one hour ten. *Richard II,* I,iii,260.

³   I was a journeyman to grief? *Richard II,* I,iii,273. (More at BANISH-MENT AND EXILE.)

⁴ For gnarling sorrow hath less power to bite
The mad that mocks at it and sets it light. *Richard II,* I,iii,291. (John of Gaunt to Bolingbroke, his son. For Bolingbroke's thoughts on the power of positive thinking, see THOUGHT.)

⁵ Each substance of a grief hath twenty shadows. *Richard II,* II,ii,14.

⁶ You may my glories and my state depose,
But not my griefs; still am I King of those. *Richard II,* IV,i,191. (Richard to the usurper Bolingbroke, who becomes Henry IV. Here Richard is refusing to pretend that he is abdicating cheerfully.)

⁷ How soon my sorrow hath destroyed my face. *Richard II,* IV,i,290. (Richard in the mirror scene. He was, incidentally, reputed to be exceptionally handsome, and Shakespeare followed this tradition.)

⁸ Sorrow breaks seasons and reposing hours,
Makes the night morning and the noontide night. *Richard III,* I,iv,76.

⁹ Is there no pity sitting in the clouds
That sees into the bottom of my grief? *Romeo and Juliet,* III,v,198.

¹⁰   Weep I cannot,
But my heart bleeds. *The Winter's Tale,* III,iii,50.

¹¹   I'll queen it no inch farther,
But milk my ewes, and weep. *The Winter's Tale,* IV,iv,453. (The shepherd-ess Perdita renouncing her prince. Before the play is over, happily, she will discover her own royal heritage.)

See also DEATH AND GRIEF; DEPRESSION; DESPAIR; HAPPINESS; STOICISM; SUFFERING; WEEPING.

SOUL

¹² I do not set my life at a pin's fee,
And for my soul, what can it do to that,
Being a thing immortal as itself? *Hamlet,* I,iv,65. (Hamlet deciding to follow the apparition of his father that is beckoning to him. The ghost, he reasons, can do him no harm.)

¹³ O my prophetic soul! *Hamlet,* I,v,40. (Hamlet upon learning that his uncle is his father's murderer.)

¹ Every subject's duty is the King's, but every subject's soul is his own. *Henry V*, IV,i,181.

² My soul's palace is become a prison. *Henry VI, Part Three*, II,i,74.

³ Mine eternal jewel. *Macbeth*, III,i,68. (The *jewel* is the soul.)

⁴ Well, God's above all; and there be souls must be saved, and there be souls must not be saved. *Othello*, II,iii,99.

⁵ Poor soul, the center of my sinful earth. *Sonnet 146*, 1.

S P A C E .   See STARS; STAR WARS.

SPECTATORS

⁶ I'll be a candleholder and look on. *Romeo and Juliet*, I,iv,38. (Romeo declining to join the dance. A *candleholder* would be a servant or other person, holding a light for others. Shakespeare identifies the phrase as proverbial. The previous line reads, "I am proverbed with a grandsire phrase.")

S P E E C H .   See PUBLIC SPEAKING; SLANDER; TALK.

SPEED

⁷ Celerity is never more admired
Than by the negligent. *Antony and Cleopatra*, III,vii,24.

⁸ O, for a horse with wings! *Cymbeline*, III,ii,49.

⁹ With wings as swift
As meditation or the thoughts of love. *Hamlet*, I,v,29.

¹⁰ Make haste: the better foot before! *King John*, IV,ii,170.

¹¹ The affair cries haste,
And speed must answer it. *Othello*, I,iii,271.

¹² With all convenient haste. *Richard III*, IV,iv,443. (*Convenient haste* means "appropriate haste." In *The Merchant of Venice*, III,iv,56, the phrase is rendered "with all convenient speed." This is similar to the legal term "with all deliberate speed," made famous in *Brown vs. the Board of Education*, the case that brought desegregation to U.S. schools.)

¹³ They stumble that run fast. *Romeo and Juliet*, II,iii,94. (More at CAREFULNESS; see also below.)

[1] Too swift arrives as tardy as too slow. *Romeo and Juliet,* II,vi,15. (More at LOVE AND LOVERS.)

See also EAGERNESS.

SPORTS

[2] Trivial fond records. *Hamlet* I,v,99. (A nice description of the kinds of facts sports buffs collect. See MEMORY.)

[3] A hit, a very palpable hit. *Hamlet,* V,ii,282. (A ruling by the courtier acting as judge in the duel between Hamlet and Laertes. Stage swordplay can be dangerous. In Paul Rudnick's 1991 production of *I Hate Hamlet,* actor Evan Handler walked off the stage and out of the theater after being rapped in an undisciplined sword swipe by Nicol Williamson. Mr. Williamson, in the role of the ghost of John Barrymore, had it just right. Theater scholar John Otis in a letter to the *New York Times* said that William Adams, stage manager for Barrymore's 1900 production of *Hamlet,* told him that Barrymore frequently cut, bruised, and terrified the actors playing Laertes. In London, one threw down his foil and fled.)

[4] *King.* What treasure, uncle?
Exeter. Tennis balls, my liege. *Henry V,* I,ii,258. (The tennis balls were sent from the dauphin to the young King Henry V. The king was soon enough playing in the French court. The game, incidentally, was court tennis, which is played indoors; the court and the rules are different from those of the modern game.)

[5] They laugh that win. *Othello,* IV,i,124.

[6] There be some sports are painful. *The Tempest,* III,i,1.

See also RIDING.

SPRING

[7] It was a lover and his lass,
With a hey, and a ho, and a hey nonino,
That o'er the green cornfield did pass
In springtime, the only pretty ringtime,
When buds do sing, hey ding a ding, ding.
Sweet lovers love the spring. *As You Like It,* V,iii,13.

[8] When daisies pied and violets blue
And lady-smocks all silver-white
And cuckoo-buds of yellow hue
Do paint the meadows with delight,

The cuckoo then, on every tree,
Mocks married men; for thus sings he, "Cuckoo!" *Love's Labor's Lost*,
V,ii,895. (From the happy, if slightly bawdy, song that ends the play. The
cuckoo's call, of course, is a version of "cuckold." See also SEX.)

¹ Rough winds do shake the darling buds of May. *Sonnet 18*, 3. (More at
MORTALITY.)

² From you I have been absent in the spring,
When proud-pied April, dressed in all his trim,
Hath put a spirit of youth in everything. *Sonnet 98*, 1.

³ The uncertain glory of an April day. *The Two Gentlemen of Verona*, I,iii,85.
(More at LOVE AND LOVERS.)

⁴ More matter for a May morning. *Twelfth Night*, III,iv,148.

⁵ When daffodils begin to peer,
With heigh the doxy over the dale,
Why, then comes in the sweet o' the year,
For the red blood reigns in the winter's pale.
The white sheet bleaching on the hedge,
With heigh the sweet birds, O how they sing! *The Winter's Tale*, IV,iii,1.
(The sight of sheets bleaching on the hedge gladdens the shepherd Au-
tolycus, not only as a sign of spring, but also because he steals them—theft
of linen was a common crime in Elizabethan England. Autolycus is named
after a son of Mercury, skilled in thieving. The *pale* refers to an enclosure.
The phrase *the doxy over the dale* may be a pun. The term *dale* or *dell* refers
to a virgin as well as a valley, so this may be a light tribute to the free doxy
over the restrained virgin.)

See also PLANTS AND FLOWERS.

STARS

⁶ But I am constant as the Northern Star,
Of whose true-fixed and resting quality
There is no fellow in the firmament.
The skies are painted with unnumbered sparks,
They are all fire. *Julius Caesar*, III,i,60. (Caesar in a characteristically self-
satisfied mood. The metaphor reflects an interest in astronomy, common
among educated Elizabethans. On the Continent, the Copernican revolution was underway. Kepler was already doing major work in the 1590s,
when *Julius Caesar* was written. On the other hand, astrology was still
widely accepted. When Calphurnia speaks of comets as portents—see
GREATNESS—Shakespeare presents this as a normal view. Meteors were
conceived as exhalations; see RUIN.)

¹   It is the stars,
The stars above us, govern our conditions. *King Lear,* IV,iii,33. (An example of the identification of the stars with destiny, a common view, but
usually rejected in Shakespeare. See EXCUSES, quote from *King Lear*.)

²   These blessèd candles of the night. *The Merchant of Venice,* V,i,220.

³ The music of the spheres! *Pericles,* V,i,232. (A reference to the concept,
dating back to Pythagoras, that all solid bodies, including the planets, emit
musical sounds. The result is a transcendent celestial harmony.)

See also FATE; HEAVENS, THE; RESPONSIBILITY; STAR WARS.

STAR WARS

⁴ Combat with adverse planets in the heavens! *Henry VI, Part One,* I,i,54.
(The duke of Bedford is making the now-familiar point that combat with
aliens is a pleasanter prospect than dealing with civil strife. The whole
sentence reads: "Prosper this realm, keep it from civil broils, / Combat
with adverse planets in the heavens!")

STOICISM

⁵   'Tis good to be sad and say nothing. *As You Like It,* IV,i,8.

⁶ No man bears sorrow better. *Julius Caesar,* IV,iii,146.

⁷ I am tied to the stake, and I must stand the course. *King Lear,* III,vii,55.
(Gloucester, at the mercy of Regan, compares himself to a bear or bull
baited by a *course,* or relay of dogs. A few moments later, Regan's husband,
the duke of Cornwall, blinds Gloucester, bragging: "Out vile jelly. /
Where is thy luster now?" l.84.)

⁸ Many can brook the weather that love not the wind. *Love's Labor's Lost,*
IV,ii,34. (*Brook* means "endure.")

STORIES

⁹ And thereby hangs a tale. *As You Like It,* II,vii,28. (More at TIME. The
phrase reappears in *The Merry Wives of Windsor,* I,iv,147; *The Taming of
the Shrew,* IV,i,55; *The Two Noble Kinsmen,* III,iii,41; *Othello,* III,i,8. One
may speculate that it had appeal for Shakespeare, whose world teemed
with stories.)

¹⁰ I could a tale unfold whose lightest word
Would harrow up thy soul. *Hamlet,* I,v,15. (More at FEAR.)

1   In this harsh world draw thy breath in pain,
To tell my story. *Hamlet,* V,ii,349. (Hamlet to Horatio. More at NEWS.)

2   So shall you hear
Of carnal, bloody, and unnatural acts,
Of accidental judgments, casual slaughters,
Of deaths put on by cunning and forced cause,
And, in this upshot, purposes mistook
Fallen on the inventors' heads. All this can I
Truly deliver. *Hamlet,* V,ii,381. (Horatio immediately begins to fulfill
Hamlet's dying request—see quote above—to tell the true story of the
events that led to his death. In isolation, the passage sounds rather like an
author's pitch to a fiction editor.)

3   It is a tale
Told by an idiot, full of sound and fury
Signifying nothing. *Macbeth,* V,v,26. (More at LIFE.)

4 I will a round unvarnished tale deliver
Of my whole course of love. *Othello,* I,iii,90. (Othello preparing to explain
his relationship with Desdemona. *Round* means "blunt.")

5 Her father . . .
. . . questioned me the story of my life
From year to year, the battle, sieges, fortune
That I have passed. *Othello,* I,iii,127. (More below.)

6 Wherein I spoke of most disastrous chances,
Of moving accidents by flood and field,
Of hairbreadth scapes in the imminent deadly breach,
Of being taken by the insolent foe
And sold to slavery, of my redemption thence. *Othello,* I,iii,133. (Hearing
this exciting story, requested by her unwise father, Desdemona falls in love
with Othello. His adventures even included strange encounters with "the
Cannibals that each other eat, / The Anthropophagi, and men whose
heads / Grew beneath their shoulders," l.142.)

7 My story being done,
She gave me for my pains a world of kisses. *Othello,* I,iii,157. (More at
LOVE AND LOVERS.)

8 An honest tale speeds best being plainly told. *Richard III,* IV,iv,358.

9 Your tale, sir, would cure deafness. *The Tempest,* I,ii,106.

10 A sad tale's best for winter; I have one
Of sprites and goblins. *The Winter's Tale,* II,i,25.

STORMS. See WEATHER.

STRENGTH. See COMPETITION; POWER; SUCCESS.

STUPIDITY. See FOOLS; INSULTS.

STYLE. See EFFETENESS; FASHION; GRACE; MANNERS.

SUCCESS

1   I came, saw, and overcame. *Henry IV, Part Two,* IV,iii,42. (Falstaff quoting Julius Caesar's *"Veni, vidi, vici."*)

2 The force of his own merit makes his way. *Henry VIII,* I,i,64. (The duke of Norfolk speaking of Cardinal Wolsey. The duke of Buckingham and his nephew take a less flattering view.)

3   Lowliness is young ambition's ladder,
Whereto the climber upward turns his face;
But when he once attains the upmost round,
He then unto the ladder turns his back,
Looks in the clouds, scorning the base degrees
By which he did ascend. *Julius Caesar,* II,i,22. (For *lowliness* in the first line read "humility.")

4   Let none presume
To wear an undeservèd dignity.
O that estates, degrees, and offices
Were not derived corruptly, and that clear honor
Were purchased by the merit of the wearer! *The Merchant of Venice,* II,ix,38.

5 They laugh that win. *Othello,* IV,i,124.

6 They well deserve to have
That know the strongest and surest way to get. *Richard II,* III,iii,198.

7 O the fierce wretchedness that glory brings us! *Timon of Athens,* IV,ii,30. (Flavius speaking of the disappointment that can accompany wealth and success. "Riches point to misery and contempt," he continues, l.32; instead of true friends, the rich have just a "dream of friendship," l.34. This becomes more apparent after one has lost all one's money, as Timon did.)

See also AMBITION; BOLDNESS; COMPETITION; FORTUNE; GREATNESS; OPPORTUNITY; ORGANIZATION; POWER; RICH, THE; RUTHLESSNESS.

SUFFERING

¹ Thou art a soul in bliss; but I am bound
Upon a wheel of fire, that mine own tears
Do scald like molten lead. *King Lear,* IV,vii,46. (The wheel of fire was an
instrument of torture symbolic of hell.)

See also ADVERSITY; DEATH; INJUSTICE; SORROW AND SADNESS.

SUICIDE

²   I will be
A bridegroom in my death, and run into it
As to a lover's bed. *Antony and Cleopatra,* IV,xiv,99. (Antony before falling
on his sword. See also below.)

³   Then is it sin
To rush into the secret house of death
Ere death dare come to us? *Antony and Cleopatra,* IV,xv,79. (Cleopatra—
the question is rhetorical.)

⁴   It is great
To do that thing that ends all other deeds,
Which shackles accidents and bolts up change. *Antony and Cleopatra,*
V,ii,4. (Cleopatra deciding on suicide.)

⁵ To be, or not to be: that is the question:
Whether 'tis nobler in the mind to suffer
The slings and arrows of outrageous fortune,
Or to take arms against a sea of troubles,
And by opposing end them. To die, to sleep—
No more—and by a sleep to say we end
The heartache, and the thousand natural shocks
That flesh is heir to! 'Tis a consummation
Devoutly to be wished. To die, to sleep—
To sleep—perchance to dream: ay, there's the rub,
For in that sleep of death what dreams may come
When we have shuffled off this mortal coil,
Must give us pause. There's the respect
That makes calamity of so long life:
For who would bear the whips and scorns of time,
Th' oppressor's wrong, the proud man's contumely,
The pangs of despised love, the law's delay,
The insolence of office, and the spurns
That patient merit of th' unworthy takes,
When he himself might his quietus make

With a bare bodkin? Who would fardels bear,
To grunt and sweat under a weary life,
But that the dread of something after death,
The undiscovered country, from whose bourn
No traveler returns, puzzles the will,
And makes us rather bear those ills we have,
Than fly to others that we know not of? *Hamlet,* III,i,56. (The prince's
thoughts on suicide, probably the most famous soliloquy in the history of
drama. The *rub* is an uneven spot on the ground that deflects a bowling
ball. *Mortal coil* may be interpreted as the flesh, or body, encircling the soul
or, in another meaning, as worldly turmoil. The sentence *There's the respect
/ That makes calamity of so long life* translates "That's the consideration that
makes us endure calamity for so long." Finally, a *bodkin* is a dagger, a *fardel*
is a burden, and a *bourn* is a region.

In his film version of *Hamlet,* Laurence Olivier used a controversial
subtitle: *A Story of a Man Who Could Not Make Up His Mind.* In a filmed
interview, shown posthumously on the Arts and Entertainment network in
December 1990, entitled "To Be Hamlet," Sir Laurence explained that he
picked up that line from a Gary Cooper movie, in which Cooper describes
the play in those words.)

[1] Life, being weary of these worldly bars,
Never lacks power to dismiss itself. *Julius Caesar,* I,iii,96. (Cassius to
Casca. But rather than suicide, Cassius is proposing the assassination of
Caesar.)

[2] Every bondman in his own hand bears
The power to cancel his captivity. *Julius Caesar,* I,iii,101. (Casca agrees
with Cassius that suicide is always a possibility. He also agrees that he
would rather kill Caesar.)

[3] Why should I play the Roman fool, and die
On mine own sword? *Macbeth,* V,viii,1.

See also DEATHBED STATEMENTS AND FINAL WORDS; DEPRESSION.

SUMMER

[4] For now, these hot days, is the mad blood stirring. *Romeo and Juliet,* III,i,4.
(Benvolio predicting that on a hot day brawling is apt to break out between
the followers of the Capulets and the Montagues.)

[5] Summer's lease hath all too short a date. *Sonnet 18,* 4. (More at
MORTALITY.)

[1] The summer's flower is to the summer sweet. *Sonnet 94,* 9. (More at VIRTUE.)

[2] Why this is very midsummer madness. *Twelfth Night,* III,iv,58.

SUSPICION

[3] There is something in the wind. *The Comedy of Errors,* III,i,69.

[4] Something is rotten in the state of Denmark. *Hamlet,* I,iv,90.

SWEARING.   See OATHS; PROMISES; TALK, PLAIN AND FANCY.

SYCOPHANCY.   See FLATTERY AND SYCOPHANCY.

T

TALK

1   Give me leave
To speak my mind, and I will through and through
Cleanse the foul body of the infected world. *As You Like It,* II,vii,58.

2 Answer me in one word. *As You Like It,* III,ii,222. (A surefire laugh line, given the questions preceding: "What did he when thou saw'st him? What said he? How looked he? Wherein went he? What makes he here? Did he ask for me? Where remains he? How parted he with thee? And when shalt thou see him again?")

3 Ill deeds is doubled with an evil word. *The Comedy of Errors,* III,ii,20. (Lucinda advising Antipholus of Syracuse not to add insult to injury by letting his wife know of his infidelity.)

4   I wear not
My dagger in my mouth. *Cymbeline,* IV,ii,78. (Translation: I don't insult and threaten people—but I am armed.)

5 Give it an understanding but no tongue. *Hamlet,* I,ii,250. (Translation: Pay attention, but do not speak of what you see. In the next scene, l.59 reads: "Give thy thoughts no tongue"; more at WISDOM, WORDS OF.)

6   To expostulate
What majesty should be, what duty is,
Why day is day, night night, and time is time,
Were nothing but to waste night, day and time. *Hamlet,* II,ii,86. (Polonius tediously leading up to the comment below.)

[1] Brevity is the soul of wit. *Hamlet* II,ii,90.

[2] His sweet and honeyed sentences. *Henry V,* I,i,50. (*Sentences* may be read as "sayings.")

[3] Men of few words are the best men. *Henry V,* III,ii,37.

[4] "The empty vessel makes the greatest sound." *Henry V,* IV,iv,71. (A boy summons a proverb to comment on the blustering Pistol.)

[5] Speak on, but be not over-tedious. *Henry VI, Part One,* III,iii,43.

[6] Things are often spoke and seldom meant. *Henry VI, Part Two,* III,i,268.

[7] If I chance to talk a little wild, forgive me;
I had it from my father. *Henry VIII,* I,iv,26. (Lord Sands, apologizing none too sincerely for the pass he is about to make at Anne Bullen [Boleyn] and another lady of the court. This scene is sometimes attributed to John Fletcher rather than Shakespeare.)

[8] 'Tis well said again,
And 'tis a kind of good deed to say well.
And yet words are no deeds. *Henry VIII,* III,ii,152.

[9] Mend your speech a little,
Lest you may mar your fortunes. *King Lear,* I,i,96. (Lear to Cordelia.)

[10] These
That . . . are reputed wise
For saying nothing. *The Merchant of Venice,* I,i,95.

[11] Gratiano speaks an infinite deal of nothing. *The Merchant of Venice,* I,i,114. (More at REASONS.)

[12] Have I lived to stand at the taunt of one that makes fritters of English? *The Merry Wives of Windsor,* V,v,146. (Falstaff making fun of the Welsh parson Sir Hugh Evans.)

[13] Shall quips and sentences and these paper bullets of the brain awe a man from the career of his humor? *Much Ado About Nothing,* II,iii,236. (Benedick resolves to marry Beatrice despite the teasing that will come his way because of his earlier public vow to remain a bachelor forever. *Sentences* means "sayings"; *career* means "course.")

[14] Mere prattle without practice. *Othello,* I,i,23. (Iago accuses his rival Cassio of talking a good game without experience: "Mere prattle without practice / Is all his soldiership.")

[1] Talkers are no good doers. *Richard III*, I,iii,350. (A murderer delivers this opinion.)

[2]   O madness of discourse,
That cause sets up with and against itself. *Troilus and Cressida*, V,ii,139. (Troilus deplores ambivalence and inconsistency in discourse—and in Cressida.)

[3] Bid me discourse, I will enchant thine ear. *Venus and Adonis*, 145.

See also ARGUMENTS; BRAGGING; FLATTERY; LISTENING; NONSENSE; PRAISE; PUBLIC SPEAKING; RUMOR; SLANDER; TALK, PLAIN AND FANCY; WIT; WORDS.

TALK, PLAIN AND FANCY

[4]   Mince not the general tongue. *Antony and Cleopatra*, I,ii,106. (Translation: Don't mince your words.)

[5]   I do not much dislike the matter, but
The manner of his speech. *Antony and Cleopatra*, II,ii,116. (The person with the bad manner of speech is Enobarbus, who is actually exceptionally eloquent. However, as a soldier, he is also blunt, too much so evidently for Octavius Caesar, who voices this complaint. See also CLEOPATRA for Enobarbus's description of her barge on the Nile.)

[6] When a gentleman is disposed to swear, it is not for any standers-by to curtail his oaths. *Cymbeline*, II,i,11.

[7] We must speak by the card, or equivocation will undo us. *Hamlet*, V,i,139. (Hamlet is reacting to the blunt literalness of the gravedigger, who when asked for whom the grave is intended, answers, "One that was a woman, sir; but, rest her soul, she's dead," l.137. "How absolute the knave is," Hamlet bursts out. When he refers to speaking *by the card*, he means a compass card, with exact directions.)

[8]   I must speak in passion, and I will do it in King Cambyses' vein. *Henry IV, Part One*, II,iv,386. (Falstaff mocking the bombastic, semitragical style of Thomas Preston's play *King Cambyses*.)

[9]   A good mouth-filling oath. *Henry IV, Part One*, III,i,256. (Hotspur urging his wife, as a lady, to swear straight out and leave off using fancy phrases like "in sooth," which is short for "in God's truth." Falstaff, too, has no time for the mealy-mouthed. See below.)

[10] A rascal, yea-forsooth knave! *Henry IV, Part Two*, I,ii,38. (Falstaff is describing someone contemptible. A *yea-forsooth knave* would use such a namby-pamby expression instead of a hearty oath. See also above.)

[1] Out with it boldly: truth loves open dealing. *Henry VIII,* III,i,39. (Queen Katherine to Cardinal Wolsey. He replies, *"Tanta est erga te mentis integritas, regina serenissima . . ."* "O, good my lord, no Latin," pleads the queen, l.42.)

[2] For mine own part, it was Greek to me. *Julius Caesar,* I,ii,283. (A joke by Casca. He refers to a speech by Cicero—in Greek, of course. Actually the historical Casca probably did understand Greek.)

[3] For I have neither wit, nor words, nor worth,
Action nor utterance, nor the power of speech
To stir men's blood. I only speak right on. *Julius Caesar,* III,ii,223. (From Mark Antony's eloquent funeral speech for Caesar. Note the phrase *right on.*)

[4] 'Tis my occupation to be plain. *King Lear,* II,ii,94.

[5] A man . . .
That hath a mint of phrases in his brain. *Love's Labor's Lost,* I,i,163. (The man is Don Adriano de Armado, described in the cast of characters as "a fantastical Spaniard.")

[6] A man of fire-new words, fashion's own knight. *Love's Labor's Lost,* I,i,177. (*Fire-new words* are newly fired, or newly coined, words. Armado again [see above], but Walter Pater observed that this phrase more aptly describes the speaker, Berowne. A. L. Rowse has identified Berowne with Shakespeare himself.)

[7] Remuneration? O that's the Latin word for three farthings. *Love's Labor's Lost,* III,i,137.

[8] *Moth.* They have been at a great feast of languages and stolen the scraps. *Costard.* O, they have lived long on the alms-basket of words. I marvel thy master hath not eaten thee for a word; for thou art not so long by the head as *honorificabilitudinitatibus.* Thou art easier swallowed than a flapdragon. *Love's Labor's Lost,* V,i,39. (A *flapdragon,* also called *snapdragon,* is a raisin in a drink of brandy or strong liquor set alight. The idea is to snatch out the burning raisin and pop it in one's mouth. There is a memorable winged flapdragon among John Tenniel's illustrations for Lewis Carroll's *Through the Looking Glass.*)

[9] The posteriors of this day, which the rude multitude call the afternoon. *Love's Labor's Lost,* V,i,89. (Armado speaks. The admiring Holfernes responds, "The word is well culled, chose, sweet and apt, I do assure you, sir, I do assure," l.93.)

[1] Taffeta phrases, silken terms precise,
Three-piled hyperboles, spruce affectation,
Figures pedantical. *Love's Labor's Lost,* V,ii,407.

[2] "Convey," the wise it call. "Steal?" Foh, a fico for the phrase! *The Merry Wives of Windsor,* I,iii,28. (*Fico* means "fig.")

[3] Here will be an old abusing of God's patience and the King's English. *The Merry Wives of Windsor,* I,iv,5. (For *old* read "great.")

[4] This is the short and the long of it. *The Merry Wives of Windsor,* II,ii,60.

[5] She speaks poniards, and every word stabs. *Much Ado About Nothing,* II,i,245.

[6] He was wont to speak plain and to the purpose, like an honest man and a soldier; and now is he turned orthography; his words are a very fantastical banquet. *Much Ado About Nothing,* II,iii,18. (Benedick speaks of Claudio in love. *Orthography* can be read as "phrasemaker.")

[7] Rude am I in my speech,
And little blessed with the soft phrase of peace. *Othello,* I,iii,81. (Othello speaks; see also PUBLIC SPEAKING.)

[8] Speak to me as to thy thinkings,
As thou dost ruminate, and give thy worst of thoughts
The worst of words. *Othello,* III,iii,131. (Othello to Iago, of all people.)

[9] Grace me no grace, nor uncle me no uncle. *Richard II,* II,iii,86.

[10] My hair doth stand on end to hear her curses. *Richard III,* I,iii,303.

[11] An honest tale speeds best being plainly told. *Richard III,* IV,iv,358.

[12] How, how, how, how, chopped-logic? *Romeo and Juliet,* III,v,150. (Juliet's father utterly bewildered by her confused, enigmatic remarks about being thankful but not proud. "Thank me no thankings, nor proud me no prouds," the poor man continues, l.153.)

[13] Who you are and what you would are out of my welkin; I might say "element," but the word is overworn. *Twelfth Night,* III,i,58. (*Welkin* means "sky." This may be a dig at Ben Jonson, who was unduly fond of the word *element.*)

See also ARGUMENTS; EDUCATION; NONSENSE; PUBLIC SPEAKING; TRUTH.

TAXES

[14] And daily new exactions are devised,
As blanks, benevolences, and I wot not what. *Richard II,* II,i,249. (*Blanks*

were blank orders for payment on which the king's agents could fill in any amounts. *Benevolences* were forced loans, actually introduced not by Richard II, but by Richard III in 1473.)

TEMPTATION

[1] O, thou . . . art indeed able to corrupt a saint. *Henry IV, Part One,* I,ii,94. (Falstaff to Prince Hal.)

[2] How oft the sight of means to do ill deeds
Make deeds ill done! *King John,* IV,ii,219.

[3]   Why do I yield to that suggestion
Whose horrid image doth unfix my hair
And make my seated heart knock at my ribs,
Against the use of nature? *Macbeth,* I,iii,134. (Macbeth is shaken to discover that the witches' prophecy that he will be king has turned his imagination to the murder he must commit to win the throne. He only briefly considers the possibility that success may not require violence: "If chance will have me King, why, chance may crown me, / Without my stir," l.143.)

[4]   The primrose way to the everlasting bonfire. *Macbeth,* II,iii,19. (From the porter's speech. In ancient times, Bion observed, "The road to Hades is easy to travel." Hamlet speaks of "the primrose path of dalliance"; see ADVICE.)

[5]   'Tis one thing to be tempted, Escalus,
Another thing to fall. *Measure for Measure,* II,i,17.

[6] The tempter or the tempted, who sins most? *Measure for Measure,* II,ii,163.

[7] *Desdemona.* Wouldst thou do such a deed for all the world?
Emilia. The world's a huge thing; it is a great price for a small vice. *Othello,* IV,iii,69. (The deed is adultery. Desdemona cannot believe that there are women who would be so unkind to their husbands; see also SEX.)

[8]   Tempt not a desperate man. *Romeo and Juliet,* V,iii,59.

[9]   Sometimes we are devils to ourselves
When we will tempt the frailty of our powers,
Presuming on their changeful potency. *Troilus and Cressida,* IV,iv,95.

See also LIMITS; WEAKNESS.

TENNIS.   See SPORTS.

THEATER

[1] The King's a beggar now the play is done. *All's Well That Ends Well,* Epilogue, 1. (The king of France becomes a mere actor and begs for applause: "Your gentle hands lend us, and take our hearts," l.6.)

[2] Antony
Shall be brought drunken forth, and I shall see
Some squeaking Cleopatra boy my greatness
In the posture of a whore. *Antony and Cleopatra,* V,ii,218. (Cleopatra imagining how she and Antony will be played on the Roman stage. A boy would be given her part.)

[3] All the world's a stage,
And all the men and women merely players. *As You Like It,* II,vii,139. (More at LIFE.)

[4] Come, give us a taste of your quality. Come, a passionate speech. *Hamlet,* II,ii,440. (Hamlet to the players.)

[5] The play, I remember, pleased not the million; 'twas caviary to the general. *Hamlet,* II,ii,446. (*The general* means "the masses.")

[6] Let them be well used, for they are the abstract and brief chronicles of the time. *Hamlet,* II,ii,534. (Hamlet referring to the actors.)

[7] What's Hecuba to him, or he to Hecuba,
That he should weep for her? *Hamlet,* II,ii,569. (Hamlet commenting on an actor's capacity to weep on cue, while Hamlet himself, facing real tragedy, is silent.)

[8] The play's the thing
Wherein I'll catch the conscience of the King. *Hamlet,* II,ii,616.

[9] Speak the speech, I pray you, as I pronounced it to you, trippingly on the tongue. But if you mouth it, as many of our players do, I had as lief the town crier spoke my lines. Nor do not saw the air too much with your hand, thus, but use all gently, for in the very torrent, tempest, and (as I may say) whirlwind of your passion, you must acquire and beget a temperance that may give it smoothness. O, it offends me to the soul to hear a robustious periwig-pated fellow tear a passion to tatters, to very rags, to split the ears of the groundlings, who for the most part are capable of nothing but inexplicable dumb shows and noise. I would have such a fellow whipped for o'erdoing Termagant. It out-herods Herod. Pray you avoid it. *Hamlet,* III,ii,1. (The start of Hamlet's instructions to the players—probably the most famous prose passage in Shakespeare's works. Termagant and Herod were characters in medieval mystery plays. *Terma-*

gant was an imaginary deity, supposedly worshiped by Moslems. Because
this creature was clad in a long robe, it was confused with a female. Hence
the term came to mean a shrewish woman. *Groundlings* were the members
of the audience who paid the cheapest admission; they stood in the pit.)

[1] Be not too tame neither, but let your own discretion be your tutor. Suit
the action to the word, the word to the action, with this special observance,
that you o'erstep not the modesty of nature. For anything so o'erdone is
from the purpose of playing, whose end, both at the first and now, was and
is, to hold, as 'twere, the mirror up to nature; to show virtue her own
feature, scorn her own image, and the very age and body of the time his
form and pressure. Now, this overdone, or come tardy off, though it makes
the unskillful laugh, cannot but make the judicious grieve, the censure of
the which one must in your allowance o'erweigh a whole theater of others.
O, there be players that I have seen play, and heard others praise, and that
highly (not to speak it profanely), that neither having th' accent of Christians, nor the gait of Christian, pagan, nor man, have so strutted and
bellowed that I have thought some of Nature's journeymen had made men,
and not made them well, they imitated humanity so abominably. *Hamlet,*
III,ii,17. (*Pressure* means "shape," "image." As for that "poor player that
struts his hour upon the stage," see LIFE, the quote from *Macbeth.*)

[2]   Let those that play your clowns speak no more than is set down for
them, for there be of them that will themselves laugh, to set on some
quantity of barren spectators to laugh too, though in the meantime some
necessary question of the play be then to be considered. That's villainous
and shows a most pitiful ambition in the fool that uses it. *Hamlet,* III,ii,40.
(In Elizabethan theater there was some conflict between the demands of
the new, serious playwrights and the broad style of performance characteristic of the late Middle Ages. Actors tended to ham it up inappropriately.
The most famous ad-libbing clown, a favorite of the queen, was Richard
Tarlton. Shakespeare may have been taking him a bit to task here. Tarlton
may also have been the model for Yorick.)

[3] Play out the play. *Henry IV, Part One,* II,iv,484.

[4] O for a Muse of fire, that would ascend
The brightest heaven of invention:
A kingdom for a stage, princes to act,
And monarchs to behold the swelling scene! *Henry V,* Prologue,1. (More
below.)

[5]   Can this cockpit hold
The vasty fields of France? Or may we cram
Within this wooden *O* the very casques

That did affright the air at Agincourt? *Henry V,* Prologue, 11. (A continuation of the breathtaking opening lines; see above. Which theater is referred to by "this wooden *O*" is a matter of scholarly debate. Presumably the stage was round or perhaps octagonal. The theater might have been the new Globe, rebuilt in 1599, the year the play was written, or the Curtain theater, which Shakespeare's company used from 1597 to 1599. *Casques* are helmets. Paraphrased, the lines mean: Can this stage hold even the helmets—much less the warriors—that frightened all at Agincourt?)

1   Yet sit and see,
Minding true things by what their mockeries be. *Henry V,* IV,Chorus, 52. (The last line of the Chorus's description of the opposing armies on the night before the battle of Agincourt. *Mockeries* means "imitations," and the invitation summarizes the purpose of theater.)

2 'Tis ten to one this play can never please
All that are here. Some come to take their ease,
And sleep an act or two. *Henry VIII,* Epilogue, 1.

3   *Cassius.* How many ages hence
Shall this our lofty scene be acted over
In states unborn and accents yet unknown!
Brutus. How many times shall Caesar bleed in sport? *Julius Caesar,*
III,i,111.

4 *Quince.* Marry, our play is, "The most lamentable comedy, and most cruel death of Pyramus and Thisby."
Bottom. A very good piece of work, I assure you, and a merry. *A Midsummer Night's Dream,* I,ii,11. (Later this lamentable comedy becomes a "very tragical mirth," V,i,57. Bottom begs to play Thisby, promising, "I'll speak in a monstrous little voice," I,ii,53. He'd also like to play the lion, explaining that he will modify his voice so that the roars do not frighten the ladies; see below.)

5   I will aggravate my voice so that I will roar you as gently as any sucking dove; I will roar you an 'twere any nightingale. *A Midsummer Night's Dream,* I,ii,81. (Bottom doesn't always find exactly the word he's looking for. By *aggravate* he means "moderate.")

6 Come now, what masques, what dances shall we have,
To wear away this long age of three hours
Between our aftersupper and our bedtime?
Where is our usual manager of mirth?
What revels are in hand? Is there no play,
To ease the anguish of a torturing hour? *A Midsummer Night's Dream,*
V,i,32. (More below.)

¹ What masque? What music? How shall we beguile
The lazy time, if not with some delight? *A Midsummer Night's Dream,*
V,i,40.

² The best in this kind are but shadows. *A Midsummer Night's Dream,*
V,i,212. (*This kind* refers to plays and/or players.)

³ All that I have to say is to tell you that the lanthorn is the moon; I, the man
in the moon; this thorn bush, my thorn bush; and this dog, my dog. *A
Midsummer Night's Dream,* V,i,257. (In the hilarious production of "Pyramus and Thisby" that concludes *A Midsummer Night's Dream,* this actor
explains his function to the noble audience. He is soon complimented by
Hippolyta: "Well shone, Moon. Truly, the moon shines with a good
grace," l.268.)

⁴ This passion, and the death of a dear friend, would go near to make a man
look sad. *A Midsummer Night's Dream,* V,i,289. (An explanatory aside from
Theseus in response to the hysteria that the actor playing Pyramus displays
upon discovering Thisby's bloodstained mantle.)

⁵ No epilogue, I pray you; for your play needs no excuse. Never excuse. *A
Midsummer Night's Dream,* V,i,357.

⁶ If we shadows have offended,
Think but this, and all is mended:
That we have but slumbered here,
While these visions did appear. *A Midsummer Night's Dream,* V,i,425.

⁷ As in a theater the eyes of men,
After a well-graced actor leaves the stage,
Are idly bent on him that enters next,
Thinking his prattle to be tedious. *Richard II,* V,ii,23. (The ignored prat-
tler is the deposed Richard II; the well-graced actor is the usurper Bolingbroke, the future Henry IV. Shakespeare, theater-wise, avoided this
predicament for his actors, for example, with terrific entrance lines.)

⁸ 　　Canst thou quake and change thy color,
Murder thy breath in middle of a word,
And then again begin, and stop again,
As if thou wert distraught and mad with terror? *Richard III,* III,v,1. (Rich-
ard referring to the tricks of a tragedian. The role of Richard, incidentally,
was created by Shakespeare's friend Richard Burbage. When Laurence
Olivier did the role, he modeled himself on the legendary boy-wonder
producer Jed Harris. See also below.)

[1] Tut, I can counterfeit the deep tragedian,
Speak and look back, and pry on every side,
Tremble and start at wagging of a straw,
Intending deep suspicion. Ghastly looks
Are at my service, like enforcèd smiles. *Richard III,* III,v,5. (Buckingham answering Richard—see above—shows himself equally familiar with the actor's trade.)

[2] And if the boy have not a woman's gift
To rain a shower of commanded tears,
An onion will do well for such a shift. *The Taming of the Shrew,* Induction,i,124.

[3]   A kind
Of excellent dumb discourse. *The Tempest,* III,iii,38. (The dancing and gestures of the surreal beings that bring a banquet to the shipwrecked king of Naples and his companions.)

[4] Our revels now are ended. These our actors,
As I foretold you, were all spirits and
Are melted into air, into thin air;
And, like the baseless fabric of this vision,
The cloud-capped towers, the gorgeous palaces,
The solemn temples, the great globe itself,
Yea, all which it inherit, shall dissolve,
And, like this insubstantial pageant faded,
Leave not a rack behind. We are such stuff
As dreams are made on, and our little life
Is rounded with a sleep. *The Tempest,* IV,i,148. (Near the end of his life, Shakespeare in this magnificent passage identifies the role of theater and imagination with the dreamlike nature of life itself. *All which it inherit* is all that exists in the world. A *rack* is a wisp of a cloud.)

[5] Like a strutting player, whose conceit
Lies in his hamstring, and doth think it rich
To hear the wooden dialogue and sound
'Twixt his stretched footing and the scaffoldage. *Troilus and Cressida,* I,iii,153. (Here Shakespeare mocks the kind of bad actor whose imagination [*conceit*] lies far from his brain, and whose technique depends largely on striding noisily around the stage. As much as Shakespeare must have suffered at the hands—or feet—of clumsy thespians, Elizabethan actors were called upon to master such an enormous repertory that it was no wonder if some resorted to hoary tricks of the trade. Edward Alleyn, for example, a lead actor with the Admiral's Men, memorized and retained seventy roles in three years.)

¹ He does it with a better grace, but I do it more natural. *Twelfth Night,* II,iii,83. (Sir Andrew Aguecheek referring to Sir Toby Belch's singing and clowning.)

² He must observe their mood on whom he jests,
The quality of persons, and the time;
And, like the haggard, check at every feather
That comes before his eye. This is a practice
As full of labor as a wise man's art;
For folly that he wisely shows, is fit;
But wise men, folly-fall'n, quite taint their wit. *Twelfth Night,* III,i,63. (A fine exposition of the rigorous art of the professional clown, or comedian. A *haggard* is an untrained hawk. *Check at* means "follow after." In some editions the first word in this line is not *and* but rather *not.*)

³ *Exit, pursued by a bear. The Winter's Tale,* III,iii,57. (A delightful stage direction, signaling the abrupt end of poor Antigonus.)

THINNESS

⁴ O, give me the spare men, and spare me the great ones. *Henry IV, Part Two,* III,ii,278. (Falstaff on the value of thin men in battle: they present smaller targets and they can retreat faster. See also FATNESS.)

THOUGHT

⁵ There is nothing either good or bad but thinking makes it so. *Hamlet,* II,ii,253.

⁶ Thus conscience does make cowards of us all,
And thus the native hue of resolution
Is sicklied o'er with the pale cast of thought,
And enterprises of great pitch and moment,
With this regard their currents turn awry,
And lose the name of action. *Hamlet,* III,i,83. (From the "to be or not to be" soliloquy; see SUICIDE. Here *conscience* in the first line means "awareness," "the ability to think." *Pitch* is a term from falconry referring to height. The *regard* that undermines action is thought and consciousness in general, and more specifically, fear of the unknown and fear of death.)

⁷ Cudgel thy brains no more about it. *Hamlet,* V,i,57.

⁸ Thy wish was father, Harry, to that thought. *Henry IV, Part Two,* IV,v,92. (More at CHILDREN.)

⁹ Faster than spring-time showers comes thought on thought. *Henry VI, Part Two,* III,i,337. (The next line is "And not a thought but thinks on dignity,"

with *dignity* meaning rank. The speaker is the duke of York, a very ambitious politician.)

¹   Merciful powers,
Restrain in me the cursèd thoughts that nature
Gives way to in repose! *Macbeth,* II,i,7.

² Faith, thou hast some crotchets in thy head now. *The Merry Wives of Windsor,* II,i,149. (*Crotchets* are strange ideas.)

³ O, who can hold a fire in his hand
By thinking on the frosty Caucasus?
Or cloy the hungry edge of appetite
By bare imagination of a feast?
Or wallow naked in December snow
By thinking on fantastic summer heat?
O, no! the apprehension of the good
Gives but the greater feeling to the worse. *Richard II,* I,iii,293. (Bolingbroke's impatient reaction to his father's advice to look on the bright side of banishment, and think positively.)

⁴   Nimble thought can jump both sea and land. *Sonnet 44,* 7.

⁵ Thought is free. *The Tempest,* III,ii,128. (*Free* in the sense that it is not in the power of outside authority to control it. The same phrase is used in *Twelfth Night,* I,iii,68. More at REBELLION.)

See also IMAGINATION; INSPIRATION; MIND.

TIME

⁶ The inaudible and noiseless foot of Time. *All's Well That Ends Well,* V,iii,41. (More at OLD AGE.)

⁷   "It is ten o'clock.
Thus we may see," quoth he, "how the world wags.
'Tis but an hour ago since it was nine,
And after one hour more 'twill be eleven;
And so, from hour to hour, we ripe and ripe,
And then, from hour to hour, we rot and rot;
And thereby hangs a tale." *As You Like It,* II,vii,22. (Spoken by "melancholy Jaques." For Jaques' most famous speech, see the "seven ages of man" speech at LIFE.)

⁸ Time travels in divers paces with divers persons. *As You Like It,* III,ii,304. (Einstein demonstrated that time travels in divers paces for persons on fast-moving spaceships as opposed to those on planet Earth. Rosalind, of

course, refers to the perception of time. Thus, time "gallops" with a thief to the gallows, but "ambles" with those who are rich and contented.)

[1] For ever and a day. *As You Like It,* IV,i,138. (Orlando's estimate of how long his love will last. Jaques, the pessimist, senses time flying [two quotes above]. Orlando, the lover, has lost all sense of time. Rosalind, the realist, points out that time's pace is relative; see quote above.)

[2] Take thy fair hour, Laertes. Time be thine,
And thy best graces spend it at thy will. *Hamlet,* I,ii,62.

[3] Unless hours were cups of sack, and minutes capons, and clocks the tongues of bawds, and dials the signs of leaping houses, and the blessed sun himself a fair hot wench in flame-colored taffeta, I see no reason why thou shouldst be so superfluous to demand the time of the day. *Henry IV, Part One,* I,ii,7. (Prince Hal's slam-bang opening speech, delivered in answer to Falstaff's simple question "What time of day is it, lad?" The term *dials* refers to sundials, *leaping houses* to brothels.)

[4] "Past and to come seem best, things present worst." *Henry IV, Part Two,* I,iii,108. (The quote is a proverb.)

[5]   He weighs time
Even to the utmost grain. *Henry V,* II,iv,137.

[6] So minutes, hours, days, months, and years,
Passed over to the end they were created,
Would bring white hairs unto a quiet grave. *Henry VI, Part Three,* II,v,38. (From a speech in which the king longs to be a simple shepherd, estimating the hours of his life and how they will be spent, until a peaceful death concludes his time on earth. See also COUNTRY LIFE.)

[7]   Cormorant devouring time. *Love's Labor's Lost,* I,i,4. (The cormorant is a ravenous sea bird that eats fish in large numbers.)

[8] Time and the hour runs through the roughest day. *Macbeth,* I,iii,147.

[9] Tomorrow, and tomorrow, and tomorrow
Creeps in this petty pace from day to day,
To the last syllable of recorded time. *Macbeth* V,v,19. (Macbeth realizing that his life is wearisome; see LIFE.)

[10] This will last out a night in Russia,
When nights are longest there. *Measure for Measure,* II,i,133.

[11] Time's glory is to calm contending kings,
To unmask falsehood and bring truth to light. *The Rape of Lucrece,* 939.

¹ I wasted time, and now doth Time waste me:
For now hath Time made me his numb'ring clock;
My thoughts are minutes. *Richard II,* V,v,49. (The imprisoned king, minutes before his murder.)

² Like as the waves make towards the pebbled shore,
So do our minutes hasten to their end. *Sonnet 60,* 1.

³ Time doth transfix the flourish set on youth,
And delves the parallels in beauty's brow. *Sonnet 60,* 9.

⁴ When I have seen by Time's fell hand defaced
The rich proud cost of outworn buried age. *Sonnet 64,* 1. (*Cost* means "splendor.")

⁵ Time hath, my lord, a wallet at his back,
Wherein he puts alms for oblivion,
A great-sized monster of ingratitudes.
Those scraps are good deeds past, which are devoured
As fast as they are made, forgot as soon
As done. *Troilus and Cressida,* III,iii,145. (Here and below, Ulysses bemoans the fleeting existence of good deeds, which are quickly forgotten, passing into oblivion. Only what is new is admired.)

⁶ For time is like a fashionable host,
That slightly shakes his parting guest by the hand,
And with his arms outstretched, as he would fly,
Grasps in the comer. The welcome ever smiles,
And farewell goes out sighing. Let not virtue seek
Remuneration for the thing it was. For beauty, wit,
High birth, vigor of bone, desert in service,
Love, friendship, charity, are subjects all
To envious and calumniating time. *Troilus and Cressida,* III,iii,165.

⁷   That old common arbitrator, Time. *Troilus and Cressida,* IV,v,223.
(More at ENDINGS.)

⁸ O Time, thou must untangle this, not I;
It is too hard a knot for me t'untie. *Twelfth Night,* II,ii,40.

⁹   Thus the whirligig of time brings in his revenges. *Twelfth Night,* V,i,378.

¹⁰   There's time enough for that. *The Winter's Tale,* V,iii,128.

See also FUTURE, THE; HISTORY; PAST, THE; PRESENT, THE; SPEED.

TIMELINESS.   See ACTION, PROMPT; SEASONS.

TIMES.   See BAD TIMES; PEACE.

TOMORROW.   See FUTURE.

TRAVEL

1   Travelers must be content. *As You Like It,* II,iv,17. (More at HOME.)

2 Farewell, Monsieur Traveler. Look you lisp and wear strange suits, disable all the benefits of your own country, be out of love with your nativity, and almost chide God for making you that countenance you are; or I will scarce think you have swam in a gundello. *As You Like It,* IV,i,31. (Rosalind making fun of an all too familiar type of traveler. For *disable* read "disparage," for *gundello,* "gondola.")

3   Aboard, aboard, for shame!
The wind sits in the shoulder of your sail. *Hamlet,* I,iii,55.

4   'Tis ever common
That men are merriest when they are from home. *Henry V,* I,ii,271.

5 Now spurs the lated traveler apace
To gain the timely inn. *Macbeth,* III,iii,6.

6 I'll put a girdle round about the earth
In forty minutes. *A Midsummer Night's Dream,* II,i,175. (Puck setting out to obtain the flower "love in idleness" for Oberon; see PLANTS AND FLOWERS.)

7 Such wind as scatters young men through the world
To seek their fortunes farther than at home,
Where small experience grows. *The Taming of the Shrew,* I,ii,49.

8 O mistress mine, where are you roaming?
. . .
Trip no further, pretty sweeting;
Journeys end in lovers meeting,
Every wise man's son doth know. *Twelfth Night,* II,iii,40,43.

9 Then westward ho! *Twelfth Night,* III,i,136.

10   Let him spend his time no more at home,
Which would be great impeachment to his age,
In having known no travel in his youth. *The Two Gentlemen of Verona,* I,iii,14. (*Impeachment* means "detriment.")

See also BANISHMENT AND EXILE; HOME; SEPARATION; SHIPS AND SAILING.

TREASON

[1] Supposition all our lives shall be stuck full of eyes;
For treason is but trusted like the fox. *Henry IV, Part One,* V,ii,8. (The earl of Worcester concluding that he must continue in the path of rebellion despite a peace offer from the king. The meaning of the couplet is that the treason will not be forgotten, the rebels will always be watched.)

[2] Whilst bloody treason flourished over us. *Julius Caesar,* III,ii,194. (More at JULIUS CAESAR.)

[3] Thus treason works ere traitors be espied. *The Rape of Lucrece,* 361.

[4] His treasons will sit blushing in his face,
Not able to endure the sight of day. *Richard II,* III,ii,51.

[5]   A nest of traitors. *The Winter's Tale,* II,iii,80.

See also BETRAYAL.

TRICKS.   See CRAFTINESS.

TROUBLE

[6] Marry, this is miching mallecho; it means mischief. *Hamlet,* III,ii,142. (*Miching mallecho* translates "sneaking mischief.")

[7] One woe doth tread upon another's heel.
So fast they follow. *Hamlet,* IV,vii,163. (See also SORROW AND SADNESS, *Hamlet,* IV,v,78.)

[8]   Every cloud engenders not a storm. *Henry VI, Part Three,* V,iii,13. (But see the quote from *Richard III* below.)

[9] Nor heaven nor earth have been at peace tonight. *Julius Caesar,* II,ii,1.

[10]   Mischief, thou art afoot,
Take thou what course thou wilt. *Julius Caesar,* III,ii,262.

[11] My flocks feed not, my ewes breed not,
My rams speed not, all is amiss. *The Passionate Pilgrim,* xvii,1.

[12]   When clouds are seen, wise men put on their cloaks;
When great leaves fall, then winter is at hand;
When the sun sets, who doth not look for night? *Richard III,* II,iii,32.

[13]   Thou art wedded to calamity. *Romeo and Juliet,* III,iii,3. (Friar Lawrence speaking of Romeo.)

[14] How cams't thou in this pickle? *The Tempest,* V,i,281.

See also ADVERSITY; DANGER; DECLINE; SORROW AND SADNESS; TYRANNY.

TROY.   See CITIES.

TRUST

[1]   Love all, trust a few. *All's Well That Ends Well*, I,i,68. (More at WISDOM, WORDS OF.)

[2] More should I question thee, and more I must,
Though more to know could not be more to trust. *All's Well That Ends Well*, II,i,207. (The king of France here accepts Helena as his physician. As he admits, the leap of trust has made the rest of the interview no more than a formality.)

[3]   What trust is in these times? *Henry IV, Part Two*, I,iii,100.

[4] *Buckingham.* Trust nobody, for fear you be betrayed.
Say. The trust I have is in my innocence,
And therefore am I bold and resolute. *Henry VI, Part Two*, IV,iv,58. (Lord Say is shortly thereafter beheaded by Jack Cade's revolutionaries.)

[5]   Oftentimes, to win us to our harm
The instruments of darkness tell us truths,
Win us with honest trifles, to betray us
In deepest consequence. *Macbeth*, I,iii,123. (The last line means "in the most important matter." The method attributed here to the instruments of darkness is the classic approach of the con man and counterintelligence agent.)

See also WISDOM, WORDS OF.

TRUTH

[6] 'Tis not the many oaths that makes the truth,
But the plain single vow that is vowed true. *All's Well That Ends Well*, IV,ii,21.

[7] Your bait of falsehood take this carp of truth,
And thus do we of wisdom and of reach,
With windlasses and with assays of bias,
By indirections find directions out. *Hamlet*, II,i,63. (Polonius instructing a servant on how to discover whether Laertes, who is studying abroad, is living too wild a life. Polonius advises using indirection, and even false statements, to elicit truthful information. A *windlass* refers to a circuitous method; *assays of bias,* a bowling term, refers to taking a curved path.)

[8] Mark now how a plain tale shall put you down. *Henry IV, Part One*, II,iv,254. (Hal warning Falstaff that the simple truth is about to come out.)

[1] Tell truth and shame the devil. *Henry IV, Part One,* III,i,58.

[2] Truth's a dog must to kennel; he must be whipped out, when Lady the Brach may stand by the fire and stink. *King Lear,* I,iv,114. (*Brach* means "bitch.")

[3]   Truth is truth
To the end of reckoning. *Measure for Measure,* V,i,45.

[4] Truth will come to light. *The Merchant of Venice,* II,ii,79. (More at CRIME.)

[5]   In the end truth will out. *The Merchant of Venice,* II,ii,80.

[6] Truth hath a quiet breast. *Richard II,* I,iii,96.

[7]   Simple truth miscalled simplicity. *Sonnet 66,* 11.

See also TALK, PLAIN AND FANCY.

TYRANNY

[8]   Each new morn
New widows howl, new orphans cry, new sorrows
Strike heaven on the face. *Macbeth,* IV,iii,4.

[9]   Our country sinks beneath the yoke;
It weeps, it bleeds, and each new day a gash
Is added to her wounds. *Macbeth,* IV,iii,39.

[10]   The snares of watchful tyranny. *Macbeth,* V,viii,67. (More at BANISHMENT AND EXILE.)

[11] 'Tis time to fear when tyrants seems to kiss. *Pericles,* I,ii,79.

See also CENSORSHIP; INJUSTICE; POWER.

UGLY PEOPLE.   See INSULTS.

UNHAPPINESS.   See COMPLAINTS; DEPRESSION; ENVY;
HAPPINESS; JEALOUSY; SORROW AND SADNESS;
WEEPING.

UTILITY
[1] It did me yeoman's service. *Hamlet,* V,ii,36. (More at WRITING.)

See also VALUE.

UTOPIA
[2] *Gonzalo.* In the commonwealth I would by contraries
Execute all things. For no kind of traffic
Would I admit; no name of magistrate;
Letters should not be known; riches, poverty,
And use of service, none; contract, succession,
Bourn, bound of land, tilth, vineyard, none;
No use of metal, corn, or wine, or oil;
No occupation; all men idle, all;
And women too, but innocent and pure;
No sovereignty.
Sebastian. Yet he would be king on it. *The Tempest,* II,i,152. (*By contraries*
means "in ways the opposite of what usually is done." *Service* refers to

work done by servants. *Succession* refers to inheritance. *Bourn* refers to boundaries or property lines. The passage is closely derived from a passage by Montaigne in his essay "Of the Cannibals," 1580, an important source for the ideas underlying this play. The speaker, Gonzalo, is kindly but limited. Sebastian immediately sees a problem in this paradise.)

V

VALOR.   See BOLDNESS; COURAGE; DISCRETION; VIRTUE.

VALUE

1   Small to greater matters must give way. *Antony and Cleopatra,* II,ii,11.

2   There is nothing either good or bad but thinking makes it so. *Hamlet,* II,ii,253.

3 I have been worth the whistle. *King Lear,* IV,ii,29. (Goneril's expression of satisfaction with herself refers to the proverb "It is a poor dog that is not worth the whistling." Her husband replies, "You are not worth the dust which the rude wind / Blows in your face," l.30.)

4 The jewel that we find, we stoop and take it
Because we see it; but what we do not see
We tread upon, and never think of it. *Measure for Measure,* II,i,24.

5 All that glisters is not gold;
Often have you heard that told. *The Merchant of Venice,* II,vii,65. (Bart-lett's *Familiar Quotations* traces this proverb back to a Latin translation of a sentence in Aristotle's *Elenchi:* "Yellow objects appear to be gold.")

6 I would not have given it for a wilderness of monkeys. *The Merchant of Venice,* III,i,115. (Shylock speaking of a turquoise ring given him by his wife, stolen by his daughter.)

1   What we have we prize not to the worth
Whiles we enjoy it; but being lacked and lost,
Why, then we rack the value, then we find
The virtue that possession would not show us
Whiles it was ours. *Much Ado About Nothing,* IV,i,217.

2 What win I if I gain the thing I seek?
A dream, a breath, a froth of fleeting joy.
Who buys a minute's mirth to wail a week?
Or sells eternity to get a toy?
For one sweet grape who will the vine destroy? *The Rape of Lucrece,* 211.
(Tarquin reasoning that he should abandon his designs on Lucrece.)

3 Men prize the thing ungained more than it is. *Troilus and Cressida,* I,ii,301.

4 What's aught but as 'tis valued? *Troilus and Cressida,* II,ii,52.

VANITY

5 He wants nothing of a god but eternity and a heaven to throne in.
Coriolanus, V,iv,24.

6 I am not in the roll of common men. *Henry IV, Part One,* III,i,42. (Glendower insists that portents at his birth—comets and earthquakes—proph-
esied his future supernatural greatness. See also OCCULT, THE.)

7   There was never yet fair woman but she made mouths in a glass. *King
Lear,* III,ii,35. (*She made mouths in a glass* means "she tried out different
expressions in front of a mirror.")

8 "I am Sir Oracle,
And when I ope my lips, let no dog bark!" *The Merchant of Venice,* I,i,93.

9 Light vanity, insatiate cormorant,
Consuming means, soon preys upon itself. *Richard II,* II,i,38.

10 Being so great, I have no need to beg. *Richard II,* IV,i,308.

11 What a sweep of vanity comes this way. *Timon of Athens,* I,ii,134. (The
curmudgeon Apemantus commenting on the entrance of Athenian ladies,
done up as Amazons, dancing and playing lutes.)

12 Like madness is the glory of this life. *Timon of Athens,* I,ii,136. (Apemantus
again; see above. The term *glory* here means "vanity" or "vainglory.")

See also CONSPICUOUS CONSUMPTION; PRIDE.

VARIETY

[1] Her infinite variety. *Antony and Cleopatra,* II,ii,242. (More at CLEOPATRA.)

VICE.   See CRIME; DANGEROUS PEOPLE; EVIL; MORALITY; SEX; WILD AND WANTON PEOPLE.

VICTORY.   See COMPETITION; SUCCESS.

VIGILANCE

[2]   Some must watch, while some must sleep. *Hamlet,* III,ii,279.

[3]   I am as vigilant as a cat to steal cream. *Henry IV, Part One,* IV,ii,59.

See also CONSPIRACY.

VILLAINS.   See CRIME; DANGEROUS PEOPLE; EVIL.

VIOLENCE

[4]   His sword can never win
The honor that he loses. *All's Well That Ends Well,* III,ii,97.

[5] Thou has done a deed whereat valor will weep. *Coriolanus,* V,vi,133. (The deed is the assassination of Coriolanus.)

[6] Let me be cruel, not unnatural;
I will speak daggers to her, but use none. *Hamlet,* III,ii,403. (Hamlet preparing to speak with his mother.)

[7] How now? A rat? Dead for a ducat, dead! *Hamlet,* III,iv,24. (Hamlet as he stabs Polonius through the arras [curtain].)

[8] I am not yet of Percy's mind, the Hotspur of the North: he that kills me some six or seven dozen Scots at a breakfast, washes his hands, and says to his wife, "Fie upon this quiet life! I want work." *Henry IV, Part One,* II,iv,102. (Prince Hal joking about Hotspur's warrior mentality. Hal kills Hotspur at the battle of Shrewsbury.)

[9] There is throats to be cut, and works to be done. *Henry V,* III,ii,114. (Captain Macmorris describing the business of war.)

[10]   When blood is their argument? *Henry V,* IV,i,145.

[11] Speak hands for me! *Julius Caesar,* III,i,76. (Casca attacking Caesar.)

[12] Woe to the hand that shed this costly blood! *Julius Caesar,* III,i,258. (Antony over the body of Caesar.)

¹ There is no sure foundation set on blood,
No certain life achieved by others' death. *King John,* IV,ii,104.

² It is a damnèd and a bloody work,
The graceless action of a heavy hand. *King John,* IV,iii,57.

³ Your sword is bright, sir; put it up again. *King John,* IV,iii,79.

⁴ Then, kill, kill, kill, kill, kill, kill! *King Lear,* IV,vi,189.

⁵   If the assassination
Could trammel up the consequence, and catch,
With his surcease, success; that but this blow
Might be the be-all and the end-all—here,
But here, upon this bank and shoal of time,
We'd jump the life to come. But in these cases
We still have judgment here; that we but teach
Bloody instructions, which, being taught, return
To plague th' inventor. *Macbeth,* I,vii,2. (*Trammel up* means "catch up, as
in a net"; *his surcease* seems to refer to Duncan's death; *jump* means "take
a chance on." Macbeth's argument is that if the assassination could be
accomplished without lingering consequences in this world, then he'd take
a chance on retribution in the next world. But, he reminds himself, there
may still be consequences here; having used violence, one may find oneself
eventually a victim of violent retribution. Followed by a reference to
"even-handed justice." See also ACTION, PROMPT and JUSTICE.)

⁶ O horror, horror, horror! Tongue nor heart
Cannot conceive nor name thee. *Macbeth,* II,iii,66. (Macduff upon finding
Duncan murdered.)

⁷ Bloody thou art, bloody will be thy end. *Richard III,* IV,iv,195. (The
duchess of York to her son Richard III.)

See also CRIME; PASSION; POWER; REVOLUTION; RUTHLESSNESS; WAR.

VIRTUE

⁸ O infinite virtue, comest thou smiling from
The world's great snare uncaught? *Antony and Cleopatra,* IV,viii,17.

⁹ Honesty coupled to beauty is to have honey a sauce to sugar. *As You Like
It,* III,iii,29. (A quip by Touchstone on virtue in women.)

¹⁰   Keep you in the rear of your affection,
Out of the shot and danger of desire.
The chariest maid is prodigal enough

If she unmask her beauty to the moon.
Virtue itself scapes not calumnious strokes.
The canker galls the infants of the spring
Too oft before their buttons be disclosed,
And in the morn and liquid dew of youth
Contagious blastments are most imminent.
Be wary then; best safety lies in fear. *Hamlet,* I,iii,34. (Laertes advising Ophelia to mistrust Hamlet's love. The *canker* is a cankerworm, and *buttons* are buds.)

[1] Assume a virtue, if you have it not. *Hamlet,* III,iv,161.

[2] There lives not three good men unhanged in England; and one of them is fat, and grows old. *Henry IV, Part One,* II,iv,130. (Falstaff on the subject of Falstaff.)

[3]   A good heart, Kate, is the sun and the moon. *Henry V,* V,ii,167. (The king to Princess Katherine of France.)

[4] A heart unspotted is not easily daunted. *Henry VI, Part Two,* III,i,100.

[5]   In thy face I see
The map of honor, truth, and loyalty. *Henry VI, Part Two,* III,i,202.

[6] Virtue finds no friends. *Henry VIII,* III,i,126.

[7]   Be just, and fear not.
Let all the ends thou aim'st at be thy country's,
Thy God's, and truth's. Then if thou fall'st, O Cromwell,
Thou fall'st a blessed martyr. *Henry VIII,* III,ii,446. (Cardinal Wolsey to his servant Cromwell. The speech may have been written by John Fletcher rather than Shakespeare.)

[8] Men's evil manners live in brass; their virtues
We write in water. *Henry VIII,* IV,ii,45. (Similar to the more famous line from Antony's funeral oration for Caesar; see below.)

[9]   This man,
This good man—few of you deserve that title. *Henry VIII,* V,iii,137.

[10] The evil that men do lives after them,
The good is oft interrèd with their bones. *Julius Caesar,* III,ii,77. (From Antony's funeral oration for Caesar; more at JULIUS CAESAR. See also the quote above from *Henry VIII,* IV,ii,45.)

[11] His life was gentle, and the elements
So mixed in him that Nature might stand up

And say to all the world, "This was a man!" *Julius Caesar,* V,v,73. (Antony speaking over the body of Brutus.)

[1] A man of sovereign parts he is esteemed,
Well fitted in arts, glorious in arms.
Nothing becomes him ill that he would well. *Love's Labor's Lost,* II,i,44. (Translation: A man of princely qualities, he is esteemed, accomplished in the arts, glorious in battle, he does nothing poorly that he wishes to do well.)

[2]   This Duncan
Hath borne his faculties so meek, hath been
So clear in his great office, that his virtues
Will plead like angels trumpet-tongued against
The deep damnation of his taking-off. *Macbeth,* I,vii,16. (Macbeth reflecting on the virtues of the king whom he is considering assassinating. *Faculties* means "powers"; *clear* means "spotless." Other quotes from this soliloquy are at ACTION, PROMPT; AMBITION; CRIME; and JUSTICE.)

[3] Some rise by sin, and some by virtue fall. *Measure for Measure,* II,i,38.

[4] The hand that hath made you fair hath made you good. *Measure for Measure,* III,i,182.

[5] Virtue is bold, and goodness never fearful. *Measure for Measure,* III,i,211.

[6] I never did repent for doing good. *The Merchant of Venice,* III,iv,10.

[7] How far that little candle throws his beams!
So shines a good deed in a naughty world. *The Merchant of Venice,* V,i, 90.

[8]   Never anything can be amiss,
When simpleness and duty tender it. *A Midsummer Night's Dream,* V,i, 82.

[9] Are you good men and true? *Much Ado About Nothing,* III,iii,1.

[10]   A maid
That paragons description and wild fame;
One that excels the quirks of blazoning pens. *Othello,* II,i,61. (The subject is Desdemona, a maid who exceeds her description and very favorable fame, one who excels the ingenuities of written praise.)

[11]   He was not born to shame.
Upon his brow shame is ashamed to sit. *Romeo and Juliet,* III,ii,91.

1   Captive good attending captain ill. *Sonnet 66,* 12. (Virtue's subservience is one of the wrongs that make the poet weary of life.)

2 They that have power to hurt and will do none,
That do not do the thing they most do show,
Who, moving others, are themselves as stone,
Unmovèd, cold, and to temptation slow;
They rightly do inherit heaven's graces
And husband nature's riches from expense;
They are the lords and owners of their faces,
Others but stewards of their excellence.
The summer's flow'r is to the summer sweet,
Though to itself it only live and die. *Sonnet 94,* 1. (This sonnet is open to a number of interpretations. William Empson argued in *Some Versions of Pastoral* that the meaning is that the virtuous control their emotions and are indifferent to temptation. Although cold, their excellence is real and their success deserved. But if they do fall, they may become worse than ordinary people, for "Lilies that fester smell far worse than weeds," l.14.)

3   'Tis the mind that makes the body rich,
And as the sun breaks through the darkest clouds
So honor peereth in the meanest habit. *The Taming of the Shrew,* IV,iii, 170.

4 He lives in fame that died in virtue's cause. *Titus Andronicus,* I,i,391.

5 His heart and hand both open and both free,
For what he has he gives, what he thinks he shows. *Troilus and Cressida,* IV,v,100.

6 Is it a world to hide virtues in? *Twelfth Night,* I,iii,127.

7 Dost thou think, because thou art virtuous, there shall be no more cakes and ale? *Twelfth Night,* II,iii,114.

8 In nature there's no blemish but the mind;
None can be called deformed but the unkind.
Virtue is beauty. *Twelfth Night,* III,iv,379.

9 He is complete in feature and in mind
With all good grace to grace a gentleman. *The Two Gentlemen of Verona,* II,vi,72.

See also GRACE; HONOR; INNOCENCE; KINDNESS; LOYALTY; MORALITY; NOBILITY; WISDOM; WISDOM, WORDS OF.

VISION

[1] It adds a precious seeing to the eye. *Love's Labor's Lost,* IV,iii,332. (*It refers to love.*)

[2]   Argus, all eyes and no sight. *Troilus and Cressida,* I,ii,30.

See also PERCEPTION.

VOWS.   See OATHS; MARRIAGE; PROMISES.

WALES AND THE WELSH

1   The devil understands Welsh. *Henry IV, Part One,* III,i,231. (Hotspur, whose patience has been tried by the self-important Welsh chieftain Glendower. See also another quote from the scene at MUSIC.)

WAR

2 The end of war's uncertain. *Coriolanus,* V,iii,141. (For *end* read "outcome.")

3 Every jack-slave hath his bellyful of fighting. *Cymbeline,* II,i,21.

4 We go to gain a little patch of ground
That hath in it no profit but the name. *Hamlet,* IV,iv,18.

5 I would 'twere bedtime, Hal, and all well. *Henry IV, Part One,* V,i,125. (Falstaff to the prince at the start of the battle of Shrewsbury. Hal reminds him that he owes God a death; see DEATH.)

6   Full bravely hast thou fleshed
Thy maiden sword. *Henry IV, Part One,* V,iv,129. (Hal, the Prince of Wales, to his brother John after the battle of Shrewsbury. Historically, these young warriors were age sixteen and fourteen. Shakespeare makes them a little older.)

7 We fortify in paper and in figures,
Using the names of men instead of men,

Like one that draws the model of an house
Beyond his power to build. *Henry IV, Part Two,* I,iii,56. (Good projections
on paper will not win the fight on the battlefield. Lord Bardolph warning
that in armed rebellion, nothing can be left to chance; careful and realistic
planning is needed. See PLANNING for an earlier passage from this speech.)

1   For God's sake, go not to these wars! *Henry IV, Part Two,* II,iii,9.

2   I have in equal balance justly weighed
What wrongs our arms may do, what wrongs we suffer,
And find our griefs heavier than our offenses. *Henry IV, Part Two,* IV,i,67.
(A pompous, if familiar, defense of war offered by the Archbishop of York,
whose given name was Richard Scroop.)

3 God, and not we, hath safely fought today. *Henry IV, Part Two,* IV,ii,121.
(A superficially pious remark, but in context outrageous. With this comment Prince John excuses breaking his pledge of leniency and executing
the rebels. The part is written for someone older than the prince actually
was at this time, age fourteen.)

4 Now all the youth of England are on fire,
And silken dalliance in the wardrobe lies. *Henry V,* II, Chorus,1. (From
the opening of this act, describing the preparations for the invasion of
France. The second line means that the young men have put aside flirta-
tions and entertainments as one would pack away a silk garment.)

5 Once more unto the breach, dear friends, once more;
Or close the wall up with our English dead!
In peace there's nothing so becomes a man
As modest stillness and humility;
But when the blast of war blows in our ears,
Then imitate the action of the tiger:
Stiffen the sinews, conjure up the blood,
Disguise fair nature with hard-favored rage;
Then lend the eye a terrible aspect. *Henry V,* III,i,1. (The king, urging on
his soldiers to capture Harfleur. In the first line, *unto* is often misquoted
as *into.* More below.)

6 I see you stand like greyhounds in the slips,
Straining upon the start. The game's afoot!
Follow your spirit; and upon this charge,
Cry, "God for Harry, England and Saint George!" *Henry V,* III,i,31.
(Laurence Olivier perfectly captured the ecstatic patriotism of *Henry V* in
his 1944 film. He had first played the role in 1937. In another, stranger
wartime production, in England in 1916 and 1921, Marie Slade did the
play with an all-woman cast, herself appearing as Henry. There were

various reasons for such an oddity, one being the shortage of young Englishmen in that era.)

[1]   I know the disciplines of war. *Henry V,* III,ii,143. (Captain Fluellen is referring to the Roman disciplines of war, which he believes to be still valid.)

[2] From camp to camp, through the foul womb of night,
The hum of either army stilly sounds;
That the fixed sentinels almost receive
The secret whispers of each other's watch.
Fire answers fire, and through their paly flames
Each battle sees the other's umbered face.
Steed threatens steed, in high and boastful neighs
Piercing the night's dull ear; and from the tents
The armorers accomplishing the knights,
With busy hammers closing rivets up,
Give dreadful note of preparation. *Henry V,* IV, Chorus,4. (The French and English camps on the night before the battle of Agincourt, October 25, 1415. For *paly* read "pale"; for *umbered,* "shadowed"; for *battle,* "army"; for *accomplishing,* "equipping." Later in the passage, the Chorus describes the king walking among the troops—"The royal captain of this ruined band," l.29. See also HENRY V.)

[3]   There are few die well that die in a battle. *Henry V,* IV,i,144.

[4] They have said their prayers, and they stay for death. *Henry V,* IV,ii,56. (The constable of France describing the sickly English troops before the battle of Agincourt. The English won, however. See below and also SOLDIERS.)

[5] This day is called the Feast of Crispian:
He that outlives this day, and comes safe home,
Will stand a-tiptoe when this day is named,
And rouse him at the name of Crispian. *Henry V,* IV,iii,40. (The king rousing the English army going into the battle of Agincourt. More below. See also SOLDIERS.)

[6] Then will he strip his sleeve and show his scars,
And say, "These wounds I had on Crispin's day."
Old men forget; yet all shall be forgot,
But he'll remember, with advantages,
What feats he did that day. *Henry V,* IV,iii,47. (The young king, age twenty-seven, promising his men a place in history if they survive the day's fighting. The English, with some 6,000 men, were facing an army of about 25,000. *Crispin* and *Crispian* were brothers and martyrs, d. A.D. 286. See also below and under HONOR and SOLDIERS.)

¹ We few, we happy few, we band of brothers;
For he today that sheds his blood with me
Shall be my brother. *Henry V,* IV,iii,60. (Henry's message to his men
going into the battle of Agincourt.)

² And gentlemen in England, now abed,
Shall think themselves accursed they were not here;
And hold their manhoods cheap whiles any speaks
That fought with us upon Saint Crispin's day. *Henry V,* IV,iii,64. (The
great victory was a slaughter in a muddy field, but with opportunities for
soldiers to enrich themselves that those at home might perhaps have
envied. For a marvelous description of the Agincourt encounter, see John
Keegan's *The Face of Battle.* Kenneth Branagh's Henry V, in his wonderful
1989 movie, captured the more brutal aspects of the war and the king
himself.)

³ Lean Famine, quartering Steel, and climbing Fire. *Henry VI, Part One,*
IV,ii,11. (The weapons of siege warfare.)

⁴ O piteous spectacle! O bloody times! *Henry VI, Part Three,* II,v,73. (The
king in the midst of battle in the civil war. He has just seen a boy realize
that he has inadvertently killed his own father; see PRAYERS.)

⁵ A curse shall light upon the limbs of men;
Domestic fury and fierce civil strife. *Julius Caesar,* III,i,262. (Antony predicting civil war. Shakespeare's generation was still haunted by memories
of the bloody Wars of the Roses.)

⁶ All pity choked with custom of fell deeds. *Julius Caesar,* III,i,269. (Antony
again.)

⁷ Cry "Havoc," and let slip the dogs of war. *Julius Caesar,* III,i,273. (From
the passage quoted twice above.)

⁸ War! War! No peace! Peace is to me a war. *King John,* III,i,39.

⁹ *First Witch.* When shall we three meet again?
In thunder, lightning, or in rain?
Second Witch. When the hurlyburly's done,
When the battle's lost and won. *Macbeth,* I,i,1. (The witches' riddles
convey the confusion of war. Macbeth in his first appearance, fresh from
the battlefield, says, "So foul and fair a day I have not seen," I,iii,38.)

¹⁰ Had I power, I should
Pour the sweet milk of concord into hell,
Uproar the universal peace, confound
All unity on earth. *Macbeth,* IV,iii,97. (Malcolm speaks.)

[1] Hang out our banners on the outward walls.
The cry is still "They come!" Our castle's strength
Will laugh a siege to scorn. *Macbeth,* V,v,1. (Perhaps the most effective
dramatization of the warfare in this play and of Macbeth as warrior is in
Akira Kurosawa's *Throne of Blood,* titled in Japanese *The Castle of the
Spider's Web.* The movie is only loosely based on the play, but fully
captures its spirit.)

[2] I begin to be aweary of the sun,
And wish the estate of the world were now undone.
Ring the alarum bell! Blow wind, come wrack!
At least we'll die with harness on our back. *Macbeth,* V,v,49.

[3] I have no words:
My voice is in my sword. *Macbeth,* V,viii,6. (Macduff to Macbeth. See also
below.)

[4]   Lay on, Macduff;
And damned be him that first cries "Hold, enough!" *Macbeth,* V,viii,33.

[5]   O now, forever
Farewell the tranquil mind! Farewell content!
Farewell the plumed troops, and the big wars
That makes ambition virtue! O, farewell!
Farewell the neighing steed and the shrill trump,
The spirit-stirring drum, th' ear-piercing fife,
The royal banner, and all quality,
Pride, pomp, and circumstance of glorious war!
And O you mortal engines whose rude throats
Th' immortal Jove's dread clamors counterfeit,
Farewell! Othello's occupation's gone! *Othello,* III,iii,344. (Othello, a great
commander, with his life unraveling, regrets the ruin of his marriage and
the loss of his career. The *mortal engines* are cannon.)

[6]   He is come to open
The purple testament of bleeding war. *Richard II,* III,iii,93. (Richard on
Bolingbroke's rebellion.)

[7]   Tumultuous wars
Shall kin with kin and kind with kind confound;
Disorder, horror, fear, and mutiny,
Shall here inhabit, and this land be call'd
The field of Golgotha and dead men's skulls. *Richard II,* IV,i,140. (A
recurring theme: the horror of civil war. Here the bishop of Carlisle reacts
to Bolingbroke's rebellion against Richard II.)

¹ Religious canons, civil laws are cruel;
Then what should war be? *Timon of Athens,* IV,iii,61. (The embittered Timon urging Alcibiades to make war ruthlessly.)

² We were not all unkind, nor all deserve
The common stroke of war. *Timon of Athens,* V,iv,21. (An Athenian senator reminding Alicibiades that even a just war hurts the innocent as well as the guilty.)

³   The ministers and instruments
Of cruel war. *Troilus and Cressida,* Prologue, 4.

⁴ War and lechery confound all! *Troilus and Cressida,* II,iii,77. (See also SEX, *Troilus and Cressida,* V,ii,192.)

⁵ What's past and what's to come is strewed with husks
And formless ruin of oblivion. *Troilus and Cressida,* IV,v,165. (King Agamemnon speaking in the midst of the Trojan war.)

See also DEFENSE; PEACE; RESISTANCE; RETREAT; REVOLUTION; RUTHLESS-NESS; SOLDIERS; STAR WARS; VIOLENCE; WAR AND PEACE.

WAR AND PEACE

⁶   The latter end of a fray and the beginning of a feast fits a dull fighter and a keen guest. *Henry IV, Part One,* IV,ii,80. (Falstaff, who is not in a hurry to get into action at the battle of Shrewsbury.)

⁷ In war was never lion raged more fierce,
In peace was never gentle lamb more mild. *Richard II,* II,i,173. (The reference is to Richard's father, the Black Prince.)

⁸ Grim-visaged War hath smoothed his wrinkled front,
And now, instead of mounting barbèd steeds
To fright the souls of fearful adversaries,
He capers nimbly in a lady's chamber
To the lascivious pleasing of a lute. *Richard III,* I,i,9. (From Richard's opening soliloquy, which begins "Now is the winter of our discontent." See PEACE. *Front* means "forehead." *Barbèd* means "armored.")

⁹ Make war breed peace. *Timon of Athens,* V,iv,83. (This is what Alcibiades promises to accomplish if Athens allows him peaceful entry.)

See also DEFENSE; PEACE; WAR.

WAR CRIMES.   See GUILT (first quote from *Henry V*); WAR.

WEAKNESS

[1] Now am I, if a man should speak truly, little better than one of the wicked. *Henry IV, Part One,* I,ii,97. (Falstaff working up to one of his many vows to reform.)

[2] Who so firm that cannot be seduced? *Julius Caesar,* I,ii,312.

[3] The weakest kind of fruit
Drops earliest to the ground. *The Merchant of Venice,* IV,i,115.

[4] The weakest goes to the wall. *Romeo and Juliet,* I,i,15. (Proverbial. Part of a series of word plays on *wall.* The meaning: The weakest are pushed back.)

[5] I am a feather for each wind that blows. *The Winter's Tale,* II,iii,152.

See also FAILINGS; TEMPTATION.

WEATHER

[6] 'Tis bitter cold,
And I am sick at heart. *Hamlet,* I,i,8.

[7] *Hamlet.* The air bites shrewdly; it is very cold.
Horatio. It is a nipping and an eager air. *Hamlet,* I,iv,1.

[8] Comes a frost, a killing frost. *Henry VIII,* III,ii,355. (Part of Wolsey's farewell to greatness; see GREATNESS.)

[9] Blow, winds, and crack your cheeks. Rage, blow! *King Lear,* III,ii,1. (The king's curse on mankind and the storm merge in a raging crescendo. Lear calls down "oak-cleaving thunderbolts," l.6, and "all-shaking thunder," l.7. The entire passage is given at DESPAIR AND RAGE.)

[10] Here's a night pities neither wise man nor fools. *King Lear,* III,ii,12.

[11] I tax not you, you elements, with unkindness. *King Lear,* III,ii,16. (Lear, addressing the wind and rain, acknowledges that unlike his daughters, they owe him no kindness.)

[12] The wrathful skies
Gallow the very wanderers of the dark
And make them keep their caves. *King Lear,* III,ii,43. (The earl of Kent describes this overwhelming storm. See the quotes above. *Gallow* means "frighten.")

[13] The rain it raineth every day. *King Lear,* III,ii,77. (The same phrase, which refers to life's adversity, is used in *Twelfth Night,* V,i,394.)

¹ Poor Tom's a-cold. *King Lear,* III,iv,150.

²   This place is too cold for hell. *Macbeth,* II,iii,17.

³ Untimely storms makes men expect a dearth. *Richard III,* II,iii,35. (A *dearth* is a famine.)

⁴ Like a red morn that ever yet betokened
Wrack to the seaman, tempest to the field,
Sorrow to the shepherds, woe unto the birds,
Gusts and foul flaws to herdmen and to herds. *Venus and Adonis,* 453.
(The same concept as in the adage "Red sun at night, sailors delight; red sun in morning, sailors take warning.")

See also SPRING; SUMMER; WINTER.

WEEPING

⁵   The big round tears
Coursed one another down his innocent nose
In piteous chase. *As You Like It,* II,i,38. (A wounded deer is weeping.)

⁶ O lady, weep no more. *Cymbeline,* I,i,93.

⁷ Like Niobe, all tears. *Hamlet,* I,ii,149. (Hamlet describing his mother's demeanor at the funeral of his father. The tears dried quickly. Niobe, by the way, wept for her dead children.)

⁸ To weep is to make less the depth of grief. *Henry VI, Part Three,* II,i,85.

⁹ If you have tears, prepare to shed them now. *Julius Caesar,* III,ii,171. (Brilliant use of suggestion by Mark Antony, delivering the funeral oration for Caesar.)

¹⁰   Let not women's weapons, water drops,
Stain my man's cheeks. *King Lear,* II,iv,276. (Lear holding back tears. See also below.)

¹¹   You think I'll weep.
No, I'll not weep.
I have full cause of weeping, but this heart
Shall break into a hundred thousand flaws
Or ere I'll weep. O Fool, I shall go mad! *King Lear,* II,iv,281.

¹²   I will weep no more. *King Lear,* III,iv,17.

¹³ How much better it is to weep at joy than to joy at weeping. *Much Ado About Nothing,* I,i,27.

¹ I am not prone to weeping, as our sex
Commonly are. *The Winter's Tale,* II,i,108. (Queen Hermione is speaking.)

See also SORROW AND SADNESS.

WHYS. See REASONS.

WILD AND WANTON PEOPLE

² Let us be Diana's foresters, gentlemen of the shade, minions of the moon. *Henry IV, Part One,* I,ii,25. (Falstaff to Prince Hal.)

³ We have heard the chimes at midnight, Master Shallow. *Henry IV, Part Two,* III,ii,220. (Falstaff reminiscing over long nights of eating, drinking, and so on.)

⁴   A ruffian that will swear, drink, dance,
Revel the night, rob, murder, and commit
The oldest sins the newest kind of ways? *Henry IV, Part Two,* IV,v,124.

⁵   He is given
To sports, to wildness, and much company. *Julius Caesar* II,i,188. (Brutus assessing Mark Antony.)

⁶ Wine loved I deeply, dice dearly; and in woman out-paramoured the Turk. *King Lear,* III,iv,91. (Edgar speaks.)

⁷ When night dogs run, all sorts of deer are chased. *The Merry Wives of Windsor,* V,v,240.

⁸   You are one of those that will not serve God if the devil bid you. *Othello,* I,i,105.

⁹ His days are foul and his drink dangerous. *Timon of Athens,* III,v,74.

See also DANGEROUS PEOPLE; FUN AND FUN PEOPLE; PASSION; SEX.

WILL

¹⁰   His will is not his own. *Hamlet,* I,iii,17. (More at HIGH POSITION.)

¹¹ Our bodies are our gardens, to the which our wills are gardeners. *Othello,* I,iii,315.

See also CHOICE; DECISION, MOMENT OF; EXCUSES.

WINNING. See COMPETITION; SUCCESS.

WINTER

¹ When icicles hang by the wall,
And Dick the shepherd blows his nail,
And Tom bears logs into the hall,
And milk comes frozen home in pail.
. . .
When all aloud the wind doth blow,
And coughing drowns the parson's saw,
And birds sit brooding in the snow,
And Marian's nose looks red and raw,
When roasted crabs hiss in the bowl,
Then nightly sings the staring owl,
"Tu-whit,
Tu-who!" a merry note,
While greasy Joan doth keel the pot. *Love's Labor's Lost,* V,ii,913,922.
(From the song that ends the play, a marvelous picture of winter in rural
England. In the second line, Dick is blowing on his nails to warm his hand.
The *parson's saw* is his sermon.)

²   You have such a February face,
So full of frost, of storm, and cloudiness? *Much Ado About Nothing,*
V,iv,41.

³   The winter of our discontent. *Richard III,* I,i,1. (More at PEACE.)

See also CHRISTMAS; WEATHER.

WISDOM

⁴   Full oft we see
Cold wisdom waiting on superfluous folly. *All's Well That Ends Well,*
I,i,110. (In paraphrase: Often we see wisdom, threadbare and cold, serv-
ing useless folly.)

⁵   The little foolery that wise men have makes a great show. *As You Like
It,* I,ii,86. (The notion that wise men may be foolish and fools are often
wise is a frequent theme in Shakespeare. See FOOLS.)

⁶ Thou speak'st wiser than thou art ware of. *As You Like It,* II,iv,55. (Rosalind to the professional fool Touchstone, who is, in fact, well aware of his
own wisdom, but too wise to show it.)

⁷ Young in limbs, in judgment old. *The Merchant of Venice,* II,vii,71. (Also,
"I never knew so young a body with so old a head," IV,i,162.)

See also EXPERIENCE; FOOLS; WIT.

WISDOM, WORDS OF

1   Love all, trust a few,
Do wrong to none; be able for thine enemy
Rather in power than use, and keep thy friend
Under thy own life's key. Be checked for silence,
But never taxed for speech. *All's Well That Ends Well,* I,i,68. (*Be able for
thine enemy* etc. means "be as strong as your enemy, but do not use that
power." Here the countess of Rousillion advises her son, Bertram. The
passage is similar to Polonius's advice to Laertes. See below.)

2 And these few precepts in thy memory
Look thou character. Give thy thoughts no tongue,
Nor any unproportioned thought his act.
Be thou familiar, but by no means vulgar.
Those friends thou hast, and their adoption tried,
Grapple them unto thy soul with hoops of steel.
. . .
. . . Beware
Of entrance to a quarrel; but being in,
Bear't that th' opposèd may beware of thee.
Give every man thine ear, but few thy voice;
Take each man's censure, but reserve thy judgment.
Costly thy habit as thy purse can buy,
But not expressed in fancy; rich, not gaudy,
For the apparel oft proclaims the man.
. . .
Neither a borrower nor a lender be,
For loan oft loses both itself and friend,
And borrowing dulleth edge of husbandry.
This above all, to thine own self be true,
And it must follow, as the night the day,
Thou canst not then be false to any man. *Hamlet,* I,iii,58,65,75. (Scholars
suggest that Polonius, who speaks here, was modeled after Lord Burghley,
chief adviser to Elizabeth I and state treasurer from 1572 to 1598. Burgh-
ley, a shrewd bourgeois statesman, wrote a book, *Certain Precepts, or
Directions,* with advice resembling that given here. Burghley was an enemy
of Essex, while Shakespeare's patron, the earl of Southampton, was one of
Essex's friends and admirers. This probably explains Shakespeare's unkind portrayal of Burghley-Polonius, named, in an earlier version of the
play, Corambis, which means "tedious iteration.")

3 Wake not a sleeping wolf. *Henry IV, Part Two,* I,ii,158.

4 Trust none;
For oaths are straws, men's faiths are wafer-cakes,

And Hold-fast is the only dog, my duck. *Henry V*, II,iii,51. (Wisdom from Pistol. The last line derives from the proverb "Brag is a good dog, but Hold-fast is a better.")

¹ Ill will never said well. *Henry V*, III,vii,118. (The first entry in a proverb-quoting contest between the constable of France and the duke of Orleans. The rest are "There is flattery in friendship," l.119; "Give the devil his due," l.121; "a fool's bolt is soon shot," l.127.)

² Have more than thou showest,
Speak less than thou knowest,
Lend less than thou owest. *King Lear*, I,iv,21.

³ Keep thy foot out of brothels, thy hand out of plackets, thy pen from lenders' books, and defy the foul fiend. *King Lear*, III,iv,97. (*Plackets* are openings in skirts.)

⁴ He's mad that trusts in the tameness of a wolf, a horse's health, a boy's love, or a whore's oath. *King Lear*, III,vi,18.

See also ADVICE; COMMON SENSE; PRUDENCE; RISK.

WIT

⁵ The dullness of the fool is the whetstone of the wits. *As You Like It*, I,ii,52.

⁶ Brevity is the soul of wit. *Hamlet*, II,ii,90. (Said by Polonius, who, despite this insight, rambles on with his customary verbosity, provoking Queen Gertrude to plead, "More matter, with less art," l.95.)

⁷ What, in thy quips and thy quiddities? *Henry IV, Part One*, I,ii,46. (Falstaff to Hal. Paraphrase: What, in a witty mood, are you?)

⁸ I am not only witty in myself, but the cause that wit is in other men. *Henry IV, Part Two*, I,ii,10. (Falstaff speaking. As a fat man and a rogue, he is the butt of endless jokes.)

⁹ His wit's as thick as Tewksbury mustard. *Henry IV, Part Two*, II,iv,246. (Falstaff is complimenting the mustard, but not the wit.)

¹⁰ Your wit's too hot, it speeds too fast, 'twill tire. *Love's Labor's Lost*, II,i,119. (Berowne to Rosaline. A. L. Rowse identifies these two characters with Shakespeare himself and the "dark lady" of the sonnets.)

¹¹ A jest's prosperity lies in the ear
Of him that hears it, never in the tongue
Of him that makes it. *Love's Labor's Lost*, V,ii,862.

¹ How every fool can play upon the word! *The Merchant of Venice,* III,v,43. (We would say "can play upon words" or "can make puns.")

²   There's a skirmish of wit between them. *Much Ado About Nothing,* I,i,60. (The warring wits are Beatrice and Benedick.)

³ He doth indeed show some sparks that are like wit. *Much Ado About Nothing,* II,iii,185.

⁴   We work by wit, and not by witchcraft. *Othello,* II,iii,372. (Instead of *wit,* we would probably say "brains" or "intelligence.")

⁵ Look, he's winding up the watch of his wit; by and by it will strike. *The Tempest,* II,i,14.

⁶ God give them wisdom that have it, and those that are fools, let them use their talents. *Twelfth Night,* I,v,14. (*Talents* means "native wit.")

See also COMMON SENSE; JOKES; TALK.

WOLSEY, CARDINAL

⁷ He was a scholar, and a ripe and good one;
Exceeding wise, fair-spoken, and persuading;
Lofty and sour to them that loved him not,
But to those men that sought him, sweet as summer. *Henry VIII,* IV,ii,51. (Griffith speaking in defense of Cardinal Wolsey, who died ruined and disgraced.)

WOMEN

⁸ Age cannot wither her, nor custom stale
Her infinite variety. *Antony and Cleopatra,* II,ii,241. (More at CLEOPATRA.)

⁹   A woman is a dish for the gods. *Antony and Cleopatra,* V,ii,274. (The sentence concludes: "If the devil dress her not." *Dress* refers both to preparing, as food, and dressing in clothes.)

¹⁰   Heavenly Rosalind! *As You Like It,* I,ii,279. (Orlando in love. George Bernard Shaw, reviewing the play in 1896, wrote: "Rosalind is to the actress what Hamlet is to the actor—a part in which, reasonable presentability being granted, failure is hardly possible.")

¹¹   If ladies be but young and fair,
They have the gift to know it. *As You Like It,* II,vii,37.

¹² The fair, the chaste, and unexpressive she. *As You Like It,* III,ii,10. (Rosalind as described by a stricken Orlando. *Unexpressive* means "beyond the

power of words to describe." Nevertheless he gives it a try, as in "From the east to western Ind, / No jewel is like Rosalind," l.88.)

¹ Do you not know that I am a woman? When I think, I must speak. *As You Like It,* III,ii,247.

² A woman's thought runs before her actions. *As You Like It,* IV,i,133. (Specifically, here, thought of marriage.)

³ I know a wench of excellent discourse,
Pretty and witty; wild and yet, too, gentle. *The Comedy of Errors,* III,i,109. (This charming person—the Courtesan—is a much lesser character in Shakespeare's play than in his source, Plautus's *Menaechmi.*)

⁴   Frailty, thy name is woman. *Hamlet,* I,ii,146.

⁵   Women fear too much, even as they love. *Hamlet,* III,ii,172. (From the play written by Hamlet to trap the king.)

⁶   A poor lone woman. *Henry IV, Part Two,* II,i,32.

⁷ You are the weaker vessel, as they say, the emptier vessel. *Henry IV, Part Two,* II,iv,61. (Mistress Quickly to Doll Tearsheet. The term *weaker vessel* is derived from *I Peter* 2:17, "Giving honor unto his wife as unto the weaker vessel.")

⁸ She-wolf of France. *Henry VI, Part Three,* I,iv,111. (This is Margaret of Anjou, wife of Henry VI, the villainess of this trilogy on the War of the Roses. See also below. Historically, there was another she-wolf of France married to an English king: Isabella, wife of Edward II.)

⁹ O tiger's heart wrapped in a woman's hide! *Henry VI, Part Three,* I,iv,137. (The speaker is the duke of York; the woman is Margaret of Anjou; see also the quote above. The line is important evidence in dating the play, because Robert Greene in *The Groatsworth of Wit,* written in 1592, parodied it in an attack on Shakespeare: "There is an upstart crow, beautified with our feathers . . . with his tiger's heart wrapped in a player's hide." More at SHAKESPEARE.)

¹⁰ Women are soft, mild, pitiful, and flexible. *Henry VI, Part Three,* I,iv,147. (The duke of York on the subject of women. He concludes that Margaret of Anjou [see above] cannot be of this gender, for she is "stern, obdurate, flinty, rough, remorseless," l.42. *Pitiful,* incidentally, means "full of pity.")

¹¹ I am a simple woman. *Henry VIII,* II,iv,106. (Queen Katherine, contending with Cardinal Wolsey. Later she exclaims, "Alas, I am a woman friendless, hopeless!" III,i,80.)

¹ I have a man's mind, but a woman's might.
How hard it is for women to keep counsel! *Julius Caesar,* II,iv,8. (The second line means "How hard it is for a woman to keep a secret." This hardly rings true, considering that Portia is one of the stronger characters in the play. But Shakespeare was working from Plutarch's *Lives,* in which Portia in this scene, overcome by worry as she awaits news of the assassination attempt, collapses as if dead.)

²   Ay me, how weak a thing
The heart of woman is! *Julius Caesar,* II,i,39. (Portia in the same scene as above. This weak-hearted woman later commits suicide by swallowing lighted coals.)

³   A will! A wicked will;
A woman's will; a cankered grandam's will! *King John,* II,i,193. (*Will* as in the legal document, not the psychic faculty.)

⁴   Thou art a fiend,
A woman's shape doth shield thee. *King Lear,* IV,ii,66. (The fiend is Goneril. The speaker is her husband.)

⁵ ·   Her voice was ever soft,
Gentle and low, an excellent thing in woman. *King Lear,* V,iii,274. (Lear speaking of his daughter Cordelia.)

⁶   A child of our grandmother Eve, a female; or, for thy more sweet understanding, a woman. *Love's Labor's Lost,* I,i,259.

⁷ From women's eyes this doctrine I derive:
They are the ground, the books, the academes,
From whence doth spring the true Promethean fire. *Love's Labor's Lost,* IV,iii,301. (Berowne, who may represent Shakespeare himself, finds the study of women more rewarding than the study of books. More below. The second quote below repeats the theme in a more famous passage.)

⁸ For where is any author in the world
Teaches such beauty as a woman's eye? *Love's Labor's Lost,* IV,iii,311.

⁹ From women's eyes this doctrine I derive.
They sparkle still the right Promethean fire;
They are the books, the arts, the academes,
They show, contain, and nourish all the world. *Love's Labor's Lost,* IV,iii,349.

¹⁰ Why, you are nothing then: neither maid, widow, nor wife? *Measure for Measure,* V,i,177. (The duke is questioning Mariana, and is astonished that she denies being a virgin, wife, or widow. As she seems respectable, he can think of no identity for her.)

¹ She has brown hair, and speaks small like a woman? *The Merry Wives of Windsor,* I,i,47. (*Small* means "quietly.")

² He . . . curses all Eve's daughters—of what complexion soever. *The Merry Wives of Windsor,* IV,ii,18.

³ Wives may be merry, and yet honest too. *The Merry Wives of Windsor,* IV,ii,100.

⁴   You are pictures out of door,
Bells in your parlors, wildcats in your kitchens,
Saints in your injuries, devils being offended,
Players in your housewifery, and housewives in your beds. *Othello,* II,i,108. (Iago speaks. *Pictures* are painted, pretty, and silent. *Bells* are ever-sounding. *In your injuries* means "when injuring someone else." *Housewifes in bed* probably means "hard workers in bed.")

⁵ She that was ever fair, and never proud;
Had tongue at will, and yet was never loud. *Othello,* II,i,146. (From a passage in which Iago describes an ideal woman. As for her final fate, see below.)

⁶ To suckle fools and chronicle small beer. *Othello,* II,i,158. (Iago's summary of woman's work. The last phrase refers to keeping account of food supplies. Desdemona replies "O most lame and impotent conclusion," l.159.)

⁷   The world hath not a sweeter creature! She might lie by an emperor's side and command him tasks. *Othello,* IV,i,185. (Othello speaking of Desdemona, shortly before he murders her.)

⁸ Relenting fool, and shallow, changing woman! *Richard III,* IV,iv,431.

⁹ A woman moved is like a fountain troubled,
Muddy, ill-seeming, thick, bereft of beauty. *The Taming of the Shrew,* V,ii,142. (*Moved* means "upset," "angry." A tamed Kate discovers cosmetic advantages in keeping one's temper. See also MARRIAGE and MEN AND WOMEN.)

¹⁰   For several virtues
Have I liked several women. *The Tempest,* III,i,42.

¹¹ She is a woman, therefore may be wooed;
She is a woman, therefore may be won. *Titus Andronicus,* II,i,82. (The most famous of a group of related couplets, including "Gentle thou art, and therefore to be won; / Beauteous thou art, therefore to be assailed," *Sonnet 41,* 5; "She's beautiful and therefore to be wooed; / She is a woman, therefore to be won," *Henry VI, Part One,* V,iii,78; and "Was ever woman

in this humor wooed? / Was ever woman in this humor won? *Richard III,* I,ii,227. The similarity of expression has also been used to link the poem "Willobie His Avisa" with Shakespeare and the mysterious H.W., who may have been the author of the poem. In it, H.W. says to his friend "W.S.": "She is no Saynt, she is no Nonne / I thinke in tyme she may be wonne.")

1   Women are angels, wooing;
Things won are done. *Troilus and Cressida,* I,ii,298. (More at SEX.)

2 Brother, she is not worth what she doth cost
The keeping. *Troilus and Cressida,* II,ii,51. (Hector, speaking of Helen of Troy, tries to puncture Troilus's inflated notions of the importance of romantic love and knightly honor.)

3   She is a pearl
Whose price hath launched above a thousand ships
And turned crowned kings to merchants. *Troilus and Cressida,* II,ii,81. (Troilus speaking of Helen of Troy. Similar to Christopher Marlowe's "Was this the face that launched a thousand ships, / And burnt the topless towers of Ilium?" Marlowe's *Doctor Faustus* dates from about 1588, while *Troilus and Cressida* was written about 1601–1602. Shakespeare, of course, knew Marlowe's work. In *All's Well That Ends Well,* I,iii,71, Shakespeare wrote of Helen, "Was this fair face the cause, quoth she, / Why the Grecians sacked Troy?" In *Troilus and Cressida,* Helen, like Cressida, is a shallow character, hardly worth a quarrel, much less a war.)

4   Women are as roses, whose fair flower,
Being once displayed, doth fall that very hour. *Twelfth Night,* II,iv,38. (The duke to Viola, who is disguised as a boy. She answers: "And so they are; alas, that they are so. / To die, even when they to perfection grow," l.40. More at LOVE AND LOVERS.)

5 I have no other but a woman's reason:
I think him so because I think him so. *The Two Gentlemen of Verona,* I,ii,23. (Lucetta explaining her recommendation of Proteus as lover for her mistress Julia.)

6   Maids, in modesty, say "no" to that
Which they would have the profferer construe "ay." *The Two Gentlemen of Verona,* I,ii,55.

See also BEAUTY; CLEOPATRA; LOVE AND LOVERS; MARRIAGE; MEN AND WOMEN; ROMEO AND JULIET; SEX.

WONDERS

[1] That would be ten days' wonder at the least. *Henry VI, Part Three,* III,ii,113.

WORDS

[2] I love not many words. *All's Well That Ends Well,* III,vi,86.

[3]　　These are but wild and whirling words. *Hamlet,* I,v,133.

[4] A rhapsody of words! *Hamlet,* III,iv,49. (*Rhapsody* is used in the negative sense of a meaningless flow.)

[5] Words are no deeds. *Henry VIII,* III,ii,154. (More at TALK.)

[6] Zounds! I was never so bethumped with words. *King John,* II,i,466.

[7] They have lived long on the alms-basket of words. *Love's Labor's Lost,* V,i,41. (More at TALK, PLAIN AND FANCY.)

[8] The words of Mercury are harsh after the songs of Apollo. *Love's Labor's Lost,* V,ii,931. (Translation: Clever words are unwelcome after fine music. The conclusion of the play.)

[9]　　His words are a very fantastical banquet. *Much Ado About Nothing,* II,iii,20. (More at TALK, PLAIN AND FANCY.)

[10] How long a time lies in one little word. *Richard II,* I,iii,212. (The word is the king's reduction of Henry Bolingbroke's banishment from ten years to six.)

[11] These words are razors to my wounded heart. *Titus Andronicus,* I,i,315.

[12] Words pay no debts. *Troilus and Cressida,* III,ii,56.

[13] Words, words, mere words, no matter from the heart. *Troilus and Cressida,* V,iii,108.

[14] They that dally nicely with words may quickly make them wanton. *Twelfth Night,* III,i,14.

See also EDUCATION; NAMES; READING *(Hamlet);* TALK; TALK, PLAIN AND FANCY.

WORK

[15] To business that we love we rise betime
And go to it with delight. *Antony and Cleopatra,* IV,iv,20. (See also the quote from *Macbeth* below.)

¹ Thou art not for the fashion of these times,
Where none will sweat but for promotion,
And having that, do choke their service up. *As You Like It,* II,iii,59.
(Orlando praising his faithful, aged servant Adam by contrasting him to
the majority of workers, interested only in promotion.)

² I am a true laborer; I earn that I eat, get that I wear, owe no man hate,
envy no man's happiness, glad of other men's good, content with my harm.
As You Like It, III,ii,73. (By *content with my harm* Corin the shepherd
means that he is not unhappy with the burdens of his life.)

³ Shipwrights, whose sore task
Does not divide the Sunday from the week. *Hamlet,* I,i,75. (From a
passage in which a soldier, Marcellus, comments on what appear to be
hurried preparations for war. The work goes on not only all week, but all
night as well: "This sweaty haste / Doth make the night joint-laborer with
the day," l.77.)

⁴ Some must watch, while some must sleep. *Hamlet,* III,ii,279.

⁵ There is no ancient gentlemen but gardeners, ditchers, and gravemakers.
They hold up Adam's profession. *Hamlet,* V,i,30. (*Hold up* means "uphold." A common thought with revolutionary overtones. Thus the anonymous verse "When Adam delved and Eve span / Who was then a
gentleman?" was quoted by John Ball to rally the men at Blackheath in
1381 during Wat Tyler's Peasant Rebellion. See also GARDENS, *Henry VI,
Part Two.*)

⁶ And follows so the ever-running year
With profitable labor to his grave. *Henry V,* IV,i,281. (The king speaking
of the peasant who works from dawn to nightfall and then sleeps to dawn
and begins again, "Winding up days with toil and nights with sleep," l.284.
Winding up is the equivalent of "passing" or "spending.")

⁷ A surgeon to old shoes. *Julius Caesar,* I,i,26. (A cobbler describes himself.)

⁸ That which ordinary men are fit for, I am qualified in, and the best of me
is diligence. *King Lear,* I,iv,35. (The earl of Kent in disguise, applying with
characteristic modesty for service with King Lear.)

⁹ Why, all delights are vain, but that most vain
Which, with pain purchased, doth inherit pain. *Love's Labor's Lost,* I,i,72.
(The reference is to study, which is painful to do and results in weak eyes
and headaches. But the line is applicable to any hard or tedious work that
impairs well-being. On the damage to eyesight, l.77 reads, "Light seeking
light doth light of light beguile," which means "Eyes seeking knowledge
cause weakened sight.")

¹ The labor we delight in physics pain. *Macbeth,* II,iii,52. (Meaning: The work we love cures pain. See also the quote from *Antony and Cleopatra* above.)

²   My nature is subdued
To what it works in, like the dyer's hand. *Sonnet 111,* 6.

WORLD

³   There's place and means for every man alive. *All's Well That Ends Well,* IV,iii,354. (Exposed as a shameless, cowardly braggart—see BRAGGING—Parolles cheers himself up with this observation.)

⁴   The golden world. *As You Like It,* I,i,115. (More at LEISURE.)

⁵ O, how full of briers is this working-day world! *As You Like It,* I,iii,11.

⁶ "Thus we may see," quoth he, "how the world wags." *As You Like It,* II,vii,23. (More at TIME.)

⁷ Thou seest we are not all alone unhappy:
The wide and universal theater
Presents more woeful pageants than the scene
Wherein we play in. *As You Like It,* II,vii,136. (The "universal theater" becomes in *King Lear* a "stage of fools." See below.)

⁸   All the world's a stage,
And all the men and women merely players. *As You Like It,* II,vii,139. (More at LIFE.)

⁹ How weary, stale, flat, and unprofitable
Seem to me all the uses of this world! *Hamlet,* I,ii,133. (More at DEPRESSION and below.)

¹⁰   'Tis an unweeded garden
That grows to seed.
Things rank and gross in nature
Possess it merely. *Hamlet,* I,ii,135. (Hamlet on the ugliness of the world. *Merely* means "entirely.")

¹¹ Vain pomp and glory of this world, I hate ye. *Henry VIII,* III,ii,365. (From Cardinal Wolsey's farewell to greatness; see GREATNESS.)

¹² Mad world! Mad kings! Mad composition! *King John,* II,i,561. (*Composition* means "compromise," in this case, the marriage of Blanch of Spain, niece of King John of England, to the dauphin of France. The speaker is Richard Plantagenet, a character invented by Shakespeare. He continues with a disillusioned recognition of the role of self-interest in human affairs; see SELF-INTEREST.)

¹ The thorns and dangers of this world. *King John,* IV,iii,141.

² When we are born, we cry that we are come
To this great stage of fools. *King Lear,* IV,vi,184. (A dark version of the view in *As You Like It* that "all the world's a stage." See LIFE.)

³ I hold the world but as the world . . .
A stage, where every man must play a part,
And mine a sad one. *The Merchant of Venice,* I,i,77. (For the "all the world's a stage" speech from *As You Like It,* see LIFE.)

⁴ O wicked, wicked world. *The Merry Wives of Windsor,* II,i,20.

⁵ Why, then the world's mine oyster,
Which I with sword will open. *The Merry Wives of Windsor,* II,ii,2.

⁶ All places that the eye of heaven visits
Are to a wise man ports and happy havens. *Richard II,* I,iii,274. (John of Gaunt advising his son Bolingbroke to take advantage of banishment to learn more about the world. He adds, "There is no virtue like necessity," l.277.)

⁷ O brave new world. *The Tempest,* V,i,183. (More at HUMAN NATURE AND HUMANKIND.)

⁸ The world is but a word;
Were it all yours to give it in a breath,
How quickly were it gone! *Timon of Athens,* II,ii,162. (The good servant Flavius to Timon, who has wasted and given away vast property.)

⁹ I am sick of this false world. *Timon of Athens,* IV,iii,380.

¹⁰ This world's a city full of straying streets,
And death's the market place where each one meets. *The Two Noble Kinsmen,* I,v,15. (Lines possibly by Shakespeare, possibly by John Fletcher.)

See also LIFE.

WORRY.   See ANXIETY AND WORRY.

WRITING

¹¹ I once did hold it, as our statists do,
A baseness to write fair, and labored much
How to forget that learning, but, sir, now
It did me yeoman's service. *Hamlet,* V,ii,33. (Hamlet to Horatio. *Statist* means "statesman." *Fair* means "well" or "clearly." What Hamlet wrote

was a document ordering the bearers' death. This he substituted for the document that Rosencrantz and Guildenstern were bearing from the king, ordering Hamlet beheaded.)

[1] Devise, wit; write, pen; for I am for whole volumes in folio. *Love's Labor's Lost,* I,ii,182.

[2] The quirks of blazoning pens. *Othello,* II,i,63. (More at VIRTUE.)

[3] Let there be gall enough in thy ink. *Twelfth Night,* III,ii,50.

See also MEDIA AND MESSAGES; POETRY; READING; STORIES.

YORICK. See MORTALITY.

YOUNG IN SPIRIT, THE

[1] You that are old consider not the capacities of us that are young. *Henry IV, Part Two,* I,ii,180. (White-haired Falstaff to the Chief Justice. Falstaff includes himself among the older young people: "We that are in the vaward [vanguard] of our youth," l.182. The Chief Justice is outraged: "Have you not a moist eye, a dry hand, a yellow cheek, a white beard, a decreasing leg, an increasing belly? Is not your voice broken, your wind short, your chin double, your wit single, and every part about you blasted with antiquity?" l.187. See also OLD AGE.)

YOUTH

[2] Natural rebellion done in the blade of youth,
When oil and fire, too strong for reason's force,
O'erbears it and burns on. *All's Well That Ends Well,* V,iii,6. (*Blade* as in blade of grass. Some editions attempt to improve on Shakespeare by rendering this as *blaze.*)

[3]   My salad days,
When I was green in judgment. *Antony and Cleopatra,* I,v,73.

[4]   He wears the rose
Of youth upon him. *Antony and Cleopatra,* III,xiii,20.

¹ He had rather see the swords and hear a drum than look upon his schoolmaster. *Coriolanus,* I,iii,58.

²   In the morn and liquid dew of youth
Contagious blastments are most imminent. *Hamlet,* I,iii,41. (Shakespeare is likening the innocence of youth to the tenderness of a young plant, vulnerable to contagious blights. More at VIRTUE.)

³ Youth to itself rebels, though none else near. *Hamlet,* I,iii,44. (The concluding line from the passage quoted above. Laertes is remarking that youth is bent on rebellion—to its own peril.)

⁴   You speak like a green girl,
Unsifted in such perilous circumstance. *Hamlet,* I,iii,101. (Polonius to his daughter, Ophelia. *Unsifted* means "untried.")

⁵   It is common for the younger sort
To lack discretion. *Hamlet,* II,i,116.

⁶ A very riband [ribbon] in the cap of youth. *Hamlet,* IV,vii,77.

⁷   Youth, the more it is wasted, the sooner it wears. *Henry IV, Part One,* II,iv,401.

⁸ As full of spirit as the month of May. *Henry IV, Part One,* IV,i,100. (More at SOLDIERS. See also below for another May figure of speech.)

⁹   In the very May-morn of his youth. *Henry V,* I,ii,120.

¹⁰ How green you are and fresh in this old world! *King John,* III,iii,145.

¹¹ *Lear.* So young, and so untender?
Cordelia. So young, my lord, and true. *King Lear,* I,i,108. (Lear is disappointed that Cordelia does not avow more love for him. She replies that she is honest. To his grief, he fails to realize her implication that her sisters are not so.)

¹² Young blood doth not obey an old decree. *Love's Labor's Lost,* IV,iii,216.

¹³   An unlessoned girl, unschooled, unpracticed;
Happy in this, she is not yet so old
But she may learn. *The Merchant of Venice,* III,ii,159.

¹⁴ Young in limbs, in judgment old. *The Merchant of Venice,* II,vii,71. (Also, "I never knew so young a body with so old a head," IV,i,162; and see below.)

¹⁵ How much more elder art thou than thy looks! *The Merchant of Venice,* IV,i,250. (This and the two quotes above are references to Portia, disguised as a male lawyer.)

[1] He capers, he dances, he has eyes of youth, he writes verses, he speaks holiday, he smells April and May. *The Merry Wives of Windsor,* III,ii,62. (*He speaks holiday* etc. translates "He speaks happily, he smells of spring.")

[2] So wise so young, they say do ne'er live long. *Richard III,* III,i,79. (The wise youth is Prince Edward. The speaker is his uncle Richard, who will make certain that the prediction is fulfilled.)

[3] Some say thy fault is youth, some wantonness,
Some say thy grace is youth, and gentle sport. *Sonnet 96,* 1.

[4] Young men, whom Aristotle thought
Unfit to hear moral philosophy. *Troilus and Cressida,* II,ii,166. (Hector refers to a passage in Aristotle's *Nicomachean Ethics,* I,3. The philosopher actually spoke of "political" philosophy, but the translation was often rendered as Shakespeare has it, for the subject was political ethics. Aristotle thought that a young man's inexperience and passions would render him unlikely to benefit from lectures in this subject. Even more unlikely is that Hector, who lived in the thirteenth century B.C., would have had anything to say about Aristotle, born nine centuries later.)

[5] Not yet old enough for a man nor young enough for a boy; as a squash is before 'tis a peascod, or a codling when 'tis almost an apple. *Twelfth Night,* I,v,155. (A *squash* would be an immature pea pod, or peascod. A *codling* is an immature apple.)

[6] Then come kiss me, sweet, and twenty,
Youth's a stuff will not endure. *Twelfth Night,* II,iii,52 (More at LOVE AND LOVERS.)

[7] When that I was and a little tiny boy,
With hey, ho, the wind and the rain,
A foolish thing was but a toy,
For the rain it raineth every day. *Twelfth Night,* V,i,391.

[8] Two lads that thought there was no more behind
But such a day tomorrow as today,
And to be boy eternal. *The Winter's Tale,* I,ii,63. (*Behind* means "to come." See also INNOCENCE.)

[9] I would there were no age between ten and three-and-twenty, or that youth would sleep out the rest; for there is nothing in the between but getting wenches with child, wronging the ancientry, stealing, fighting. *The Winter's Tale,* III,iii,58.

See also CHILDREN; FUN AND FUN PEOPLE; GENERATIONS; INNOCENCE; MATURITY; YOUNG IN SPIRIT, THE.

Index

boy: my heart, sweet b., shall be thy
sepulcher 52:5
the b. was the very staff of my age 25:6
this wimpled, whining, purblind, wayward
b. 150:3
to be b. eternal 326:8
when that I was and a little tiny b. 326:7
boys: as flies to wanton b., are we to the
gods 145:5
braggart: every b. will be found an ass 20:1
brave: O b. new world 121:1
brain: b. . . . the soul's frail dwelling house
20:3
brains: cudgel thy b. no more 284:7
breach: once more unto the b. 303:5
breath: what fine chisel could ever yet cut b.
187:2
breed: this happy b. of men 70:10
brevity: b. is the soul of wit 274:1
briers: how full of b. is this . . . world 2:4
bright: so quick b. things come to confusion
151:7
bringer: the first b. of unwelcome news
188:8
Britain: B.'s a world by itself 69:9
brothels: keep thy foot out of b. 313:3
brother: into the world like b. and b. 73:6
brothers: we happy few, we band of b. 305:1
Brutè: et tu, B.? 18:7
Brutus: B. is an honorable man 118:7
poor B. 6:7
Buckingham: B., the mirror of all courtesy
165:4
budge: I'll not b. an inch 233:7
buds: the darling b. of May 181:8
build: when we mean to b. 209:3
bull: the savage b. doth bear the yoke 167:11
burglary: flat b. 38:6
buried: whose to be b. in it? 46:2
burr: I am a kind of b. 207:7
business: every man hath b. 21:2
great b. must be wrought ere noon 21:4
my b. was great 21:6
to b. that we love we rise betime 63:1
butchers: be sacrificers, but not b. 37:1
buttonhole: let me take you a b. lower 129:2
buy: dispraise the thing that you desire to b.
21:7
by: "b. and b." is easily said 221:7

cabin: make me a willow c. at your gate
159:6
Caesar: C. hath wept 135:6
C. must bleed for it 135:2
great C. fell 135:7

how many times shall C. bleed in sport?
281:3
imperious C., dead and turned to clay
181:4
not that I loved C. less 204:15
O Julius C., thou art mighty yet 135:8
O mighty C.! Dost thou lie so low? 135:3
the . . . ides have come—ay, C., but not
gone 42:3 (note)
upon what meat doth this our C. feed
135:1
cakes: no more c. and ale? 300:7
calamity: thou art wedded to c. 289:13
calfskin: hang a c. on those recreant limbs
128:9
Caliban: C. has a new master 96:8
calumny: thou shalt not escape c. 231:9
Cambyses: in King C.'s vein 275:8
camp: from c. to c. 304:2
candied: let the c. tongue lick absurd pomp
90:7
candies: the devil c. all sins o'er 121:7 (note)
candle: how far that little c. throws his
beams! 299:7
out, out brief c! 145:7
candleholder: I'll be a c. 264:6
candles: those blessed c. of the night 267:2
candy: a c. deal of courtesy 90:9
cannibals: the C. that each other eat 268:6
(note)
caper: I can cut a c. 41:1
capers: he c., he dances 326:1
he c. nimbly in a lady's chamber 307:8
caps: they threw their c. 110:6
captain: the royal c. of this ruined band
112:8
captains: call to me all my sad c. 98:1
care: c. is no cure 10:2
c. keeps its watch in every old man's eye
198:1
c. killed a cat 10:6
golden c. 10:1
so wan with c. 9:10
tender loving care 137:4
the raveled sleave of c. 256:10
the windy side of c. 10:5
where c. lodges 198:1
cares: his c. are now all ended 46:12
carry-tale: some c., some please-man 129:1
Casca: you are dull, C. 128:4
Cassius: C. has a lean and hungry look 43:2
forever, and forever, farewell, C. 85:7
cast: I have set my life upon a c. 236:2
to set the . . . wealth of all our states all at
one? c. 235:10

death (*cont.*)

hold d. awhile at the arm's end 44:9

I fain would die a dry d. 253:6

lightning before death 51:1 (note)

make d. proud to take us 44:7

nothing can we call our own, but d. 50:7

O proud D. 46:6

seeking d., find life 49:5

so bad a d. 47:5

so many years of fearing d. 48:1

the dread of something after d. 270:5

the sense of d. is most in apprehension 49:6

the stroke of d. is as a lover's pinch 44:8

the sure physician, D. 45:6

the worst is d., and d. will have his day 50:5

they have said their prayers, and they stay for d. 304:4

they'll give him d. by inches 224:8

this fell sergeant, D. 46:4

thou owest God a d. 46:9

'tis strange that d. should sing! 48:5

to rush into the secret house of d. 270:3

what we fear of d. 146:2

where d.'s approach is seen so terrible 47:5 (note)

when men are at the point of d. have they been merry! 51:1

deaths: cowards die many times before their d. 47:10

deceased: the young gentleman . . . is indeed d. 50:1

deceit: O that d. should dwell in such a . . . palace, 144:1

deed: a d. of dreadful note 37:7

a d. whereat valor will weep 296:5

a d. without a name 75:6

if one good d. in all my life I did 76:1

yet but young in d. 78:3

deeds: foul d. will rise 35:6

unnatural d. do breed unnatural troubles 75:8

defect: men carrying . . . the stamp of one d. 79:2

defense: in cases of d. . . . weigh the enemy more mighty 55:1

defenses: d., musters, preparations should be maintained 54:13

deformed: he is d., crooked, old and sere 127:3

degree: the heavens themselves . . . observe d. 200:5

oh, when d. is shaked 201:1

take but d. away, untune that string 201:2

delay: make no d. 2:1

delays: d. have dangerous ends 55:2

delights: all d. are vain 320:9

Denmark: something is rotten in the state of D. 74:4

desert: use every man after his d. 165:1

desire: d. my pilot is 57:3

desires: black and deep d. 6:5

desolation: a careless d. 55:7

despair: I shall d. 57:5

my ending is d. 57:7

desperate: diseases d. grown 170:4

devil: a d., a born d. 44:4

d. hath power to assume a pleasing shape 12:5

eye of childhood fears a painted d. 49:2

give the d. his due 313:1 (note)

he's a very d. 44:5

he will give the d. his due 221:9

must have a long spoon [to] eat with the d. 41:6

seem a saint when most I play the d. 122:2

the d. candies all sins o'er 121:7 (note)

the d. can cite Scripture 121:8

we do sugar o'er the d. himself 121:7

write "good angel" on the d.'s horn 223:8

devils: from all such d., . . . deliver us! 219:9

Diana: let us be D.'s foresters 310:2

dice: Hercules and Lichas play at d. 23:2

did: thou canst not say I d. it 107:3

die: a man can d. but once 46:11

all that lives must d. 45:7

d. two months ago, and not forgotten yet? 52:2

d. we must 47:7

few d. well that d. in a battle 304:3

if I must d. 49:7

live 1000 years, I shall not find myself so apt to d. 48:2

that I shall d. is true, but for thy love . . . no 260:4 (note)

to d. and go we know not where 49:8

to d., even when they to perfection grow 318:4 (note)

to d., to sleep 270:5

what blessings I have . . . that I should fear to d.? 51:7

died: had I but d. an hour before this chance 237:10

men have d. . . . but not for love 148:9

dies: he d. and makes no sign 47:4

he that d. pays all debts 51:1

digestion: now good d. wait on appetite 92:4

things sweet to taste prove in d. sour 92:13

digestions: unquiet meals make ill d. 111:5

the apprehension of the g. 72:2
the g. is oft interred with their bones 298:10
the hand that hath made you fair hath
made you g. 299:4
there lives not three g. men unhanged in
England 298:2
this g. man 298:9
goodness: g. in things evil 3:1
undone by g. 138:3
governed: woe to that land that's g. by a
child! 103:2
grace: g. me no g. 277:9
O, mickle is the powerful g. that lies in
plants 186:3
O momentary g. of mortal men 103:7
what a g. was seated on this brow 103:4
grave: a g. unto a soul 254:4
a little, little g., an obscure g. 115:5
almost no g. allowed me 237:4
renowned be thy g. 45:4
the g. doth gape for thee thrice wider 87:12
gravemaking: 'a sings in g. 46:1
graves: let's talk of g., of worms, and
epitaphs 50:6
gravity: what doth g. out of his bed at
midnight? 196:7
Graymalkin: I come, G. 8:3
great: a g. man's memory may outlive his life
half a year 52:2
being so g., I have no need to beg 295:10
build their evils on the graves of g. men
140:7 (note)
for he was g. of heart 191:9
O, that I were as g. as is my grief 238:5
pacts and sects of g. ones 105:4
some are born g., some achieve greatness
105:6
spare me the g. ones 104:4
what g. ones do, the less will prattle of
189:9
greater: small to g. matters must give way
294:1
greatest: g. scandal waits on g. state 115:1
he that of g. works is finisher 258:1
greatness: a long farewell to all my greatness
104:7
be not afraid of g. Some are born great
105:6
g. knows itself 104:3
g. that will overwhelm thee 5:6
I have touched the highest point of all my
g. 104:6
the abuse of g. 217:8
Greek: it was G. to me 276:2
green: how g. you are 325:10
you speak like a g. girl 325:4

green-eyed: jealousy It is the g. monster
132:4
greenwood: under the g. tree 33:3
grief: a plague of sighing and g. 262:4
as full of g. as age 197:5
each substance of a g. 263:5
g. makes one hour ten 263:2
I was a journeyman to g. 16:4
my g. lies onward 3:12
no pity . . . that sees into the bottom of
my g.? 263:9
O, that I were as great as is my g. 238:5
perked up in a glistering g. 109:5
the g. that does not speak 262:9
'tis unmanly g. 51:10
griefs: my g., I am still King of those 263:6
some g. are medicinable 261:11
what private g. they have 262:6
grows: everything that g. holds in perfection
but a little moment 181:7
grudge: the ancient g. I bear him 234:8
guests: unbidden g. 106:1
guilt: so full of artless jealousy is g. 106:5
guilty: it started, like a g. thing 106:2
suspicion always haunts the g. mind 107:1

habit: use doth breed a h. 108:3
habitation: a local h. and a name 124:6
hags: you secret, black and midnight h.! 75:6
hair: scanted men in h. 16:2
hairs: how ill white h. becomes a fool 196:10
halcyon: h.'s days 205:10
half: he is the h. part of a blessed man 167:7
hand: O, that I were a glove upon that h.
158:8
will all [the] ocean wash this blood clean
from my h.? 107:2
woe to the h. that shed this costly blood!
296:12
hands: now join your h. 5:1
speak h. for me! 296:11
your gentle h. lend us 279:1 (note)
hang: h., beg, starve, die in the streets 25:11
let them h. 224:7
let them h. themselves in their own straps
230:1
that would h. us, every mother's son 107:7
hanging: h. and wiving goes by destiny 167:8
many a good h. prevents a bad marriage
169:3
happiness: one mutual h. 169:5
to look into h. with other men's eyes! 109:3
happy: h. in that we are not overhappy 171:3
h. man be his dole 109:7
this h. breed of men 70:10
hard: these h. hearts 239:8

mad: I'll curb her m. and headstrong humor 164:7 (note)
  m. as a March hare 164:5
  m. world! m. kings! 321:12
  so, it will make us m. 163:9
  that he's m., 'tis true 162:3
madman: sharp weapons in a madman's hands 217:4
madmen: lovers and m. have such seething brains 124:6
madness: great wits are sure to m. near allied 163:2 (note)
  his m. is poor Hamlet's enemy 163:4
  m. in great ones must not unwatched go 163:3
  m., yet there is method in it 34:7
  O m. of discourse 275:2
  O, that way m. lies 163:6
  this is very midsummer m. 272:2
magic: this rough m. I here abjure 195:3
maid: a m. that paragons description 299:10
maiden: a m. never bold 126:6
  be something scanter of your m. presence 173:4
  in m. meditation 126:5
maids: m. are May when they are m. 166:5
  m., in modesty, say "no" 318:6
majesty: magic in thy m. 165:10
  when m. falls to folly 214:9 (note)
makes: it m. us, or it mars us 1:3
malady: the greater m. 3:6
malcontents: the Mars of m. 30:5
malice: deep m. makes too deep incision 111:1
man: a good m. . . . he is sufficient 80:5
  ah, where's my m.? 172:11 (note)
  a little worse than a m. 129:6
  a m. of sovereign parts he is esteemed 299:1
  a m. more sinned against than sinning 126:4
  a m.'s life is a tedious one 172:6
  a m. whose blood is very snow-broth 67:7
  a m. whose blood is warm within 98:4
  an honest exceeding poor m. 216:7
  a poor old m. 197:5
  a slight unmeritable m. 128:5
  a very foolish, fond old m. 197:7
  away, slight m.! 128:7
  care keeps its watch in every old m.'s eye 198:1
  every m. shall eat in safety under his own vine 206:2
  he was a m., take him all in all 172:7
  I could have better spared a better m. 83:2

if it be m.'s work, I'll do it 172:8
I know thee not, old m. 83:3
I must also feel it as a m. 67:6
is m. no more than this? 120:3
let him pass for a m. 80:4
m. delights not me 56:2
m. is a giddy thing 120:9
m., more divine, the master of all these 172:5
m., proud m. . . . plays such fantastic tricks 120:6
O, what may m. within him hide 120:7
such a m. as this I dreamt of 172:2
such a m., so faint, so spiritless 128:1
the inward m. 13:5
the state of a man, like to a little kingdom 36:8
the state of m. in divers functions 200:4
this good m. 298:9
this bold bad m. 75:1
this is the state of man 104:7
this m. is now become a god 105:1
this was a m.! 298:11
to give the world assurance of a m. 103:5
unaccommodated m. 120:4
weak, and despised old m. 197:6
were m. but constant 173:1
what a piece of work is a m. 119:10
what a pretty thing m. is 172:10
what is a m. 120:2
you a m.! You lack a m.'s heart 172:4
mankind: how beauteous m. is 121:1
manner: to the m. born 108:1
mannish: m. cowards 172:3
many: the mutable, rank-scented m. 223:4
March: mad as a m. hare 164:5
  the ides of M. 42:3
marigold: the m. that goes to bed with the sun 211:6
marriage: good hanging prevents a bad m. 169:3
  hasty m. 167:2
  honor, riches, m. blessing 169:1
  let me not to the m. of true minds admit impediments 154:5
  m. vows as false as dicers' oaths 221:8
  O curse of m. 132:6
  there were no fear in marriage 166:2
married: a young man m. 166:3
  Benedick the m. man 167:10 (note)
  we will be m. a Sunday 159:4
  whose weakness m. to thy stronger state 166:6
marry: I do m. that I may repent 166:1
Mary-buds: winking M. begin to ope their golden eyes 209:4

mask: the m. of night is on my face 191:3
masons: singing m. building roofs of gold 8:1
masque: what m.? what music? 282:1
masters: we cannot all be m. 142:6
matter: more m., with less art 313:6 (note)
May: as full of spirit as the month of M. 259:7
in the very M.-morn of his youth 325:9
more matter for a M. morning 266:4
the darling buds of M. 181:8
meaning: with best m. have incurred the
worst 3:8
means: the sight of m. to do ill deeds 278:2
measure: M. still for M. 136:7
medicine: a m. that's able to breathe life into
a stone 170:2
medicines: m. to make me love him 170:5
meditation: in maiden m. 126:5
melancholy: a m. of mine own 55:8
I am as m. as a gib-cat 262:3
I can suck m. out of a song 182:2
memory: a great man's m. may outlive his
life half a year 104:2
a noble m. 72:7
from the table of my m. I'll wipe away all
. . . records 171:6
I'll note you in my book of m. 171:8
m., the warder of the brain 171:9
the m. be green 171:4
these are begot in the ventricle of m.
176:5
'tis in my m. locked 171:5
men: are you good m. and true? 299:9
give me the spare m. 104:4
in the catalogue ye go for m. 129:3
I wonder m. dare trust themselves with m.
121:2
m. are April when they woo 166:5
m. are as the time is 120:5
m. are flesh and blood 10:3
m. are m.; the best sometimes forget 79:8
m. must endure their going hence 48:8
m. should be what they seem 117:6
m.'s vows are women's traitors! 173:3
m. were deceivers ever 172:9
not three good m. unhanged in England
298:2
no trust, no faith, no honesty in m. 172:11
O, you are m. of stones 52:6
this happy breed of m. 70:10
you are not wood, . . . not stones, but m.
67:4
mercy: m. but murders 175:2
how shalt thou hope for m.? 174:4
no more m. in him . . . than milk in a
male tiger 239:5

nothing emboldens sin so much as m.
175:3
sweet m. is nobility's true badge 175:4
the quality of m. is not strained 174:5
we do pray for m. 175:1
with half so good a grace as m. does 174:3
merit: the force of his own m. makes his way
269:2
mermaid: heard a m., on a dolphin's back 183:6
merrier: a m. man . . . I never spent an
hour's talk 98:3
merry: a m. heart goes all the day 110:4
as m. as the day is long 109:8
I am not m. 109:11
if to be old and m. be a sin 82:7
rather . . . a fool to make me m. than
experience to make me sad 78:2
that m. wanderer of the night 81:1
messenger: winged m. of heaven 7:1
mickle: O, m. is the powerful grace that lies
in plants 186:3
midnight: let's mock the m. bell 98:1
we have heard the chimes at m. 310:3
midsummer: this is very m. madness 164:4
mightiness: how soon this m. meets misery
104:5
military: will maintain his argument as well as
any m. man 259:9
milk: pour the sweet m. of concord into hell
305:10
the m. of human kindness 137:5
mince: m. not the general tongue 275:4
thy honesty and love doth m. this matter
189:7
mind: all things are ready, if our m. be so
176:3
a m. content 109:4 (note)
a mote . . . to trouble the m.'s eye 198:5
canst thou not minister to a m. diseased
170:9
farewell the tranquil m. 57:4
I am not in my perfect mind 197:7
in my m.'s eye 176:2
in nature there's no blemish but the m.
300:8
m. is tossing on the ocean 10:4
my m. is troubled 10:10
O what a noble m. is here o'erthrown! 108:4
the tempest in my m. 176:4
'tis the m. that makes the body rich 300:3
minds: the marriage of true m. 154:5
mine: what's m. is yours 158:1
minutes: so do our m. hasten to their end
287:2
so m., hours, days, months, and years 286:6

that struts and frets his hour upon the s. 145:7

the world . . . a s. where every man must play a part 322:3

this great s. of fools 322:2

stand: I must s. the course 267:7

s. fast 207:5

star: a star danced, and under that was I born 109:10

I am constant as the Northern S. 266:6

that give a name to every fixed s. 64:7

the moist s. 179:2

Star-chamber: a s. matter 141:6

stars: cut him out in little s. 158:10

the fault, dear Brutus, is not in our s. 233:10

the s. above us govern our conditions 267:1

two s. . . . in one sphere 30:3

starveling: you s., you eel-skin 127:1

state: an old man broken with the storms of s. 101:4

steal: "s."? Foh, a fico for the phrase! 277:2

will s. . . . an egg out of a cloister 59:2

stomach: a man of an unbounded s. 47:9 (note)

stone: the s. shall cry out of the wall 38:4 (note)

stones: s. have been known to move and trees to speak 37:8

the very s. prate of my whereabout 37:4

you blocks, you s. 128:3

stories: tell sad s. of the death of kings 115:4

to tell sad s. of my own mishaps 196:5

storms: untimely s. 309:3

story: tell my s. 188:6

my s. being done 268:7

the s. of my life 268:5

strange: s. bedfellows 3:14

strangers: desire we may be better s. 127:2

strawberry: s. grows underneath the nettle 2:8

streets: I have walked about the s. 27:3

strength: to have a giant's s. 217:10

strongest: they . . . that know the s. and surest way to get 269:6

strumpet: the s.'s plague 248:2

transformed into a s.'s fool 245:5

strutting: like a s. player 283:5

study: I am slow of s. 79:7

s. is like the heaven's glorious sun 64:7

s. what you most affect 65:6

stuff: we are such s. as dreams are made on 146:4

stumble: they s. that run fast 264:13

style: so quiet and so sweet a s. 103:3

suck: I have given s. 240:1

suckle: to s. fools and chronicle small beer 317:6

sudden: he's s. if a thing comes in his head 125:2

suggestion: they'll take s. as a cat laps milk 107:11

why do I yield to that s. 278:3

suit: s. the action to the word 280:1

sulphurous: the s. pit 247:2

summer: shall I compare thee to a s.'s day? 181:8

s.'s flower is to the summer sweet 272:1

s.'s lease hath all too short a date 181:8

Saint Martin's s., halycon's days 205:10

thy eternal summer shall not fade 181:8 (note)

sun: arise, fair s., and kill the envious moon 236:4

be it s. or moon or what you please 14:1

herein will I imitate the s. 112:4

men shut their doors against a setting s. 54:11

s. . . . looks on alike 73:7

the s. that warms you here shall shine on me 244:9

superfluous: in the poorest thing s. 160:9

supper: that nourishment which is called s. 92:3

surgeon: a s. to old shoes 320:7

with the help of a s. 59:6

suspicion: s. always haunts the guilty mind 107:1

swan: I am the cygnet to this pale faint s. 48:5

sweet S. of Avon! 250:8

swanlike: a s. end, fading in music 183:1

swear: do not s. at all 222:3

O, s. not by the moon 251:4

when a gentleman is disposed to s. 275:6

swearest: if thou s., thou mayst prove false 222:1

swears: when my love s. that she is made of truth 154:7

sweat: where none will s. but for promotion 320:1

sweet: good night, sweet Prince 109:1

parting is such s. sorrow 85:9

s., s., s. poison 91:4

sweets to the s.! 210:3

s. Swan of Avon! 250:8

things s. to taste prove in digestion sour 92:12

thy bridal bed to have decked, s. maid 85:3 (note)

two w. placed together 165:3
w. are as roses 155:8
w. are angels, wooing 318:1
w. are made to bear 130:1
w. are soft, mild, pitiful 315:10
w. fear too much 315:5
w. may fall 173:8
w.'s weapons, water drops 309:10

won: I think in time she may be won
    [wonne] 317:11 (note)
things w. are done 249:3

wonder: ten days' w. at the least 319:1

wonderful: O w., w., and most w. 110:5

woodbine: so doth the w. . . . gently entwist
    210:6

woods: what I know of the divine science
    . . . I learnt in w. 185:4 (note)
w. more free from peril than the . . .
    court 33:1

wooed: who w. in haste 168:6
was ever woman in this humor w.? 248:8

word: but a choleric w. 261:3
every w. stabs 277:5
how every fool can play upon the w.!
    314:1
ill deeds is doubled with an evil w. 273:3
how long a time lies in one little w. 319:10
suit the action to the w., the w. to the
    action 280:1
the most immodest w. 63:7
the w. is overworn 277:13
the w. is well culled 276:9 (note)

words: a few of the unpleasantest w. 189:6
a man of fire-new w. 276:6
a rhapsody of w.! 319:4
give thy worst of thoughts the worst of w.
    277:8
his w. are a very fantastical banquet 319:9
his w. are bonds 222:5
I love not many w. 319:2
I was never so bethumped with w. 319:6
men of few w. are the best men 274:3
my w. fly up, my thoughts remain below
    218:6
the alms-basket of w. 319:7
these are but wild and whirling w. 319:3
these w. are razors 319:11
the w. of Mercury are harsh 182:8
they that dally nicely with w. 319:14
w. are no deeds 274:8
w. pay no debts 319:12
w., w., mere w. 319:13

work: a damned and a bloody w. 297:2
the w. we have in hand, most bloody 36:6
what w. is here! 191:5 (note)

works: he that of greatest w. is finisher 258:1

world: aweary of this great w. 71:3
all the w.'s a stage 144:6
darkling stand the varying shore [*or* star]
    of the w.! 57:8
I am fled from this vile w. 52:9
I am sick of this false w. 322:9
I hold the w. but as the w. . . . a stage 322:3
lord of the whole w.? 5:3 (note)
mad w.! mad kings 321:12
O brave new w. 322:7
one touch of nature makes the whole w.
    kin 121:3
the excellent foppery of the w. 76:10
the golden w. 321:4
the rack of this tough w. 48:9
there is a w. elsewhere 68:5
there's nothing in this w. can make me joy
    145:4 (note)
the thorns and dangers of this w. 322:1
the w. is but a word 322:8
the w.'s a city full of straying streets
    322:10
the w.'s mine oyster 322:5
the golden w. 203:8
this w. is grown so bad 15:7
thus we may see . . . how the w. wags
    285:7
vain pomp and glory of this world 321:11
weary, stale, flat and unprofitable . . . the
    uses of this w.! 55:10
wicked, wicked w. 322:4
w. is still deceived with ornament 13:2
you have too much respect upon the w.
    199:3
you in my respect are all the w. 158:2

worm: the smallest w. will turn 228:9

wormwood: that's w. 2:7

worry: never hurry, never w. 22:1 (note)

worst: if you be afeard to hear the w. 189:2
the w. is not so long as we can say "This
    is the w." 3:7

worth: I have been w. the whistle 294:3
you are not w. the dust 294:5 (note)

would: we w. and we w. not 6:8

wound: it is good for your green w. 92:2
    (note)

wracks: a thousand fearful w. 253:4

wrinkles: w. forbid! 195:8

write: a baseness to w. fair 322:11
devise, wit; w., pen 323:1

yea-forsooth: a . . . y. knave! 275:10

years: I am declined into the vale of y. 175:7
that vanity in y. 196:8